Working w

Michael Harding DFAstrol.S h
1983 and Chairman of the Astro............................. since 1984. He
is also Chairman of the Association of Professional Astrologers and
teaches Techniques for the Faculty of Astrological Studies and is on
its council. He has run workshops in England and abroad and
contributes regularly to the *Astrological Association Journal*. He is
currently writing *Hymns to the Ancient Gods*, which is a re-analysis of
the relationship between astrology and the unconscious, seen from a
non-Jungian perspective. He began to study astrology in 1979 while
working in a psychiatric day centre, and initially saw it purely from
a 'psychological' perspective. Experience of its other uses demonstrated that it is far richer and more profound than any single
psychological system.

Charles Harvey has been a full-time consultant astrologer, teacher,
lecturer and writer since 1966 when he gained his Diploma
(DFAstrol.S) from the Faculty of Astrological Studies. He was
Faculty Vice-President from 1977 to 1986. He has been President of
the Astrological Association since 1973, and Chairman of the
Urania Trust since 1982. He worked closely with John Addey in
developing the harmonic approach to astrology, and has been
active in promoting Reinhold Ebertin's work on cosmobiology,
collaborating on the translation of the supplement to *Combination of
Stellar Influences* in 1969 and of *Pluto* (1990). His *Mundane Astrology*,
written together with Baigent and Campion, is the authoritative
work in the field. He was a major contributor to *Recent Advances in
Natal Astrology*, to the *Larousse Encyclopaedia of Astrology*, and to *The
Future of Astrology*, and is currently working on *The International
Astrological Handbook*. He is married to fellow astrologer and consultant Suzanne Lilley and they have two sons.

CONTEMPORARY ASTROLOGY
Advisory Editor: Howard Sasportas

WORKING WITH ASTROLOGY

The Psychology of Harmonics, Midpoints and Astro*Carto*Graphy

MICHAEL HARDING AND CHARLES HARVEY

ARKANA

ARKANA

Published by the Penguin Group
27 Wrights Lane, London W8 5TZ, England
Viking Penguin Inc., 40 West 23rd Street, New York, New York 10010, USA
Penguin Books Australia Ltd, Ringwood, Victoria, Australia
Penguin Books Canada Ltd, 2801 John Street, Markham, Ontario, Canada L3R 1B4
Penguin Books (NZ) Ltd, 182–190 Wairau Road, Auckland 10, New Zealand

Penguin Books Ltd, Registered Offices: Harmondsworth, Middlesex, England

First published 1990
1 3 5 7 9 10 8 6 4 2

Made and printed in Great Britain by
Richard Clay Ltd, Bungay, Suffolk
Filmset in 10/12pt Linotron Baskerville by
Rowland Phototypesetting Ltd, Bury St Edmunds, Suffolk

Acknowledgements

The authors would like to thank their colleagues and students who directly or indirectly gave them help and encouragement with this work, particularly Melanie Reinhart, Howard Sasportas, Sue Tompkins and Gaila Yariv. For assistance with specific points our thanks go to Marian Davison, Jamie McPhail, Udo Rudolph, and Dr Rick Tarnas. Our most grateful thanks go to Sheila Healey for her help in clarifying many points for the case history in Chapter 20. We are also indebted to Jim Lewis for kindly providing us with ACGs for many individuals and also with commentaries from his clients. We are most grateful to James Hillman for permission to include the quotation from *Anima* on pp. 270–71, and for allowing us to use his birth chart. MH would like to thank Judith Harding for her invaluable research and her considerable patience, and for producing all the illustrations. Finally deepest gratitude from CH to Douglas Sissons for his help and kindness, and to Suzi for her ever-receptive ear, illuminating comments and advice.

Contents

Acknowledgements   vi

Introduction (*Michael Harding and Charles Harvey*)   1

PART ONE: MIDPOINTS

1   The Origin and Development of Midpoints and the Concept of Planetary Symmetries (*Charles Harvey*)   7

2   Calculating Midpoints (*Michael Harding*)   19

3   The Cardinal/Fixed/Mutable Sort (*Michael Harding and Charles Harvey*)   40

4   The Inner Marriage: The Sun/Moon Midpoint (*Charles Harvey*)   57

5   Analysing Three Factors (*Michael Harding and Charles Harvey*)   77

6   Interpreting Midpoint Trees (*Michael Harding and Charles Harvey*)   100

7   Transits (*Michael Harding and Charles Harvey*)   117

8   Midpoints in Mundane Astrology (*Michael Harding*)   140

9   Midpoints in Other Harmonics (*Michael Harding*)   150

10   Starting to Use Midpoints (*Michael Harding*)   163

PART TWO: HARMONICS

11   Introducing Harmonics (*Michael Harding*)   169

12   Consciousness: The Number 5 and the 5th Harmonic (*Charles Harvey*)   184

13   The 7th Harmonic – Whatever Turns You On
     (*Michael Harding*)   224
14   The 9th Harmonic (*Charles Harvey*)   253
15   The Harmonics of Manifestation (*Charles Harvey*)   285
16   Starting to Use Harmonics (*Michael Harding*)   300

PART THREE: ASTRO*CARTO*GRAPHY

17   Astro*Carto*Graphy (*Michael Harding and Charles
     Harvey*)   307

PART FOUR: CASE HISTORIES

18   James Joyce (*Michael Harding*)   335
19   Zelda Fitzgerald (*Michael Harding*)   365
20   Practice Makes Perfect: A Case Study (*Charles
     Harvey*)   390
21   Looking Ahead (*Michael Harding and Charles Harvey*)   423

'Solution' to the midpoint case   443
Appendix 1: Computer Program   445
Appendix 2: Table of Equivalents   450
Appendix 3: Addresses for Further Information   452
Appendix 4: Chart Data   455

General Index   459
Name Index   465
Midpoints Index   471

Introduction

When we set up a chart we are confronted with the problem of having to interpret it. We do this by mentally ascribing certain 'values' to the planets according to how they are arranged within the three cycles or circles we are examining: the circle of the zodiac which lets us know which *sign* the planet is in, the diurnal circle which tells us in what *house* the planet is and the aspect circle which tells us which *aspect phase* the planet is in. Looking at a planet in this way we begin to get a feel of what it is 'doing' in the individual chart. A Sun square to Mars, for instance, will immediately tell us that we have the map of an individual who will need to express energy in a forceful way. The relationship of the Sun to Mars in the aspect circle tells us that this need to express personal energy will be there regardless of how the two bodies are placed in the other two cycles.

The circle of the zodiac will give us a lot of extra information about the nature of that particular Sun and Mars. Depending on how they are placed we will decide that this need for self-expression will be either particularly forcefully expressed, moderately expressed or even hard to express, and consequently more likely to be turned inwards. When we come to look at the diurnal circle which gives us the houses, we get a chance to see in what area of life the Sun/Mars energy is likely to emerge and we may then also choose to modify our feelings as to how strongly or weakly we believe the $\odot$–σ force will be expressed in that individual's life. The diurnal circle is the fastest changing of the three cycles and thus 'fine-tunes' the planetary energies most precisely. Even a 'weak' Mars comes into prominence four times a day when it approaches and passes the angles and may temporarily become extremely assertive in individuals born during these periods. Obviously, both the Sun and Mars will be making aspects to other planets as well, and we shall also take these into account. But for the moment our basic problem remains the same for astrologers today as it has always been: how to judge 'what type of Mars' we are looking at, and how to find reliable methods which allow us to make this assessment as quickly and accurately as possible.

We have all seen from our own experience, and particularly from the work of the Gauquelins, how important this 'fine-tuning' effect of the diurnal circle really is when it comes to examining how a planet will operate in the world. But even this is not enough, as Eastern astrologers have known for centuries. A planet can easily spend two or more hours in the same house, and if this is the most we can hope to 'fine-tune' a nativity then it says little for our claim that each human being is an expression of a precise moment in time and space. Indeed, at certain periods of the day at some latitudes it would be possible to set two charts nearly two hours apart which under conventional analysis would produce the same interpretation, the planets having not changed houses and any aspects to the angles just changing from applying to separating – a shift of emphasis very little used or commented upon. Viewed in other ways, however, the most profound changes could be revealed, changes which pin-point very precisely the complex and shifting nature of planetary energy as it relates to the angles during the planets' apparent orbits around the Earth. These methods are *not* difficult to apply – particularly with the advent of computers – and in a number of respects are easier to learn and use than many more traditional and less accurate approaches. Yet these methods allow us to make much more precise judgements in all areas of astrology in ways which literally and visually reflect the constantly changing relationship of our Earth to the planets. These methods are known as midpoints and harmonics and they, more than any other approach, focus on revealing what type of planet we are looking at when we sit down to confront the chart.

Midpoints and harmonics are generally regarded as modern astrological methods despite the fact that they have been used for a very long time – for thousands of years in the case of harmonics. They are also seen as something 'advanced' which can only appeal to the most experienced and technically-minded of astrologers. But above all, they are seen as 'techniques', with the implication that this somehow makes them different from the rest of astrology or useful only when other methods fail and something really exotic is called for to save the day. This view is not only wrong, but indicates a failure to grasp the fact that *all* astrological methods are techniques and unless the astrologer is aware of *why* he or she uses one particular technique rather than another there is a real danger that the resulting chart is the creation of ideas which are not understood or else actually erroneous. If we do not understand what we are doing, and why we are doing it, then it becomes increasingly unlikely that we shall be able to understand what results from it.

One of the commonest errors in astrological literature, particularly that written for beginners, is the statement that the birth chart is an accurate map of the planets as they appear from a specific place on the surface of the Earth, set for a specific moment in time. It is not. It is a distorted attempt to fit a highly-complex set of geometric relationships into a simple diagram. The method for doing this, which omits the majority of planetary relationships in favour of simplifying a few of them, is the first technique of all: the zodiac. But when we draw a circle and place the planets around it we are choosing to measure their relationship to one another in only one of several possible ways, and in doing so are simultaneously distorting those relationships as measured by the remainder. This is not an exercise in semantics or a rarefied argument over abstruse astronomical facts, but an illustration of the most fundamental issue in astrology: how we lay out our information and the criteria we use for the methods we employ will finitely determine what we can expect to discover. In other words, what you get is what you *see*.

In the following chapters we shall see how the use of midpoints and harmonics can show us what each planetary story can be and what specific information each different perspective has to offer us. We feel certain that when you begin to work with these methods your astrology will take on ever deeper vitality and become a daily, moment-by-moment source of revelation.

These are not sterile analytical techniques fit only for research, but come closer than anything else to capturing the constantly

changing dynamics of our relationship with the cosmos and consequently can bring us closer than anything else to the real nature of
astrology.

Michael Harding and Charles Harvey
March 1989

PART ONE

Midpoints

CHAPTER 1

The Origin and Development of Midpoints and the Concept of Planetary Symmetries

CHARLES HARVEY

It is easy to fall into the trap of thinking of astrology as though it were a revealed body of knowledge about which we already know everything. This attitude is no doubt encouraged by the fact that astrology does indeed deal with real universal principles and archetypes. What is often overlooked, however, is that our understanding and perception of the nature of these principles is, like all knowledge, forever developing and evolving. During the past few decades of exuberant growth in astrology, a confusing profusion of new ideas have been emerging on all sides. The student who wants to steer a clear path through this jungle of new possibilities is entitled to know something of the track record of the techniques he is being encouraged to embrace and to know which ideas are likely to prove the most fruitful. For this reason it seems appropriate to begin our study of midpoints and planetary symmetries with a look at their historical and contemporary development.

An examination of astrological history shows that midpoints, those zodiacal positions which lie exactly half-way between any two chart positions, are not new. They have in fact been used to some extent for many centuries, and the larger underlying concept of planetary symmetries has been with us in some form since at least the time of the Greeks. An examination of contemporary practice shows that today midpoints offer one of the most powerful and clearly defined tools for chart analysis, and for understanding the way in which the cycles of the planetary principles unfold time and eternity within the cosmos and within the individual and collective psyche. Indeed, as we shall see later, when linked with harmonics, midpoints promise to be one of the most important keys to unravelling the cosmic code which links Above and Below.

War is ever the spur to invention. To refine his timings for the military campaigns of the Count of Montefeltro, Guido Bonati (1223–1300), the one-time Professor of Mathematics at Bologna and Paris, seems to have been the first astrologer to consider the zodiacal point exactly half-way between each pair of planets in a chart. Guido's highly successful invasion charts are the first known use of such midpoints. While it is possible that he may have observed the efficacy of such midpoints from his own first-hand experience, their use may well go back much earlier. As a keen student of Arab astrology, Bonati would have been familiar with the Part of Fortune and the many other Arabic parts. He may have derived his ideas on midpoints from the same source. The use of parts goes back to at least 300 BC, and, as we shall see later, can be seen as one particular form of the concept of symmetry which lies at the root of midpoints and what the great twentieth-century pioneer Alfred Witte (2 March 1878–2 August 1941) was to call 'planetary pictures'.

In fact, such midpoints and parts continued to be used in a piecemeal way throughout the Middle Ages and down through the nineteenth century. However, little formal or theoretical attention seems to have been given to them by most practising astrologers. Even experimentalists like Childrey and Goad, during the brief flowering of scientific astrology in the second half of the seventeenth century, did not attempt to evaluate them as far as we know.

Probably the most commonly-used Arabic part is that of the Part of Fortune, calculated by the Ascendant + Moon − Sun formula. It is usually described as representing that point where the Moon would be if the Sun was on the Ascendant, and indeed it does. But if we look at the resulting geometry more closely we can see that we can equally consider Fortuna to mark the precise zodiacal position which brings the Sun, Moon and Ascendant into an exact symmetrical relationship with each other. Figure 1.1 shows the geometry involved in Alfred Witte's chart. Originally there were two distinct formulas for this part, or lot as it was called. If the birth was by day the Ascendant + Moon − Sun formula,

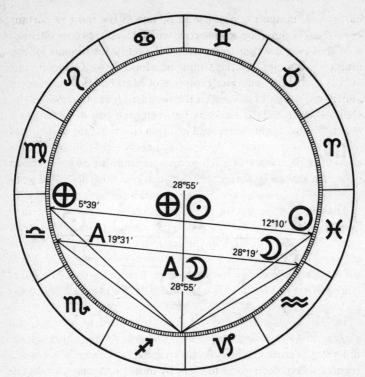

Figure 1.1 The Part of Fortune is said to be that point where the Moon would be if the Sun were exactly rising. But it will also be seen that Fortuna's position is such that it creates a symmetrical picture between Sun, Moon and Ascendant, such that the midpoint ☽/AS = ☉/Fortuna.

illustrated in Figure 1.1, was the one used. But if the birth took place during the hours of darkness the formula Ascendant − Moon + Sun, giving the position shown in Figure 1.2, was used. This second formula produces what is now called the Part of Spirit. In either case we can see that what is actually happening with such parts is that they are setting up a symmetrical planetary picture between these vital elements in the chart and bring them all into resonance. As we can see in Figure 1.1, the axis of symmetry falls where the Moon/Ascendant midpoint exactly conjoins the Sun/ Part of Fortune midpoint. Likewise in Figure 1.2 we see that the

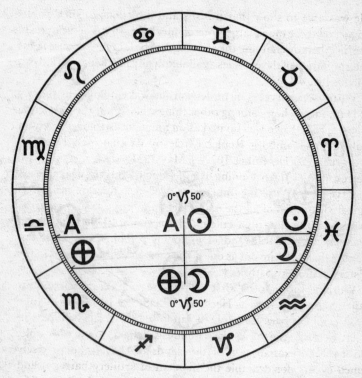

Figure 1.2 As with the Part of Fortune, the Part of Spirit brings Sun, Moon and Ascendant together into a symmetrical picture such that ⊙/AS = ☽/Fortuna.

axis of symmetry falls where the Sun/Ascendant midpoint exactly conjoins the Moon/Fortuna midpoint.

Alfred Witte was the first person really to get to grips with the idea of midpoints, and of planetary symmetries in general. He spent his life investigating the interpretation of such symmetries and patterns of relationships using a movable dial, which will be described more fully later. This dial allowed Witte and his colleagues to identify quickly in any chart the way whole series of symmetrical midpoints and sensitive points (alias parts) were inter-relating and resonating around the chart, binding the ideas and energies of the planets involved together in unique patterns.

He was able to show that transits and directions to such points trigger off these much larger interconnected patterns of meaning in the life, thereby enabling the astrologer to be far more precise in his interpretation of the energies available at any particular period in a client's life.

Witte was a surveyor by profession and was employed by the city of Hamburg, where, among other things, he set out the municipal airport. In 1913 he was invited as an amateur astrologer to give a talk to the Hamburg Kepler Circle by its chairman Friedrich Sieggruen (20 December 1877–4 May 1951). This meeting with Sieggruen was the beginning of a life-long friendship which seems to have given Witte the impetus he needed to develop his astrological ideas. And of all the many ideas and insights to come from Witte's extraordinarily fertile mind, his elaboration of the idea of planetary symmetries and of midpoint combinations must undoubtedly mark him out as one of the most important figures in the history of modern astrology.

Working through the First World War with Sieggruen and his other colleagues, such as Hermann Lefeldt (29 June 1899–1 June 1977) and Ludwig Rudolph (9 January 1893–14 July 1982), in what became known as the Hamburg School, Witte was able, through the examination of thousands of charts and precisely timed events, for example the moment of artillery barrages and explosions on the Western Front, to produce perhaps the first major advance in interpretational techniques since Ptolemy.

Taking 'problem' charts which did not obviously reveal the known qualities of the moment, Witte found on close examination that appropriate chart factors, which were not necessarily in any conventional aspect, were forming symmetrical 'pictures' and midpoint combinations within tight orbs. Thus he noticed that artists often tended to have the Mercury/Venus midpoint involved with the MC; that where the Sun was involved in the midpoint there was a possible gift for the plastic arts, such as sculpture, and where the Moon was involved painting talent was to the fore. By contrast he noted that Uranus with Mercury and Venus tended to give mathematical talent, as did, for example, the MC and/or the Moon when involved in a symmetrical midpoint picture with Mercury and Uranus. Likewise Witte and his colleagues noted

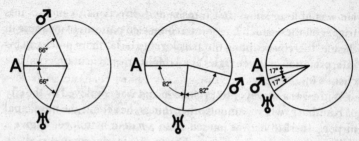

Figure 1.3 Three different symmetrical pictures involving AS, Mars, Uranus. In each case the middle factor is equidistant from the other two and is therefore on their midpoint. Though no traditional aspects are involved, Witte found all such pictures associated with sudden releases of energy such as sudden outbursts of anger, explosions and accidents.

that the charts of accidents showed the symmetrical arrangements of the Ascendant with Mars and Uranus, such as the Ascendant or Mars being on the Ascendant/Uranus midpoint or Uranus being on the Mars/Ascendant midpoint. As we shall see later, he subsequently came to realize that such midpoint combinations could also be activated when planets were in hard aspect, 45°, 90°, 135°, or 180° to the midpoint.

During his life Witte generalized his findings into an entirely new system of astrology which emphasized the paramount importance of such 'planetary pictures' in understanding the chart of any moment. He first began writing up these ideas and observations in astrological periodicals in 1919. Then in 1928, after a further decade of study and research, he published, together with Lefeldt, a summary of his findings in their major systematized dictionary, *Regelwerk fuer Planetenbilder* (*Rules for Planetary Pictures*), a work which, in revised editions, continues to be the corner-stone of the Hamburg School today.

However, despite Witte's desire to simplify and rationalize astrological interpretation, and to bring astrology into the twentieth century, his ideas appeared too radical and, in a pre-computer age, too technical, for the mainstream of traditionalists. Outside of Germany his ideas made some slow headway in the USA. But in general his work was ignored by most students until well after the Second World War. His concepts only really began to penetrate the astrological establishment in the 1950s and 60s, in a distilled form, through the work of one of Witte's most brilliant students, Reinhold Ebertin (16 February 1901, 4.40 a.m. MET, 14W58, 51N09 – 'early hours' 14 March 1988).

Ebertin, the son of one of Germany's most outstanding astrologers, Elsbeth Ebertin (1880–1944), while recognizing the technical genius of Witte, gradually became dissatisfied with the lack of any attempt on Witte's part in *Rules* to grapple with the deeper underlying psychological principles involved. It was these shortcomings that Ebertin set out to remedy with such success in his magnum opus *The Combination of Stellar Influences*, which he first published in card index form in 1940. In this brilliant work, affectionately known in English as *COSI* (pronounced 'cosy'), Ebertin discards Witte's and Sieggruen's hypothetical planets, the use of antiscia, and multiple systems of house division, and focuses on the interpretation of midpoint combinations pure and simple. Using the cumulative experience of his own research and that of the many contributors to his monthly journal *Neue Sternblatter* (from 1933 *Mensch im All*), he was able to expand and clarify the main body of Witte's work on psychological lines, making *COSI* one of the single most important works on astrological interpretation ever written.

Such is the strength of the language barrier that while these ideas were developing fast in Germany they moved into the English-speaking world only very slowly. In 1924 in Britain Charles Carter (31 January 1887–4 October 1968) mentioned the importance of midpoints in his *Encyclopaedia of Psychological Astrology* in connection with degree areas, and in 1929 Vivian E. Robson (26 May 1890–1939) devoted a chapter to midpoints in his *The Radix System*. The influential E. H. Bailey, writing in the *British Journal of Astrology* of September 1930 on what he called 'the important question of midpoints', stated his 'intention to make greater use of them in dealing with horoscopes each month', which he did. But, no doubt because of the time-consuming calculations and the natural conservatism of students, progress was slow.

In the USA progress was much the same though technically more full-blooded. Enthusiastic explanatory articles on Witte's work began to appear in the astrological press in the early 1930s, and an unauthorized translation by Hans Niggemann of Witte's *Rules for Planetary Pictures* appeared in 1932, while in June 1939 Richard Svehla published his lucid little *Introduction to the Uranian System of Astrology*, which, had it not been for the war, could have inspired many more students with the immense value of midpoints and planetary pictures.

It was not to be, however, and the real breakthrough of these ideas into mainstream astrology did not begin in fact until Alfred G. Roosedale made his masterly translation of Ebertin's *The Combination of Stellar Influences* in 1960, a translation which some say actually improves upon the original. Roosedale, a German-Jewish refugee, was a brilliant inventor, astrologer and linguist 'with a mind like Einstein' who moved in astrological and Gurdjieff-Ouspensky circles in London immediately after the war. Though little else is known of his astrology, it was through his translation of Ebertin that *COSI* soon became a classic textbook on both sides of the Atlantic and has proved to be the key to bringing midpoints increasingly into the mainstream of English-speaking astrology.

Meanwhile in Germany, following the war, Ebertin adopted the name cosmobiology for his systematic approach to astrology in order to separate it from astrology's connotations of Sun sign columns and TV entertainers. In 1956, to continue his work of clarifying the astrological tradition, he founded the Aalen Cosmobiological Academy. With the eminent physicist Professor Rudolf Tomaschek (23 December 1895, 14.00 MET, Nudweis – 8 February 1966) as its first president, the Academy soon became a focus for valuable research. Although not as active as it was, the Academy continues to hold annual conferences and has published valuable yearbooks. In his quest for the demonstrable essentials of astrology Reinhold Ebertin abandoned house division and stripped away much of what he called the 'medieval ballast' from astrology, while at the same time continuing to be a technical innovator in the Witte mould. Astrologers have particular reason to thank him for the development of graphic ephemerides, which enable one to see at a glance a comprehensive picture of the movements of the transiting planets and transiting midpoints to the natal chart. His development of the concept of midpoints in declination has opened up the interpretation of the previously neglected third dimension of the chart: the distance of planets north and south of the Celestial Equator.

In recent years various of Ebertin's colleagues have further broadened the scope of the Academy's work. Dr Theodor Land-scheidt, a High Court judge, physicist and mystic, has made outstanding contributions to the understanding of the relationship of the planets to solar activity, as shown in his remarkable recent book *Sun-Earth-Man*. He has also shown the importance of the planetary nodes in natal chart interpretation. Dr Hans-Jorg Walter in his yet untranslated work *Entschuesselte Aspektfiguren* (Encoded Aspect Figures) draws together the systematic use of midpoints with Addey's concept of harmonics. Of especial significance is the work of Ebertin's son Dr Baldur Ebertin (b. 21 July 1933). He is a child psychologist and homeopath as well as an outstanding astrologer/cosmobiologist. He continues to develop his father's work and has produced an amplified version of *COSI*[1] which includes a wider range of medical and depth psychological interpretations for each planetary combination.

At the same time the Hamburg School has remained extremely active in Hamburg under the leadership of Ludwig Rudolph's son Udo Rudolph (b. 14 December 1921). It continues to elaborate on Witte's original work and has published a remarkable *Lexicon* by Ruth Brummund (b. 26 September 1921), which indexes every combination in Witte-Lefeldt's *Rules* together with the observations given in the many studies published in their quarterly journal *Hamburger Hefte*. However, while the school has keen students from Thailand to the USA, who work with the full range of ideas that Witte advanced, such as his advocacy with Sieggruen of eight hypothetical planets yet to be discovered, the systematic use of planetary antiscia, and six simultaneous systems of house division, these techniques are still only practised and understood by re-latively few members of the astrological community at large and it may be several more decades before Witte's work is seen in perspective. The main English-language periodical devoted to these ideas is *Uranian Forum*, a well-produced bi-monthly with an international range of contributors.

Since Roosedale's translation of *COSI* and the advent of the computer the English-speaking world has played an increasing part in the development of Witte's and Ebertin's ideas. Doris Greaves in Melbourne, Australia has done much to champion the cause there and encourage a deeper integration between midpoints and traditional approaches. In 1965 Charles Harvey persuaded A. R. Brown, a computer programmer in the Astrological Association, to write a program which would calculate and sort all the midpoints into 45° and 90° 'sorts' and to make this program, the first of its kind, available to the community through the AA. Such programs were later to become standard features of the pioneering computer software houses and services for astrologers in the USA such as Neil F. Michelsen's Astro-Computing Services and Dr Gregg Howe's Astro-Numeric Services in 1974, Michael Erlewine's Matrix Company in 1977, and Robert Hand's Astro-Graphics (now Astrolabe) in 1978. Such services not only saved students an enormous amount of time but they quickly opened up a whole new world of interpretational subtleties and precision comparisons between charts that had not been touched upon by Witte or Ebertin.

While hitherto it had been the normal practice to identify midpoints visually with the aid of a circular 90° or 360° 'dial'[2] and simply draw or write planetary pictures without reference to their exact positions, with the advent of the computer Charles Harvey was able to suggest that the actual sequence of the midpoints was important in their interpretation, revealing deeper levels of psychological conditioning and habitual patterns of expectation. Likewise he was able to show, as Charles Carter had suggested back in 1924, that the charts of family members with known genetic and psychological inheritance often showed the same midpoints in the same degree areas. This kind of approach is currently in the process of being linked with Addey's concept of harmonics and promises to open further avenues for refining our understanding of the chart.

While midpoints have developed over the past seventy years as an increasingly precise tool, we cannot close this short survey without mentioning the broader, and closely related, work of the great Russian-born astrologer Alexandre Volguine (Novay-Praha, Russia, 03.32.45 GMT, 3 March 1903–June 1976), who fled to France with his family after the Revolution. Using his remarkable collection of charts which he built up while he was editor of the leading French journal *Les Cahiers Astrologiques*, Volguine developed the more general concept of encadrement, which has been variously translated as 'planetary containment', 'inbetweenity' or 'framing'. He found that each planet or angle seems to be coloured and conditioned by the planets falling immediately adjacent on either side of it, regardless of how far away they are on each side and even though the central factor might be signs away from the actual midpoint. Using the usual ten planets, Volguine considered the significance of each of their thirty-six possible containments, i.e. each planet in a chart has one of the other nine planets before it in the zodiac and another one after it, giving thirty-six possible variations for each planet. He likewise researched the forty-five possible containments of the MC and Ascendant. (There are nine more possible containments for the angles because any two of the ten planets can bracket the angle.) His observations on the significance of such containments closely parallel those found for midpoints. Thus, for example, Volguine found that the individual with the Sun between Mercury and Mars would be assertive, good at debate and forceful leadership. Unlike midpoints, he found that this applied even when Mercury might be only a few degrees on one side of the Sun and Mars several signs away on the other.

After years of study Volguine concluded that containments are as important as sign or house positions for understanding the way in which a planet will manifest. His work, *L'Encadrement Planétaire*, has been developed in the USA by John Sandbach and Ronn Ballard in their book *Planets in Containment*. They consider twice the number of possible containments used by Volguine as they distinguish between the order of the planets. They, for example, suggest that there are important differences between someone with the sequence Mercury-Sun-Mars and the sequence Mars-Sun-Mercury. The former, they found, would, as it were, put thoughts into action with force and vigour, the latter would find this more difficult and could vitalize others but would tend to lack consistency in his efforts. In emphasizing the actual sequence of the planets Sandbach and Ballard hark back to the work of Marc Edmund Jones and Michael Meyer, who considered which of

Moon, Mercury, Venus, or Mars rose ahead of the Sun as of significance in how the individual deals with career matters.

Undoubtedly the general principle of containment is a valid one and, like the sequencing of midpoints, it helps to remind us that though we examine charts spatially as though they were static geometries, each moment is in fact a dynamic process in which all the planetary principles are subtly interrelated. The implications of containment for the general idea of midpoints is that those midpoints in a chart which are also containments are likely to be of especial importance for the individual and the manifestation of that particular moment. To fully evaluate such ideas, and to include the subtleties implied by harmonic theory, future workers on midpoints and planetary pictures will require not only a formidable collection of good data but great patience and breadth and depth of vision. In the meantime let us now explore further some of the interpretational riches that have already been discovered by our predecessors and how we may most effectively use them to enhance our work for our clients.

NOTES

1. Baldur R. Ebertin, *Kosmobiologische Diagnostik. Die kosmischen Strukturen und Rhythmen in uns*, 3 vols. in loose-leaf format. Published by Ebertin Verlag, Freiburg, 1978–1984. Baldur Ebertin has also recently published *Das ABC der Kosmobiologie*, Ebertin Verlag, Aalen, 1989, an excellent guide to working with cosmobiological methods. He has also published a major work on his own clinical experience with reincarnation therapy using the cosmobiological approach to astrology as a basic tool; *Reinkarnation und neues Bewußtsein*, 2nd enlarged edn, Ebertin Verlag, Freiburg, 1989.
2. See p. 454 for details of a leaflet on the 90° dial.

CHAPTER 2

Calculating Midpoints

MICHAEL HARDING

To begin at the beginning: a midpoint is precisely what it says it is – the point exactly midway between any two planets. The planets' positions are measured in Celestial Longitude and then the point half-way between them is found. In a circle there are always *two* half-way points – located in the longer and the shorter arc – as can be seen in Figure 2.1. The exact midpoint is always located in the *shorter* arc. It is at the midpoint that the combined energies of the two planets come together. A third planet at the midpoint of two others – such as the Moon in Figure 2.2 – will act as a factor that brings these energies together and through which they will tend to be expressed. This contact can come via a conjunction to the midpoint, an opposition or square to it, or through a semi-square or sesquiquadrate aspect to that point. A transit or progression by

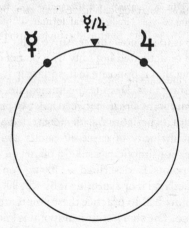

Figure 2.1 The Mercury/Jupiter midpoint lies half-way between Mercury and Jupiter and is written as ☿/♃.

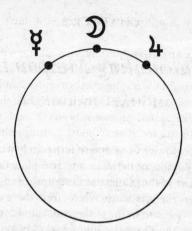

Figure 2.2 The Moon on the Mercury/Jupiter midpoint. This is written as ☽ = ☿/♃; a maximum orb of +/− 2° is allowed.[1]

any of these aspects to this midpoint can also act during the course of life as a trigger to release the latent energy of the pair which can be expressed as an event or an experience. This is the basic theory of midpoints. It is not complex, it is not confusing and everything else from now on is just fine-tuning. There is probably no other profound astrological idea that can be explained so simply.

The next step is to see how this sensitive point – the midpoint – can be triggered or activated not only by a planet conjunct it, but also by any planet that is opposite to it, square to it, semi-square to it or sesquiquadrate to it. Despite the immediate, logical reaction that the actual midpoint *directly* between any two planets should be the most powerful, experience has demonstrated again and again that in the vast majority of cases *all* points can be considered equally effective. For simplicity's sake, a planet on any one of these eight possible points is described as being 'on the midpoint' whether it is exactly on it or aspecting it by 45°, 90°, 135° or 180° as illustrated in Figure 2.3. In practice these points are always treated as being the same. The shortest-arc midpoint is known as the *direct midpoint* and the other seven points are the *indirect midpoints*. You now have virtually all the technical information you need to know about the theory of midpoints. We can now start putting it into practice.

Unless you are an out-and-out masochist, you will be using your computer to perform the task of actually calculating midpoints and printing them out, but it *is* important to understand fully what we are actually doing when we are locating and using these points. We are looking for the actual midpoint between each pair of planets and then looking to see if that point is conjunct, semi-square, square, sesquiquadrate, or opposite any other planet. Any multiple of the 45° aspect, in fact, which will pull together the combined energies of the planets we find.

We are looking for patterns which form an eightfold or 8th harmonic pattern in the circle of the zodiac, and seeing how this pattern relates to the various planets and personal points in the chart. The principle of the number 8 is like all numbers based on multiples of 2, the principle of manifestation in the world. In the case of 8, this principle works particularly powerfully and almost always relates to concrete, tangible events. It's important to recall that from a psychological point of view behaviour is also an event.

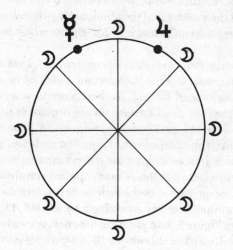

Figure 2.3 The Moon falling at any multiple of 45° from the ☿/♃ midpoint is said to be 'on the ☿/♃ midpoint'.

A person is always *doing* something in the world, even when fast asleep. When using midpoints we are focusing on this principle and examining how it operates in life and thus we are concentrating on those parts of the personality which are most likely to be operative and express themselves, consciously or unconsciously, through events.

By concentrating on how this eightfold rhythm binds the planetary energies together we go quickly to the core of the chart. Planetary energies or principles are seen to operate not just by themselves – by looking at each individual planet in turn as in conventional astrology and generally noting only a few aspects – but by seeing each planet as it relates to all the others and seeking their actual midpoints as the focus of their combined energies.

To start, we need to find that midpoint. This is simply done by taking the absolute longitude of both planets, adding them together and dividing by 2. The absolute longitude is the actual degrees and minutes each planet is from 0° Aries. Thus if the Sun is 4° 30′ of Aries it has an absolute longitude of 4° 30′. If another planet lies at 14° 20′ of Aries it has an absolute longitude of 14° 20′. To find their midpoint we just add the two numbers together and divide by 2. In other words, their combined absolute longitude is 18° 50′ and their midpoint (the absolute longitude divided by 2) is 9° 25′. Their midpoint, then, is 9° 25′ of Aries which is written 9 ♈ 25.

In another case we may find a planet at 12 ♉ 13 and this has an absolute longitude of 42° 13′. A second planet at 16 ♐ 42 has an absolute longitude of 256° 42′. If these figures are added together they produce 298° 55′. Dividing that by two gives us 149° 28′ or 14 ♌ 29. Thus 14 ♌ 29 is the midpoint of these two factors. Sometimes this method of calculating the midpoint produces an answer that is 180° away from the correct figure, the opposite side of the chart in fact. But this is easily spotted simply by looking at what must be the logical position. Remember, when we are stating the *specific* midpoint of two planets we are always referring to this shortest-arc figure – the shortest distance between the planets concerned. In Figure 2.1 we see the Mercury/Jupiter midpoint. Notice again that it is in the shortest arc between these two planets. It is written ☿/♃, with the faster-moving planet written first.

Figure 2.2 shows the Moon exactly on the Mercury/Jupiter mid-point. This is written $☽ = ☿/♃$. But what does it actually *mean*?

If we go through this planetary picture step by step, treating it similarly to a triple conjunction, it has a lot to tell us. For a start, the Moon is the focus of both Mercury and Jupiter. The Moon represents our past, our emotional reactions and our gut-feelings. Images of women in general and the mother archetype in particular are intimately connected with this symbol. It is also the centre through which much of our inner-life finds somatic expression. The Moon often channels those energies which we can express 'naturally' in life. Thus it is often a key factor in health issues, both physical and mental, and a centre around which much of our partially conscious material gravitates.

The Mercury/Jupiter contact we are looking at tells us that it is *through* this lunar symbol that the principles of Mercury and Jupiter are going to be expressed. The first thing we recognize is that we are basically looking at how this person's *feelings* are going to modulate the expression of ideas in some form or other. We are not looking at him from the point of view of his drives (Mars) or his goals (MC) but are trying to discover something about his emotional responses towards life in so far as they connect to both Mercury and Jupiter.

Starting at a very simple level, Mercury will represent communication in all its forms and Jupiter will seek wisdom and philosophical authority. At a superficial level we have someone who may talk a lot, perhaps one for whom discussing philosophical or religious ideas is a natural part of their emotional needs. These two planets are connected to the Moon – thus whatever ideas are discussed are bound to have a strong emotional component. The man will think as much with his stomach as with his head. Emotional reactions will play a very large part in his own personal philosophy in some way or another, and this response may involve inflated feelings or ideas, or express emotional needs and longings that are rooted in his past.

The Mercury/Moon contact can bring a rapidly changing quality to the expression of language and ideas. In fact Ebertin uses the expression 'a lively exchange of thoughts' as part of his interpretation of this combination. Moon/Jupiter, however, often tends to be a little more excessive. People with strong Moon/ Jupiter contacts can run the risk of 'preaching' to others – the religious or philosophical qualities of Jupiter seem to come out one way or another whatever happens – and putting all three factors together we could be looking at someone who could really run off at the mouth in a rather overbearing fashion should the mood (the Moon) take him. There can be issues of *excess* in these areas. Excessive talking, dominating, self-righteous ideas and so on. There is also the possibility of a rather maudlin sentimentality – extreme feelings – or we could be looking at quite a skilled orator with an instinctive (Moon) ability to put feelings into words and sway the crowd. We can twist the triptych this way and that to begin with, experimenting with the manner in which each aspect can be exaggerated, but we keep coming back to the same basic images. Moods, ideas and philosophies are inextricably inter-twined and will interact together continuously. Thus the simple diagram of $\mathbb{D} = \mathring{\varphi}/\mathrm{4}$ provides us with a considerable amount of very useful information in quite a specific area and we shall return to it later.

As we have seen, the midpoint lying exactly between any two planets can be activated by a radical or transiting planet which is exactly on it, or which is an exact multiple of 45° away from it. Thus the Moon 45° away from the $\mathring{\varphi}/\mathrm{4}$ midpoint is for sim-plicity's sake described as being 'on the midpoint' of Mercury /Jupiter. This is also the case if it is 90° away, 135° away or opposite it at 180° distance. Figure 2.3 shows the Moon at the various multiples of 45° from the Mercury/Jupiter midpoint. The orbs used are very close: 2° if midpoints to the Sun, Moon, Ascendant or MC are being examined, 1.5° if the midpoint is made to any of the planets or the node. It is very important to keep to these orbs and not be tempted to stretch a point to make something fit nicely. However, if one of the factors were to involve either the Ascendant or MC and you felt very strongly from experience that they *should* be included in the equation, then this could suggest that the time of the chart is slightly incorrect. In this way midpoints can be used for rectification purposes, using the transiting angles as we shall see in Chapter 3.

In Figure 2.4, both the Moon and the node are on the $\mathring{\varphi}/\mathrm{4}$

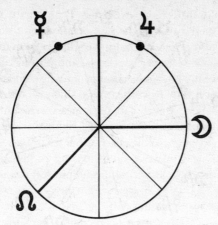

Figure 2.4 Here both the Moon *and* the node fall on the ☿/♃ midpoint.

midpoint. The other possible positions are unoccupied by natal factors and thus can only be stimulated by future transits or progressions. We would write this combination as ☽ = ☊ = ☿/♃ or ☽ and ☊ = ☿/♃. Either will do, but do avoid ☽ + ☊ = ☿/♃. This use of '+' could be very confusing as it is part of the Hamburg School's own notation and would mean something quite different.

Figure 2.5 demonstrates exactly why the 90° dial was invented! Here there are only three bodies drawn in – Moon, Mercury and Jupiter – but already a confusing number of sensitive midpoint degrees can be located around the circle of the zodiac. If all the planets and all their midpoints had been inserted in the diagram, then in *each* 45° segment of the circle we would have a 'reflection' of the thirteen main natal factors and the seventy-eight midpoints they combine to produce. The importance of each planetary pair being repeated in the same sequence every 45° will be examined later; in the meantime let us return to this basic idea of each factor and each midpoint being found *once* in each 45° section of the zodiac.

Imagine that we drew Figure 2.6 accurately to scale on a large sheet of paper. With every planet and every midpoint inserted in its proper place we could very easily see if the Sun was 2° away from any particular midpoint. Having noted which midpoints fell within

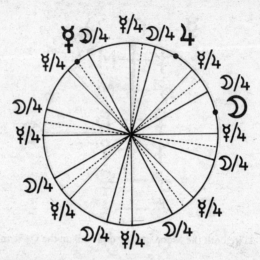

Figure 2.5 Midpoints created by just three factors, the Moon, Mercury and Jupiter.

this orb we could list the example given as $\Psi/M = \sigma/M = \odot = \varphi/\hbar = \Psi/\mathbb{P} = \sigma/\mathbb{P} = \mathbb{H}/\Psi = \sigma/\mathbb{H}$ (Figure 2.7). The list would be like this because the Ψ/M and σ/M midpoints came *before* the Sun in the zodiac sequence, and were within 2° of it, and $\varphi/\hbar$ out to $\sigma/\mathbb{H}$ came *after* the Sun in the circle of the zodiac and likewise fell within the 2° orb.

After listing all the midpoints to the Sun, we would then move on

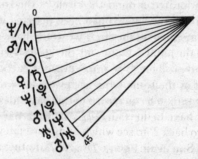

Figure 2.6 Any 45° section of the chart contains a reflection of *all* the chart factors and their midpoints. Here we see those midpoints within a 2° orb of the Sun (not to scale).

Figure 2.7 Here the same solar midpoints as in Figure 2.6 are laid out on a midpoint tree. The dot shows where the Sun falls in the zodiacal sequence.

to noting those contacts made by the Moon, those contacts made by the angles, and then go through all the planets and the node similarly noting the midpoints each factor is contacting, one by one. With the Moon's nodes being exactly opposite each other, the node is seen as a single factor as far as midpoints are concerned, though it retains the dual quality of representing a point in which energy can flow either in or out of an individual's life, generally through the process of relationships.

This 45° segment of the circle which contains all the planetary pairs as well as the planets themselves can be referred to as the *45° sort*. Computers which have an option for midpoint work will list all the planets and pairs in such a 45° sequence, from 0° to 45°. This can be used to see quite quickly which midpoints contact which planets. All we have to do is identify the position of the Sun in the sort and then go back 2° to see which midpoints fall within orb. We then locate the Sun again and go *forward* 2°, noting once more any combinations that fall within this range. These are *all* the midpoints made to the Sun. As we are looking at a *sequence* which repeats every 45°, we need to make one further check should a planet fall right at the end or the beginning of the 45° sort. If it falls at the *end* of the sort we check backwards as before to see which midpoints come within orb and then start at the *beginning* of the sort to count forwards. If the planet falls right at the start of the sort then we count *forward* as normal but see which pairs fall within orb right at the *end* of the sort as well. The 45° sort can be thought of as a circle, which of course has no start or end. The cycle repeats continuously as does the circle of the zodiac.

We have now arrived at the point where we have identified how each natal factor is actually keyed in to a number of planetary energies all round the zodiac and listed which combinations are actively involved. In other words we have taken the first step to describing 'what sort of Sun' we are talking about and thus begun the process of defining in detail how these specific variations can be delineated. In this case we see that the Sun is configured with seven planetary combinations, all adding something to our total picture of the solar principle and making it a very different picture – because of its involvement with the angles – from the Sun of someone born only a few minutes earlier or later that same day. Before going any further with how we arrange and examine the various midpoints we have located for all the planets, we should examine how we might interpret these midpoints to the Sun.

In this particular case there are a considerable number of these contacts. In fact some of them are 'hit' by other factors than the Sun, but for the moment we'll stay just with what the Sun is doing in the chart, and what type of solar principle is being expressed. Remembering that midpoints are seen as a kind of triple-conjunction with the central planet bringing the energies together and in turn being qualitatively altered by those energies, we can start to look at what this 'fine print' is telling us.

The Sun is the individual's basic source of energy and its function in the psyche is to focus and to integrate. Thus the quality and nature of someone's Sun as described by the midpoints to it will tell you a lot about how they 'organize and integrate' their life and the energies they will use in their basic striving towards self-expression. Here we see that the Sun is configured with Neptune and the MC – it is on the Ψ/M midpoint. Assuming that the time of birth is correct, this will suggest someone who will seek to 'make a career' or use the qualities of Neptune to establish themselves in the world. The qualities of Neptune will merge with the Sun and be projected as some form of goal or aim in that person's life. The MC is particularly important in midpoint work, not just because it is one of the angles, but because experience demonstrates that when a planet is configured with the Ascendant or MC it is almost certainly going to be expressed in that person's life. It is as if they are very specifically attuned to the nature of whatever planetary energies connect to the angles. The angles make a planet's energy *personal* and thus liable to be expressed strongly in the world, probably because the contact is defined by the world itself. In Chapter 17 we shall examine this idea more fully through the use of Astro*Carto*Graphy.

To recap: in using just *one* midpoint we have already established something very important about our client: he will probably need to seek a career or aspire towards a goal in which the energies of Neptune can be fully expressed. The next midpoint, $\odot = \male/M$, says the same sort of thing except that it is now Mars that is going to be used in a similar manner. Martian qualities will come strongly to the fore in this individual's striving to manifest himself in his chosen direction. His ego is *consciously* (MC) tied in with his personal energy (Mars) and the wish to express it in the self-integrating process (Sun).

Taking these first two midpoints together, we can get an image of someone who consciously seeks and aspires to merge personal energy and will with the much larger collective energies of Neptune. Unless high ideals have been cultivated, this is a difficult one to live with. Most Mars/Neptune contacts are hard to handle as their respective qualities – and needs – are so different. There is often a risk of confusion and deception – either deliberately or just arising from the very nature of the energies involved. Mars is a selfish, focused energy seeking immediate and direct expression; Neptune wishes all to share the sublime. Mars/Neptune contacts seem to occur in the charts of those people concerned with issues such as healing and mysticism as well as those involved with narcotics or more exotic sexual activities. Relationships can be highly 'addictive' as well. They are often romanticized and over-idealized, or there can be an almost fatal attraction to underdogs,

losers and emotional gamblers where sexual desire becomes confused with fantasies and ideals become blurred with the imagined
goals of the Gods. There can also be a strong 'show-biz' or
rock-star quality to this combination, where the glamour and hype
allows the performer to legitimately 'deceive and seduce' his
audience and lead a multiplicity of unreal lives as well as expressing the well-known Neptunian affinities with art in all its many
forms.

But our subject also has $\odot = ♀/♄$, which is a more sobering
combination. It suggests that the life will in some way focus on
relationships which are sad or serious. Relationships that are very
important; hard to form and hard to break. Relationships that may
have something binding about them, and something solitary.
Venus/Saturn can also relate to a negative or fearful self-image or
to actual poverty; emotional 'hard times' in fact. The need to
control emotions – or women – may be present, perhaps through
the process of taking on some form of responsibility for them. Next
comes $\odot = ♆/♇$ and another strong indication that we are dealing
with someone whose manner of personal integration (the Sun) is
keyed in to much larger collective forces. Neptune is here once
again, and now we also find Pluto involved as well. Thus the
images of dissolving and transcending which we associate with
Neptune merge with the need for the harder and more forceful
Pluto experience of death and rebirth and the probably emotional
catharsis that can accompany it. Taken together, the Self needs to
be associated with profound and possibly mystical changes which
could induce different or altered states of consciousness, perhaps
related to issues which bring together mass ideals (Neptune) in an
extremely powerful (Pluto) and moving manner.

The next midpoint, $\odot = ♂/♇$, brings a lot of intense drive and
energy into the picture. Mars/Pluto is hard, focused sexual/
assertive energy with considerable force behind it. Unlike Neptune, Mars finds in Pluto a resonant partner. Personal energy and
drive are not likely to be dispersed and fragmented with this
contact, rather amplified and channelled. As the Sun is also
configured with the Neptune/Uranus midpoint, we now have all
three outer planets, each representing different areas of the collective unconscious, directly connected with the Sun. $♅/♆$ again

reinforces the idea of strange, mystical states which may have a highly-charged or magical quality about them, as if ordinary consciousness has in some way to be broken down for something truer and more personal (Uranus) to break through. Finally, the Sun is also on the Mars/Uranus midpoint, and like the ♂/♇ this is another potential power-point. Mars and Uranus are very much planets of energy and activity. The personal will is reinforced with Uranus and the individual is likely to act forcefully and rashly, seeking immediate and unconsidered action. It's the sort of configuration you might find in the chart of someone who likes hang-gliding, motor racing or karate – life just has to have that edge of danger or it becomes boring. It is a factor that demands action and attention and is not happy in the back row waiting its turn.

If we start putting all this together we begin to get an image of someone who at their centre will be strongly drawn towards the forces of the collective unconscious, and whose personal will and drive is likely to be intimately bound up with his goals in seeking the expression of these energies. This is someone with a capacity for making the fullest use – for good or ill – of Mars and Neptune energies, and someone who is able – with ♂/♇ and ♂/♅ – to take very forceful and powerfully decisive action when the need or desire arises. Among all this there is also a sense of sadness or hardship as far as personal relationships are concerned.

Overall we have a picture of an individual who *needs* in some way to use the energies symbolized by the transpersonal planets forcefully and to apply them to find his own centre and fulfilment. Approaching the chart for the first time in this way we have already quite a strong feeling about what the Sun is 'doing'. We have done it just by looking at the midpoint pictures as a series of multiple conjunctions and used our understanding of astrological symbolism in a very straightforward manner to set out the kind of story these pictures might tell. Without using conventional aspects, signs or houses we have already amassed some very clear astrological images.

The next thing to be looked at is the fact that in this case Saturn *also* forms midpoint aspects to the majority of the same planetary pairs configured with the Sun – refer to Figure 2.8 to check this out.

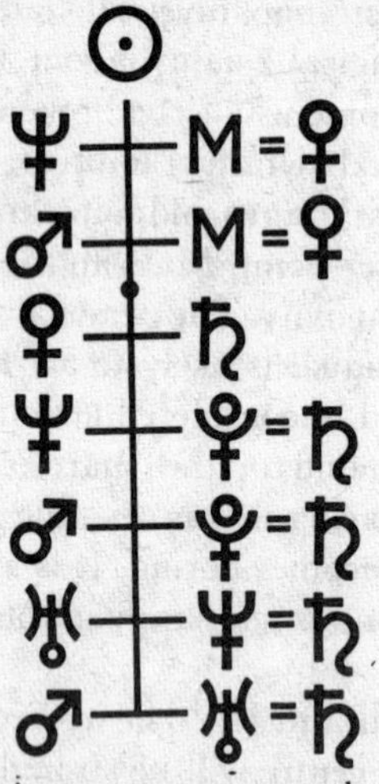

Figure 2.8 In this midpoint tree, or structure, the first two solar midpoints are also hit by Venus and the last four by Saturn.

So how do we handle all these contacts and what does it all tell us?

When two or more planets are on the same midpoint, their combined energies will work together – or at odds with – each planetary pair. Which way it goes will depend a lot on the actual planets involved and, most importantly, on the level of consciousness of each individual and his capacity to recognize his behaviour and to make appropriate choices. For instance, Mars and Saturn contacts can indicate problems with self-assertion versus authority or parental figures. This can lead to the well-known 'stop-go' approach towards life, where every personal action is in some way doubted or feared and the individual lives in dread of the cold hand of disapproval slapping down his every move. Used in another way, Mars and Saturn can bring disciplined energy to every endeavour and make this the hallmark of someone who battles to overcome every obstacle and seeks to express in a concrete and solid form the results of his own personal drive and expression.

If Mars was together with Jupiter we would have two planets which had much more in common. Both are to do with assertion and expansion, albeit in different areas of life, but the basic energies are much more compatible. The possible problems are not those of conflict or contradiction, but of excessive enthusiasm, impatience and the general attitude of raising the individual's personal desires to a level which others could easily find intrusive. In this case we find that Venus also joins the Sun on Ψ/M and ♂/M. This strongly suggests that this individual will tend to focus himself around relationships and that these will enter very strongly into the areas of life in which Mars and Neptune operate.

Where before we saw the Sun alone with these pairs and suggested that the individual's goals and ambitions will draw these energies to him, or that he will seek out areas of life in which he can operate professionally with these energies, we now can add to this sentence 'with other people'. Venus configured in this way with the Sun brings home the importance of this individual connecting other people with his own goals (the MC) and also suggests that the people in question are more likely to be female. People are very important to this person. Keeping in mind that we suggested ☉ = ♀/♄ could indicate someone whose relationships might be in some way sad or estranged, we can now place greater emphasis on how important relationships are and consequently how they may actually turn out. With Saturn coming into the picture once more, this time combining directly with the Sun on the ♂/♇, ♅/Ψ and ♂/♅ midpoints, the sense of authority, discipline or formality is strengthened. This could be someone whose life is either focused around issues of being controlled by others, or focuses their life around the need to control *them*.

The ♄ = ♂/♇ and ♄ = ♂/♅ have a very strong 'controlling' feel about them. In both cases strong, powerful and self-willed energies are being brought together by Saturn and either disciplined and focused or held in check and repressed. There is a sense of force, of repression or *fear* about what these drives may bring in their wake. Taken by itself, ♄ = ♂/♇ or = ♂/♅ could indicate an extremely disciplined worker, someone capable of exceptional single-mindedness with the sort of 'disciplined ruthlessness' that many a top business executive may have. Taken together with what we already have started to see of our individual, it would seem more likely that these energies would seek expression in trying to control or use the strong Uranus/Neptune and Pluto components we have established as being a main factor in the life of the native. If Venus is brought into this as well, the need to relate via these energies in one way or another would seem highly probable, and with such a strong Saturn (and the ☉ = ♀/♄ also present) there could well be a need to control others – perhaps out of fear – but in some way the issue of *authority* in these areas is very likely to emerge very strongly during the course of the native's life.

At this point you should go over the Sun structure, looking at each pair step by step, and see if you feel that any combination has not been fairly dealt with. Write down anything you think has been missed out, bearing in mind that we are working with the basic planetary principles as a series of multiple conjunctions as they relate to the solar principle. We are *not* looking to the native's emotional responses – for these we would look to midpoints made to the Moon – neither are we looking at Mercury midpoints to see in what way he is able to communicate his drives and goals. We're just sticking to a basic analysis of how our native will tend to 'organize' his life, and in what manner it will be natural for him to operate if left to his own devices. If there is anything you feel has been left out, write it down now.

Obviously a person's background, upbringing and environment will all contribute to the manner in which someone will express their chart, whichever technique you use to analyse it, and this clearly has to be borne in mind. However, the basic planetary principles *will* be expressed on one level or another in the course of life. For some that ☽ = ☿/♃ we looked at first will represent a person whose most profound feelings might be expressed in religious or philosophical pursuits or who has a literal 'love of learning' and the need to develop spiritual growth out of their emotional drive towards wisdom. Another may simply prattle away about whatever he happens to be feeling at any one moment and another may even project it, being attracted towards a woman who might act as a teacher or be the type of person whose projections compel him to be forever seeking yet another guru in yet another country. But however disparate these examples might be, the symbolism is clearly there using very straightforward astrology and, using one final technique utilized in midpoint analysis, there is something else we can do to give us a clearer understanding of *how* a planetary picture may be expressed in life. This is called 'sequencing'.

Up to now we have paid no attention to the actual order in which the midpoints fall, but studies over the past twenty years have shown that the actual sequence of midpoints can be very important indeed. To understand this more fully, take another look at Figure 2.6, in which one 45° segment of the circle is drawn. This 45° sort shows the actual order in which the midpoints fall around the zodiac and thus the *order in which they are hit by transits, directions and progressions*. Every day the angles will each contact every combination eight times, each month the Moon will contact them eight times, each year the Sun will also contact them eight times and so on out through the planets. While there will obviously be periods when planets are retrograde, the vast majority of transits will be following that same sequence, first hitting one midpoint pair and then the next and so on. This can have an effect within the individual of laying down a specific pattern of behaviour. Such a pattern might emerge as the result of experiencing certain events or feelings as tending to follow one another as this sequence is triggered again and again in the same order. Eventually we may come to expect such events as inevitable and even unconsciously precipitate them.

Psychologically, what we see happening here is the Pavlov-type response which is self-reinforcing and is known by behaviourists as *operant conditioning* and, in one form, by depth psychologists as *reaction formation*. As one type of event, thought or feeling tends to follow upon another, the individual gradually comes to *expect* such a sequence of experiences as inevitable and unconscious patterns of behaviour can develop. What we can learn about a person from studying the sequence of midpoints in the chart can profoundly affect the way in which we assist our clients to confront important issues in a counselling situation and – very specifically – how we approach predictive work.

This idea of sequencing is not new to astrology, but its use in midpoints allows for a much more specific and focused approach. The zodiac itself is a sequence, and many astrologers have commented on the way the signs mirror the unfolding process of life from the outrush of Aries to the closing moments of the Piscean dissolve. A close conjunction in a natal chart will often respond to a transit in a similar manner. Many people born close to one of the Jupiter/Saturn conjunctions, for instance, have markedly different responses to transits if the Jupiter falls before the Saturn in the zodiac compared to those born shortly after the same conjunction, when it is Saturn that is triggered first. For those with Jupiter applying to the conjunction of Saturn it is often a question of having to face the cold reality of Saturn after a too-hasty or over-optimistic response. For those with Jupiter separating from the conjunction the result is often to get the just reward for all the hard work done when Saturn was transited first! In midpoint work this basic idea is just the same, but applied with greater attention to detail as there are more planetary energies to consider and much tighter orbs. Let us look again at Figure 2.7, which depicts the Sun structure of our chart, and view it in the light of this idea of sequence.

We see that in the habitual cycle of experience first the Ψ and σ midpoints with the MC would be hit and lastly the σ/H on which Saturn also sits. In fact, in the actual chart Saturn is one minute from an exact contact with σ/H. Such a structure laid out in this format is called a midpoint tree, and is a straightforward depiction of how the midpoints fall in the zodiac relative to the planet we are examining, in this case the Sun. The 'star' in the tree structure indicates where the Sun itself falls in the sequence – check that again in Figure 2.6 – and of course the midpoints just above and just below the Sun's position are the two which are in reality closest to the Sun's own position. In many cases these two may be particularly powerful.

Looking down the tree in this way we can immediately get some idea of how an individual may experience his life unfolding on the solar level. The strong Neptune and Mars contacts with the Midheaven suggest that his first solar response might be towards creating for himself a goal in which he can express these energies as we have already discussed. The need to formalize relationships (φ/$\hbar$) comes next, or perhaps the flighty dreams of Neptune come down to earth with a crash – a typical experience when Saturn follows Neptune in a tree structure – and authority (Saturn) comes into the picture as this planet now *also* triggers the remaining midpoints. The emphasis on control particularly on $\male/\pluto$ and $\male/\uranus$ is extremely strong – is this how life was experienced? For a man who spent virtually all his formative years in prison, this is a particularly apt diagram; authority always has the last word. No matter what dreams or ambitions there may be, control of the basic life and sexual forces ($\male/\pluto$ and $\male/\uranus$) would always seem to be their final outcome. Such a pattern was to have disastrous consequences when it came to be sketched out years later on a much wider canvas.

Life for our native had been an aimless succession of petty crimes which from the age of sixteen until the age of thirty-two had resulted in almost continual incarceration. Much of the time in prison was spent learning to play the guitar or studying Scientology, Buddhism and other mystical interests. At one time he was actually taking a Dale Carnegie course on self-improvement and public speaking. Again and again the basic patterns of the Sun structure are repeated; music, mysticism, the lack of female company ($\female/\saturn$), all in a controlled and ordered environment. The $\moon = \mercury/\jupiter$ mentioned at the beginning of this chapter also comes from his chart – the public speaker with religious interests on a Dale Carnegie course!

Prison records tell us that he was released from jail on 21 March 1967 at 8.15 a.m. in San Pedro, California. At that moment the transiting Ascendant was exactly on his Sun and thus of course hitting all the midpoints we have been examining, while the transiting Uranus was just 5′ from an exact contact with the radical $\saturn/M$ midpoint (which occurs in the Jupiter tree). $\uranus = \saturn/M$ is a very powerful image of a sudden release from confinement – Ebertin gives 'great emotional excitability' for this contact, and one which can only be amplified by occurring on the Jupiter structure. The solar pattern that had been learned during years of confinement was about to be replayed for real in the world outside the walls.

Charles Manson *did* 'make a career' of Neptune and Mars. His was a dark version of the religious aspirations that resulted from the blending of those two planets. He became his own Son of Man, his own Christ. Where he was controlled, he became the controller, where he was denied freedom and pleasure he became the evangelist of sex and drugs, deliberately using these as devices to control his followers (Ψ/M, ♂/M). Where he had been the victim, he became the saviour. From his position of power he took revenge on women for his own mother's failings – she had been a prostitute (♀/♄) whose own spells in prison had deprived the young Manson of any hope of a stable childhood. This particular pattern was repeated very precisely when Manson himself lived for a period on the earnings of two women he had inveigled into prostitution. This was, in fact, an active ambition of his. In his autobiography, *Without Conscience*, he describes how he always saw himself being a 'big shot' through successful pimping. For someone with ☉ = ♀/♄ the image of striving to obtain worldly credibility through controlling prostitutes is singularly apt.

Finally he took the ultimate revenge; the ♄ = ♂/♇ and ♄ = ♂/♅ spells out again how the pattern of authority and control was for him always the way to 'end the matter'. For Manson, that was how self-expression had *always* worked out. His brief spells of freedom and self-expression through crime had *always* resulted in punishment and denial of his own life. 'Prison,' he said at his trial, 'is my father.' His biography describes the brutality and sadism inflicted on him during his formative years in youth correction institutes, and when *he* became the warder – and thus took on the Saturn role – the pattern was exactly the same. He saw himself as a mixture of Christ, the Devil and a rock singer. His final failure to get anyone to take his music seriously led him to coerce a group of his women followers to murder the occupants of a secluded house, owned by the record producer who had last rejected his work.

Manson himself did not see his actions as criminal. Despite the fact that he is believed by the prosecuting attorney to have killed over thirty people, his behaviour could always be justified through his own religious ideas. ☽ = ☿/♃ suggests someone whose belief systems might depend solely on personal feelings rather than objective observation, and Manson was an extreme expression of this. The dark core of his philosophy is almost completely summed up by that complex of Sun, Venus and Saturn aspects to the Ψ/M midpoint through to the final ♂/♅ as it spells out his notorious statement: 'You really have to love people to kill them.' The potential power of his ☉ = ♄ = ♂/♇ for ritual killing is an echo of the English sex-killer Neville Heath, who, with an identical pattern on his solar axis, commited two particularly sadistic murders in 1947.

While Manson's is obviously an extreme case – and a fuller understanding of his drives would require much more observation than we have put in here – his life nevertheless illustrates clearly how midpoints to the basic solar energy source can pin-point very precisely different aspects of the drive to fulfilment and the sequence in which this may be expressed in life. In other words, midpoints tell us almost at a glance 'what type of Sun' we are looking at and in what order the basic life of the individual may strive to create its own unique expression in the world. In the following chapter this idea of following the flowing sequence of events will be more fully explored.

NOTE

1. When working with midpoints a maximum orb of + /– 2° is allowed for the personal points, ⊙, ☽, MC, AS, when they are on a midpoint. For all other chart factors a maximum orb of + /– 1°30′ is allowed. An orb of + /– 2° is also allowed for any factor in aspect to a midpoint involving two personal points, i.e. ⊙/☽, ⊙/M, ⊙/AS, ☽/M, ☽/AS, or MC/AS. The same orb is normally given for all hard aspects, no distinction being made between 45°, 90°, or 0°. Remember, these are the *maximum* orbs. If you use a maximum orb of 8° for a conjunction, opposition, trine or square in traditional chart work and consider 2° a close aspect, then c.30′ is a close aspect for a midpoint involving the personal points, and c.22′ is a close aspect for midpoints involving other chart factors. As always, the tighter the orb, the more powerful the combination is likely to prove. The orbs for transits and progressions should not normally be more than 30′.

CHAPTER 3

The Cardinal/Fixed/Mutable Sort

MICHAEL HARDING AND CHARLES HARVEY

As we have seen, sequencing midpoints in their zodiacal order gives us a deeper understanding of the inner dynamics of astrology; they can show us how events come to be created, how they emerge and manifest in the world, and even hint at their outcome. But this approach is not confined to the process of interpreting only those midpoints which are permanently activated by being in contact with the natal planets, but can be extended to examine *all* the chart's midpoints on a day-to-day or even minute-by-minute basis as the transits of the planets and the diurnal angles trigger off one combination after the other. In such a way we can begin to come to grips with the great potential for change and creativity that all too often lies hidden within the horoscope, and work with the chart in terms of its own dynamics as they are revealed by these very specific patterns.

The vast majority of the birth chart lies unseen under the conventional astrologer's gaze, with whole segments of the map – generally the signs and houses – being treated as large grey areas in which anything can happen so long as it is vaguely related to the business of that particular portion. This is something of a problem, as a transiting planet may reside for months or even years in one of the twelve divisions and, if conventional wisdom is to be believed, it must continue to sing its own song with no rise of pitch or change of tempo while all sorts of events which are clearly related to its nature may be going on all over the place with little regard to house or sign. Everyday experience constantly confirms this, so what on earth is actually happening?

Each day we are forced to recognize that events and their emotional counterparts are taking place in our lives all the time whether we like it or not. Sometimes these are of great importance but generally they are not and our lives tend to be filled with trivial, though often temporarily demanding, occurrences. We may get a letter which pleases or annoys us, a phone call which requires some minor but necessary decision to be taken. A sudden change in the state of the weather may please or depress us, a bus may just be missed or a train delayed. In short, every day of our life we either take part in or are a witness to dozens of incidents which affect us emotionally one way or another, and if we can take time to reflect on them they show us again and again the continual state of flux in which we all exist. A state of affairs which, if we really do believe in the basic astrological tenet of 'as above, so below', must somehow reflect the caprices of the planets. Even without any great dramas, the simple processes of everyday life should offer us major insights into the way astrology works even if the events themselves are of no real or lasting consequence. But does it really happen that way?

If we get down to our chart at the end of the day, is Mercury always trine to our third house cusp when we get cheerful news? Did Saturn suddenly hop on to our Descendant when some issue of loss occurred? Did Jupiter really make a quick personal trip to our Uranus when we had a sudden bright idea, only to be followed by yet another visitation of Saturn an hour later (this time to Neptune) when we realized we couldn't afford it? From a midpoint view the answer is *Yes – that's exactly what does happen!* As we shall shortly see.

The conventional approaches towards the analysis of events and personality tend to see the chart in large undifferentiated areas illuminated by the occasional aspect, but otherwise somewhat devoid of real life. Large areas of longitude can lie barren as a winter field, in which transiting planets seem to be left to wander about like lost sheep waiting to make some clear-cut, officially approved aspect with at least the Part of Fortune. And if things happen during these periods of celestial limbo, if the sheep are clearly heard to be bleating, then the astrologer is forced to scrabble about in his box of tertiary progressions or assorted asteroids in the hope of finding something that may explain the noise. The real problem, however, lies not with the sheep, the asteroids or the progressions. It all comes down to *how the field is laid out*. As has been suggested earlier – what you get is what you *see*.

The Cardinal/Fixed/Mutable sort is a method of laying out

planetary information so that we can see at a glance how these hidden dynamics of the chart are responding to daily transits, progressions or lunations. Moreover, we can use this same sort both to rectify a chart virtually to the second or to come to a much deeper understanding of how very specific aspects affect us. All too often events occur in our lives when – according to the ephemeris – there is nothing 'there' to explain them. Using this particular sort can be quite an eye-opener, as it enables us to see that planetary energies are far more active in the chart than may have been previously realized and that these energies combine to resonate again and again around the zodiac. In fact, using the full range of midpoints which we all have in our charts, we can begin to see that the energies of a specific planet can be triggered by a transit far more frequently than conventional approaches allow and that these transits can correlate with remarkable precision with events and occurrences in our lives.

If we come back to the basic idea of midpoints discussed in the previous chapter – that each planetary pair resonates eight times around the circle of the zodiac, every 45° in fact – then a planet moving through just 45° of its cycle will aspect every pair once. Similarly the Moon will trigger each pair about every three and a half days and the MC and Ascendant every three hours – and the transits of these angles can prove to be very important indeed.

Generally speaking, the transits of the Ascendant and the Midheaven are not treated with any particular regard in ordinary astrological work; which is strange considering how much emphasis is placed on their progressed positions when inevitably there can be room for doubting the precise accuracy of the stated positions. In midpoints, however, they are fundamental for understanding how the psychology of the planets operates within us. For again and again we shall see that it is the moment by moment triggering of planetary pairs by the two angles which will bring into sudden high relief the energies of the planets concerned. The MC hitting ♃/♅ for instance, often correlates with a feeling of elation or relief; it is the classic point of 'good fortune' when energies which have been held in check for some reason are suddenly released in a burst of enthusiasm. The individual can experience the principle of Jupiter at such a time very strongly indeed – although Jupiter itself is by transit nowhere to be seen! This is not to suggest that its current transiting position is of no account, rather that the orthodox approach of concentrating almost exclusively on Jupiter's house position, when no conventional aspect is formed, ignores the full spectrum of its radical potential and consequently our own ability to experience its effects in the everyday course of life – as our own ordinary experiences force us to admit that we actually do. The conventional approach towards the interpretation of transits is to say, in effect, 'What is the planet *doing* to me?' The use of midpoints makes us more aware that we have the planet already there within us all the time and instead stresses the question, 'How do I experience its principle now?' The planet may well be 'doing' something as well, but that is the second stage and will be looked at more fully in Chapter 6.

In using midpoints we are concentrating much more on the dynamics that exist between the individual and the cosmos, or in mundane work between the event and the country in which it occurs, as a continual process of interaction. Every twenty-four hours each part of our chart is touched by the Ascendant and the Midheaven eight times, and experience suggests that if an event is building up in our life which symbolizes specific planetary energies, then these transits of the angles are as likely – indeed *more* likely – to herald its exact arrival as the transits of the planets themselves.

The easiest way to test this one out is to create a Cardinal/Fixed/Mutable sort of all the midpoints in your chart and see how they are actually activated by transits. All that is needed to create this sort is the once-only task of putting the midpoints into a slightly different sequence, according to how they fall in each Cardinal, Fixed or Mutable sign. This work can be done by hand or by using the computer program specially written for this task which is to be found in Appendix 1 (p. 445). But before using the program it is advisable to go through the process manually at least once so that you have a clear idea of what is going on and how we are using this particular midpoint sort.

As its name suggests, the Cardinal/Fixed/Mutable sort shows us how each pair of midpoints falls in each of the triplicities. It is created simply by finding out which midpoints fall in which of the triplicities and then listing their positions in one of three columns. Because each of these qualities is either opposite or square to one another – think of the Cardinal cross, the Mutable dilemma and so on – it follows that a midpoint which falls as 0 Aries also falls at 0° Cancer, 0° Libra and 0° Capricorn. Thus by looking at only one of each of the triplicities we can see what is going in in *each* of them. The only real calculation needed – and this is very simply done in one's head or with any calculator – is in finding the indirect (45°-away) midpoint for each pair and putting that into the picture as well. For instance, a midpoint at 0° Aries will also occur at 15° Taurus, being 45° away, and having found this we enter its position in the Fixed column. There is no need to go on to locate its further repetition at 15° Leo, 15° Scorpio and 15° Aquarius, for these are also all square to one another and thus treated identically. Remember, the actual minutes of each pair's longitude are always going to be the same, so it is just a matter of adding 45° to each combination to find the indirect position.

The first stage in creating the sort is to calculate the seventy-eight midpoints in the standard 360° sort – to show their actual positions in the circle of the zodiac – entering '360' as the choice of sort or dial on most computer programs will give you a print-out of this information. Working from the print-out, first split the midpoints up into the triplicities and then find the indirect midpoint for each pair by adding 45° to each combination in turn. With this data you can list all the midpoints as they fall in sequence from 0° 0' to 29° 59' of each sign so that you end up with a list that looks like Figure 3.1. Note that the three columns will very rarely be of equal length; this is of course simply a reflection of how the planets themselves are dispersed unequally around the zodiac. In some examples there may be nearly twice as many midpoints in one column as in another. It is also useful to add into this list both the direct and indirect positions of the planets and angles themselves for additional information. Make a number of photocopies of this sort and you can begin to take a new look at your life.

What we now have is the ideal tool for checking transits in a very precise and detailed manner, allowing in some cases for extremely accurate predictions to be made as well as providing one of the best tools for rectifying a questionable birthtime. All that we need to do

```
OIL SPILL
24 MAR 1989/ 0:4 AM/ 61 N 7/ 146 W 16 / ZONE: 10  / ALASKA
==CARDINAL================FIXED================MUTABLE==
```

CARDINAL			FIXED			MUTABLE		
MO/NN	0	4	ME/MA	0	31	JU/AS	0	10
ME/AS	0	7	SO/AS	0	58	MO/UR	0	21
***VE	0	48	VE/JU	1	27	MO/MC	1	20
MO/MA	1	44	UR/AS	1	43	NN/AS	1	26
SO/VE	2	16	AS/MC	2	42	***JU	2	7
ME/NE	2	40	VE/NN	2	44	MA/AS	3	5
VE/UR	3	1	SO/JU	2	56	JU/NN	3	23
ME/SA	3	8	JU/UR	3	40	MO/NE	3	52
***SO	3	45	SO/NN	4	12	ME/PL	3	56
VE/MC	3	59	VE/MA	4	23	MO/SA	4	21
SO/UR	4	29	JU/MC	4	39	***NN	4	40
***UR	5	13	UR/NN	4	57	MA/JU	5	3
SO/MC	5	28	MO/PL	5	9	MA/NN	6	19
UR/MC	6	12	NE/AS	5	14	VE/PL	7	49
PL/AS	6	31	SA/AS	5	43	***MA	7	58
VE/NE	6	32	SO/MA	5	51	SO/PL	9	17
VE/SA	7	1	NN/MC	5	55	UR/PL	10	1
***MC	7	11	MA/UR	6	36	ME/AS	10	38
SO/NE	8	0	JU/NE	7	11	PL/MC	11	0
JU/PL	8	28	MA/MC	7	35	ME/JU	12	35
SO/SA	8	29	JU/SA	7	40	NE/PL	13	33
UR/NE	8	45	NE/NN	8	28	ME/NN	13	51
SA/UR	9	13	SA/NN	8	56	SA/PL	14	1
MO/NE	9	16	MA/NE	10	7	VE/AS	14	30
NE/MC	9	43	MA/SA	10	36	ME/MA	15	31
PL/NN	9	45	MO/AS	11	51	SO/AS	15	58
SA/MC	10	12	ME/VE	11	56	VE/JU	16	27
MA/PL	11	24	SO/MC	13	24	UR/AS	16	43
***NE	12	16	MO/JU	13	48	AS/MC	17	42
SA/NE	12	45	ME/UR	14	8	VE/NN	17	44
MO/VE	13	8	***PL	14	49	SO/JU	17	56
***SA	13	13	MO/NN	15	4	JU/UR	18	40
SO/MO	14	37	ME/MC	15	7	SO/NN	19	12
JU/AS	15	10	MO/MA	16	44	VE/MA	19	23
MO/UR	15	21	SO/VE	17	16	JU/MC	19	39
MO/MC	16	20	ME/NE	17	40	UR/NN	19	57
NN/AS	16	26	VE/UR	18	1	MO/PL	20	9
MA/AS	18	5	ME/SA	18	8	NE/AS	20	14
JU/NN	18	23	VE/MC	18	59	SA/AS	20	43
MO/NE	18	52	SO/UR	19	29	SO/MA	20	51
ME/PL	18	56	SO/MC	20	28	NN/MC	20	55
MO/SA	19	21	UR/MC	21	12	MA/UR	21	36
MA/JU	20	3	PL/AS	21	31	JU/NE	22	11
MA/NN	21	19	VE/NE	21	32	MA/MC	22	35
VE/PL	22	49	VE/SA	22	1	JU/SA	22	40
SO/PL	24	17	SO/NE	23	0	***ME	23	3
UR/PL	25	1	JU/PL	23	28	NE/NN	23	28
***MO	25	29	SO/SA	23	29	SA/NN	23	56
ME/AS	25	38	UR/NE	23	45	MA/NE	25	7
PL/MC	26	0	SA/UR	24	13	MA/SA	25	36
ME/JU	27	35	MO/MA	24	16	MO/AS	26	51
NE/PL	28	33	NE/MC	24	43	ME/VE	26	56
ME/NN	28	51	PL/NN	24	45	SO/ME	28	24
SA/PL	29	1	SA/MC	25	12	MO/JU	28	48
VE/AS	29	30	MA/PL	26	24	ME/UR	29	8
			SA/NE	27	45			
			MO/VE	28	8			
			***AS	28	12			
			SO/MO	29	37			

Figure 3.1 An example of the Cardinal/Fixed/Mutable sort, much reduced, as produced by an Astrocalc program.

to use this sort is to look at the ephemeris and see what was going on at a date that concerns us and then enter the transiting planets' positions (and those of the angles if we have an exact time) as they fall in each of the triplicities to see exactly what is really going on. Mars is suddenly no longer just 'in the 4th House' or 'in Aquarius'; it is instead at a very precise spot and perhaps activating a specific midpoint in a way which can well manifest in life as an equally specific event. The angles themselves, if we are looking at a precisely-timed moment in our life, can be very telling. No longer is the MC 'somewhere near our Jupiter' or whatever. It will almost certainly fall very close to a planetary pair and thus point to *exactly* what was going on in our life at the time. This is micro-astrology, where we can begin to put our chart under the microscope and take a look at what until now has been a completely hidden world.

The first use of this sort can be a somewhat sobering experience and can perhaps remind us of when we first approached astrology somewhat sceptically and discovered that a complete stranger knew slightly more about us than we may have cared to admit! When we get a good idea we like to think that it is 'us' who gets it, rather than perhaps something which *happens* to us. If we discover that the MC is exactly on the ☿/♅ at the moment when we had an astrological insight we may be tempted to think that the insight was having us, almost as if the meridian was waiting for the first suitable person to come round on the carousel! So let's have a look at some similar, real examples from accurately-timed events over which the participants would have little apparent control. Remember the orb we are using for the MC is 2°, which is the equivalent of eight minutes of time; though aspects to the Ascendant also have an orb of 2° this may reflect a change of more or less than eight minutes of time depending on the rising sign and the latitude.

A climber reaches the top of a volcano (Figure 3.2) and the MC is on his own ♇/AS midpoint. Literally, he becomes conscious

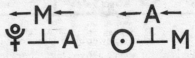

Figure 3.2 The transiting MC comes to the natal ♇/AS midpoint at the same time as the transiting AS hits ☉/M.

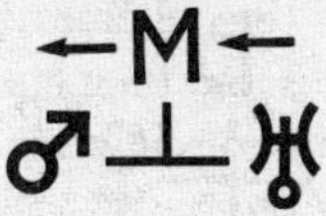

←M←
♂⊥♅

Figure 3.3 The MC hits ♂/♅ at the moment of an accident. This combination frequently occurs in accidents, operations and explosions.

(MC) of the relationship between Pluto and the environment (AS). The transiting Ascendant is also on his ☉/M midpoint – the conscious goal has been reached at a particular point on the earth's surface.

A mechanic is slightly injured (Figure 3.3) when electrical equipment he is working on suddenly explodes – as the MC hits his ♂/♅ midpoint. This midpoint is often implicated in accidents, operations or explosions, and someone with strong aspects to the ♂/♅ midpoint may well be accident-prone or have an 'explosive' personality.

A four-year-old boy (Figure 3.4) prone to sudden outbursts of activity has ♃ = ♅/AS = ☉/AS = ♂. Repeatedly as the transiting angles come to this picture he is prone to suddenly fly off the handle. For example, when ♃ by transit was on this picture and was joined by the transiting AS the boy excitedly rushed forward to grab a toy from his younger brother. As he did so he gashed his forehead on an intervening table. This is highly characteristic of the way in which at present this energy picture is expressing itself. But by being aware of this pattern and the form it takes, it is possible for the parents to encourage the positive use of

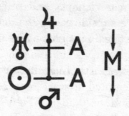

Figure 3.4 The MC crossing a powerful structure of midpoints to Mars and Jupiter in the chart of a very active child. Note that both Sun and Uranus aspect the radical Ascendant; this contact with the angles would suggest that the energy *will* find expression in the environment.

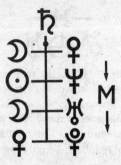

Figure 3.5 Saturn 'grounds' an inspirational (☉/Ψ) and insightful (☽/♅) combination within powerful indicators of deep emotions (☽/♀ and ♀/♇). Transits to this structure have correlated with profound and mystical insights.

this highly dramatic and competitive pattern of energies through games and play acting.

A man who has ♄ = ☽/♀ = ☉/Ψ = ☽/♅ = ♀/♇ (Figure 3.5) is given to moments of sudden poetic inspiration and insight when the transiting angles trigger this picture. By deliberately noting when this picture is going to be especially activated by slower transits and transiting angles, it has been possible to choose such moments to obtain insights into the ideas, issues, and personal blockages encapsulated in this seed pattern. For example, when the transit MC configured the 1988 ♄–0–♅ on this picture this man was meditating on the concept of unity when he experienced an overwhelming flood of highly illuminating and transformative poetic imagery, of great richness and intensity, which lasted several minutes before subsiding. By the deliberate use of such moments it is possible to gain insights which might normally arise but rarely.

A man who had been a strict vegetarian for many years had out of politeness attempted to eat some steak provided by a well-meaning host, and become ill (Figure 3.6). On his way to the bathroom he collapsed vomiting and was rendered temporarily unconscious. This occurred at exactly the moment that transit MC reached his Ψ/♇ = ☉. Of this combination *COSI* says 'throwing in the sponge' and 'a sensitive physique . . . proneness to

Figure 3.6 Solar energy brings together Neptune and Pluto. A transit to this point resulted in temporary unconsciousness – one way to get to the depths!

external influences. Peculiar diseases as a consequence of over-indulgence . . .' Such an event when understood in this way alerts the individual to a deeper picture of personal sensitivity with its implications on the psychological and spiritual as well as the simply physical level.

☽/♂ is related by Ebertin to 'the unconscious direction of the muscular movements' and to 'reactions of the emotional life such as blushing'. (See also Chapter 19, the case history of Zelda Fitzgerald.) For ☽/♂ = ♅ *COSI* gives 'quick irritability, a quick and violent temper'. A five-year-old girl with this combination was on her way to a ballet lesson with her mother when a friend asked her mother whether the girl would like to come to tea. Her mother said this was impossible because of the ballet class. Shortly afterwards the little girl collapsed with an extremely acute muscular cramp in her calf and was unable to go on to the class. At that moment the transit MC was exactly on the ☽/♂ = ♅ (Figure 3.7). Later, when, on the evidence of the astrology of the moment, the mother was asked what the little girl had been angry about, the mother said that she had not been in any way angry. When the astrologer, persisting, asked the girl the same question, she burst

Figure 3.7 A burst of anger correlated with a transit to this powerful indicator of emotional responsiveness.

out that she was furious because she had been stopped from going to tea by 'silly old ballet'. Obligingly her 'unconscious muscular movements' had translated her anger into an appropriate cramp which had made dancing impossible!

Such insights can alert the individual, or the parent in this case, to the likelihood that, unless allowed to be expressed in some more direct way, there will be ready displacement of anger into physical symptoms which could have longer-term consequences. In this particular case the girl in adolescence was for a period acutely anorexic and this was in all probability closely related to her inability to express her own anger at parental problems which were happening at this time.

At 7.30 p.m. on 24 March 1974 a chauffeur-driven car was proceeding down the Mall in London when its progress was blocked by a car in front. The MC at this moment was at 8.28 Cancer exactly on the natal $\odot = \mathbb{D}/\sigma = \mathbb{H}$ of the woman sitting in the back seat, while the AS was on her $\hbar/\text{AS} = \Psi/\Omega = \odot$, while the M/AS was exactly with her $\odot$ (Figure 3.8). At this time (MC) we might expect some kind of sudden potentially violent, personal, emotional upsets, and at this place (AS) the possibility of situations which could bring to the fore her potential for personal self-control and for meeting with Neptunian types. While these angles cross this point every day, also in the sky at this point in space time was $\odot/\text{AS} = \mathbb{P} = \sigma/\mathbb{H}$, a highly violent and unstable combination which fell on the distinguished lady's natal $\odot/\mathbb{P}$, a point which promises both 'the qualities of leadership' and 'physical suffering . . . danger to life'. As the limousine drew to a halt a gun was thrust through the window and a man tried to wrench open the door and hijack the car. During the next few minutes a life and

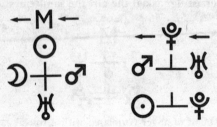

Figure 3.8 Various factors transited at the time of an attempted kidnap.

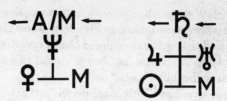

Figure 3.9 Transits of the A/M midpoint and Saturn to factors in Boris Becker's natal chart at the moment he loses his title.

death struggle ensued in which several shots were fired, seriously wounding the chauffeur and injuring a policeman and Princess Anne's bodyguard. That Princess Anne came through this ordeal can perhaps in part be put down to the fact that Jupiter, the 'Great Protector', was only 9′ away from its exact return to its natal place on the ⊙/☽ and ♄/♇ midpoints.

At 4.55 p.m. on 27 June 1987 the MC/AS 'at this time and place' axis of the moment at Wimbledon was exactly with Boris Becker's Ψ = ♀/M. Of the possible manifestations of this combination *COSI* says, '. . . renunciation, the state of being unsatisfied and unhappy . . . the suffering of the soul . . .' At this moment the twice-crowned tennis champion was knocked out in the fourth round of the championships by an unknown Australian. That Saturn in the sky at this time was also exactly (6′) from Becker's ♃/♅ = ⊙/M no doubt had much to do with what *COSI* describes as 'sudden disadvantages, losses' and 'the tendency to withdraw or retire, the mood of sadness' (Figure 3.9).

Figure 3.10 shows that the M = ♂/Ψ of the moment was on

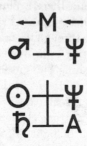

Figure 3.10 President Nixon resigns as the transiting M = ♂/Ψ contacts his ♄/AS midpoint.

natal $h/M = \odot/\Psi = h/AS$ exactly at the moment that President
Nixon made his speech resigning as President of the USA. Again
and again we find that accurately timed charts reveal graphically
the inner workings of events, be they a record of some simple
everyday event or the fall of kings.

Let us look at a case in a little more detail, using the Cardinal/
Fixed/Mutable sort. Figure 3.11 is the C/F/M sort for Christa
MacAuliffe, the teacher who was killed when the Space Shuttle
exploded on 28 January 1986. Alongside her natal midpoints have
been written in the transits for that moment. Looking at the
Mutable column we can see that Saturn is within 3′ of her $\odot/\mathbb{D}$
midpoint. In the next chapter we shall go further into the meaning
of this most important point and see that it can be as powerful as
any personal planet in the chart. The $\odot/\mathbb{D}$ midpoint can be
thought of as a 'centre' or focus of personal energy in which both
the masculine and feminine elements of the psyche come together.
A Saturn transit to this point will almost invariably mark a sober
and serious time of life and occasionally – as in Christa's case – its
termination. The symbolism is very clear, and no astrologer could
in all honesty encourage someone to undertake a dangerous
venture at such a time.

Of course one cannot and should not make such a definite
statement from one chart factor alone, but a glance at some of the
other transits which show up so clearly using this method can only
back up the initial concern that the Saturn aspects provide. $\female =$
$\female/\Omega$ indicates a shared and perhaps tragic destiny, and Christa's
own $\female/M$ midpoint – her own personal experience and awareness
of the Pluto energy – is being literally illuminated by the transiting
Sun on that day. Ebertin describes the $\female/M$ midpoint as having the
potential for 'sudden ruin through the misuse of power, a crisis . . .
in life, a turn in one's destiny'. The Sun is symbolically picking the
day. Looking at the transiting Pluto itself, we see it is within a few
minutes of her own $\male/\female$ midpoint, with $\mercury$ only a degree away $=$
$\odot/\uranus$ (another midpoint associated with sudden events, often of a
military nature and with a strong element of risk, and Mercury, of
course, is clearly symbolic of flight). Both these transiting planets
are clustered around the node, that point of shared fate or communication, and, as it turned out, the Ascendant itself touched that

CHRISTA MACAULIFFE
2 SEP 1948/ 9:13 PM/ 42 N 22/ 71 W 4 / ZONE: 5 / BOSTON

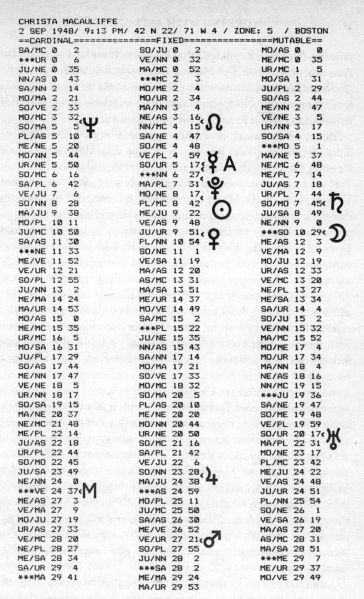

```
==CARDINAL===============FIXED================MUTABLE==
SA/MC  0  2      SO/JU  0  2      MO/AS  0  0
***UR  0  6      VE/NN  0 32      ME/MC  0 35
JU/NE  0 35      MA/MC  0 52      UR/MC  1  5
NN/AS  0 43      ***MC  2  3      MO/SA  1 31
SA/NN  2 14      MO/ME  2  4      JU/PL  2 29
MO/MA  2 21      MO/UR  2 34      SO/AS  2 44
SO/VE  2 33      MA/NN  3  4      ME/NN  2 47
MO/MC  3 32      NE/AS  3 16      VE/NE  3  5
SO/MA  5  5      NN/MC  4 15      UR/NN  3 17
PL/AS  5 10      SA/NE  4 47      SO/SA  4 15
ME/NE  5 20      SO/ME  4 48      ***MO  5  1
MO/NN  5 44      VE/PL  4 59      MA/NE  5 37
UR/NE  5 50      SO/UR  5 17      NE/MC  6 48
SO/MC  6 16      ***NN  6 27      ME/PL  7 14
SA/PL  6 42      MA/PL  7 31      JU/AS  7 18
VE/JU  7  6      MO/NE  8 17      UR/PL  7 44
SO/NN  8 28      PL/MC  8 42      SO/MO  7 45
MA/JU  9 38      ME/JU  9 22      JU/SA  8 49
MO/PL 10 11      VE/AS  9 48      NE/NN  9  0
JU/MC 10 50      JU/UR  9 51      ***SO 10 29
SA/AS 11 30      PL/NN 10 54      ME/AS 12  3
***NE 11 33      SO/NE 11  1      VE/MA 12  9
ME/VE 11 52      VE/SA 11 19      MO/JU 12 19
VE/UR 12 21      MA/AS 12 20      UR/AS 12 33
SO/PL 12 55      AS/MC 13 31      VE/MC 13 20
JU/NN 13  2      MA/SA 13 51      NE/PL 13 27
ME/MA 14 24      ME/UR 14 37      ME/SA 13 34
MA/UR 14 53      MO/VE 14 49      SA/UR 14  4
MO/AS 15  0      SA/MC 15  2      SO/JU 15  2
ME/MC 15 35      ***PL 15 22      VE/NN 15 32
UR/MC 16  5      JU/NE 15 35      MA/MC 15 52
MO/SA 16 31      NN/AS 15 43      MO/ME 17  4
JU/PL 17 29      SA/NN 17 14      MO/UR 17 34
SO/AS 17 44      MO/MA 17 21      MA/NN 18  4
ME/NN 17 47      SO/VE 17 33      NE/AS 18 16
VE/NE 18  5      MO/MC 18 32      NN/MC 19 15
UR/NN 18 17      SO/MA 20  5      ***JU 19 36
SO/SA 19 15      PL/AS 20 10      SA/NE 19 47
MA/NE 20 37      ME/NE 20 20      SO/ME 19 48
NE/MC 21 48      MO/NN 20 44      VE/PL 19 59
ME/PL 22 14      UR/NE 20 50      SO/UR 20 17
JU/AS 22 18      SO/MC 21 16      MA/PL 22 31
UR/PL 22 44      SA/PL 21 42      MO/NE 23 17
SO/MO 22 45      VE/JU 22  6      PL/MC 23 42
JU/SA 23 49      SO/NN 23 28      ME/JU 24 22
NE/NN 24  0      MA/JU 24 38      VE/AS 24 48
***VE 24 37      ***AS 24 59      JU/UR 24 51
ME/AS 27  3      MO/PL 25 11      PL/NN 25 54
VE/MA 27  9      JU/MC 25 50      SO/NE 26  1
MO/JU 27 19      SA/AS 26 30      VE/SA 26 19
UR/AS 27 33      ME/VE 26 52      MA/SA 27 20
VE/MC 28 20      VE/UR 27 21      AS/MC 28 31
NE/PL 28 27      SO/PL 27 55      MA/SA 28 51
ME/SA 28 34      JU/NN 28  2      ***ME 29  7
SA/UR 29  4      ***SA 28  2      ME/UR 29 37
***MA 29 41      ME/MA 29 24      MO/VE 29 49
                 MA/UR 29 53
```

Figure 3.11 The Cardinal/Fixed/Mutable sort for Christa MacAuliffe for the moment of the *Challenger* explosion. Note the factors clustering around her node (which is also on America's node), the ♄ = ☉/☽ and the fact that *both* Mercury and Uranus are hitting the same natal combination.

point as *Challenger* exploded (that degree of the Fixed signs is also America's own node, but more of that later); while Jupiter on the ♂/♃ midpoint adds another pointer towards an explosive picture. When a transiting planet touches a midpoint which includes its radical position as one of the pair, then there is a very strong tendency for the principle of that pair to be strongly exaggerated. It is like reinforcing like; no one can doubt that Mars and Jupiter together can bring risks of carelessness, recklessness and fire.

If we look more closely at the Mutable sort again we see that Uranus is *also* = ☉/♅. In other words, it is conjunct Mercury in the 45° sort and must be one multiple of that phase away. It is in fact almost exactly 45° from the planet of flight. So in reality we find ☿ = ♅ = ☉/♅. This is not a pattern which can encourage confidence where matters of flight or risk are involved, and when we come to the last transiting planet in the Fixed column, Mars at 27° 17' = ☿/♀ and ♀/♅, we see the picture of flight, energy, sudden events and shock again repeated. The ♀/♅ midpoint is an especially sensitive one to consider. Ebertin connects it mainly with birth – either literally or symbolically – but it also indicates feelings of shock or having to face the unexpected. Mars here may be a good indicator of excitement or even extreme pleasure for someone whose feet are on the ground, but for someone who is sitting on top of what is effectively a bomb it is a less than happy aspect. Furthermore, that transiting Mars is less than half a degree away from her natal Saturn; in other words it is beginning to activate all the midpoints connected to her own Saturn. Christa was born with ♄ = ☿/♀ = ♀/♅ and thus it is *this* energy which Mars is actually triggering. Furthermore, Neptune was nearly 45° from Saturn when Christa was born and thus Neptune is *also* on these same midpoints radically and *also* being triggered by transiting Mars. And it was the combined energies of Saturn and Neptune which more than anything else caused the loss of *Challenger*.

At the very moment that *Challenger* exploded, Mercury, Uranus, Pluto and the Ascendant *all* fell on the ♄/♆ midpoint of the moment. Thus the principles of Saturn and Neptune were being very powerfully activated by the other two outer planets as well as by the planet of flight and by the point describing the actual position on Earth at which the event took place – the Ascendant. *Challenger* exploded because intense cold made it impossible for a sealing ring to expand and thus gases leaked out with fatal results! One would be hard-pressed to see planetary energies more clearly and unambiguously expressed. The last part of the equation, the transiting Midheaven for the moment itself, is a harder one to read in this particular case because of Christa's own unique synastry with the chart of the USA. Her Venus, on which the MC falls = ☿/AS (the enjoyment of communication and the 'flight of ideas') and is also exactly opposite America's own Mercury (flight, again) at 24 ♋ 12. America *also* has Mercury 45° of its natal Uranus and thus the *Challenger* explosion takes place on the very day when the two planets which represent flight and innovation are repeating their phasing in America's own birth chart, and it is almost certainly *this* radical pattern which the MC for the moment is picking up. The placement of Christa's own Venus at this unique point indicates more than anything else how she was to symbolize everything that was lost with the destruction of *Challenger*.

While the chart for the loss of *Challenger* is a strong one even using conventional analysis, the use of midpoints brings to the surface factors that would otherwise remain unseen. In using the Cardinal/Fixed/Mutable sort we can bring out key points at a glance. For instance, the full Moon on 26 January – two days prior to the launch – at 5 ♌ 45 fell within minutes of the sensitive nodal point already referred to, while the Ascendant for that full Moon was at 26 ♌ 52 – exact to the minute of the ☿/♀ midpoint that was so strongly activated on the day. The lunation MC at 24 ♉ 32 is just 6′ from that other equally marked midpoint – ♂/♃. Again and again lunations, progressions and transits which otherwise can be seen as just falling in one house or another actually pick out key energies which clearly manifest in the world in a very precise manner. With these two methods of laying out the 45° sort, first the midpoint trees to locate the dominant patterns which affect and alter the way in which the focusing planet operates and second the C/F/M sort which reveals the full range of midpoints as they fall within each of the signs and allows us to see how the chart is resonating to transits moment by moment, we have two very important tools which we can use to examine in depth how the chart's potential unfolds in time. These two simple techniques form the basis of all midpoint work and the information they can give us is considerable. In the following chapters we shall see how to utilize these techniques, and how to make best use of the information they reveal.

CHAPTER 4

The Inner Marriage: The Sun/Moon Midpoint

CHARLES HARVEY

Like two partners in a relationship, the Sun and the Moon form the twin foci around which the dynamics of any chart revolve. The 'lights' can be seen to represent the male and female, conscious and unconscious, active and passive, yin and yang, the purposeful and practical potentialities of every moment. As we know, in any chart analysis a full consideration of these bodies and their relationship to each other can often reveal some of the most fundamental issues in the individual's life.

When we consider the actual Sun/Moon midpoint we will see that we have one point which represents the total fusion of these two ideas, a point where the potent process symbolized by these bodies can interact with other planetary principles releasing enormous creative power within the individual life. This creative power arises because the Sun/Moon midpoint is, as it were, the point of *conjunctio* of the alchemists, that point of 'inner marriage' where inner masculine and feminine can potentially join in creative union. This is that point in the chart where the individual can relate to the world 'wholeheartedly', 'body and soul', 'heart and mind', where they can 'get themselves together' and 'give themselves' to their life with abundant creative energy and joyous self-surrender to their larger purpose. Looking at this in terms of recent psycho-physiological findings, we can see that the Sun/ Moon midpoint symbolizes that point where the otherwise almost autonomous left and right hemispheres of the brain have the potential to interact. At this interface the left-hand side 'masculine', logical, verbal, intellectual faculties and the 'feminine', emotional, musical, intuitive faculties can come together, resulting in an upsurge of creative energy.[1]

In our daily life we can experience the significance of the interaction of the Sun and Moon levels in those moments when we are about to fall asleep or when we are just waking. Such moments can be enormously creative as these two different aspects of the psyche fleetingly interact and we gain semi-conscious access to the unconscious. For example, so powerfully productive were such times for the young Descartes that at the monastery where he was being educated he was allowed to stay in bed, contrary to all the rules of the Order. Likewise times of 'falling in love' or indeed 'falling out of love' are celebrated the world over by the poetry, music and general creativity that they produce as male and female elements of the psyche interact. Many are the artists, such as Goethe, who have become addicted to such sweet inspirations.

This potential for 'inner marriage' is present in all of us but it would seem to be particularly active in those whose Sun/Moon midpoint is occupied by a third chart factor or factors.[2] This additional factor appears to act as a catalyst or focal point for this process of inner fusion. When this happens the whole of the life will tend to become concentrated and at the same time suffused with the qualities of this third factor or factors. Indeed, the more someone with an occupied Sun/Moon midpoint works with the principle of the third factor the more their life will seem to 'come together'.

A similar catalytic effect can be observed when an otherwise unoccupied Sun/Moon is triggered by transit, especially by the station of an outer planet, or by a progression or direction. Such periods can produce a temporary experience of greater focus and purposefulness and integration through working with the energies of the triggering planet. Things can begin to 'connect' that have previously gone their own paths. Likewise such times can deeply permeate the circumstances and situation of the life with the planetary principle involved. The woman with Mars stationary on her Sun/Moon may suddenly become uncharacteristically forceful and self-assured, the previously rigidly orthodox man with Neptune transiting this point may soften and become open to new ideas, or they may become temporarily 'all at sea' and beguiled by dubious schemes and relationships. Hence an awareness of what is going on at this point, by transit and progression, can have a profound bearing on how we approach a counselling situation and how we present chart information to our client.

The importance of this midpoint cannot be over-stressed. It is as prominent as any personal planet – after all, it focuses the energy of the two most powerful ones – and it is missed out at some considerable peril. A client may have any number of bodies in fire signs, but if Saturn sits firmly on the ☉/☽ midpoint then the overwhelming chance is that the astrologer who blithely ignores this in favour of a discourse on how those fiery energies ought to be operating in the client's life risks spending two hours collecting egg on his or her face – and doing a second-rate job into the bargain. So before going on to discuss methods of using midpoints in general, we ought to take a much closer look at specific examples which highlight the ☉/☽ midpoint in action.

Examining Figure 4.1 by traditional methods, it is doubtful that the crucial importance of Jupiter would be noted. Indeed, a close angular Saturn trine Sun in Capricorn and Mercury in Aquarius, with Aquarius, a traditionally Saturn ruled sign, rising, suggests that the Jupiter principle will be very much in the background. Beyond its rulership of the MC and its exalted position in Cancer, Jupiter's lack of traditional aspect, with only a weak semi-square to Saturn, would again lead us to play down its importance. Only the close quintile to Neptune, the bi-quintile to the Ascendant and semi-quintile to the node would alert the observant student to Jupiter's potential power in shaping an individual born at this moment, as we shall see in Chapter 12 on the 5th harmonic chart.

Indeed, Lois Rodden says of this natal chart in her *Portraits of Women*: 'The chart makes as little sense as did her short life.' This is the chart of Janis Joplin, who said, 'I'd rather have ten years of "superhypermost" than live to be seventy sitting in some goddam chair watching TV.' It is the chart of the singer who burnt herself out in five years of such a 'superhypermost' of passionate singing, drugs, drink, and a final heroin overdose at the age of twenty-seven. Whatever her angular Saturn and Capricorn Sun meant in terms of her professionalism and craft as a performer, they were undoubtedly subservient to her 'superhypermost'[3] desire to 'create a swelling feeling in her audience' so descriptive of Jupiter in Cancer in the 5th house.

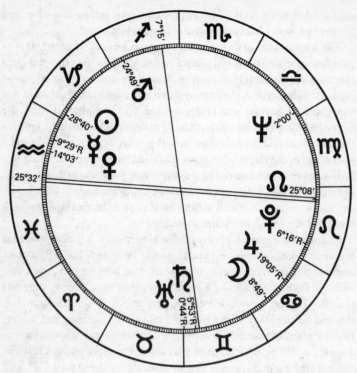

Figure 4.1 Janis Joplin: a seemingly Saturnine chart which Lois Rodden says 'makes as little sense as did her short life'.

But in addition to this, as Figure 4.2 shows, Jupiter is in fact square the Sun/Moon midpoint with an orb of only 21'. This immediately indicates that the Jupiter principle will be at the very heart of this person's life and be the principle around which their life will revolve. Looking at Jupiter's other midpoints, we find that it is only 5' from the −135− ♅/M, 3' from −45− Ψ/♇ and 20' from the opposition of ♀/♂. This gives us the picture ☉/☽ = ♅/M = ♃ = Ψ/♇ = ♀/♂.

Translating this story we could say of ☉/☽ = ♃, 'I centre myself body and soul, soul and spirit around the expansion of my abundant feelings', and ♅/M = ♃, 'I aspire to expand my power to assert myself in the world as an individual and do so with immense optimism and the power to succeed', and $\text{♃} = \text{♆}/\text{♇}$, 'my sense of my own potential for creating joy draws upon deep collective powers and a desire to transcend the merely ordinary and express a universal all-embracing love', and $\text{♃} = \text{♀}/\text{♂}$, 'my powers of expansion come coupled with a strong creative passion and strong physical appetites'.

In this picture we see a classic example of how a relatively long-term and impersonal picture $\text{♃} = \text{♆}/\text{♇}$, which in itself is a fair description of a transcendental 'superhypermost', is made immediately personal by its involvement with $\text{♅}/\text{M}$, the individual power to make one's way in the world, and then focused at the very centre of the individual's personal dynamic by its involvement

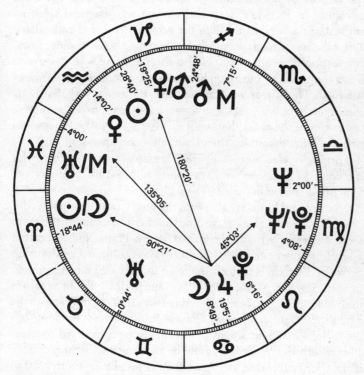

Figure 4.2 Janis Joplin: showing the central importance of ♃'s placement $-90-\;\text{☉}/\text{☽} = \text{♅}/\text{M} = \text{♆}/\text{♇} = \text{♀}/\text{♂}$.

with ☉/☽. If ♃ = Ψ/♇ can in an ideal form produce a deep love for humanity it can obviously also at a personal level lead to excesses in such things as drink and drugs which can temporarily induce a sense of transcendent euphoria and ecstasy.

It is of interest to note that the astrologer Pamela Crane, of *Draconic Astrology* fame, was born only six hours thirty-three minutes after Janis Joplin.[4] She of course shares the ♃ = Ψ/♇ = ♀/♂, but the ☉/☽ has moved on 1° 55' and is now 1° 26' from ♃ but only 23' from ♄ which is but 13' from ☊/M. This of course puts a very different emphasis on this aspect of the chart pattern, making for a far more serious and grounded approach to the possibilities of these underlying ♃ pictures which will be seen with the benefit of a Saturnine perspective. This comes out most obviously in Pamela's deep and earnest religious and spiritual enthusiasm as well as through the general dedicated enthusiasm and idealism which pervades her teaching and healing work. Interestingly enough, Pamela also sings and she is not averse to being centre-stage, but again her approach is more purposeful and subdued. Though, as we shall see later, the actual way that Janis Joplin put over her songs would necessarily have to do more with the angles of the chart than with this ☉/☽ level which has to do with the inner dynamic rather than the outer expression.

Turning now to a quite different example, we see in Figure 4.3 the chart of someone who was born with Saturn conjunct the Sun/Moon midpoint (orb 27') and Pluto −135− the midpoint (orb 2'); Saturn and Pluto are also with the Sun/Uranus midpoint with orbs of 24' and 5'. Thus, according to our criteria, this life should in some way revolve round the idea of Saturn-Pluto. Note again that apart from the close ☽−90−♅ there is no traditional relationship between these chart factors, though Saturn makes a wide quintile to both Sun and Moon (orbs 1° 23' and 2° 16'). While Saturn is undoubtedly strong, being placed in its exaltation and close to the MC at the Gauquelin point of maximum intensity, its close (orb 29') −135− to Pluto would not normally be considered to place Pluto centre-stage, though again the alert student might note that, if the time is accurate, the Ascendant is bi-quintile Pluto (2° 09') and that the Sun is septile Uranus (59') and tri-septile Pluto (33').

Ebertin, writing in *COSI* long before this chart became avail-

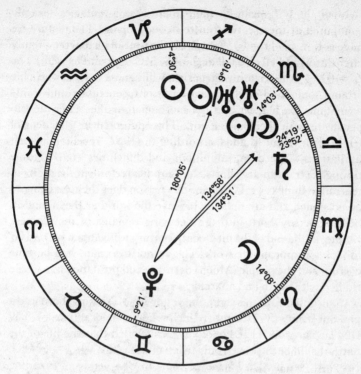

Figure 4.3 ☉/☽ = ♄ = ♇ reveals the focus of this man's life in a way that traditional methods cannot.

able, speaks of Saturn/Pluto as, inter alia, to do with 'tenacity, toughness, endurance, the capability to make record efforts of the highest possible order, the ability to perform the most difficult work with extreme self-discipline, self-denial and renunciation' and a 'tendency to violence, a fanatical adherence to one's principles once they have been adopted'. He also says of it, 'the participation in achievements brought about by large groups or masses of people . . . silent activity, the process of growing spiritually and mentally . . . the application of force or compulsion . . .' To this we might add that ♄–♇ in its highest form also suggests the professional eliminator and regenerator, the alchemist and transformer of base metal into gold.

What does it mean to have these 'heavy energies' exactly configured at the creative centre of one's being? The picture we have is $h = \odot/\text{⯞} = \odot/\mathbb{D} = \text{P}$. (If the time of birth were slightly later this would all also fall at the AS/MC midpoint as well.) The $h = \odot/\mathbb{D} = \text{P}$ certainly suggests a willingness to focus one's life around some kind of Herculean tasks of regeneration and transformation, the heavier and the more onerous the better, and to persevere with them to the end. The additional involvement of $\odot/\text{⯞}$ with h and P adds, according to *COSI*, 'rebellion against limitations of freedom, inhibitions and difficulties are overcome through extraordinary efforts' and 'a radical reformer, the desire to rearrange things . . .' Whatever this person does they are going to be no slouch and are unlikely to leave the world as they found it. Such a person born into the decaying remains of the Chinese Empire at the end of the nineteenth century would not have had far to look for appropriate work. The authorities (Sun) had become corrupt and the people (Moon) destitute and the nation as a whole riddled with death and anarchy.

Confronted with this sight, the young Mao Tse-tung, born into a peasant family (26 December 1893, c.7.30 a.m. local time = 23.59 GMT, Siangton, 112E47, 27N55), concluded that the life of the nation could be improved only by revolution ($\text{P} = \odot/\mathbb{D} = \odot/\text{⯞}$). Inspired (see his 7th harmonic chart in Chapter 13) by reading China's history (h) and the romances of heroes and brigands, he decided to devote himself to obtaining an education so that he could give himself as effectively as possible to politics and the systematic preparation for revolution. In 1920 he read Marx's *Manifesto* and married an active communist, who was executed in 1930. ($\odot/\mathbb{D}$ can also represent the outer marriage as well as the inner, and here with $h = \text{P}$ is suggestive of danger of violence and drastic events in this connection.) In August 1927 Mao organized an unsanctioned uprising and only just escaped execution. Expelled from the party, he retreated into the mountains with 1,000 followers revealing, the *Encyclopaedia Britannica* tells us, 'his great organizational talents, his ingenuity, determination, and powers of endurance in undertaking guerrilla attacks' and his 'astonishingly meticulous sense of duty, tireless energy, and considerable genius as a political and military strategist . . .'

In October 1934 Mao began his famous 6,000-mile year-long 'Long March' with the remains of his Red Army to the north-west of China, a feat of endurance archetypal of $h-P$, as too was his notorious tendency to drive people to their limit and beyond. But this $h-P$ feat seems to have been crucial in establishing his *de facto* leadership of the Chinese Communist Party during the march in January 1935 – indeed, the whole of his case history is a classic case of someone who comes into his own and goes from strength to strength the more he works with these central energies.

Even after the revolution and the establishment of Communist China in 1949, Mao had no intention of allowing China to settle down. He saw 'his' 600 million peasants as 'the greatest creative force in the world' and deliberately released social discontent and criticism to sustain his central concept ($P = \odot/\mathbb{D} = \odot/\mathbb{H}$) of the 'permanent revolution'. What was it Ebertin said about 'achievements brought about by large groups or masses of people' and the 'radical reformer with the desire to change things . . .'?

Undoubtedly revolution and transformation and the ability for a hard, patient ruthlessness in bringing it about were at the heart of this remarkable man who was the architect and alchemist of modern China. Yet it is also noteworthy that in considering the creative aspect of Sun/Moon, and the fact that this brings together the masculine and feminine aspects of the psyche, Mao was also famous for his poetry and for using it as a vehicle for his revolutionary message, and that as an extraordinarily tough military man he equally expressed a distinctly 'feminine quality' which was an important part of his chemistry as a leader. Likewise we can see the constant interaction of this whole Sun/Moon axis in Mao's repeated attempts to revitalize the revolutionary spirit by sending the leaders (Sun) back to work at the grass roots level (Moon), and through his Cultural Revolution, by which he attempted 'to reanimate the party organizations at all levels by altering the spirit of the party bureaucracy and its relation with the masses'.

It would be an exaggeration to say that Mao's chart is entirely unintelligible without this midpoint, but it certainly transforms our understanding of it and places centre-stage energies which might otherwise be less obviously emphasized. However, in the case of Adolf Hitler his chart remains an almost complete enigma

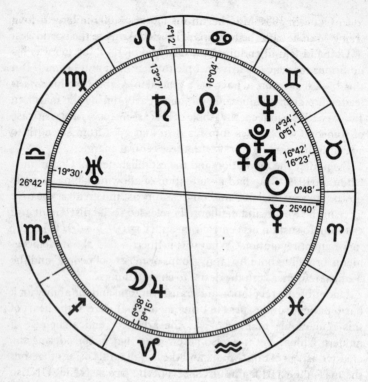

Figure 4.4 Hitler's traditional chart: it tells us about his painting and love of architecture but little about his revolutionary, demonic and destructive aspect.

without the use of midpoints and harmonics. Figure 4.4 shows Hitler's natal chart. Figure 4.5, opposite, shows his Sun/Moon tree. Here is a man who drew upon almost demonic archetypal forces of revolution, elimination and regeneration. By no normal approach can we see the potentially pivotal role played by Uranus-Pluto in this chart. Using midpoints their central importance is self-evident. The actual sequence reads: $\odot/\mathcal{D} = \mathrm{H} = \odot/\mathfrak{Q} = \mathrm{P} = \mathfrak{Q}/\Omega = \mathcal{D}/M = \Omega/AS = \mathfrak{Q}/M$. This is a clear indication that not only is the radical transformative energy of Uranus-Pluto central to the whole way in which this individual centres his life, but that it is also intimately connected with his success in life ($\odot/\mathfrak{Q}$), his deepest feelings about the future (☽/M) and the way he will communicate with others (☿/Ω) and the world around him (Ω/AS) his grandiose plans (♃/M).

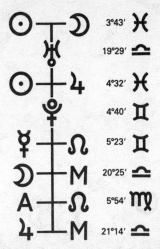

Figure 4.5 Hitler's ☉/☽ axis reveals how he could harness Uranian and Plutonian power with such devastating effect.

THE COMBINATIONS SUN/MOON = NEPTUNE

As we can see from the example of Hitler, simply having a planet at the midpoint of Sun/Moon does not mean that we will automatically become a highly integrated person around the principle of that planet or planets. Nor does it mean that these principles will necessarily be well used. Charts cannot speak of good or ill. The use we make of our planetary patterns will depend predominantly upon our ideals, our culture, our social and educational upbringing and the general level of our consciousness. The man born into a tribe whose rites of initiation into adulthood include the killing of enemy tribesmen will probably work with a dominant Mars in a very different way to someone with more or less the same chart born into an affluent western Quaker family!

The habitual level of consciousness of an individual is of course impossible to determine from the birth chart alone and is in any

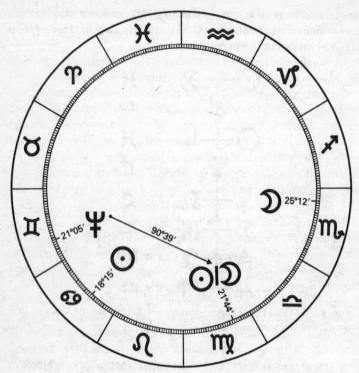

Figure 4.6 'Legs' Diamond, bootlegger and narcotics baron, shows one way in which to focus one's life around Ψ at the physical level.

case a difficult concept to measure. It ranges from complete self-absorption and the need for self-assertion, self-preservation, and self-expression, through to complete absorption into the not-Self and mystical at-one-ment. The person who is preoccupied at the physical level, as we all tend to be in childhood and notably in adolescence, will energize his possibilities very differently from the way he will when operating on a more mental level. Likewise, the person who has chosen to give up personal ambition for a life of devotion and prayer may not be entirely free of physical needs but the focus of his purpose and intention will be very different. In western society most people will oscillate somewhere in between these extremes, with the nature of their work and their educational level usually playing an important part in determining their habitual level of consciousness.

There is not space here to consider every Sun/Moon combination in detail, but the examination of some different examples of Sun/Moon = Neptune will serve to illustrate this point.

Starting at the physical end of the spectrum, the racketeer and bootlegger 'Legs' Diamond (Figure 4.6) shows Neptune at work as the deceiver. Of Diamond the *Encyclopaedia Britannica* says that he 'was noted as a well-dressed man-about-town who frequented night-clubs and Broadway shows and kept several mistresses. As a deadly killer and enforcer, he worked for various crime bosses before becoming head of his own bootleg and narcotics rackets in 1927. The ensuing gang wars – with Dutch Schultz as his chief rival – resulted in Diamond's murder in an Albany, N.Y., boarding house in 1931.' We may note here in this parable of Neptune how his life moved, always on the physical level, from agent to organizer. At his own level he could be said to have 'come into his own' when involved with Neptunian issues!

Equally on a physical level, but viewed from the level of intellect, we find Jacques Yves Cousteau (Figure 4.7), b. 11 June 1910, 13.15 Paris time, Saint André, Gironde, with $\odot/\mathbb{D} = \Psi$ and also $= \mathbb{\emptyset}$. Cousteau is the greatest living authority on modern deep-sea diving and a pioneer of underwater photography, a combination which surely must be as Neptunian as you can get. He tells us in his first book *The Silent World*, published in 1953, how on a summer's day 'one Sunday morning in 1936 at Le Mourillon, Toulon', when already a powerful swimmer, he took his first dive using goggles and 'my eyes were opened to the sea'. He became instantly 'obsessed by the incredible realm of oceanic life waiting to be known'. He goes on: 'sometimes we are lucky enough to know that our lives have been changed, to discard the old, embrace the new, and run headlong down an immutable course'. Such a sense of purpose and identification seems to be a common experience of the individual who has 'found' himself at this Sun/Moon midpoint. It is notable how not only has Cousteau's life entirely centred around the sea but his wife Simone and their two sons Jean-Michel and Philippe all regularly dive with him, so that his outer as well as his inner marriage, Sun-Moon, is equally centred about Neptune. The

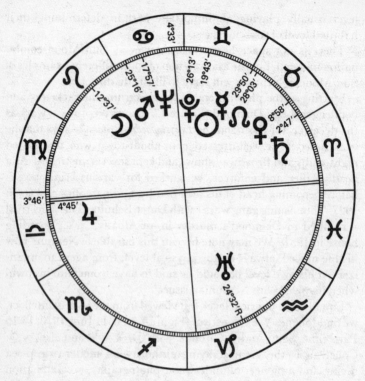

Figure 4.7 Jacques Cousteau's ☉/☽ = Ψ shows how to centre one's life around Ψ in a more literal way.

first chapter of *The Silent World* is entitled 'Menfish', and with his 'Underwater Research Group' and his invention of the aqualung Cousteau can be seen as one of the great pioneers of Neptune's kingdom. It is interesting to note that while his MC is only in wide conjunction (2° 32') with the actual midpoint of Ψ/♇, in Volguine's terms it is 'contained' by these planets, which so aptly reflects 'underwater research'. Beginning to move from the physical to the emotional and artistic levels of expression, we find that the famous forger of Old Masters Tom Keating, Figure 4.8, has this combination together with Jupiter for good measure; the 'up market' fraud, as it were. In his highly entertaining autobiography in which he candidly admits his frauds he does, however, reveal that when he was forging paintings he would be 'taken over and possessed' by the 'spirit' of the deceased artist. He records occasions when he painted dozens of Samuel Palmers, Degas, and other Impressionists, like a medium taking down automatic writing. His life is a study of Neptune at the reins.

Moving to the more artistic and emotionally expressive levels of Neptune, we find this combination for example in that romantic singer of calypso Harry Belafonte. It is joined by Venus in the case of Leonard Bernstein, who has spoken eloquently about the nature of his inspiration and how it 'lifts him out of space and time'. His constant uncertainties and confusion as to the orientation of his own sexuality is a typical expression of the potential dilemma

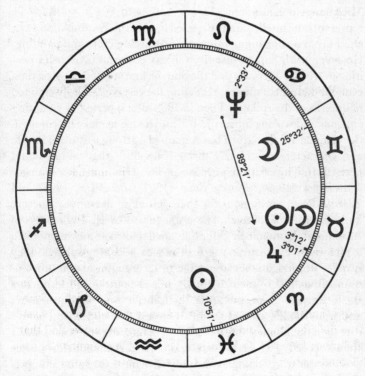

Figure 4.8 Tom Keating, the master forger, shows ⊙/☽ = ♃ = Ψ both as grand deceiver and medium.

present in this combination. That one of Bernstein's most inspired and successful musicals was *West Side Story*, based on the theme of Romeo and Juliet, is classic of this Sun/Moon = Neptune arche-type, while its hit song, 'Maria', almost amounts to a hymn to Neptune as romantic muse. In this connection we may note that that brilliant student of agriculture who became the greatest romantic actor produced by Hollywood, Rudolph Valentino, has this same planetary picture. He dreamt of farms in California but it was through Neptune he lived and died. We may also note here Sarah Miles, the actress for whom paranormal and visionary experiences have become commonplace and whose first such experience occurred while she was filming *The Sailor Who Fell from Grace with the Sea*! Continuing in the Neptunian realm of celluloid, Michelangelo Antonioni (Figure 4.9) with $\odot/\mathrm{D} = \Psi = \mathrm{2L}$ represents the intellectually directed level of this combination. As a child his first consuming interests were architecture and painting. However, with Saturn just risen in the powerful Gauquelin pos-ition in trine to Mercury and the Sun, he first studied classics, then economics and commerce, revealing the reserved, self-disciplined hallmarks of that planet. Then in 1939 after a period of 'haunting cinemas and writing film criticism' he decided to make his career in the cinema. While Saturn has remained a strong feature of his life and character, it is clearly through his films that he has found himself and his central purpose in life. His films, for example *L'Avventura* (1959), *Deserto Rosso* (1964), *Blow Up* (1966) and *Zabriski Point*, are famous for their 'puzzling narrative structure and obscurity of motive'. The critic John Russell Taylor says of Antonioni: 'Human beings for him are depicted as moving parts in a pictorially exquisite pattern of moods and atmospheres; they wander around unable to engage in meaningful action, uncom-municative, lost in their dreams, while the outside world mirrors the feelings they never express, their alienation from one another and from the life around them.' It is said that under Antonioni's direction the film became a metaphor of human experience, rather than a record of it. Taylor says again: 'After Antonioni few people saw a water tower or a plastic dump with quite the same unappre-ciative eyes; in his films a new kind of beauty was revealed in the mechanical jungle of the twentieth century.' Note how the very

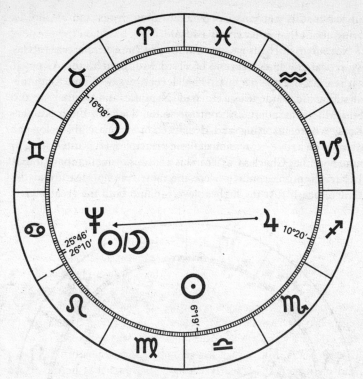

Figure 4.9 Michelangelo Antonioni, ☉/☽ = ♃ = Ψ, used film to reveal the beauty in water towers and plastic dumps.

subjects that Antonioni transfigures are Neptune-Saturn images: a water tower and a plastic dump! Taylor continues: 'His reputation stood at its highest when the impact of his new, personal vision was most immediate, between *L'Avventura* (1959) and *L'Eclisse* (1962), in both of which a young woman, portrayed by the exquisite, mysterious Monica Vitti, unsuccessfully seeks in romance a means of coping with the emptiness in her life.'

Others whose lives have centred in different ways around the creative imagination of Neptune are John Buchan, one of the founders of the tradition of spy stories, and Jimi Hendrix, whose life speaks volumes about the power of Neptune when combined with Mars to produce inspirational energy while at the same time all too readily becoming dependent upon drugs and alcohol to bring about that inner creative fusion.

Not surprisingly as we move to the psychic and spiritual realms we repeatedly find Neptune involved with Sun/Moon. As noted earlier, at the passively psychic level we saw Tom Keating's mediumistic tendencies. He had Neptune and Jupiter at the Sun/Moon midpoint. By contrast so too does Elizabeth Kubler-Ross, whose inspiring and deeply compassionate work for the dying is an active expression of these principles. (It is interesting to note here that Charles Carter in his analysis of death reported that Jupiter-Neptune contacts were the most common feature at the time of death!) At the highest level we find both the great mystic

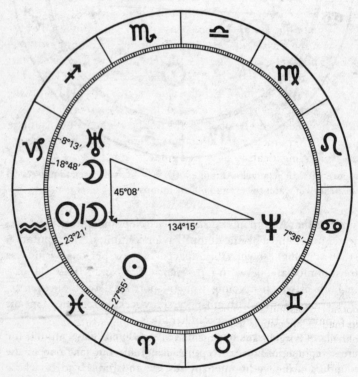

Figure 4.10 Adolf Eichmann with $\odot / \mathbb{D} = \text{Ħ} = \Psi$ shows how Ψ visions can turn to nightmares when the collective is unleashed.

and mistress of prayer, meditation and contemplation St Teresa of Avila, and the visionary St Thérèse of Lisieux. The great occultist Rudolf Steiner may also have had this combination, if his normally recorded birth data is correct. Alice Bailey, who took down the voluminous teachings of the discarnate Tibetan known as DK, has Neptune within 23′ of her Sun/Moon midpoint at noon on her day of birth, indicating a strong probability that she was born within a few hours of noon. Sri Aurobindo, the seer, poet and Indian nationalist who originated the philosophy of cosmic salvation through spiritual evolution, can be seen as representative of this combination both at its most transcendent and most practical.

Lest we get swept away by the higher promises of Neptune, it is perhaps salutary to end by reminding ourselves of the obsessive quality of Neptunian visions when placed at the very heart of an individual's life. Its devastating consequences are evidenced by the case of Adolf Eichmann, who master-minded the nightmare of the Nazi 'Final Solution' (Figure 4.10). He also had Uranus almost exactly with this combination, a visionary autocrat as it were. The case of Mark Chapman, who became fatally obsessed with the Neptunian figure of John Lennon to the extent that in some senses he believed he was Lennon, again testifies to the all-consuming power of Neptune on this all-important midpoint when there are no over-riding ideals to serve as a guide.

NOTES

1. For further discussion on left and right brains see R. Ornstein, *The Mind Field*, Viking Press, New York, 1976, and other works. This balance between right and left hemispheres, Sun and Moon, is not of course exclusive to individuals. We can see the same principle at work within the collective where mind/emotion splits can be observed on a large scale and notably in totalitarian regimes. We can see parliamentary democracy with its built-in 'opposition' as a safeguard against this potential social schizophrenia. It is significant that totalitarian regimes find it that much easier to institute a social divorce between thinking and feeling, and are the most adept at double-think, and at repressing unwanted elements.
2. The phrase 'occupied by' seems to imply a static relationship between the three factors involved. Of course in fact every birth chart is a 'freeze

frame' of a constantly interweaving dynamic of cycles. The power of midpoints would seem to derive from the close dynamic interactions of multiple cycles that they reveal.

3. Quoted by Pamela A. F. Crane in her valuable study of Janis Joplin in *Draconic Astrology*, Aquarian Press, 1987, p. 158. She does not, however, use midpoints or harmonics in this study but suggests that the chart is best understood in terms of the draconic zodiac, itself a special form of harmonic chart (see Chapter 21).

4. Pamela A. F. Crane, op. cit.

CHAPTER 5

Analysing Three Factors

MICHAEL HARDING AND CHARLES HARVEY

When approaching the analysis of a chart using midpoints we are looking at their relationship to the thirteen chart factors – Sun, Moon, planets, node and angles – which together will typically generate about seventy distinct midpoint combinations in the average chart. At first glance this can seem something of an information overkill compared to the dozen or so conventional aspects used in the natal chart. In fact, this isn't really the case. The usual chart analysis takes into immediate consideration signs, houses, elements and triplicities for each planet, and when these permutations are applied to each body they generate *more* possibilities than the seventy or so offered on the midpoint trees. However, they will not be so readily discernible nor so clearly laid out nor so precisely measured. Anyone who doubts this should try – without first sitting down to think about it – to explain *exactly* why a specific conclusion is reached about any personal planet in their own chart using the traditional approaches. The breadth of meaning inherent in any sign or house allows for a wide spectrum of possibilities, further enlarged by the rulers and dispositors tugging at our attention from around the chart. Midpoints can focus in on an immediate message, generally providing a simpler way of getting accurate, precise information.

As with any other approach, it is practice which eventually pays off, but it will certainly help to de-mystify the initial approach to the wealth of information presented if midpoints are approached in a reasonably logical manner. All midpoints are equal, but some are certainly more equal than others! Going straight to those which offer the most pertinent information will quickly supply the skeleton on which the framework of the chart can be constructed. In this chapter we shall be looking at some of the key factors to take into consideration before trying to make sense of all the thirteen midpoint trees which the typical chart produces.

In this respect it is important to recognize that not all midpoint pairs on the midpoint structure are going to be experienced *all* the time. As with every other chart factor, we are born with these contacts and have them for life. Transits, or our growing awareness of the planetary energies the natal pair represent, will trigger most of them for the first time at one point or another. Similarly, the simple process of *denial* operates very effectively in keeping certain of our traits from impinging on our consciousness! While experience suggests that most midpoints on the tree *are* experienced, and tend to be experienced in their sequence, this is not a fixed rule.

There can be a 'gap' – dumb note – in the cycle when no immediate connection can be made with a particular pair. How this situation should be treated during the consultation depends a lot on *which* midpoints are 'missing'. Outer planet combinations may simply represent large areas of collective energies which are not focused around specific character traits or experiences. More personal contacts which are not recognized should be noted; their symbolism may emerge unexpectedly or the individual expression of them may be significantly different from the usual to escape our immediate attention. In either event, we should still be left with sufficient clearly recognizable combinations to work effectively with the chart using the messages they give us. Assessing the relative importance of those messages will depend on our understanding of the hierarchy of significance we can create from the various possible contacts.

We have already looked at some length at the ☉/☽ midpoint and noted its importance. This is the first midpoint to look out for. While every chart *has* a ☉/☽ midpoint waiting to be triggered by transits and progressions, not every chart will have it activated by a third body from the word go. If the Sun/Moon midpoint aspects one of the natal planets then this is the first factor to examine. However, if, as is more common, there is no radical aspect to the Sun/Moon midpoint then determining what is next in importance will depend almost solely on how accurate your chart data is.

When looking at Manson's chart in Chapter 2 we noted the importance of the planet/angle midpoints. That is, the midpoints made by each planet and the node to both the Ascendant and the MC. Clearly, these change very quickly – typically just six minutes difference in time will pull a factor in or out of orb, or eight minutes if we're examining midpoints to the Sun, Moon or the angles themselves. This is tight, and assuming an accurate time we have immediate access to very precise information. When the angles lock into the picture, the planetary energy they trigger is far more likely to be expressed in life than a three-planet combination by itself. Which of course prompts us to ask what the AS/MC midpoint itself can offer us.

Alfred Witte saw the Midheaven as relating to the *time* of an event and the Ascendant to its *place*. The AS/MC midpoint itself he described as representing the idea of 'at this time and place'; in effect, how an event is brought into being at its own precise moment. The Ascendant refers to our 'persona' or our response towards the world while the MC depicts our aims and goals. Obviously, there is much more to these two points than this as we shall see in the next chapter, but for the moment let's take them at this basic level. Seen together in this way we have a picture of how we may orientate ourselves in life and the way in which we might actualize our conscious or professional ambitions. In some respects this can be seen as the point where our conscious Ego (MC) is brought together with the way in which we tend to respond to the world (AS). A planet aspecting this point may tell us exactly how we do this.

If the Sun/Moon midpoint is the balance point of our masculine and feminine sides – the fulcrum of our own 'inner marriage' – then the Ascendant/Midheaven midpoint will focus more on the way we self-actualize moment by moment. In this respect the term used in Gestalt psychology, the 'here and now', captures the immediacy of this point with some clarity. A planet on the AS/MC midpoint is something like a direct hit. The individual will almost certainly use that energy constantly in life, generally thriving on it, for example as Margaret Thatcher with her ♂ = AS/MC thrives on the cut and thrust of political life, has an intense dislike of compromise and consensus and takes an unashamedly aggressive stance (despite ☉, ☿ and ♀ in Libra) towards every issue she faces. As with the ☉/☽ midpoint the AS/MC is also highly sensitive to transits and progressions and for the purposes of rectification is an excellent method of handling both angles at the same time.

Midpoint combinations which involve the angles when the chart is known to be accurate are powerful indicators that the planetary energies involved are most likely to be expressed in the world. This is particularly true if one of the factors is either the Sun or the Moon, as in $\hbar = \mathbb{D}/M$, suggesting an ability to reflect seriously on emotions and use them in some way as part of one's goals in life. Such a pattern exists in the chart of the writer F. Scott Fitzgerald. His wife Zelda Sayre also wrote extensively (see Chapter 19 for a short case history), but her real passion was for dancing and her $♀ = ♅/AS$ is a clear indicator of someone who seeks to express a highly original and somewhat erratic persona in a harmonious and balanced manner. The next midpoint she has on the Venus tree is $♇/M$, which suggests someone who will strive obsessively to use the Venus principle to become successful at whatever cost to herself, a fact vividly borne out by her life's experience.

Because of the need for an accurate birth-time to make real use of planet/angle midpoints we sometimes see the best examples of their power in mundane charts. Where times *are* available, they are frequently correct to the second. Thus the combinations $M = ♂/♅$, $♅ = ♀/AS = ♇/AS$ and $♀ = ♇/AS = ☉/AS$ all appear at the moment the space shuttle *Challenger* exploded. The $♂/♅$ midpoint occurs again and again in the charts of accidents, operations and sudden moments of physical stress and is one of several midpoints needing close attention by those interested in medical astrology.

In 1980 a group of terrorists took over the Iranian Embassy in London, holding many people as hostages. The killing of one of their captives led to a spectacular rescue bid by the SAS on 5 May at 6.25 p.m. GMT. A prominent feature in the sky at the time was a close Mars/Jupiter conjunction with its promise of 'successful martial activity'. The angles for the moment of attack (Figure 5.1) focus this 'here and now' with the combinations $M = ♃/AS = ♂/AS$; a graphic image of a group of soldiers bursting into a building. The Ascendant comes to $= \hbar = ♇/M$ – another powerful image of the event, especially as all but one of the terrorists was killed during the rescue. In the same chart we also have $♅ =$

Figure 5.1 The SAS storms the Iranian Embassy.

♃/M = ♂/M; again the Mars/Jupiter combination reappears, this time tied in with the planet that more than any other stands for sudden intervention, Uranus. In fact the ♃/M midpoint was exact to the minute with Uranus at the moment the SAS blew open the windows of the Embassy and stormed inside. Such events do not occur in a vacuum. The transiting angles act as 'the final wards in the lock', releasing the longer-term underlying planetary pictures.

This is vividly illustrated by another embassy siege incident (Figure 5.2), which occurred at 10.20 a.m. BST on 17 April 1984 in St James's Square, London, when WPC Yvonne Fletcher was murdered by a shot fired from the Libyan People's Bureau. Throughout the day ♅, which is so often involved in sudden eruptions of energy from the collective, was at 13° 11' Sag activating the midpoints: ♀/♄ 28♑01 = ♃/♄ 13♐29 = ☉/♇ 29♑12 = ♂/♆ 14♐25. This gives us a picture of strong explosive emotional tension (♅ = ♀/♄) joining longer-term social pressures and tensions (♅ = ♃/♄) connected with revolutionary power struggles (♅ = ☉/♇) and sudden 'sneak' attacks for 'idealistic' or

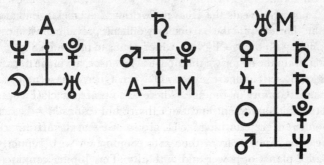

Figure 5.2 The murder of WPC Yvonne Fletcher.

misguided ends ($\text{H}\!\!\!\text{I} = \sigma/\Psi$). Also exact during the day was the picture $\hbar$ 14♏16 = σ/P 14♏09, symbolic of contained and directed violent energy which can either be focused into intense hard work or which can, as *COSI* puts it, create 'the desire to overcome difficulties and obstacles at all costs forcibly'.

As the shot rang out at 10.20 a.m. the MC had reached 14♓19, having just passed −90− $\text{H}\!\!\!\text{I}$, and was within 7′ of $\odot/\text{P}$ (of which *COSI* says 'the experience of physical interference or violence . . .') and 6′ of σ/Ψ ('dependence on sub-conscious influences'). At the same moment the AS was at 15♋40 = Ψ/P 1♐06 = $\!)\!/\text{H}\!\!\!\text{I}$ 1♐10. Of the possible manifestations of Ψ/P *COSI* says 'the pursuit of fantastic ideas' and 'confusion, a grievous loss', while of $\!)\!/\text{H}\!\!\!\text{I}$ *COSI* says 'sacrifices for the attainment of special aims' and 'states of fear and anxiety' and with AS, 'an upsetting experience'.

Simultaneously the MC/AS at 14♉59 had just passed over $\hbar$ = σ/P, indicating that 'at this time and place' the idea of 'overcoming difficulties and obstacles forcibly at all costs' could be released. We may also reflect that $\hbar$ can represent 'the police' and the forces of order, and that here we see σ/P, which negatively can manifest as force and brutality, focused on this point.

At exactly the same time that WPC Fletcher was shot, a policeman was also shot in North London in a completely unconnected incident, 'unconnected' that is in any normal sense. Cosmically we might say that they are different manifestations of the same pattern of ideas.

Turning to a happier event, the coronation of Queen Elizabeth II on 2 June 1953, which, as far as we know, was not chosen by astrologers, reveals the Heavens writing their message loud and clear. This despite the particularly difficult prevailing astrological climate with the $\hbar-\Psi$ cycle, which seems to play such an important part in the history of the House of Windsor, having just reached its conjunction phase exactly 90° the Queen's Ascendant and square Uranus in the sky. There are numerous close contacts between the moment and the nativity but just taking the actual moment of the crowning, at 11.32 a.m., we find the MC, marking the time, only 9′ from the exact conjunction with Jupiter, the 'royal' planet of power and authority. This Jupiter conjunct the MC (Figure 5.3) falls exactly in 45°/135° to the Queen's Ω = AS =

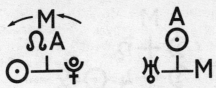

Figure 5.3 The Coronation of Queen Elizabeth II.

$\odot$/P. Of $\mathfrak{2}\!\!\!/$/Ω *COSI* says 'entering into advantageous associations', of $\mathfrak{2}\!\!\!/$/AS it says 'successes or expressions of recognition', of $\mathfrak{2}\!\!\!/$ = Ω/AS it says, inter alia, 'the sharing of enjoyments and joyful occasions together with other people . . .', and of $\mathfrak{2}\!\!\!/$ = $\odot$/P 'successful striving for power . . . a person who establishes his position in life successfully . . .' Here we should note that the natal $\odot$/P = AS = Ω foreshadows 'sudden advancement in life' and 'the ability to establish and consolidate one's own position as a leader . . .' The transiting MC times the exact moment when this picture became manifest.

The Ascendant of the moment, marking the place, is exactly square transit Sun, which is elevated within 6° of Jupiter and the MC. These focus exactly, 6' and 10', on the Queen's ⚥/M, a midpoint which represents, inter alia, 'the power of assertion' and 'the power to make one's way in life successfully'. AS = $\odot$ = ⚥/M could be translated as 'the focus of this place (AS) and this day ($\odot$) are upon manifesting this individual's (MC) power of assertion and authority (⚥)'.

The MC/AS of the moment, 'at this time and place', was only 13' off the exact 45° from the transiting $\odot$/$\mathfrak{2}\!\!\!/$, the significator of monarchs, 'powerful people' and the attainment of 'social and religious power'. We must not forget that at this moment Elizabeth was being crowned not only Queen but 'Defender of the Faith' and Head of the Church of England.

At the moment that Princess Diana and Prince Charles were declared 'man and wife', 11.17 a.m. on 29 July 1981, at Westminster (Figure 5.4), we find for the time: $\mathcal{D}$/$\hbar$ = $\mathcal{D}$/$\mathfrak{2}\!\!\!/$ = M = $\mathcal{D}$/σ, a combination speaking of both seriousness and joy. The $\mathcal{D}$/$\mathfrak{2}\!\!\!/$ = M, described in *COSI* as, inter alia, 'popularity . . . the happy wife . . . the bride', is exactly conjunct Diana's own $\odot$ which is natally with φ = $\mathcal{D}$/φ = $\mathcal{D}$ = ⚥/Ω. Of $\odot$ = $\mathcal{D}$/φ *COSI* says 'marital love'

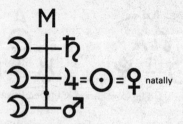

Figure 5.4 The marriage of Prince Charles and Princess Diana.

and for $M = \mathcal{D}/\sigma$ 'getting married'! For the place we find: $\hbar/M = AS = \varphi/\Psi = 4/M$. $\hbar/M = AS$ expresses the solemnity of the occasion, $\varphi/\Psi = AS$ expresses the fairytale setting, the idealism and romance and $AS = 4/M$ 'the experiencing of joy together with others, a festivity'. The $\odot$ representing the day itself is found in the picture $\varphi/\hbar = \varphi/4 = \odot = \varphi/\sigma = \varphi/AS$. *COSI* says of $\varphi/\hbar$ 'love unions with appreciable difference in age', of $\varphi/4 = \odot$ 'a man permeated by the joy of love, a happy man (bridegroom)', and of $\varphi/AS = \odot$ 'a love affair'.

Taking these basic principles, what might we make of an event whose time is described by: $\hbar/\Omega = M = \odot/\Psi = \varphi/\mathbb{H}$, whose place is: $AS = 4/\mathbb{H} = \odot/\mathcal{D}$ and whose 'here and now' is: $\varphi = M/AS = \mathcal{D}/\Psi = \varphi/\Omega = \mathcal{D}/4 = \odot$? A further clue: $4/M = \mathbb{H} = \mathcal{D}/\Omega = \Psi/\mathbb{P} = \varphi/\Psi = 4/\mathbb{P}$.

Analysing this we get an outline as follows:

$M = \hbar/\Omega$ = Contacts with mourning and bereavement
$M = \odot/\Psi$ = Spiritual, mystical, romantic moments
$M = \varphi/\mathbb{H}$ = A time of sudden perception, discovery
$AS = 4/\mathbb{H}$ = Fortunate discoveries, shared happiness
$AS = \odot/\mathcal{D}$ = Focus here at this day and hour
$M/A = \varphi$ = Love/beauty permeate this time and place
$\quad = \mathcal{D}/\Psi$ = Sensitive art and love
$\quad = \varphi/\Omega$ = A contact with love and art
$\quad = \mathcal{D}/4$ = Great happiness, joyful love and art
$\quad = \odot$ = Are the focus of the day here and now
$\mathbb{H} = 4/M$ = Sudden luck, success, happy discovery
$\quad = \mathcal{D}/\Omega$ = Restless and excitable people
$\quad = \Psi/\mathbb{P}$ = Unusual, mystical discoveries

= ☿/Ψ = Sudden receptivity to love and art
= ♃/♇ = Awakening to power and plutocracy

You may like to add your own translations and insights and create a summary of the picture that emerges before turning to the end of the book (pp. 443–4) where the event in question is described.

Another very important clue as to the importance of a specific midpoint is if it is triggered by two or more factors such as Uranus, Neptune and Mars all hitting the same combination as they do in Charles Manson's ♅ = Ψ = ♂ = AS/MC. This picture strongly reinforces the message we detected in his solar tree and makes the Mars/Neptune energies in particular even more personal. Not surprisingly, such multiple contacts often indicate particular talents or abilities, and at another level F. Scott Fitzgerald also has a multiple conjunction on a highly telling midpoint: AS = ☽ = ♂ = Ψ = ☿/♄. The images of emotion, inspiration, energy and self-image all cluster around what must be a classic midpoint for a professional writer, ☿/♄. This is a telling contact for the control of mental processes, of serious thought and the need to structure mental associations. Ebertin describes this point as indicating 'logical thinking, thoroughness, concentration, the ability to come straight to the point of a matter under discussion, a love of tidiness, the ability to organize, the application of method and philosophical thinking'. Despite his alcoholism and chaotic life-style, Fitzgerald was a highly organized writer who prepared very detailed diagrams and what we would now call flow-charts indicating the construction and development of his novels and how he intended to parallel the experiences of those close to him in his work. With both Mars and Neptune on this same ☿/♄ midpoint we can see – as with Manson's use of drugs with very similar configurations – the possible danger of seeking to stimulate the creative writing process with drink. One could also suggest that this particular midpoint played its part in naming the book which brought him overnight fame and fortune – *This Side of Paradise*.

Fitzgerald spoke frequently about the 'professionalism' of being a writer and was scathing of all amateurism in the field, a criticism he frequently directed towards his wife Zelda. The AS = ☿/♄ shows his personal investment in being a 'professional writer', and he clung to this self-image despite all the catastrophes which resulted from his pouring so much liquid on the creative fires. In fact the concept of 'professionalism' played a large part in his uneasy relationship with Ernest Hemingway, another writer who has AS = ☿/♄. Saturn has its doubting side – earnest, even – as has so often been noted, and the fear of failure, of an inability to match up to what the self or others expect, is very much part of Saturn in its typically self-questioning mode. With Mars on the same midpoint it is interesting to note what else was also being questioned. Fitzgerald paced himself to Hemingway like a long-distance runner, constantly assessing the differences between them at every turn of the track. The Mars energy of creative libido got caught up in this conflict with Hemingway's ultra 'macho-writer' image, finally leading Fitzgerald to ask Hemingway if he felt that his penis was too small! Hemingway did his best to reassure Fitzgerald on that score by bringing Neptune into the picture (literally) and taking him to look at the paintings and the Greek sculptures at the Louvre . . . Never let it be said that a multiple midpoint doesn't work out in a multiplicity of forms!

For his part, Hemingway has ♅ = ☉/☽ and = AS/MC and was notoriously accident-prone, surviving war-wounds, car and aircraft crashes and numerous other incidents. More importantly, with such a placement one can also feel the sense of insecurity with which he lived and the constant need to expose himself to danger or take part in sporadic bouts of violence. From a purely literary point of view, Hemingway's prose style is noted for its extreme discipline and control of emotion, expressed through his constant re-writing of key passages to get the exact effect he was after (he claims to have written the last paragraph of *A Farewell to Arms* over 100 times). All this sounds rather like Saturn again and it is indeed = ☽/☿ for that similar methodical control of feeling we recognize in Fitzgerald's approach as well as = ☿/♀.

The ☿/♀ midpoint has long been connected with the process of art, both literary and visual, as it brings together mental and physical dexterity with the desire to create beauty. Saturn here would indicate a strong need to formalize and structure the outcome; very different from ☽ = ☿/♀ which Jack Kerouac had and made it *his* ambition to write as completely from his feeling-nature as possible, aiming to record his immediate emotional response to everything he saw. Hemingway's Saturn is also = ♂/♇, and as with Charles Manson, with the same combination, he likewise had a fascination with 'ritual killing' – watching the bullfights. The same midpoint can also hint at Hemingway's doubts as to his own sexual direction, which many literary historians believe played a significant part in his suicide. However, it is another Saturn midpoint, ♄ = Ψ/AS, which for many suits him best, as through it he embodies the character of one of his most popular works, *The Old Man and the Sea*.

Having noted the importance of the ☉/☽ midpoint and, where the time is accurately known, of the AS/MC and all planet/angle configurations, we also see that multiple midpoints can be regarded as the next most important. Obviously, if the time of the chart is uncertain, one would look first to ☉/☽ and any multiple structures. Next in line are *repetitions*.

This is in itself not an idea unique to midpoints. Almost from the start we learn to spot the repetition of a theme or an idea in the chart. This could show itself as someone who has, say, Sun in Taurus *and* a strong second house *and* a prominent Venus. In midpoint work we look for a repetition of *planets*. Thus we may find ☿ = ♄/♂, ♂ = ☿/♄ and ♄ = ☿/♂. In this case, all *three* possible permutations of the planetary energies are present. These configurations are present in the chart of the teacher/astronaut Christa MacAuliffe, and even taken alone they vividly depict the main themes of her life, and indeed even hint at its final outcome.

Mercury, Mars and Saturn bring together mental and physical energy with what can be thought of here as a sense of social responsibility. Saturn would be the most important energy here, being the most powerful of the three planets, and emphasizes the sense of Christa being a 'professional communicator, a professional organizer'. Coming back to the basic idea of looking at midpoints as a series of triple conjunctions, we can suggest that here we have a woman who is an energetic communicator (☿/♂), who has a love of study and learning (☿/♄), coupled with a potential for considerable hard work and concentrated effort (♂/♄). In fact putting the three together gives us a striking picture of an energetic teacher of young children (☿/♄ again).

Although this can be seen as a good example of hindsight, there is no doubt that practice with midpoints would allow the astrologer to suggest that here we had someone who would seek out knowledge, strive to put it into a clear form and then communicate it to others, which is by no means an inappropriate observation. However, there is another side to ♂/♄ which also has to be faced.

Ebertin refers to the ♂/♄ midpoint as the 'death axis', and as each one of us has this midpoint somewhere or other in our charts it is rather important that we take a closer look at it without becoming hypochondriacs. Mars/Saturn aspects have long been known to have their problems, some of which we looked at briefly in Chapter 1. As far as the *body* is concerned, that is, our health and welfare, Mars, Jupiter and Saturn are all closely involved for they offer us images of the different processes at work within us. Mars and Jupiter clearly have to do with the processes of growth and expansion (this is not necessarily 'good', ask anyone struggling with a diet), while Saturn is clearly concerned with the habits and patterns of age and restriction. This is not necessarily bad – ask anyone who's managed to give up smoking, cut down on drink or ensured that the morning jog is taken every day come rain or shine. But habit and enthusiasm do not always see eye to eye and when there is a serious imbalance between these two principles medical problems can occur, hence Ebertin's observations that transits and/or directions to this midpoint can coincide with illness or death. In such cases it would be the *conflict* of the two principles themselves which would be stimulated. Astrologers with Freudian persuasions would also observe that sexual repression, the denial of libido and unexpressed hostilities towards the father have all been demonstrated to underlie illness and can be seen as classic manifestations of these two planets' principles.

The ♂/♄ midpoint marks the meeting point of energy and control, the brash enthusiasm of Aries and the cautious hand of Capricorn. How well they get on together in the individual chart depends almost solely on the awareness and habits of the individual concerned, and this idea of habit will be gone into much more fully in the section on Forecasting (p. 117). For the moment we can see the possibility in this combination of either an extremely powerful and focused source of energy, or a denied and frustrated libido. It is in the latter case that Ebertin's observations are the most pertinent, for such a state undoubtedly can create health problems. Although Christa MacAuliffe's ☿/♂/♄ *does* give a graphic picture of someone who literally died in flight, it would be quite wrong to assume that a ☿ = ♂/♄ means this in every chart. Coming back to the idea of repetitions, it must be noted that on the day she was killed Christa had transiting Saturn = ☉/☽ (reinforcing the principle of Saturn) and transiting Mars almost exactly square her natal Saturn emphasizing that contact yet again. Christa's Moon is at 5° Virgo 1′ and thus square to 5° Sagittarius, which is the degree associated with *flight*.

The most unusual, and perhaps the most powerful, way in which three chart factors can repeat is in the case of the Grand Trine. An exact Grand Trine with an orb less than 2° is very rare, but when formed, each angle of the trine is at the midpoint of the other two and thus the pattern combines the quality of the trine with the dynamics of the hard aspects in a classic planetary picture. This can be strong stuff and produce not an easy, relaxed pattern but a very powerful and compulsive one. Traditionalists have long pointed out that Grand Trines are not always as 'fortunate' as they're painted and in all likelihood it is the exact Grand Trine which risks fulfilling this exception most readily. Thus when midpoint structures are themselves part of another aspect pattern, such as the central planet also being the focal point of a T-square, or 45° equidistant from two others, or 30° away from both ends of a kite pattern, it has the potential for great strength within the chart and demands particular attention. In Chapter 11, when we look at harmonic charts, we shall see how other specific aspects can also considerably strengthen the importance of midpoints. Sometimes midpoints which are *closest* in orb to a planet will prove to have significant strength within the chart; in the 45° sort or on the midpoint trees these midpoints are, of course, literally the ones closest to the planet itself.

Having looked at some of the midpoints which can be considered the *most* important, we should now examine those which at first glance look less likely to operate at a personal level. In doing so we may recognize that they are nevertheless capable of highly individualistic expression, especially when triggered by transits.

Just as the current sextile between Neptune and Pluto is very much a generational pattern and to a similar extent the major aspects of Jupiter, Saturn, Neptune and Uranus to one another also more clearly refer to phases within society as a whole, so certain midpoints obviously reflect these relationships. By themselves ♅ = ♆/♇ or ♃ = ♄/♅ refer to social forces and cannot be considered 'personal' *unless the moment makes them so.* ☉ = ♃ = ♄/♅ or M = ♄ = ♆/♇ are two different pictures in which the energies of the collective have a channel to different levels of consciousness in the individual, in a similar manner to the outer planet/angle combinations we have already discussed. Just as Pluto coming to the Ascendant in the natal chart can make the energies of its sextile with Neptune very pertinent within the life of an individual born at such a moment, so too can a personal planet act as a focus for the combined energies of three slower-moving bodies in the midpoint format. In fact, quite powerful patterns can build up within the relationship of the outer planets which suddenly get triggered by the Sun, Moon or an angle – often as quite a dramatic event.

On 27 December 1985 at 8.00 a.m. GMT a terrorist bomb detonated at Rome airport. At that moment Saturn was = ♃/♅ = ♆/☊ = ♆/♇ = ♂/♆. All of them powerful, slow-moving contacts with only ♂/♆ taking in a faster-moving body. ♄ = ♂/♆ is a classic picture of the potential for ambush, betrayal or duplicity, but at the exact moment of the explosion Saturn also aligned with ☿/M and ♅/M (remember those planets in the *Challenger* explosion), thus bringing to the angles the combined cycles of the planets from Mars out to Pluto as well as the nodal contact with Neptune. Saturn itself was also at 4 ♐ 40 at the time – on the degree associated with flight.

While midpoints can bring together the cycles of the planet as a focus of their combined energy, to make it 'personal' for an individual born at a particular moment or an event taking place at a specific time, they can also help us clarify our interpretations of the cycles of the planets themselves as they appear in the birth chart.

For instance, the major phases of the planets from Jupiter outwards – their conjunctions, squares, trines and oppositions –

will remain within orb for months or even years at a time. How do we deal with this when looking at the chart of someone who has such a configuration; what is so 'special' about the moment we are obliged to examine?

The Uranus/Pluto conjunctions of 1965/6 which took place around 16° Virgo are typical of the problem astrologers face when attempting to interpret what is clearly a generational factor in the context of the natal chart. Unless these planets are angular or closely configured with one of the personal planets it can be difficult to make sense of them at this time; the generation born during the mid-1960s will need to become middle-aged before we can get a clearer understanding of what might be the main underlying 'message' of this conjunction.

Cycles do *not* repeat with perfect uniformity and pattern and there is a real danger in trying to jump the zodiacal gun with pat interpretations. Some 'cook-books' suggest that when Pluto was in Aries this was a time of much war and aggression. History teaches us that the human race was killing each other in pretty much the same manner and with much the same enthusiasm as with Pluto in Pisces or Pluto in Taurus. Trying to cut our past up into comfortable bite-size pieces does little beyond trivialize astrology and duck all the hard work needed in researching exactly what *was* going on. While it is certainly true that Pluto in Scorpio describes very accurately the AIDS epidemic, it was not in that sign when syphilis did much the same thing to Europe in the mid-1500s.

That said, we can make some generalization about the ♅/♇ conjunction in Virgo, though how this will help us to examine the individual birth chart is open to question. The last conjunction of the two planets which best summarize nuclear energy took place at 16° of the Mutables. This was the degree of the MC for the moment the atomic bomb was dropped on Hiroshima. The destiny of the generation which was born during the mid-1960s is inevitably going to be bound up in the use of nuclear power in all its forms, as well as with other manifestations of 'social revolution' – another potent Uranus/Pluto image.

For the West, 1965/6 brought a considerable amount of change within society – though nowhere near as much as that unleashed by Mao's Cultural Revolution, which began another phase of the complete transformation of the world's most populated country. At the time of writing (1988) Uranus is making the first 45° aspect in its cycle to Pluto, and the USSR is going through *its* biggest shift since 1953. The major cycles of the outer planets refer to the major cycles of the world, not the individual.

The 'electronic revolution' was also born in 1967, as was the generation that will both learn to program computers (Uranus in Virgo) as well as suffer the social consequences for good or ill of their application. The country most associated with this electronic overhaul of the world's communication, Japan, resonates like a tuning-fork to the cycle of these two planets, and indeed actually has ♃ = ♅/♇ in its post-war sovereignty chart – clearly pointing to where its fortunes lie! Not surprisingly, terrorism erupted in the world at this time as well. It has become acceptable to use violence to achieve political ends almost as a matter of course, and not just when all other avenues have been exhausted. Even such middle-class and previously 'respectable' pressure groups as animal welfare campaigners in England and anti-abortion activists in the USA have regularly used bombing campaigns to further their causes. When some of the social conflicts symbolized by these outer planets are internalized, such as those connected to the use or rejection of power or the need for dramatic, revolutionary restructuring of creative energy, the results can emerge as anorexia.

So what do we say to our clients of '67 – that they are all terrorists/computer programmers/electronic specialists/nuclear industry workers with eating disorders or just destined for permanent unemployment unless they're prepared to slave in information technology (very Uranus/Pluto!) helping the Mafia to put everything on computer?

Our problem is really one of scale. These cycles are too large and too impersonal to register much with the individual unless we look far more closely to see what gets picked up at a personal level. The midpoints made to Uranus and Pluto can reveal quite subtle and important contacts which will allow us to see how these collective energies are most likely to operate within the life. More importantly, the use of midpoints creates a clear distinction between the two planets which would otherwise be impossible. Even with the planets half a degree apart they can each pick up sufficiently different midpoints – especially with the angles – for us to get a much clearer feeling as to which planet of the pair is likely to be dominant in the life of the individual. Once the pair have separated by more than 2°, the midpoints they contact can be strikingly different and will allow us to make a much more confident analysis of what we see. The alternative is for the duo to be seen just as a conjunction which falls in one house or another, providing very limited information given the vast potential of the pair. This is an approach which can be taken with all the planetary cycles and can radically alter the way in which we see the major phases of the planets and the depth of relevant, personal meaning we can come to find in the multiplicity of their patterns.

Our immediate concern when looking at a series of midpoint trees is to seek those contacts made by the Sun and Moon, by any of the planets to the angles, by multiple or repeating contacts, by any planets which are themselves part of a strong aspect formation such as a square or a trine, or a pattern which ties in a whole series of outer planets to some personal point within the chart, or finally are the closest in orb to the central planet. Just looking at these alone will add a vast amount of information in a very easy-to-see form. After all, we are dealing only with planets and angles and using astrology in a very straightforward manner. For many students, even those quite experienced in using astrology, there can be at first a marked reluctance to trust their own inner judgement of planetary symbolism alone. This is something which can only be overcome by actually *doing* it, though simply by *listening* to what a client is saying can rapidly convince us that the planets are doing more in the chart than the main squares and trines allow. If we listen, we can start to hear the midpoints making themselves heard.

All our astrological experience tells us that each person will react slightly differently to the same planetary energies, depending on how they are able to identify and recognize the principles being expressed within them. A strong aspect may be of extreme importance in one person's life, seeming to dominate all events, while a very similar pattern may produce no particular problems in the life of another. The same holds true, of course, in the use of midpoints. But here the subtle variation of planetary contacts allows us to see very precise points within the chart and life of the native through which we can come to understand how the planetary energies are being used in the present and, more importantly, how they may express themselves in the future.

Just as the examples given earlier of F. Scott Fitzgerald, Zelda Sayre, Ernest Hemingway and Christa MacAuliffe pointed out specific character traits which inevitably manifested in the world as events, so we can hear in what our clients are saying specific references to certain midpoints in their own charts. Chances are that these midpoints will turn out to be particularly important *because* they are unknowingly being referred to, generally in connection with the reasons that brought them to an astrologer in the first place. Thus noticing and *noting* these combinations is part of the art of counselling; for it is in these patterns that many of the client's problems may lie and it will almost certainly be necessary to get the client to confront the issues symbolized by the particular structure of planets so that their energies can be experienced on different levels and utilized more creatively in life.

Such points, once identified, provide not only a focus for the astrologer to work constructively with the client, but are generally very sensitive to transits and progressions and thus invaluable for accurate and detailed predictive work and may mark key changes in the life that are as profound as those which correlate with transits to any major personal point. For our purpose here, they are also an excellent way of seeing the many forms the simple pattern of three or five planets can make, and thus an uncomplicated introduction to working with midpoints in the chart.

'I finally discovered that I drank so that I could contact my anger.' Female alcoholic (Figure 5.5).

Figure 5.5 Factors from the chart of an alcoholic.

'I don't like doing anything dangerous. Though I did once jump fully clothed into the sea in winter for a bet.' Figure 5.6 is

Figure 5.6 See text.

a woman whose job involves close contact with criminals and terrorists. And goes hot-air ballooning!

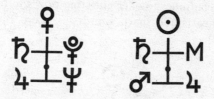

Figure 5.7 Pablo Picasso.

Figure 5.7, from the chart of Pablo Picasso, 'I'd like to live like a poor man with lots of money' and also Figure 5.8, 'For me, painting is a dramatic action in the course of which reality finds itself split apart. What counts . . . is the moment at which the universe comes out of itself and meets its own destruction.'

Figure 5.8 Pablo Picasso.

$\odot = \mathbb{D}/\mathbb{P} = \mathatmark/\hbar = \varphi/\hbar$ and $\hbar = \varphi/\sigma = \mathbb{D}/\Omega$
'Deny yourself! You must deny yourself! That is the song that never ends.' Goethe (Figure 5.9), *Faust*, Part 1.

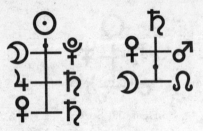

Figure 5.9 Goethe.

$$\text{☽} / ♃ = ☉ = ♂ / ♃$$

'The world continues to offer glittering prizes to those who have stout hearts and sharp swords . . .' Lord Birkenhead (Figure 5.10).

Figure 5.10 Lord Birkenhead.

$$Ψ = ☿ / ♄ = ☉ = ♃ / ♇$$

'The metaphysician . . . is a serious person, working with a serious problem, convinced of one essential fact – that the enlightenment of the human soul by discipline is possible and that the individual has within himself the substance of his own perfection, if he can recover within himself the art of regeneration.' Figure 5.11, Manly Palmer Hall, *My Books*.

Figure 5.11 Manly Palmer Hall.

$\odot - 0 = \Psi / \text{P}$

'The centre of the cyclone is that . . . place in which one can learn to live eternally. In the centre . . . one is off the wheel of Karma, of life, rising to join the Creators of the Universe . . .' Figure 5.12, John C. Lilley, psychoanalyst, author of *The Mind of the Dolphin*, in his *The Centre of the Cyclone*.

Figure 5.12 John C. Lilley.

$\odot = \mathcountersign{Y}/\text{2} = \mathcountersign{Y}/\Psi$

'A little monograph on the ashes of one hundred and forty different varieties of pipe, cigar, and cigarette tobacco' – the prolific Arthur Conan Doyle has Sherlock Holmes write this in *The Red-Headed League*, where he also speaks of a case as 'quite a three-pipe problem . . .' Holmes was of course also addicted to cocaine! Doyle (Figure 5.13) became a convinced spiritualist and wrote *A History of Spiritualism*.

Figure 5.13 Sir Arthur Conan Doyle.

$\mathcal{D} = \hbar / AS = \text{Ħ} / AS$

'Saturn is the Mother.' Figure 5.14, Bruno Huber.

Figure 5.14 Bruno Huber.

⊙/♅ = ⊙/☿ = ☽ = ♇/AS = ♆
'I am an Indian tom-tom waking all the sleepers so that they may work for their Motherland.' Figure 5.15, Annie Besant initiating the Home Rule for India League.

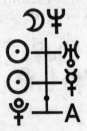

Figure 5.15 Annie Besant.

☽/♆ = M = ♃/♆
'The broad mass of the nation . . . will more easily fall victim to a big lie than to a small one . . .' 'I go the way that Providence dictates with the assurance of a sleepwalker . . .' Figure 5.16, Adolf Hitler.

Figure 5.16 Adolf Hitler.

AS = ♄/☊
'Thus we live, forever taking leave.' Figure 5.17, Rainer Maria Rilke.

Figure 5.17 Rainer Maria Rilke.

☿/M = ♃ = ☉/♅ (and ☿/♃ = ♅ = ☉/Ψ)
'I shall be an autocrat: that's my trade. And the good Lord will forgive me: that's his.' Figure 5.18, Empress Catherine the Great.

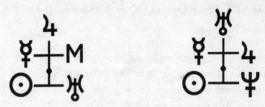

Figure 5.18 Catherine the Great.

Most of these messages are coming through very clearly. If we were to work with any of these people we should be able to home in very quickly on how they are experiencing these inner energies. From the large range of possibilities inherent in any aspect relationship we can move directly to the specific manifestations *they* experience in their own life. From there we can begin to explore with them those energies and patterns for as far as they are prepared, or need, to go. Astrologically, we are closer to their experience from the start and can move from the centre rather than approach them from the periphery of their experience.

CHAPTER 6

Interpreting Midpoint Trees

MICHAEL HARDING AND CHARLES HARVEY

The Impressionist painters broke down the images in their pictures into individual points of colour which when viewed from a distance resolved themselves once again into a complete image. This division into primary elements is the first message for simplifying the planetary pictures shown by tree diagrams. By translating each midpoint image separately and then juxtaposing them we build up a composite picture from which a total idea or series of ideas will emerge.

If we, as astrologers, find difficulty in making sense of the particular sequence of midpoints present in a tree, we can be sure that the individual who has lived through the repeated expression of a series of midpoints will in some way have made sense of them in the manifestation of their life. Simply placing the sequence of ideas represented side by side will speak volumes, enabling a client to see just how they tend to associate a particular combination of ideas, sympathies and 'colours' together in a particular part of their psyche. This basic analytical approach to interpretation also has the advantage of enabling the astrologer to suggest readily alternative ways in which certain combinations, which may have perhaps become fixated in one type of manifestation, may be re-expressed on a more creative level.

With this in mind, the simplest step for the complete beginner to midpoints is to take *COSI* and jot down notes as to the likely manifestations that have been observed by Ebertin and his colleagues. While all combinations may express themselves in both positive and negative ways, it is valuable first of all to focus on the pure ideas involved in each planetary picture. The closer we can get to the principles involved, without making value judgements, the more likely we are to be able to assist the individual to work with their deeper potential.

When working with *COSI*, rather than looking at the actual midpoint combination given on the right-hand page, it is often more useful at first to note the potential present in the midpoint as shown in the notes given on the left-hand page under 'Psychological Correspondence', 'Sociological Correspondence' and 'Probable Manifestions'. We can then of course add to these specific translations images of our own which we have found useful in getting to grips with these particular ideas in the past.

Having made this first outline picture there are several complementary ways by which we can sharpen its focus and bring out the dominant features and subtler nuances and shades of any pattern of planetary pictures. The main approaches to each tree can be summarized as follows:

1. *Sequence*: as outlined in Chapter 2, interpret each midpoint in turn and see the total 'story' that this sequence unfolds. This is the most direct and immediate means of access to a planetary tree.

2. *Closest midpoints*: as with ordinary aspects, those midpoints which are closest in orb to the central factor in the tree will usually give a particular focus and dominant colour to the tree.

3. *Personal factor combinations*: $\odot/\math답{D}$, $\odot/AS$, $\odot/M$, $\math}/M$, $\mathD/AS$ or MC/AS. These will strongly highlight the whole tree in which they are involved and draw the whole meaning of the tree into the centre of the life's expression.

4. *Combinations involving one personal factor*, i.e. those involving $\odot$, $\mathD$, MC, and AS and another chart factor: these will tend to work with and help to channel and express outer planet combinations, and personalize them.

5. *Midpoints involving the MC and AS*: these should be treated with caution unless the time of birth is known to be accurate within five minutes or so, and even then the actual sequence of these should be treated with caution (and noted as a possible source for rectification).

6. *Midpoints involving the same factor*, e.g. $\mathD = \emptyset/\emptyset = \emptyset/\Psi: =$ will place considerable emphasis on the duplicated factor.

7. *Midpoints involving paradoxical themes*, e.g. involving several ♂ combinations and several ♀ or several ♄ and several Ψ. This will demand that both sides of the paradox are integrated into the total picture and implies that both issues will come together through this particular tree.

Which trees then are important? All trees are important in terms of themselves but certain trees are always important. Thus if we need to know 'what kind of' Neptune someone has then their Neptune tree will be important. But Neptune is not necessarily an important factor for some people. However, everyone uses their solar and lunar levels at some time each day so that the Sun and Moon will always be important in any chart. Likewise the AS and MC represent vital levels of orientation which we use daily. If the time of birth is known accurately the midpoint involved with these angles will be of immense importance in understanding these levels.

To see these principles in practice let us examine some of the important midpoint pictures (Figure 6.1) of a woman born in the middle of the last century. First of all, looking generally at all four trees illustrated, we note that the ☽ is closely configured with the MC, and also with ♄ and ☿, suggesting that the life will manifest ambitions of a deep seriousness and emotional earnestness. At the

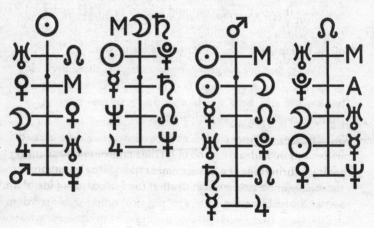

Figure 6.1 Sun, Moon, Mars and node midpoint structures.

same time we see the ♂ is very strongly placed, linking together by midpoint these MC and ☽ levels with the ☉ level, indicating someone who will find the focus of their life around a fierce drive, will-power, forcefulness, and readiness for battle. Next by contrast we may note that the ☉ links M and ☽ to ♀ by midpoint while the ☊ links these two with ♅. In sum, we have MC and ☽ themes involved at the heart of the life through ♂, at the integrated level through ♀, and at the level of contacts with others through ♅.

In the ☽–M axis itself we can expect that the reflective preoccupations and life's objectives (MC) will tend to reflect her own feelings and manifest a concern with emotional and feminine issues (☽) and that these will be thought and talked about (☿)seriously and professionally (♄). *COSI* describes this combination as 'the desire to care for others . . . great aspirations . . . inner experiences of life and the appreciation of spiritual values' and relates it to 'people with feeling and sentiment'. So emotional, feeling, and feminine issues are clearly likely to be of deep importance in the life. But in what way? Will she be drawn to poetry and romantic tales of adventure? Will she be preoccupied by the emotional needs of children? Will she be a pioneer in the area of nourishment and nurturing – a whole-food pioneer perhaps, or a fighter for child education?

Looking more closely at the tree we see that all these factors are focused in the ☉/♇ midpoint and also in the ♆/☊ midpoint. (In fact ☿ and ♄ are technically out of orbs of ♆/☊.) ☉/♇ and ♆/☊ will therefore take on a central importance in this life and will help illuminate the more specific channels for these powerful M–☽ aspirations.

COSI says of ☉/♇ that it has to do with 'the striving for power . . . consciousness of aim or objective . . . the power of attainment . . . the qualities of leadership', and that it has to do with 'pioneers, fighters, persons accustomed to rule others (martyrs to their own ideas)'. In terms of life manifestations he suggests that it can bring 'sudden advancement, the ability to establish and consolidate one's position as a leader, the realization of ideas' and that it can also bring the danger of 'physical suffering, martyrdom'. Clearly, then, this is no romantic wallflower but someone who will feel the need to fight for what she believes.

Of Ψ/Ω *COSI* has little positive to say. It refers to 'a lack of community sense' and 'peculiar or strange conduct in communal life, unreliability'. However, in terms of principles we can see that it must be related to idealistic relationships and associations, and to contacts with idealists, socialists, and those elements which emphasize sympathy, compassion, imagination and a larger more transcendent view of things. Put together with the ☉/♇, we have a picture of a pioneering idealist of some kind.

Putting this instinctive and reflective aspect of our subject to one side for the moment, we can now turn to her solar axis to see the kind of way in which she will centre her life, and the characteristic issues which she will integrate into her decision making. Starting with ♅/Ω, we see someone who will gravitate towards unusual relationships and contacts with reformers and those concerned to 'wake up' society. As *COSI* says: 'political associations advocating reforms' and the 'inclination to violence . . . becoming upset and excited along with others'.

To this, because of the common denominator ♅, we can add ♃/♅, which speaks of someone who can bring about successful changes, who can bring philosophical insight, inventive flair and organizing ability to whatever they decide to do.

By contrast with these restless energies the Sun between Venus and the Moon–MC then focuses the life on feminine and emotional issues and on ones to do with tenderness, devotion and affection, and with art, balance and justice. Finally a more forceful and possibly idealistic tone returns with the midpoint, ♂/Ψ, suggesting that this individual will gravitate towards 'crusades' and will draw upon an inspirational kind of energy and be guided by an innate sense of strategy in life's battles.

Having built up a picture of her ☽–MC and ☉ levels we now note that ♂ is with both ☉/☽ and of ☉/M, an enormously powerful pair of midpoints. While everyone's ♂ is important for revealing her capacity to assert herself as an individual, we can immediately see that individual self-assertion is a central issue for this person. This is indicative of someone who will 'get herself together' (☉/☽) through the energetic pursuit of some objective (☉/M). Surveying the whole tree we see that ♂ brings together two midpoints involving ☿ (☿/Ω and ☿/♃), and two involving Ω

($\mathaccent{}{\varphi}/\Omega$ and $\hbar/\Omega$), which indicates that φ and $\hbar$, 'deep and serious thought', and $\tiny{4}$ and Ω, 'groups with common interest', are in close hard aspect with each other and that these two aspects of the personality structure will be brought together when this individual starts to assert herself. This adds up to 'thoughtful associations for a common interest are pursued with great drive and energy'.

In sequence we find that the central martial drive ($\mathrm{\sigma}$) will tend to work in verbal, communicative, intellectual associations (φ/Ω), implying intense team-work for the realization of ideas. H/P then focuses this drive and energy around deep collective reforms and 'revolutionary' activity of some kind, giving her drive the 'super-human' and 'transpersonal' qualities. $\hbar/\Omega$ follows, indicating that this radical drive will be directed in serious associations or towards tackling difficult or repressive relationships. Then finally with $\varphi/\tiny{4}$ we see this drive manifesting through constructive ideas, oratory and successful activities generally.

Reading this tree as a story, we could say that here is an individual who pursues her conscious goals and objectives with immense drive and vigour. In so doing she feels able to throw herself totally into all that she does with great ardour and intensity. She works energetically together with others of like mind to bring about some kind of radical reform or revolution. This involves overcoming obstacles and traditional relationships but ends in successful negotiations and powerful oratorical skills.

Remembering that the Sun and Moon often represent the parents, and Sun/Moon the marriage, it may not come as a surprise to know that this girl, Emmeline Goulden, was the daughter of parents who were actively interested in radicalism and reform movements and that she was only fourteen when she attended her first women's suffrage meeting. Likewise, remembering also the Sun axis, representing both father and the men towards whom she was likely to be attracted, and her D–MC axis, we may not be entirely astonished that Emmeline fell in love with, and married at twenty, a forty-four-year-old radical, passionately interested in social reform, whose hyperactive social conscience led him to proclaim in one of his love letters that 'every struggling cause shall be ours'. Richard Pankhurst wore Principle 'like a hair shirt and wielded it like a flail'. He was determined 'to do, to be, and to suffer'.

But Emmeline was no slouch, prepared to project her will on to the men in her life. 'From the start she showed a fierce determination that the vanguard should get on with it', and that her husband should 'cease to survey the dawn from a lofty and rather smug eminence' and actually translate their ideas into actions which would bring about electoral power for women ($\mathinvisible$) ($\mathrm{D} = M = \odot/P$). She at once began suffrage work and joined the Manchester women's suffrage committee, and became active in the Independent Labour Party. The Pankhursts' home soon became a centre for political reformers, with Keir Hardie, Annie Besant, Sir Charles Dilke, and William Morris among their close friends ($\Omega = M/\mathrm{H} = \mathrm{D}/\mathrm{H} = \Psi/AS = \odot/\mathrm{Q} = \mathrm{Q}/\Psi$).

When Emmeline was thirty-nine the death of Dr Pankhurst ended their exceptionally close and congenial partnership, and she found herself in straitened circumstances with four young children to support. This she did with characteristic drive and vigour, taking on the job of registrar of births and deaths while continuing to campaign for women's suffrage. Then in 1903, when she was forty-five, she and her daughter Christabel, who was to become her mother's chief collaborator, founded the Women's Social and Political Union, which began with propaganda among Lancashire working women. In 1905, growing impatient with their slow progress, they decided to adopt more strident methods, and in October, when they were thrown out of a Liberal Party election meeting and were subsequently arrested with attendant press commotions, Emmeline suddenly realized the uses of publicity. From that time onward she adopted sensational, original, and unexpected methods ($\odot = \mathrm{H}/\Omega$, $\sigma = \mathrm{H}/P$ and also $\mathrm{H} = \sigma/M$) to draw attention to 'the cause'. Her suffragettes appeared in many kinds of disguises ($\odot = \sigma/\Psi$, $\Psi/\Omega = \mathrm{D}$) and engaged 'in conduct likely to provoke a breach of the peace', chaining themselves to railings, smashing windows, destroying property, finding every possible way to draw attention to women's lot. *COSI* says of H/P that it can be 'subversive activities, putting the gun to someone's head, the enforcement of decisions', and with σ there with her $\odot/\mathrm{D} = \odot/M$ Emmeline certainly tried to play the enforcer.

A martyr to the cause? ($\odot/P = D = M$.) Certainly . . . indeed an habitual martyr, being repeatedly arrested over a period of years, subjected to force-feeding when on hunger strike ($h = D/M = \odot/P$), and constantly in and out of prison. Her health suffered severely in consequence ($\odot = \sigma/\Psi$ can lead to an undermining of the vitality through the pursuit of idealistic causes as well as through drugs or alcohol!). She would be let out as soon as she grew too weak and re-arrested again as soon as her health began to return.

But Emmeline Pankhurst was not just one of the first, and leading, militants for a cause, she was also someone who had a deep concern for feeding and clothing children, who always took the part of the underdog, and who was concerned for all who needed rights ($D = M = \Psi/\Omega$). During the First World War, despite her own difficulties, she adopted orphans. She saw the world as her family, and after the war devoted much of her energy to lecturing on social hygiene and child welfare. On her death Baldwin described her as 'maternity pleading for her race'.

She was a woman of incredible and persistent courage (cf. σ axis) – on one occasion she walked on a protest march with a broken ankle – who was against authority on principle, but who was herself extremely autocratic and would do anything to get her own way (σ, and also $\math#{H} = \Omega/AS = \mathopen{2\!\!\mathrm{I}}/AS = \sigma/M = D/\sigma$). She was remarkably well organized ($\odot = \mathopen{2\!\!\mathrm{I}}/\math#{H}$) and was able to march 10,000 suffragettes through London in perfect order ($D-M-h-\Psi$). She was a powerful orator who spoke with a simple compassion and sincerity with a 'passionate mournful' voice ($\Psi = h = \math#{H}/\Psi = D/\mathopen{2\!\!\mathrm{I}} = \odot/P$) which flashed contemptuous asides at the objects of her disdain. If $\Psi = h = D = M = \odot/P$ is the professional orator for a cause it is also the professional traveller for a cause, and she made repeated visits to the USA to raise funds and support for the suffragette movement.

Ironically the modern women's movement have ambiguous feelings about Emmeline and prefer to remember her daughter Christabel. Perhaps they find it difficult to square the fact that during the First World War Emmeline called a truce as regards women's rights and flung all her σ energy into the war effort, recruiting, organizing munition workers, and her $D-M-\Psi-h$

energy into travelling to the USA and Russia on propaganda missions for the war. But she is perhaps forgotten even more by those who might most remember her, because after the war Emmeline, a true autocrat and believer in self-reliance, worked with great energy and devotion for the Conservative Party. Indeed, she was standing as a prospective candidate for them in Whitechapel when she died, worn out by the hardships of her life, shortly after the second Representation of the People's Act, on 14 June 1928, an individual and fighter to the last. While signs, houses, and aspects may add colour here and there to her story, the planetary pictures tell us like a strip cartoon how it was.

The next case is quite different. Figure 6.2 depicts the Sun, Saturn and MC trees for a man born during the last century to a middle-class European family. Looking at the Sun, Saturn and MC structures we ought to be able to get some idea as to how this man may choose to express himself in the world. That is, how he might tend to formalize and direct his energies towards developing his career or social standing, though in examining how this process might unfold we shall obviously learn much more about how Saturn could work in other areas of his life, and indeed what it may come to represent.

We can see at once that this Saturn is very strongly placed. It is

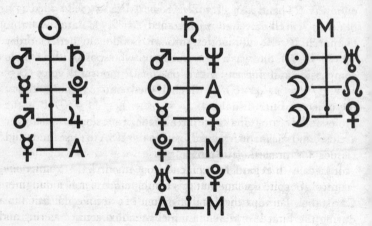

Figure 6.2 Sun, Saturn and M midpoint structures. Note that Saturn is on the AS/MC midpoint.

on both the ☉/AS and AS = MC midpoints as well as the ♇/M – the time of birth is accurate and thus we can trust these personal points. Almost at once we can decide that this is the chart of a man who is most unlikely to adopt a 'free-and-easy' attitude towards life and that in one way or another the images of Saturn will be central – almost exactly as they are on the midpoint tree itself. The Saturn anchors the personal points to ♂/Ψ and to ☿/♀ (surely not *another* alcoholic writer?) as well as contacting ♅/♇. Ebertin says of ♄ = ♅/♇, 'One-sidedness, self-will, egoism, stubbornness, hatred. Exposure to extreme pressures by others.' Obviously, such a statement can hardly be true for all the tens of thousands of people born throughout the world during the months when this combination was active, but we are not looking at such a general picture; the ♄ = ♅/♇ is firmly locked into or *in phase with* both ☉/AS and AS/MC, occupying the same degrees and strongly suggesting that something of this '♄ = ♅/♇' feeling should come through in the native's life. Just this one glimpse of Saturn alone tells us we could be dealing with a tough person, perhaps ruthless, but certainly with something in him which can stir deep feelings in others and risk the strong confrontations that Ebertin's observation suggests might happen. A quick glance at the MC tree confirms this.

The MC is configured with Mars and Uranus and = the ☉/♅ midpoint. This man is very likely to be extremely self-willed as far as his own self-direction is concerned. Mars and Uranus are not happy and relaxed energies, and with everything = ☉/♅ we could expect the need to express himself, perhaps through his career, to be strong and highly individualistic. In fact, his career might even be tied up with the very energies of Mars and Uranus themselves. But let's get back to Saturn.

With Saturn on the ♂/Ψ midpoint we get some of our earlier references to Charles Manson, in which some of the Mars/Neptune issues were raised. In Manson's case we were looking to these contacts with regard to issues to do with drugs, sexuality and control. Despite the fact that this combination is now found in the chart of a man whose whole life was one of extreme dedication to a humanitarian cause which involved much personal suffering and extreme effort, we shall soon see that such issues were exactly the same. Though sometimes, as we've noted before, midpoints can be peculiarly appropriate when it comes to pointing out specifics in an individual's life; our man with ♄ = ♂/♆ originally spent years studying fish!

♄ = ☿/♀ also gives our native the writer's control and refinement of feelings. Although he wrote extensively, this was almost exclusively of a scientific nature; however, his output did include a number of papers on the meaning and significance of art in all its forms. His *study* was filled to overflowing with examples of artifacts from all ages and corners of the world. The control here is in the *meaning* of art and the effort demanded to understand the source of its wellspring.

For ♄ = ♇/M Ebertin suggests 'The attainment of success through self-sacrifice'. The life was certainly one in which many sacrifices had to be made – of himself and others – but the combination also makes personal the contact with Pluto and thus reinforces the ♄ = ♅/♇ axis that already ties in those planets to the ☉/M and AS/MC. Once again, the issue of *power* emerges.

Turning to the solar axis we see much of the same story repeated. ☉ = ♃ = ♂/♄ – the 'death axis' we noted in the previous chapter – can also denote an authoritarian manner, a 'killer instinct' or a need to centre himself through hard or ascetic work. The 'killer instinct' referred to is another side of ♂/♄ and in many respects is a more common expression of this energy – though almost invariably modulated to a more socially acceptable level! The businessman who has to make snap 'life or death' financial decisions, the sculptor who has to place his chisel *exactly* in the right position before striking it with his mallet, the surgeon considering the correct incision or the demolition expert spending days determining the precise points to place his explosive charges, are all typical expressions of such a combination. But, as with the Sun in the chart, one has to consider if the solar axis refers exclusively to the individual or also to *his father*.

With such a strongly-placed Saturn contacting Mars on the solar tree, the ☉/AS and AS/MC itself, and with also the fact of Mars and Uranus configured with the MC, the whole issue of possible clashes with authority/father figures must be explored. The next contact on the Sun axis, ☉ = ☿/♇, suggests someone who may be prepared to risk such a voyage of discovery. The realm of Pluto needs to be explored through the psychopomp Mercury. If we had also seen abundant Neptune contacts we might have wondered if we were possibly dealing with someone with mediumistic gifts – someone who can 'talk to the dead' and use both ☿/♇ and ♂/♄ in such a manner. But these contacts are not there. Instead we have ☉ = ♂/♃ – a very healthy and buoyant configuration – and ☉ = ☿/AS, another strong indicator of the need to communicate the Self. In fact these last two pairs, far from being vague and Neptunian, complete a solar axis which has the potential for considerable physical and intellectual energy. Thus if a clash were to come with the real or symbolic father, one could expect the battle to be royally joined.

It is known that the native often saw his father as weak and ineffectual, unable to fight for his rights. His father was not always a well man (☉ = ♂/♄, ♄ = ♂/♆) and had told his son that the boy 'would never amount to much' – the image of weakness or failure clearly emanating from the father. The classical therapeutic approach might be to suggest that much of the father (as a symbol of potency and assertiveness) *was* in some ways dead or missing, though for the native it was clearly not the end of the matter. For much of his life the internal father was battled with again and again. Indeed, he went so far as to create a psychology which demanded that the Son must symbolically triumph over the Father in sexual conquest to achieve real manhood and adult sexuality. Our native is, of course, Sigmund Freud.

While Freud is now looked back on as the originator of modern psychology, during much of his life many of his contemporaries reviled him and would have put him on much the same level as Manson – citing his 'obsession' with sex, his espousal of a drug for all purposes (cocaine), and his capacity to hold to himself a passionately devoted band of disciples against all the regiments of convention. The same Saturn/Mars/Neptune issues are clearly spelled out, but operating on a much higher level; although there were several times during his life when his advocacy of cocaine caused him considerable personal problems.

It is often overlooked that Freud was almost solely responsible for introducing cocaine into the modern pharmacy. He first became interested in it during the spring of 1884 and used it regularly for at least a decade, recommending it as an antidote to depression and lethargy as well as a general stimulant. His espousal of its use in this manner was frequently attacked as irresponsible, but he did correctly identify the one area – eye-surgery – where it proved to be invaluable and this revolutionized surgical procedures almost overnight. As a researcher his $\odot = \mathrm{2\!\!\!\downarrow} = \mathrm{\sigma}/\mathrm{h}$ was also very much to the fore; while at medical school his capacity to offer highly accurate observations prior to post mortems was recognized to the degree that he was frequently able to 'localize the site of a lesion . . . [in the brain] . . . so accurately that the pathological anatomist had no further information to add'.[1] Much later in life this instinct for death was to become *thanatos* – the instinct *of* death – and led the biologically-orientated psychologist into a head-on clash with evolution.

Although there is not room here even to begin to explore some of Freud's theories of evolution and sexuality, one point should be made as it is a striking example of Freud's chart in action. Briefly, Freud believed that the individual's instinctual drives were both inherited and modified by the experiences of evolution. These experiences were handed on as a series of genetic memories and the human race unconsciously harked back to the security of 'pre-life' in the same way that he suggested that the individual unconsciously seeks the security and safety of the womb. Thus, in the final analysis, the human being and the human race seek *death* – the genetic memory of all that was before life existed. While Darwin saw evolution in purely genetic terms, Freud saw it in *libidinal* terms; that is, the successful conservation of the libido (how's that for $\mathrm{\sigma}/\mathrm{h}$?) was added to the general pool of experience and thence passed on *via* the genetic process to reinforce successful behaviour patterns.

While there are obvious contradictions in depicting evolution as seeking its own extinction, there is no doubt that humans *do* repeat early experience and that history depicts the human race with more than a passing tendency towards seeking its own destruction. Freud was pursuing this and similar ideas with remorseless logic, and saw mankind's relationship with the Sun (being the trigger of all biological cycles) as central to this theory. Thus with $\odot = \mathrm{2\!\!\!\downarrow} = \mathrm{\sigma}/\mathrm{h}$ he writes:

In the last resort, what has left its mark on the development of organisms must be the history of the earth we live on and its relation to the sun. Every modification which is thus imposed upon the course of the organism's life is accepted by the *conservative organic instincts* and stored up for further repetition . . . the aim of all life is death.[2] (Italics added.)

Seldom can one see so clearly and almost word for word how an individual has used his basic solar energy to develop himself and his ideas in the world. It is also worth noting that Freud had an obsessional fear of death, believing that certain years were potentially fatal for him. Surprisingly, given his ultra-rational approach towards anything that smacked of superstition, the dates were based on a rather suspect number theory developed by a colleague of his, Wilhelm Fliess.

While the $\sigma'/\hbar$ midpoint is clearly central to Freud's life and work, we should also look once more at his other important configuration, $\hbar = \sigma'/\Psi$. This gives us a nice image of Freud the researcher into the effects of drugs, as well as his ability to resist succumbing to their power. Despite his frequent use of cocaine there is not the slightest evidence that he was addicted to it. Indeed, the reverse psychology is true, and when in his later years he was in very considerable pain from cancer of the jaw he refused morphine again and again on the grounds that its effects clouded his thinking. His much earlier research work on the nervous systems of fish nicely illustrated another side of $\hbar = \sigma'/\Psi$ (interestingly, Jung with his $\Omega = \sigma'/\Psi$ was to write an extensive monograph on the *symbolism* of the same creature), while his long battle with cancer also depicts the type of chronic sickness which is sometimes characterized by this combination. Freud's attraction towards medicine and his need to 'scientifically' understand dreams are again obvious expressions of this midpoint combination, while his rounding on Jung that only psychoanalysis could provide 'a bulwark against . . . mysticism and occultism', as a counter against the latter's observation that Freud was making a 'religious dogma of sexuality', highlights the significance and power of this other midpoint pattern in Freud's life. It was certainly a pattern he was aware of. His biographer, Ernest Jones, records that Freud was 'in deep fear of the imaginative, and even speculative, side of his nature which he had striven so hard to repress or at least to control'.

Jung records that when he and Freud were on their way by boat to America there came a point when Freud refused to free-associate on his dreams as to do so would make him 'lose his authority'. Freud as the authority on the sexuality of dreams could not be more clearly spelled out than by $h = \sigma/\Psi$ – and on a boat as well! Another incident on that voyage again demonstrated the controlling quality of Freud's Saturn on Mars/Neptune matters, and his own problems in using it. Because of his religious upbringing, Jung was very much against the use of alcohol and even chided Freud for taking wine with a meal. Freud had frequently attempted to get Jung actually to try a glass, and during the voyage finally persuaded Jung to accept a drink. No sooner had Jung taken a sip of the wine than Freud fainted! Clearly the undercurrents of the power struggle between the two men proved a little too much to handle.

The subject of Freud's relationship with his father and his identification with the issues of authority was brought briefly to the surface by these episodes, though it obviously had been playing its part in his relationship with Jung from the start. Initially Freud saw in the Swiss doctor his spiritual son, destined to carry on the work of psychoanalysis after his death. Like Freud, Jung *also* had $\mathcal{4} = \sigma/h$. In other words, the resonance of the inner images matched the reality of later events, made all the more powerful by the striking fact that Freud's σ/h midpoint fell within 4' of Jung's Moon. In other words, at a responsive lunar level Jung would instinctively be picking up that issue again and again – it was part of *his* 'habit' too – and in due course Jung demonstrated to the full his own ability to act out the role of the father. The 'killer instinct' was present in both of them and while it is hardly surprising that he refrained from mentioning such incidents in his autobiography, Jung was capable of quite callous and brutal behaviour to colleagues and lovers. Jung's description of how he came to split with Freud, and how this event was presaged by furniture inexplicably cracking while the two men sat talking, is another graphic example of this σ/h energy at work. A sudden concentration of repressed psychic energy causes a literal fracture and symbolized for Jung the inevitability of the death of their 'father and son' relationship. On 20 April 1914 Jung wrote to Freud that he was severing all his ties with the Vienna Psychoanalytical Society; as he did so he had transiting Mars conjunct his ♃ = ♂/♄ and Freud had to contend with Uranus conjunct *his* sensitive ♄ = ♂/Ψ.

The two men first met on Sunday 3 March 1907 at 10 a.m. in Vienna (Figure 6.3). In his autobiography Jung says the meeting took place during February and that it was at 1 o'clock. This is incorrect, as the Freud/Jung letters clearly show Jung writing to Freud on 26 February suggesting meeting on the following Sunday

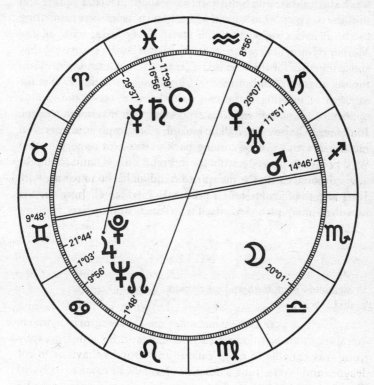

Figure 6.3 The chart for the meeting of Sigmund Freud and Carl Gustav Jung. Note the Mercury/Jupiter square and Neptune on the Sun/Moon midpoint – the two men spent thirteen hours talking about dreams!

morning, and this is confirmed in Freud's diaries. As Jung had travelled from Switzerland and was eager to impress Freud one can be reasonably certain that the appointment was kept on time. If it was, the transits give a remarkable picture.

Mercury and Jupiter were about to form an exact square and were both on Jung's ☽/♅ and AS/MC midpoints (Jung has an almost exact Moon/Uranus square natally) on the day. In Freud's case this transiting square fell on his whole Sun/Jupiter structure picking out in particular the ☿/♇ and ♂/♄. Mars was on Freud's Moon emphasizing his ☽ = ♀/♇ and on Jung's ☽/☿ midpoint. Pluto was on Jung's Mars (surely not a sexual transformation?), as was Saturn. Mars and Saturn were *also* about to form a square and thus the two men's basic natal Mars/Saturn issues were resonating to the heavens right from the start! Neverthless, with all the Mercury/Jupiter energy present as well it is hardly surprising they spoke together for thirteen hours! Interestingly, that ☿–90–♃ in the sky aligned with both the ☉/☽ midpoint and the ♆/♇ of the moment of meeting – the two pairs being exact to the minute opposite one another and thus expressing their maximum tension. In the next chapter we shall be looking more deeply into interpreting transits and will be coming back to just how important that ♆/♇ point has proved itself to be in Freud's life. That it should be aligned exactly with the 'heart and mind' of his first meeting with Jung and the formation of a relationship which changed forever how the human race views itself is strikingly appropriate.

NOTES

1. Sigmund Freud, the Standard Edition, 20.12.
2. ibid., 18.32.

CHAPTER 7

Transits

MICHAEL HARDING AND CHARLES HARVEY

Few of us would doubt the importance of seeing the chart as a whole, yet when it comes to examining transits to the natal chart many astrologers will be content to skim through the ephemeris noting 'important' dates or will laboriously list the transits of each planet month by month. Neither of these methods really gives a clear picture of what is going on in the chart as a whole, and consequently we risk missing the overall image of events. Coming back to the idea first suggested in the introduction – what you get is what you *see* – we should really choose to lay out the relationship between transits and the natal chart in a manner that gives us as comprehensive a picture as possible. In this chapter we shall be looking at the most successful method of doing this, but before starting to fill in the picture we should remind ourselves what we should be looking for.

When introducing the Cardinal/Fixed/Mutable sort in Chapter 3 we discussed the idea of the moment-by-moment transits of the angles as representing our relationship to the most basic cycle of all, the turning earth. Each day both the Ascendant and the Midheaven will trigger off each pair of midpoints seven times indirectly and once directly, reflecting the potential we have to experience the totality of our chart every twenty-four hours. Those who meditate at the *same time* each day also have the opportunity to become more deeply aware of the energy latent in each planetary pair as the diurnal contact between the angles and the planets repeats the same pattern over the course of the year – the next most important terrestial cycle. Whether we are in contact with these energies consciously or through habit, it requires only a few precisely-timed charts to demonstrate the power of these seemingly unimportant aspects; for they are the catalysts of our inner destiny and can act as triggers to our most profound experience.

But, as with so many other important ideas, we may meet them first in a more trivial guise. If we are aware of this and make a point of observing how we live our lives *from an astrological point of view* then we can come to see in the slow tread of daily events how transits of the angles as well as of the planets can reveal the inner dynamics of the chart and the deeper reaches of our potential.

It is this resonance between the static moment of the birth chart and its subsequent unravelling in time that brings our experience into being. How we approach an understanding of it is a test of our dedication as astrologers. The moment we move away from the 'cook-book' attitude towards transits and begin to explore the actual process of our existence then our astrology takes on profound philosophical and psychological importance; because astrology can *predict*. It is this ability, however imperfect it may be, that ultimately separates astrology from conventional psychotherapeutic approaches. Astrologers may choose to ignore this side of their craft, or decide to retreat into the comparative safety of Swiss metaphysics, but it is nevertheless there; and it will continue to remain there, signalling its presence every time we open an ephemeris, and surfacing afresh with each client's request for news of tomorrow.

This side of our craft is not a comfortable area, it is not complete nor well formulated and frequently has to undergo the indignity of being described in alternative terminologies. It has not developed a clear language or philosophy of its own and its results are often wrong. But for those who are prepared to accept the challenge it is one of the most exciting areas of personal research. Our experience of time is the experience of consciousness. It is this that we *really* begin to explore when we open our ephemeris and seek to relate its pages to our life.

It is clear from the way we have approached the interpretation of midpoint trees, specifically with regard to the sequencing of each individual planetary pair, that transits are an integral part of this analytic approach. Just as the individual does not exist without any reference to his surroundings, so the birth chart cannot properly be looked at without regard to its expression in time. The two are interlocked and indivisible; to suggest otherwise would be to assume that the process of life stops at the moment of birth. The analysis of the chart in its relationship to time is represented by the transits, progressions and directions made to it, and this analysis is integral to our understanding of what each chart factor is 'doing' now and how it may also operate in the future. Specific planetary energies mean different things to different individuals, and without seeking to understand each person's unique experience of his or her own transits we risk imposing on our clients our own particular patterns. To some extent, of course, this is inevitable, just as we can never recognize all our own projections, etc. But we can minimize this chance for confusion by making a clear decision to listen to what is being said to us, and by observing our own chart and those others we know well, and not jumping to the conclusions of cook-books!

For example, a man experienced the death of his father when Jupiter was exactly conjunct his own Sun. Twelve years previously, when Jupiter was within minutes of the same conjunction, a long-standing relationship broke up. Twelve years prior to that the Jupiter transit correlated with the hospitalization and death of his mother. Jupiter transits are not supposed to be like that! However, this man has the combination $\odot = \mathrm{D}/\hbar$. In other words, Jupiter conjunct the Sun is also $\mathrm{4} = \mathrm{D}/\hbar$. $\mathrm{D}/\hbar$ does not, by and large, correlate with times of great rejoicing and Jupiter has more than a passing tendency to exaggerate whatever it touches. In other words, the 'sadness/separation' issues which so often correlate with Moon/Saturn are being temporarily amplified and expanded. The astrologer familiar with using midpoints would have spotted that one a mile away and raised the issue of what the $\mathrm{D}/\hbar$ might mean to that individual before dashing off any cheerful prognostications.

The whole of our approach to the understanding of the birth chart should be in trying to discover what sort of Sun our client has, what type of Moon he or she experiences and in what manner the various energies of the planets are understood. While the use of midpoints helps this fine-tuning to a large extent, by giving us from the start a far more subtle picture of how each natal planet interacts with the rest of the chart, we still must learn to listen to how each individual responds to transits. This added awareness can give us tremendous insights into the way psychic energies are being experienced – because they are being experienced *now* and thus have all the advantages of being immediately accessible to our attention.

In the course of this chapter we shall be looking at ways transits are used together with midpoints. While it is perfectly feasible to make observations about possible events in people's lives while having absolutely no knowledge of their personality or circumstances, a thorough understanding of a person's past and present life is vitally important to make the most of what we are able to offer for the future. With such an understanding we should be able to help ourselves and others work more consciously with the energies latent in the natal chart as they are expressed and modulated by the moment.

The basic techniques of forecasting in midpoint work all make use of the four traditional methods of relating planetary cycles to the birth chart: transits, progressions, directions and lunations. By no means do all midpoint-users employ all these methods at the same time, but they will all be discussed as the potential information they can supply is enormous – indeed, at times it can be an overkill. It is for this reason that we shall try and *simplify* matters as well as point to some areas where experience suggests that the amount of information available is, at the current time, perhaps more of a hindrance than a help.

The basic planetary information supplied by looking at the transits, progressions, directions and lunations can be laid out for midpoint work in one of two ways: the Cardinal/Fixed/Mutable sort and the 45° graphic ephemeris. We have already looked at how the Cardinal/Fixed/Mutable sort is created and to use it is just a matter of seeing which planets, progressions, directions or lunations are hitting which midpoints. The problem, of course, is how to make sense of it all, and initially we would suggest concentrating only on transits and lunations.

As astrologers, the starting place for all methods and theories should be our own chart and the charts of those close to us. If we try an idea with four or five accurately-timed charts and it doesn't work with any one then the chances are that it doesn't work at all. So put these ideas to the same test.

Use the program in Appendix 1 (p. 445) to create several

Cardinal/Fixed/Mutable sorts for a number of charts and make a dozen photocopies of each of them. In this way you can mark in the transiting planets and lunation degrees for specific days you wish to examine in detail and write your notes on the back. The orbs used for transits to midpoints are very tight, generally within thirty minutes, though a degree or so can be used for lunations.

Over a period of time this can be extremely useful source material, as it is only by noting and recording the existence of important patterns that we will recognize them when they reoccur. The whole of our approach lies in detecting repeated patterns, becoming sensitive to the manner in which we experience them, learning what we may unconsciously expect of them and seeking ways in which we can make the best use of them by becoming aware of their many shades and levels. To this end the keeping of some form of personal journal is almost a prerequisite for a serious study of astrology. In it you can record briefly your daily experiences, moods and dreams, together with any exactly-timed events.

Even if what you write does not seem to make a lot of sense or be of any importance, the salient data is there and recorded. If you subsequently come to the conclusion that transiting Mars to some particular midpoint in your chart correlates with such and such a feeling then you can go back and check whether it actually *does*. Just as we said in Chapter 2 that not all midpoints are equal, so it is clear that transits are not likely to be experienced by people in a similar manner. Indeed, experience suggests that they are categorically *not*. And there is a good reason for that – we're all different.

In working with clients we will quickly recognize that certain planets don't work in the way they're supposed to (as with the Sun/Jupiter example given above) or that (a) they have very little 'effect' or (b) they seem inordinately important. The same applies for each midpoint, but we'll come back to that later; for the moment we'll stay with examining the planets themselves.

In the case of the Jupiter transiting the Sun, we saw that the key factor was the natal $\odot = \mathbb{D}/\hbar$. As the most powerful combination it 'defined' the Sun more clearly than other midpoints to the solar axis. The reason for this will be left to Part 2, when we see how certain harmonic relationships can reinforce basic midpoint combinations, but even without knowing *why*, simply listening to what is said to us while watching the factors on the midpoint trees will tell us the story. If a man has ☽/♄ as one of the combinations on his solar axis and suffers a loss every time his Sun is triggered by a Jupiter conjunction, then clearly that ☽/♄ is vitally important. If another man with ☉ = ☽/♄ who also has ☉ = ♂/♃ experiences a wonderful time driving racing cars, having love affairs and winning marathons each time Jupiter transits his Sun then clearly the ☽/♄ is of no great consequence and ♂/♃ *is*. As astrologers we are entitled to wonder why this may be the case but from a practical point of view, if we are asked to prepare a report for the next year when Jupiter hits the Sun, we have a pretty good idea what is most likely to happen. The core of all predictive work is based on this type of approach.

Our personal awareness of the many layers of planetary symbolism, of the many possibilities allowed for by including signs, houses and other major aspects are all additional information we can use to expand on the possibilities latent in each moment. But the traditional axiom that 'nothing can happen which is not promised in the radix' never holds more true than when we see how the basic patterns of experience replicate the 'type' of planet a person has, and much of what defines a planet lies on its midpoint axis.

To start off with, there are three approaches to examining transits and lunations to the natal midpoints; we can consider those which contact the angles and planets – and thus obviously also trigger all the midpoints connected with each planet – we can examine transiting planets, etc. to *each* midpoint, regardless as to whether or not it connects with a planet, and finally we can consider the transiting angles on a moment by moment basis. The aspects we will be looking for, as with all midpoint work, are all the multiples of 45°.

The idea of the transiting angles as being the 'final wards of the lock' was first put forward by John Addey and is perhaps one of the best approaches to studying our own chart. As mentioned in Chapter 3, exactly timed moments will clearly show the contact between the angles and midpoints. Using this approach over a period of time, we can come to see what parts of our chart are particularly sensitive and to which we instinctively respond. This knowledge becomes of special importance when we later begin looking at transits of the planets themselves; for we then have a much better idea how they may correlate or, indeed, whether they may prove to mean very little. The same is so with lunations.

Some people respond very strongly to the new and full Moons, and the exact degree on which they fall can be of extreme importance as the midpoints closest to that point can very often give quite a clear picture of how the lunation may express itself. For example, the full Moon prior to the first meeting of Freud and Jung fell at 8 ♏ 31. Jung has his ☿/♆ midpoint at 8° 32′ of the mutables, Freud has *his* at 8° 48′! Remember, the two men spent most of their first meeting talking about dreams. The new Moon prior to the meeting fell at 22 ♒ 53 right on Jung's ♇ = ♂/♃; one would be hard-pressed to find a more concise picture of what was about to be stimulated in his life. When the two men separated in April 1914, the new Moon at the time fell on Freud's Pluto and Jung's Sun/Neptune square, though the actual degree of the lunation hit Jung's ♃/♅ midpoint and this is a particularly interesting one to watch for all of us, as we shall see later. In looking at transits to the midpoints themselves, we have an embarrassment of riches and need to focus on what are the most significant. Listening to what your client has to say will tell you a lot about which midpoints operate most strongly in his or her chart and these should certainly be noted on the Cardinal/Fixed/Mutable sort and perhaps even drawn in on the 45° graphic ephemeris (which will be described shortly). Otherwise, certain midpoints have shown themselves to have particular importance, as we began to observe in Chapter 2. Midpoints including the angles as one of the factors, the AS/MC and ☉/☽ midpoints and any very close clustering of midpoints all hold considerable potential. This last group is harder to assess, as what they represent is literally hidden. The midpoints are not activated natally and it is only either by recording any events which trigger them by angularity or by discovering the correlation with previous transits that any clear picture may emerge. One client with five midpoint pairs within a few minutes experienced a transit of Uranus to them as particularly frightening. So much energy was released that he would wake up at night in a panic, afraid that he was about to 'turn into someone else'! Clearly for him they contained cut-off and unexpressed parts of his personality which he was not able to recognize and assimilate.

We have already noted the importance natally of the Sun/Moon midpoint. When this midpoint is occupied it is the third factor which will act as the catalytic factor, the lightning conductor through which these creative energies can be channelled. But in charts where the Sun/Moon is unoccupied the deeply integrative process symbolized by this point can be triggered into activity by transits and more especially by transits of the outer planets which can activate a particular area of the zodiac for months on end around the time of a station.

For example, a woman had Neptune repeatedly transiting this point during a period when she was becoming involved in a spiritual movement, studying transpersonal psychology and travelling overseas. In the midst of this process she not only experienced a deep change in her perception of herself but also, after a previous history of very unsatisfactory relationships, met and married a man with whom she was able to establish an extremely profound relationship on all levels. In this case we see both an inner and outer marriage being established in the life through a direct and conscious willingness to work with the Neptunian energies at a deep level.

On the other hand, in another case of a very high-powered businessman who had natal $h = MC/AS$, and who found it impossible directly to acknowledge his own strong Neptune energies, and who consequently projected them on to his marriage and business partners, this same transit coincided with a disastrous collapse of his business. This was the direct result of uncontrolled and unauthorized speculation in overseas markets by the partner. The businessman's previously secure, well-ordered world collapsed and his business had to 'go into liquidation'. The forecast and caution given to this client a year previously that 'this is a period when, if conscious steps are not taken, the very foundations of your life may seem to be undermined and things may seem to be "all at sea"' was not only appropriate, but, because it so clearly described what was 'washing over him', actually proved to be a valuable touchstone in helping this client cope with an otherwise overwhelming situation. Happily this man was able to contact his own Neptune process sufficiently to inject some real creative imagination into the final dissolution and to salvage the seeds of a new business venture from the wreck. At the same time this seeming disaster could be seen to have brought about a deeper strength and inner awareness in the life.

In these two cases the way the Sun/Moon integration was handled also reflects the midpoints immediately adjacent to the Sun/Moon. In the first case we find Sun/Moon within 3′ of Venus/Node while in the latter it is immediately adjacent to Saturn/Neptune. Whether or not this midpoint is actually occupied natally, such adjacent midpoints are extremely valuable for characterizing the way in which an individual will 'get his life together' and find his creative centre. In the former case it was a 'love relationship' which served as the major catalyst in the life. In the latter it could be said that this man comes into his own when he is 'earthing visions' and is able to express his strong practical idealism in such matters as raising large sums for charity and assisting good causes, such as alternative medicine. (Saturn/Neptune is often called the 'sickness axis' but it can be as much the concern with the sick as the sufferer and is often found in the charts of doctors.)

When Sun/Moon and MC/AS fall in the same place this can indicate a remarkable single-mindedness and the potential for becoming totally absorbed in some kind of 'mission' in life. The power of such midpoint combinations can be seen in the example of Field-Marshal Montgomery. He had these points exactly opposite each other and both within minutes of Mars/Pluto. With Sun in Scorpio, Moon in Capricorn, MC in Aries and AS in Leo he was obviously no slouch when it came to self-promotion and reaching for glory through tough aggressive challenges. But the Mars/Pluto here gives it a deeper level of 'superhuman power (force, brutality), the attainment of success through excessive effort', as *COSI* vividly puts it. It is noteworthy that Saturn was stationed exactly on this midpoint on 25 September 1942 as he was making his meticulous preparations for the battle which changed the course of the Second World War. The first orders for the battle of El Alamein were actually issued on 28 September, the actual battle beginning on 23

October. This Saturn station also encompassed his first victory of Alam Halfa which began on 31 August. Of ♄ = ♂/♇ *COSI* says: 'A person unafraid of hard work leaving no stone un-turned in the pursuit of a particular task, the desire to overcome difficulties and obstacles at all costs forcibly.' Equally appropriately Uranus was stationary on this same point throughout the Battle of Normandy, being additionally squared by Mars on 31 July 1944 as Montgomery and the Allied forces were making their first major break-out and 'the greatest achievement in military history', and Montgomery was promoted to the rank of Field-Marshal. This was, not surprisingly, simultaneously a period of the great tension and friction with the Supreme Commander, Eisenhower, as Monty's innate autocracy and rebelliousness came to the fore in no uncertain terms.

While transits of the *angles* to unaspected outer planet pairs, ♃/♄ through to ♆/♇, can be particularly illuminating, if only momentarily, as they connect us to these deeper layers of energy, transits of the planets themselves may be less significant. Indeed, as a general rule of thumb, 'reverse process' is more likely to operate. That is, transits of the angles to the outer planets can be more important than transits of the outer planets to the same pairs. Transiting Saturn coming to a radical ♅/♇ is much more of a generational experience. Transiting Saturn to a radical ☉/M, on the other hand, is certainly not. This could be a major transit if the individual concerned had problems with handling Saturn energy. Similarly, transiting Neptune to the ♃/♇ midpoint is a generational factor while transiting ♆ = ☉/♂ is not. How important this transit might be for the individual concerned will depend primarily on two factors: what the ☉/♂ is 'doing' in the chart and how well the person is able to get on with Neptune.

If the Sun/Mars aspect in the chart is a square or a trine then this will make the ☉/♂ midpoint itself of much greater importance, and will obviously mean that the transiting Neptune is now either at the midpoint of the square or trine or triggering off one corner of it. But there's a lot more to aspects than squares and trines and in the second half of this book we shall look at other aspects such as the quintile, septile and novile series, among others. There we shall see how different aspect patterns can markedly affect the way a midpoint pair might operate and alter its importance in the chart. In short, what will strengthen a midpoint pair here is if they are *already part of an existing pattern*.

The second point, how sensitive an individual is to Neptune, will have to come from your own experience with your client. While a rough guess would suggest that someone with no water in the chart or a lack of aspects to Neptune is more likely to be at sea when it arrives via a transit, this is far from a fixed rule and not a substitute for actually finding out. Someone who manifests the Saturn principle very strongly, who wants everything to arrive on schedule and even complains if his transits are late, can have one hell of a time with a minor Neptune transit while a major matter like Neptune conjunct the Sun can mean very little for someone who has lived like that all his life. Again, this means going back to the chart, seeing the 'type' of planet or midpoint and discovering the correlations with similar transits in the past. It also means taking into consideration one very important factor that 'cook-books' are notorious for omitting: humans tend to *react*.

If our archetypal Saturn businessman has a Saturn transit he will probably enjoy it. If it makes him feel bad, he will assume he deserves it for not working hard enough and think fondly of his old school. The chances are that the real recipients of his transit will be his staff. When all is said and done he will not consider it out of the ordinary. A Uranus transit is quite another matter. Uranus is supposed to bring enlightenment and a sense of adventure and the need for freedom and so on. Our businessman, however, is most unlikely to be overcome with urges to drop out and trek to Goa. Far from unknotting his tie, he is likely to pull it tighter; for something inside him is stirring and he doesn't know what it is. So, like all of us, he will tend to *react as per normal*. His basic reaction will tend to be to say to himself, 'If I sit very still and upright, doing everything very properly, be ultra-punctual and wash twice behind my ears every morning then this terrible urge to do something different will go away.' Far from loosening up, seeing new possibilities, going hang-gliding or taking up astrology, he is likely to personify Saturn to the nth degree. He could thus develop severe back problems, suffer from depression and exhaustion (sitting up straight all day is *very* tiring) and be so thrown by forcing himself to do with effort what normally comes naturally that he upsets his metabolism, and with it his own applecart. He may well under-perform at work so badly that he gets fired, become so preoccupied with needing to stand still that he gets run over, or become such a pain in his wife's neck as well that she finally clouts him and leaves with the milkman. In other words, he gets to have a classic Uranus transit.

While this is obviously an extreme case, it is not unduly exaggerated. Just as we stressed earlier the need for the astrologer to discover what each planetary energy means for the individual client, so there is the need to discover whether or not an energy is consciously experienced *at all*. Many people are so tied to one area of their chart, and so afraid of what may be lurking in its shadow, that an essential part of working with transits is learning to communicate to the client some feeling of the energies which are likely to surface in a language that the client can understand. Simply to be able to discuss it in a language that an *astrologer* can understand is no good at all.

The failure of astrologers to work at developing such a language is a definite omission, but many will use the 'sub-personality' approaches of Assagioli or the Gestalt techniques of Perls with good effect. Thus coming back to the natal chart, talking through the midpoint structures and relating them to past experiences will often induce inner recognition from the client of an emotional pattern which can be given a name. Identified in this way, it is now far easier to convey how transits may operate in a way which is genuinely useful to the client. One can now reach a point where the astrologer can discuss how a particular sub-personality, behaviour pattern, call it what you will, together with its attendant emotional issues is likely to be stimulated by the forthcoming transits. With this in mind we can start to look at the most useful technique of all for examining how transits interact with these natal energies: the 45° graphic ephemeris.

A graphic ephemeris does exactly what its name suggests – it lays out the positions of the planets in a visual manner rather than as a list of figures in celestial longitude, allowing us to see at once the broad shape of the year. It is the ideal tool for working with clients, as we can see at a glance all the points of stress for the year, where the new and full Moons are and the exact points of planetary

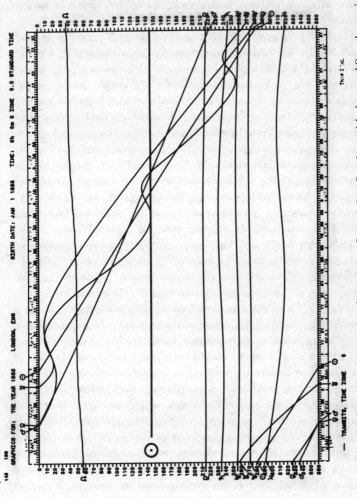

Figure 7.1 A 360° graphic ephemeris from Astro-Computing Services with the natal Sun drawn in.

stations. Using this technique there is no need to fumble through the ordinary ephemeris or laboriously write out columns of dates prior to the consultation; with the graphic ephemeris it is all *there* in front of one. So how does it work?

Figure 7.1 is a graphic depiction of the planets' positions in 1985 produced by Astro-Computing Services (see Appendix 3). On the left- and right-hand scales we can see 0° at the top and 360° at the bottom. These, of course, are the 360° of the zodiac. Along the top and bottom are the days of the year, with ten-day intervals marked in for easy reference. If we look at 215° on the left-hand scale we can see the glyph for Pluto followed by a virtually straight line; this is Pluto's position during the year. From this we can see that Pluto is practically stationary all that time at around 5° of Scorpio (215° in absolute longitude). If we now look at the top scale we can see the glyphs for Mars and Venus conjunct at the beginning of February. As they are conjunct right at the top of the page, corresponding with 0° on the left-hand scale, this means they *are* at 0°, or Aries. In other words Mars and Venus are conjunct at the beginning of February 1985 almost exactly at 0° Aries as your ordinary ephemeris will confirm. If you now carefully follow the line for Venus you will see that around 14 March it begins to level off at just over 20° and then starts to move back up the page, reaching nearly 5° by 25 April. This is, of course, a graphic representation of its retrogradation and the two points where the line turns round (14 March and 25 April) are the retrograde and direct stations. If we follow the line for the rest of the year we see there are no more retrogradations and that Venus ends the year at a little over 270°. In fact checking with the ephemeris will show that it is at 5° of Capricorn on the 31st. If you have not used a graphic ephemeris before, it would be a good idea to check the lines for *all* the planets against their position in the ephemeris now to get the feel of how it works. Remember, as the planetary lines move *down* the page, the planet is moving *direct*. If the line moves *up* the page then the planet is going *retrograde*.

So far the graphic ephemeris tells us very little, although we do get an immediate picture of how the years looks astrologically, and can note that during October and November the lines for Mercury, Venus and Mars all cross the line for Pluto. In other words, these will be days of *conjunctions*. This stands to reason; if two planets are at the same place at the same time then they must form a conjunction! This simple fact gives us the reason for using a graphic ephemeris in the first place; we can see at once when a conjunction between planets takes place – every time two lines cross. In fact, *all* possible conjunctions between *all* the planets in 1985 can be spotted with the same ease, and in a few seconds we have the same information that would otherwise require us to scour through an ephemeris for quite some time.

Now, if we draw on the position of our own planets, then we can see transits to them with the same ease. Drawn in at 145° – 25° of Leo – is a line representing our Sun. We can now see that Mercury will station conjunct it on 25 July and then again on 28 August when it will also be joined by Mars, giving us both planets conjunct the Sun at the same time. Three weeks later the Sun itself conjuncts our Sun and that is the last direct transit our Sun receives for the year. It's as simple as that. Had we drawn in *all* our planets, using the scale on each side of the graph, then we would see at a glance *all* the conjunctions we were going to experience in 1985. But what if we want to know about *other* aspects, how can the graph help us here?

Because the scale on the left- and right-hand sides is from 0° to 360° this graph can only show us conjunctions and nothing else. In using midpoints we are concerned not only with conjunctions, but with all multiples of 45°; we need a graph that shows only *these*. In other words, the 45° graphic ephemeris that is shown in Figure 7.2. Although it *looks* very different, it is actually giving us just the same information – the position of the planets throughout 1985 – but arranged in a different sequence. Instead of the 360° circle of the zodiac being graphed out, a 45° sequence is displayed in exactly the same manner as the 45° sort previously explained in Chapter 1.

A planet at 0° on the left-hand scale will either be at 0° Aries, 0° Cancer, 0° Libra, 0° Capricorn (the '90°' points) or 15° of Taurus, Leo, Scorpio or Aquarius (their '45°' equivalents). If we look at the first planet on the left-hand scale we see it is Neptune at just under 1½°. Checking with our ordinary ephemeris tells us that Neptune is in fact at 1 ♑ 23 on 1 January. The next planet down is Saturn at about 9¾° on the scale. It is in fact at 24 ♏ 47 (15° Scorpio + 9

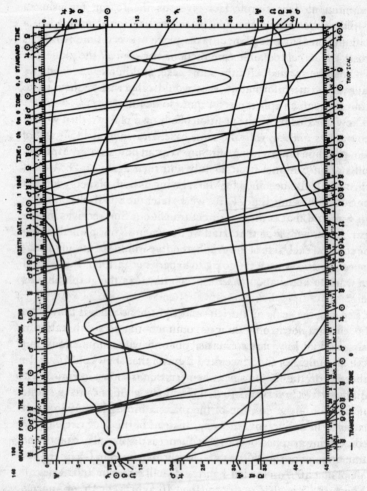

Figure 7.2 A 45° graphic ephemeris from Astro-Computing Services.

47′). If we follow the line for Saturn we see that it stations on 7 March, goes retrograde (up the page) until 25 July and then continues direct (down the page) for the remainder of the year. On 31 December it is at 20° on the scale which means this must be 5° of Sagittarius (15° Scorpio + 20° of movement). Because the graph is focusing on each planet's motion through each 45° section of the zodiac, where two lines cross is not necessarily a conjunction; it will be either that or *any* multiple of 45°. In other words, this graph allows us to see at a glance *all* aspects which are multiples of 45°. These are the aspects that particularly concern us as these relate directly to the idea of concrete manifestation in the world. If we now draw in our Sun as we did before, we will see *all* 45° aspects to it as well as the conjunctions we saw in Figure 7.1. This gives us an immediate picture of the sort of stresses placed on the Sun during the course of 1985.

To draw in a planet on this type of 45° ephemeris is very simple; just take its absolute longitude (as we did when calculating midpoints in Chapter 1) and draw a line in corresponding to that position. In our hypothetical case we placed the Sun at 25° of Leo; in other words at 145°. As our graph stops short at 45° we have to deduct multiples of 45° until we get below this figure. Thus we get 145 − 45 − 45 − 45 = 10° on the scale. With the Sun line drawn in at 10° we can now see much more than just the Mercury station we noted on 28 July; Saturn makes a hard aspect to our Sun right at the beginning of the year. On 4 January Saturn is 25° Scorpio, so the aspect is obviously a square. Because of retrogradation, Saturn makes that same aspect twice more during 1985. We can also see that in the middle of February the Sun, Mercury, Venus and Mars *all* aspect our Sun stressfully in the same few days. Checking with the ephemeris we see that these aspects are an opposition of the Sun and Mercury (both at 25° Aquarius), a sesquiquadrate from Venus (at 10° Aries on 14 February) another sesquiquadrate from Mars which is also at 10° Aries on 16 February. Draw in *all* the planets in this way and we can see at a glance how the general pattern of the year unfolds. More importantly, by actually *seeing* the movements of the planets as they relate to our chart we are less likely to fall into the trap of seeing events as separate issues which are somehow unconnected to ourselves or the flow of our life. What the graph shows us is the *process* of planetary relationships taking place and how certain issues rise and fall in prominence as the year progresses.

At this point we should look at the 45° graphic ephemeris developed by the Ebertin school, as it is slightly different from the Astro-Computing Services version. The way it is used and the planetary information is of course identical, but the Ebertin one includes more information and a helpful scale on the left-hand side which makes drawing in the natal planetary lines even easier. Figure 7.3 shows an Ebertin graph for 1987. While the right-hand column has the same 45° gradations we have already looked at (and can be used to draw in the planets in exactly the same way), the left-hand column is divided into three sections. The first section relates to all the Cardinal signs, the second to all the Fixed signs and the third to all the Mutable. The layout here is exactly the same as we described in Chapter 3 on the C/F/M sort and is a very easy way to draw in the natal lines. If the planet you wish to draw in is in a Cardinal sign then you just locate its position in the Cardinal column and draw it in. If the planet is in a Fixed sign, as our example Sun at 25° Leo is, then we use the second column and find 25° of the Fixed signs a little way down from the top, equivalent to 10° of the Cardinals. The reason for this equivalence is that 25° of any Fixed sign is an exact multiple of 45° away from 10° of any Cardinal sign. As this graphic ephemeris is effectively a 45° sort, then any two planets which are exactly 45° apart will hit the same point. Similarly 30° of a Fixed sign is – from the graphs' point of view – identical to 0° of the Mutables, as indeed the scale demonstrates.

Care needs to be taken when drawing the natal planetary lines on the graph, as errors are hard to remove. Remember, 0° of Aries is right at the top of the page, so if your planet is at only 30′ of Aries it will fall half-way between the very top line and the first scale mark. One degree of Aries (and *all* Cardinal positions) starts at the scale directly *below* the figure 1. Similarly, 0° of the Mutable signs start at the same scale which ends the Fixed signs at 30°. After all, 30° of Taurus is exactly the same as 0° of Gemini. If you spend a little while looking at the layout of the 45° graphic ephemeris you will see that what is happening is that each 45° segment of the

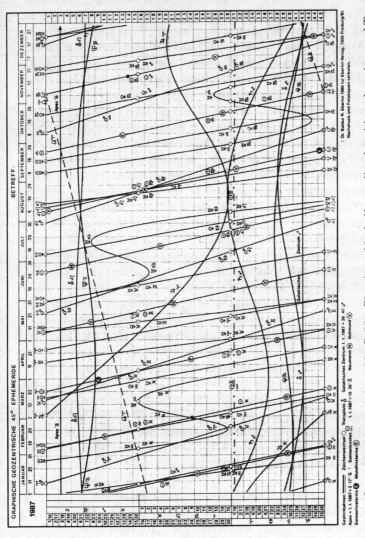

Figure 7.3 A 45° graphic ephemeris issued by Baldur Ebertin and including zodiacal positions, lunations and Transpluto.

zodiac is followed directly by the next. The first of the left-hand columns takes us to 15° of Taurus, the second from 15° of Taurus to 30° of Gemini and the third from 30° of Gemini to 0° of Cancer (and back to the first column again).

With the natal line drawn in we can also see how the lunations hit during the year. New Moons are marked with an N in a circle, full Moons with a V in a circle. Eclipses are shown as a black E or a white E depending on whether it is a solar or lunar event. The very small circles actually drawn on the planetary lines themselves indicate when a planet changes signs – see how they always correspond to a 30° mark on the left-hand scale, which obviously must indicate a change of sign. Three other points are also given. These are the Sun's node – the position where the Sun's plane intersects the plane of our galaxy – the solar apex and the galactic centre; these points will be described later. More important for the moment is to note that as this is a German graph, the sign for Uranus is like the Mars sign with a dot in the middle and the arrow pointing upwards. The position of the hypothetical planet, Transpluto, is also indicated.

Although the Ebertin graph may seem a bit more confusing to start with, as there is much more in it including the actual signs in which the planets are located (which saves you having to check with an ordinary ephemeris), it only takes a little practice to get used to reading it. Once mastered, it is the most singularly useful method available for examining transits. All the stress aspects are seen at once, both planet to planet and transit to natal. Important lunations for the whole year stand out immediately and – most importantly – you can use it with a client without breaking the flow of the consultation by flicking backwards and forwards through an ephemeris like a tourist with a train schedule trying to find the right connection on a wet Monday.

USING PROGRESSIONS AND DIRECTIONS

Both the Cardinal/Fixed/Mutable sort and the 45° graphic ephemeris can be used with any method of progressions or directions. Directed or progressed planets can be marked in on the

C/F/M sort to note which factors are currently being triggered and the same information can be drawn in on the graphic ephemeris to display visually the periods of contact. Astro-Computing Services will produce graphic ephemerides with any method of progression or direction already plotted in, but this is a simple thing to draw in by hand; all that is needed is to know the longitude of the progressed or directed body at the start and the end of the year.

If the progressed Sun begins the year at 4 ♉ 32 and ends the year at 5 ♉ 45 then this is drawn in on the graphic ephemeris exactly as a planetary line, except that instead of drawing it in as a straight line, it will slope downwards very slightly as it crosses the page. It will start on the left-hand side of the ephemeris at 4° 32′ of the Fixed signs – drawing it in at 4½° will be quite accurate enough – and finish slightly down on the right-hand side at 4° 45′ – or 4¾°. This will correspond to 34¾° on the right-hand scale. Progressed Mercury, Venus and Mars can be plotted in exactly the same way; often these planets will barely move down the page during the course of the year if they are close to a station or travelling slowly. If they are, in fact, moving retrograde, then the slope will be *up* the page and not down.

Plotting in the Moon takes a bit more time and requires a computer calculation to get high accuracy. The progressed Moon travels at different speeds through the course of the year, so just dividing up the annual motion by twelve will not provide correct monthly increments. It is best to work from twenty-four bi-monthly progressed positions calculated by a computer and then use these as the basis for your plot. Once the twenty-four positions are marked on for the year, it is a simple matter to join them up to see the complete progressed lunar cycle. As with the transiting planets already on the ephemeris, any crossing lines would indicate a hard progressed lunar aspect to a natal body – or progressed to transiting if a lunar line crosses a transit line.

Plotting information in this way reinforces the image of events or inner experience unfolding in sequence. What happens in minutes as the transiting Midheaven picks out factor after factor begins to slow down as the lunar, then the solar and finally the planetary transits are inked in. Finally the slowest of all the commonly-used astrological cycles, the progressions, continue the same motion in movements that can be so slight that a life-time can be covered by a few minutes of arc. The graphic ephemeris is probably the only method that allows us to examine these interrelating cycles, each uncoiling the same message at its own speed; occasionally coinciding in time as transits and progressions cross the same natal line within days of each other.

This graphic method of plotting transits and progressions can also be used for measuring planetary declinations, and Ebertin produces these annual graphs as well. Interestingly, this would appear to be the *first* use ever made of a graphic ephemeris, and indeed the first ever recorded use of any 'time-series' graph.

Figure 7.4 is a tenth- or eleventh-century graph found in a German manuscript, which appears to depict the declination of the Sun, Moon and known planets, although it may have other purposes as well. The grid is divided into thirty segments in one direction and twelve in the other. It is tempting to speculate that the number of degrees in each sign and the number of signs are thus *also* described, but it cannot be a straightforward graphic ephemeris as the central – solar – line is shown as a wobble. This *may* be a depiction of the sun's declination, though this obviously *cannot* be read against a 30° scale.

This graph is something of an enigma, not just to astrologers but also to students of mathematical history and statistical meth-

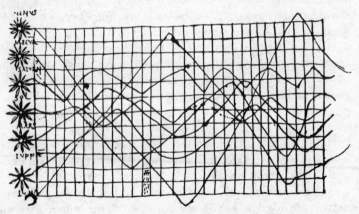

Figure 7.4 Tenth- or eleventh-century 'graphic ephemeris'.

odology, for this is the first-ever depiction of what we would now call a *time-series* graph. In other words, two different scales of measurement are brought together in time by the graphing of some form of motion – in this case planetary movement. It was not until 1779 that this idea was next used, when Johann Heinrich Lambert employed this method to depict his record of changes in soil temperature.[1]

Clearly there are few astrological techniques which can boast the impeccable historical pedigree of the graphic ephemeris![2]

NOTES

1. Edward Tufte, *The Visual Display of Quantitative Information*, Graphic Press, Connecticut.
2. For further information on the use of the graphic ephemeris, see *The Annual Diagram*, by Reinhold Ebertin. *Directions*, also by Reinhold Ebertin, covers the use of direction, and transit, in midpoint work. Both books are published by the AFA and have extensive case material.

CHAPTER 8

Midpoints in Mundane Astrology

MICHAEL HARDING

It is only comparatively recently that the emphasis in astrology has shifted from mundane to natal. Originally, virtually all the Western tradition was concerned with was predicting political and social events for kings, countries and the nobility. With such a long and illustrious history, it is perhaps not surprising that mundane astrology has remained more steeped in the traditional approaches while modern natal astrologers felt freer to experiment with a wider spectrum of techniques as well as to embrace some of the ideas current in various depth psychologies. There are some notable exceptions to this, but on the whole the main technical and philosophical developments in astrology have passed mundane by, and taken midpoints with them.

Techniques apart, perhaps the biggest difference between mundane and natal astrology is that while natal astrology concentrates on attempting to understand the current situation of an individual with reference to his or her past, mundane is almost exclusively concerned with prediction. It is in this area of attempting to foretell what is likely to happen in the world that the use of midpoints can offer most promising clues.

As with any chart, the map of any country, institution, company or similar body is rich in symbolism. If Jupiter, for instance, transits the sixth house of a sovereign state, is there about to be a rapid increase in that country's population of small animals? Is their health service about to be invaded by an army of philosophers or be controlled by corpulent civil servants? Will there be a popular mass-movement related to religious issues or will there be a boost in the state housing programme? While some of these hypotheses are more likely than others, each is symbolically correct. Small animals, the army, the health service, civil servants, state housing and the working class are all served by this one house, and unless there are some very clear natal aspects conveniently to hand, we may have considerable trouble in making sense of Jupiter's presence. A powerful midpoint lurking near the doorway, however, may give us a much clearer picture of what may be about to take place as Jupiter enters that particular abode.

Of even greater help are the aspects made by midpoints to the natal bodies; these can greatly assist in defining the nature of subsequent transits to that body – especially when we cannot rely totally on house positions due to uncertain 'birth' times. The case of the United States of America is a prime one, given that country's supreme importance in world affairs.

Despite all that has been written in astrological and historical journals over the centuries, there remains an absence of any clear contemporary evidence indicating the exact time when the Constitution of the United States was signed, and thus the crucial moment of America's self-determinism still evades us. Any chart set for a specific moment on 4 July 1776 must be regarded as speculative, however convincing subsequent transits or progressions might look. That said, there are a large number of aspects which will remain in force for the duration of the whole day – some even longer – and thus can be considered as playing a major part in the collective psyche of that country, sensitive to the ensuing triggers of time. These factors include the midpoints to the USA node (Figure 8.1), as calculated for the popular 5.10 p.m. chart giving 12 ♐ 13 rising.

There are other midpoints to the node generated by the 5.10 p.m. chart, but these include combinations connecting either the angles or the Moon and thus would not remain constant during the

Figure 8.1 Midpoints to the node in the chart for the signing of the Declaration of Independence, 4 July 1776.

day. The pattern remaining here, however, gives us a rather clear message and applies to any chart set for 4 July 1776. It shows us what specific elements of the collective the Moon's node was bringing into manifestation during those historic 24 hours.

If the node can be thought of as a sensitive point connected with a country's relationships then America's contacts with others should be dominated by differing images of the unexpected. Both ♀/♅ and ♃/♅ speak of sudden, erratic changes of fortune, hastily-taken decisions and abrupt reversals of direction. They also speak pertinently of that particular day, when the urge for self-determinism (♀/♅) manifested as a specific act which subsequently became embodied in that country's whole philosophical approach towards freedom (♃/♅). It was a freedom from another country – the node – not from some internal tyrant as was so often the case in the Old World. It is also worth noting that the ♀/♅ midpoint is strongly connected with *birth* and that the image of the 'birth of freedom' is inextricably connected with that day in Philadelphia.

The third midpoint, ♂/♆, says much about where the threat lay – with an army from overseas. Indeed, the whole issue of Independence was brought to a head over the question of how that army should be paid. From a British point of view, the war was lost through a combination of inadequate long-range logistics, confusion as to how the rebels should be treated which curtailed funds for the overseas army (the Colonialist cause had considerable support in the British Parliament) and finally Britain's favourite scapegoat – deception by the French Navy. Unclear military strategy, overseas armies and naval deception speak volumes for ♂/♆ and it is worth exploring how much they might have been embodied in America's relationships with others while promoting the desire that 'all men shall be free' (♃/♅).

♂/♆ provokes an image of unclear intent, the risk of over-idealism, the wish to impose force through stealth – or possibly experiencing such intentions from others. Issues of alcohol and drugs are both raised by the ♂/♆ contact and America, alone of Western countries, has faced both 'invasion' by bootleggers during Prohibition and massive drug-smuggling in more recent times. There is also the wholesale exporting of her home-grown Evangelism – another clear ♂/♆ issue – on a scale not seen since England's matrons sallied forth to smite the Heathen during the Victorian era. This image of invasion via the sea underlines what is perhaps the key image for this Ω = ♂/♆ combination: America's naval strength and the manner in which it is used. The dual contacts of ♀/♅ and ♃/♅ together with the ♂/♆ midpoint suggest that issues of deception, confusion and abrupt change of policy should characterize much of America's naval history. This would appear to be borne out by events to a very considerable extent.

The key degrees in this nodal contact are the position of the node itself – 6 ♌ 36 – the ♂/♆ midpoint at 6 ♌ 54, ♃/♅ at 22 ♊ 26 and ♀/♅ at 21 ♊ 01. We also need to consider the following indirect positions: the node at 21° 36′ of the Mutable signs, the ♂/♆ midpoint at 21° 54′ of the same triplicity, and also ♀/♅ at 7° 01′ and ♃/♅ at 7° 26′ of the Fixed signs. 8th harmonic transits to any of these degrees should show up at times when matters of America's naval involvement come to the fore, and these events should reflect the symbolism attached to the node.

During the Civil War America was the first country to use submarines in warfare, a form of attack that has always been described as duplicitous by those on the receiving end. It is also highly redolent of Mars/Neptune symbolism, no more so than during the early part of the Second World War when America's own submarine fleet first saw action and was bedevilled by malfunctioning torpedoes.[1]

On 23 September 1779 John Paul Jones scored a remarkable victory over the British fleet off Flamborough Head while Mars was on America's node at 22 ♐ 43, a point that Pluto was to cross during the war of 1812 – fought primarily over issues of trade and shipping. America's declaration of war against Spain, on 25 April 1898, was made with both the Sun and Neptune aspecting the node from 5 ♉ 19 and 20 ♊ 35 respectively. This war had been brought about through the sinking of the *Maine*, which blew up in Santiago harbour on 15 February of that year – Mercury at 7 ♒ 7 on the ♃/♅ midpoint. In other words, the ♃/♅ midpoint was itself reinforcing its own natal pattern. Sabotage was never proven, and President McKinley tried to avert strife, but the American public had other ideas. The *Maine* was avenged and the pattern of America being drawn into conflict through naval matters appeared to be established. The Spanish/American war effectively ended on 3 July 1898 when the Spanish fleet was destroyed off Cuba in a single engagement. Neptune was at 22 ♊ 59.

According to the *New York Journal*, the *Maine* blew up at 9.45 p.m. local time. The MC and AS for that moment are configured with both ♂/♃ and ♄/♅, while the ☉/☽ midpoint is contacting Saturn, Pluto and the node. Neptune and Mars are almost exactly 135° apart and the Sun reinforces that theme of deception by being on their midpoint – and conjunct America's Moon. Thus the ♂/♆ is crossing America's Moon as well and her public responded to the treachery it perceived.

The *New York Journal* for 25 April 1898 gives a moment-by-moment account of the day's events which culminated at 4.55 p.m. EST when Vice-President Hobart signed the Declaration of War against Spain. The resolution had been put to the Senate at 12.20 that afternoon, which resulted in a rapidly drafted bill being passed by that house at 1.20 p.m., after the briefest of discussion. At 4.50 p.m. the bill was signed by the Speaker after being passed by the House of Representatives. Five minutes later America was officially at war.

This sequence of events takes place when Mars and Neptune are *again* 135° apart and lying on the ♂/♇ midpoint at 5 ♉ 28. At 12.20 when the resolution is put to the Senate the M is conjunct that ♂/♆ with 1′! Mars is also square to the Moon by 1° 13′, and both fall across the AS/MC for the moment – an angry public response is about to be acted out in the 'here and now'. Uranus is also on the ☉/☽ midpoint. When the vote is passed by the Senate at 1.20 both the MC and Venus are conjunct ♂/☊ and ☉/♇; Venus may seem a little inappropriate until it is recalled that this was the traditional planet of victory in war in the ancient world. When the document was signed by the Vice-President at 4.55 the AS/MC was conjunct ☿/♇ (signing a document of war?) falling within 4′ of America's natal Sun. At the other end of the spectrum America had opened up trade with Japan, following Commander Perry's successful negotiations with the Japanese in 1853. On the day he sailed for Yokohama Jupiter was at 20 ♐ 38 and the north node at 20 ♐ 5.

The expedition, of course, was as much a military affair as anything and masked America's need to establish her own markets away from Europe. The Jupiter/node conjunction on her nodal axis is a good indication of which way the cookie ultimately crumbled; America was the prime beneficiary.

In the years preceding the First World War America began to increase her naval capabilities. This culminated on 16 December 1907 when President Theodore Roosevelt dispatched her battle fleet on a two-year round-the-world 'good-will visit' to test America's capacity to support her fleet at distance. On the day the ships left Annapolis Saturn stood at 21 ♓ 16 – a clear indication of limits being seriously redefined. Another key development during this period took place on 18 January 1911 when a biplane landed on the deck of the cruiser *Pennsylvania* as she lay moored off San Francisco. This precursor of the all-powerful aircraft carrier took place with Mars at 21 ♐.

As the First World War lumbered its way across Europe, America contorted itself into a position of neutrality which even the sinking of the *Lusitania* could not shift. This classic expression of Mars and Neptune has provided naval historians with a puzzle that is unlikely ever to be officially unravelled. Was the *Lusitania* armed and/or carrying ordnance? Did the British tip off the Germans as to her cargo hoping that her sinking would bring America into the war? Her sinking roused public opinion, as had the loss of the *Maine*, but the President stood firm. It took the loss of many more American merchantmen over the ensuing two years before the sinking of the *Algonquin* on 12 March 1917 (Sun 21 ♓ 21) forced Wilson to arm America's merchant fleet. When this decision had been taken on 20 March (Mercury at 20 ♓ 31 and Jupiter at 6 ♉ 45) events started to slip away to their inevitable conclusion. Just over two weeks later America had declared war on Germany, once more drawn into conflict through machinations taking place at sea.

The Second World War started for America with a single act that has since become a byword for treachery.[2] At 7.55 a.m. LT the American fleet in Pearl Harbor was attacked and destroyed as it lay at anchor. The moment the attack began the MC squared America's natal Mars and Pluto to 5 ♌ 35 conjunctioned the natal node. Revenge was to take its time, but on 6 June 1942 her navy shattered Yamamoto's battle cruisers at Midway as Venus, the traditional significator of victory, crossed 5 ♉ 11 and marked that nodal point once more. Elsewhere in the Pacific victory did not come so easily. The American landings on Tarawa Atoll between 20 and 23 October 1943 took place with Mars crossing the node at 21 ♊ 54 and cost the lives of a greater proportion of the attacking forces than any other battle in America's history. Jupiter at 21 ♍ 40 marked the loss of the USS *Franklin* during the navy's attack on the Japanese home islands on 18–21 March 1945, and on 30 July the Sun at 6 ♌ 56 marked the loss of the USS *Indianapolis* – the greatest single naval disaster since Pearl Harbor. Inexplicably – Mars/Neptune – her captain was making *no* precautionary manoeuvres while travelling in waters known to contain Japanese submarines.

In the years following the Second World War two events from the ensuing Cold War stand out. The abortive attack on the Bay of Pigs and later blockade of the Cuban mainland. The invasion and subsequent defeat at the Bay of Pigs took place with Jupiter crossing the node at 4–6 ♒ following the landings on 17 April 1961, an act which cost America dear in prestige – and a $60 billion ransom.

The blockade ordered by President John F. Kennedy was the focus of the Cuban missile crisis. It came into effect at 9 a.m. EST on 24 October 1962 with Mars at 6 ♌ 26, the Node at 5 ♌ 04 and Saturn at 4 ♒ 57 – Saturn's position is identical *to the minute* to Jupiter's on the day of the Bay of Pigs invasion. The powerful Mars/Saturn square lying across America's nodal axis is a graphic image of the armoured wall erected around Cuba by the navy.

Just as America was drawn into the First and Second World Wars by a surprise attack on her navy, so was she drawn into Vietnam. On 5 August 1964, two American warships in the Gulf of Tonkin were attacked by North Vietnamese PT boats while they were in international waters. This confrontation resulted in Congress allowing President Johnson a free hand in conducting what reprisals he chose by passing the Gulf of Tonkin Resolution – a piece of hasty (♀/♅, ♃/♅) legislation America would come to bitterly regret, as it marked the turning point of American involvement in South-East Asia. Configured with America's node on that day was the *transiting* ♂/♅ midpoint at 6 ♌ 16.

On 17 May 1987 the USS *Stark* was hit in error by an Iraqi missile in the Persian Gulf (Figure 8.2). The attack took place close to 27 N 25, 51 E 20 at 10.10 p.m. LT and produced an MC of 6 ♏ 14, very close to Pluto at 8 ♏ 05. As Saturn at 19 ♐ 28 is just over 45° away, both planets are configured with this MC giving M = ♄ = ♇ = ☉/♃, ♄/♅, ☿/♆. At first glance, ☉/♃ is one of the more cheerful of midpoints, but coupled with Saturn we can learn from Ebertin that this can result in 'a loss of good fortune, incapability and incompetence' as well as 'a lack of success and illness'. The ☿/♆ seems a particularly apt symbol for a ship attacked from the air, and this is further repeated when we see elsewhere that we have Mars almost exactly opposite the ♄/♆ midpoint. Deception or confusion clearly triggers the Mars and the next midpoint after ♂ = ♄/♆ is ♂ = ☿/AS which is not too inaccurate an image for a missile in flight. Pluto itself picks up ☉/AS, ♂/♄ and ☿/☊. The ☉/AS contact tends to confirm the accuracy of the position, as once again an angle is appropriately involved with an energy which clearly found its expression. ♇ = ♂/♄ is a classic picture seen when death and destruction take place, and we recall that Ebertin refers to the ♂/♄ midpoint as the 'death axis' and its being followed by ☿/☊ echoes again the theme of flight or the shared experience of some event which brings both Mercury and Pluto together. Uranus on the ☉/☽ midpoint is another picture which emerges again and again when sudden and unexpected events occur – by no means always unpleasant ones, but when coupled with an MC which brings Saturn and Pluto together in the

Figure 8.2 MC, Mars and Pluto structures for the attack on USS *Stark*.

way we have seen then one would be hard-pressed to see signs of pleasant surprises. At the end of the following year, attack and counter-attack took place in the same area as America responded to Iran's gunboats by blasting her oil platforms – while the transiting node was at 21 ⨉ 25.

Without doubt, the most tragic example of this tendency for transits to the node to stimulate hasty and confused responses was the shooting down of an Iranian airliner on 3 July 1988 at 6.54 a.m. GMT at 26 N 40, 55 E 20 (Figure 8.3). The MC for the moment is 21 ♊ 08, the Ascendant is 21 ♍ 22 and Mercury, depicting flight once again, is at their midpoint at 20 ♊ 56! In fact, one of the midpoints Mercury picks up is ♀/♅ – at 21 ⨉ 15. As with the attack on the *Stark*, midpoints such as ♂ = ♇ = ☿/♅ = ♅/M = ♄/AS = ♅/AS depict the sudden loss of the airliner as the result of an explosion.

In this way we can see that in taking a single, and very simple factor, we can slowly build up a very clear understanding as to what may take place when a specific degree of a chart is transited by any hard aspect. We need no complicated methods or computer programs. Just by reading the newspapers and checking reference books at a local library we can build up our case history. This approach can greatly increase the predictive possibilities of our astrology while at the same time encouraging us to directly confront what is going on in a chart, both symbolically and practically.

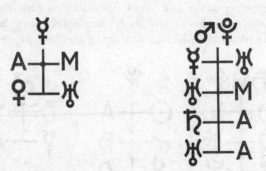

Figure 8.3 The Mercury and Mars/Pluto midpoint structures for the shooting down of the Iranian airbus by the US Navy.

NOTES

1. James M. Morris, *History of the U.S. Navy*, Bison Books, London, 1984.
2. On 5 April 1989 BBC Television transmitted a documentary on the events surrounding the attack on Pearl Harbor. Considerable evidence was put forward to suggest that both the Americans and the British knew far more about Japanese plans for the attack than has ever been admitted. It was suggested that those close to the President knew both that Pearl Harbor was to be attacked and also the actual date; nothing was done to alert the Navy in order to ensure that the attack went ahead as planned, thus forcing America into the war. If these allegations are true, then what took place not only mirrors the events surrounding the sinking of the *Lusitania* but also adds another strand to the complex weave of deceit and treachery that seems to surround American naval matters.

CHAPTER 9

Midpoints in Other Harmonics

MICHAEL HARDING

Up to now we have been examining midpoints exclusively in the 8th harmonic, but it would be wrong to think that this is anything like the final word on the matter. There are some compelling examples in a whole range of harmonics, and before exploring some of these we should remind ourselves that in using midpoints we are effectively assuming at least *two* principles are at work. The first, of course, is *number*. In other words, in using the idea of number we concentrate on the 2nd, 4th and 8th harmonics because these are the aspects of manifestation which exist in both tra-ditional and modern astrology. Probably the only reason that we take the series no further is the purely practical one of having quite enough to be getting on with without trying to make sense of the higher harmonic possibilities.

This approach is perfectly sensible. Computers have given us the power to generate print-outs like wallpaper and any random yard of harmonics will produce its quota of interesting midpoint configurations purely by chance. If we choose to go further than the 8th harmonic, we shall have to be much more selective while recognizing that the *second* principle we utilize with midpoints has nothing whatsoever to do with harmonics at all – and that is manifesting the power of the actual midpoint itself.

While a midpoint which lies, say, as the sextile point between two planets in trine to one another seems to be more potent than if no formal aspect otherwise exists, it would be quite wrong to assume that the midpoint between planets which have otherwise no classic relationship is without power. This is simply not so, and our concentrating on this fact reminds us that the principle of the midpoint has, of itself, nothing at all to do with number. The actual midpoint between two planets is potent with their combined energy regardless of how the planets face each other or in which harmonic they might coincide. The main question is simply *how potent?*

In Chapter 6 we looked at some of the ways the respective importance of midpoints can be assessed. Here we shall see how the two principles we are using, number and midpoint, can give us yet further information on the chart when used either together or separately. To do this effectively, and to avoid the risk of seeing everything anywhere, it might be useful to work initially with charts of known accuracy. We have enough going on without attempting some rectification on the side.

Looking first at the two-series of aspects we can observe them getting finer and finer as we move from the 8th harmonic to the 16th to the 32nd and to the 64th – and beyond. If we decrease our orbs proportionately then we are obviously both reducing the amount of possible midpoints and concentrating only on the closest contacts. Thus whatever comes into aspect is in tighter and tighter phase and possibly in a more powerful resonance with one another. In such a way a large number of less consequential planetary relationships may prove more important than two in a major aspect phase.

A start can be made with the chart for the world's first nuclear explosion at 12.29.21 GMT on 16 July 1945 at Alamogordo, New Mexico. The time for this explosion, code-named 'Trinity', comes from the records of the California Institute for Technology which monitored the seismic shock-wave of the bomb and is accurate to within 2 seconds.

Considering that we are looking at one of the most important and potentially destructive events ever to take place on this planet, the chart itself is not redolent of death. Saturn in the Gauquelin key-sector square to an angular Moon is probably the most immediately ominous aspect, but a Moon square Saturn repeats twice a month and we shall have to look harder than that for evidence of the ominous. In some respects the synastry with the 1776 chart for America is more striking. The Moon in the Trinity chart is within 25′ of America's Saturn, the Ascendant just 10′ away from America's natal Pluto and the MC only *one minute* away from America's Jupiter/Pluto midpoint. In fact the connection between the Trinity test, the American chart and the scientists who worked on the project is so close in so many details that the nuclear bomb can in many ways be thought of as a natural product of such interactions. However, such an explosion *did* take place and the Saturn/Pluto midpoint within 2' of the Ascendant together with ☽/♇ and ♇/M tells us we are looking at something with very heavy overtones.

These contacts are midpoints in the 8th harmonic. In the 16th, ♃/♇ and ☉/♅ are among those which also join the picture. In the 32nd harmonic ♄/M comes into frame. For the MC itself, which so often gives us an image of the event by the actual midpoints it draws in, is shown in Figure 9.1. By bringing in some of the aspects to the Ascendant, the midpoints to the MC in the 32nd harmonic – particularly ♄/♇ and ☉/Ω – say slightly more than the other harmonics. MC = AS = ♄/♇ is an extremely powerful image of the bomb's reality. Most dramatic, however, is the 64th harmonic structure that includes the radical Moon/Saturn square.

To have no less than five planets all phased together within 22.5' of arc is very rare, as we see in Figure 9.2. The Jupiter and Neptune contacts may be particularly important when the synastry sug-

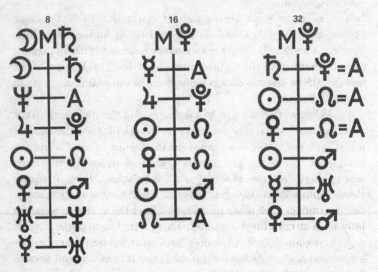

Figure 9.1 Midpoints in the 8th, 16th and 32nd harmonic for the detonation of the world's first nuclear bomb at Alamogordo.

Figure 9.2 Midpoints in the 32nd harmonic for the Alamogordo bomb. Note how no less than five planets aspect the powerful Moon/Saturn square.

gested earlier is actually applied. Einstein's Jupiter is less than a degree from America's Moon, and when Fermi initiated the world's first controlled chain reaction Jupiter was exactly opposite America's Jupiter. Oppenheimer was born with his Jupiter conjunct America's Saturn and the Trinity chart has Jupiter within a few minutes of America's Neptune. This is symbolic for the precursor of the device that was being planned even while the Trinity fission bomb had yet to be tested – the hydrogen bomb. Known by Edward Teller simply as the 'super bomb' (slight echoes of Jupiter there!), it creates energy by the Neptunian process of *fusion* with the aid of the deuterium isotope, a component of what is known as 'heavy water' and found naturally in the sea. For an image of the actual splitting of the atom at Trinity, of the shock of the moment, Uranus is on the ☉/☽ midpoint – but only in the 32nd harmonic.

Following the same idea of using the MC of a precisely-timed chart to see which harmonic draws in the most appropriate midpoints, we can look at the chart for the air crash which took place over San Diego on 25 September 1978. The crash occurred when a light aircraft collided with a Boeing 727 belonging to Pacific South-West Airways. According to the cockpit voice recorder the impact took place at 9.01.47 a.m. PDST; twenty seconds later both aircraft hit the ground. There were no survivors.

At first glance the 8th harmonic in Figure 9.3 best describes the known events; an explosion (♂/♃), the loss of life and sorrow (☉/♄) and the probable reason for the collision (☿/♆). The board of inquiry later found that the light plane was off course and

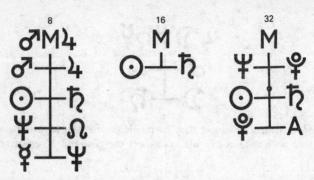

Figure 9.3 Midpoints to the MC in the 8th, 16th and 32nd harmonics for the San Diego air crash.

had not been noticed by the flight crew. Indeed, there was evidence that a *second* light plane was in the immediate vicinity and it was that one which the crew had been observing. ☿/Ψ is a very apt picture of confusions to do with light aircraft and wrong directions. The inquiry also reported that the Air Traffic Control procedures that day were confused and poorly co-ordinated. The 16th harmonic gives us little of this and it is not until we get to the rather rarefied atmosphere of the 64th harmonic (using an orb of 15′) that we get another clear image of what took place (Figure 9.4).

Except for the ☉/♄ which is within 4′ of the MC and thus appears in all pictures, each harmonic focuses on different energies which all can add something to the total picture. The question here would be one of orbs and intensities. It would suggest a model

Figure 9.4 Midpoints to the MC in the 64th harmonic for the San Diego air crash.

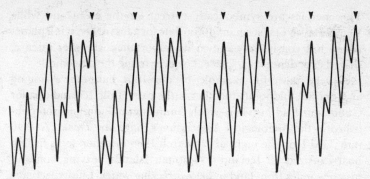

Figure 9.5 A visual image of how harmonic patterns can come together. Here the 4th, 8th, 16th and 32nd harmonics blend together to produce a powerful 'kick' every eighth cycle as they come into phase.

something like Figure 9.5 in which a varying number of shorter wavelengths combine to provide a sudden momentary peak of energy when all are phased together. This is much like the well-known phenomenon of soldiers needing to break step when crossing a bridge lest the sheer force and weight of several hundred individuals impacting on the bridge at exactly the same time have a disastrous effect.

Looking at other structures for the collision we note that, as with the Trinity explosion, it is in the 32nd harmonic that we find the picture ♅ = ☉/☽ for the first time – it is also in the 64th. On the 32nd Jupiter tree we have the structure shown in Figure 9.6.

Four planets on the AS/MC midpoint, particularly Mars, Jupiter and Saturn, say a lot about a powerful conflict of energies, and to be so closely phased with the moment of impact suggests once more that here this harmonic has something definite to add.

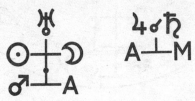

Figure 9.6 Uranus on the Sun/Moon midpoint and both Jupiter and Saturn on the AS/MC in the 32nd harmonic for the San Diego air crash.

The energies are symbolically correct for the event and while Venus may at first seem inappropriate for a loss of life, it is a planet which has consistently shown its importance wherever intense, shared experiences take place, however tragic the outcome.

A very powerful example of the 16th harmonic bringing appropriate midpoints together is the case of the Icelandic sailor Gudlaugur Fridthorsson, which Gunnlaugur Gudmundsson published in the Astrological Association's magazine *Transit*. At 9.40 p.m. GMT on the night of 11 March 1984 Fridthorsson's fishing boat capsized off Iceland's Westman Islands, leaving him and his crew miles from land in below-freezing water. Life expectancy under such conditions is under thirty minutes, and yet

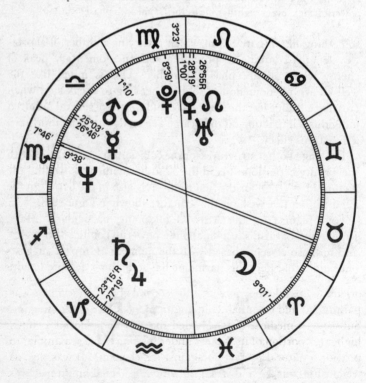

Figure 9.7 The natal chart for Gudlaugur Fridthorsson, the Icelandic sailor whose near-miraculous survival made headlines.

Fridthorsson alone managed a night swim of over six hours, a fierce battle against waves which threatened to dash him against the rocks of his home island, a climb up a steep cliff of recently-cooled lava (which can be as sharp as glass) and a three-hour walk in rain and darkness to habitation.

Even by the harsh standards of Icelandic history and the romanticism of its Sagas the feat is quite without parallel, and Fridthorsson became an immediate national hero. For a man born to be tested by the sea he has an appropriate chart (Figure 9.7). Neptune and Pluto are angular and his 12th house Mars is almost exactly at the Gauquelin 'power point' of 10° above the horizon, in a wide square to Jupiter and semi-square to Pluto. Born on the day of a full Moon, both lights pick up the ♄/♇ and ♂/♇ midpoints in both the 8th and 16th harmonics. This contact in any chart would suggest that the issue of extreme hardship and endurance will have to be confronted at some time or other in life. Here there are great reserves of energy available if they can be channelled. What is so striking about the 16th harmonic patterns is the manner in which the Sun and Moon themselves are configured with Saturn and Pluto – thus obviously heavily underlining these planetary issues – and that Saturn and Pluto are themselves on the ⊙/☽ midpoint.

This is an exceptionally powerful pattern (Figure 9.8). It would suggest, of itself, that the whole of the life is focused around the control and use of energy, its abundance and its limitation. It is never energy that is freely available; the wide square from Mars to Jupiter does not enter into this equation at all. The energy has to be tapped by force of will and there would appear to be a constant reminder of its possible denial; this is the hard Mars/Saturn contact which exists only in the 16th harmonic. In Chapter 6 we saw how Freud utilized his ⊙ = ♂/♄ to develop a death-orientated psychology in which the control of primitive forces was paramount and essential. Gudlaugur, too, conserved his energies. Subsequent medical tests revealed that his body stored a much higher proportion of its fat just under his skin like a sea animal to provide a natural protection against the elements. It was this, as well as his courage and strength, which protected him during his ordeal.

Not surprisingly, Gudlaugur's life underwent a considerable

Figure 9.8 Gudlaugur Fridthorsson's Sun/Moon midpoint in the 16th harmonic. Note how both Saturn and Pluto come together there, to be followed by both ♂/♄ and ♂/♇; a combination of intensely focused energy at the core of his psyche.

upheaval – a real sea change – after his experience. He felt that he had been guided to land by supernatural forces and has subsequently become a more religious person. This is again dramatically picked up only in the 16th harmonic, Figure 9.9. As the time of birth is not accurate to the exact minute the ♀/AS aspect may have to be ignored; however, the ☿ = ♃ = ♀/♆ is quite valid and a vivid picture of finding faith through salvation at sea. Even the Mercury to Jupiter aspect suggests the guiding voices he believed led him finally to the safety of land.

While Gudlaugur's natal Mars square Jupiter makes no 16th harmonic midpoint aspects, it is very much in evidence on the night of his ordeal, demonstrating again how the inner geometry of the birth chart seems to respond to the many phases of its external expression. Mars, Jupiter and Pluto were all part of an almost exact 16th harmonic pattern at the time the fishing boat capsized, imbuing the time with a powerful archetype of extreme physical

Figure 9.9 Gudlaugur Fridthorsson's ☿/♃ contacts in the 16th harmonic – finding his faith at sea.

endeavour. Another aspect, exact to within 9′, was a semi-square between Saturn and Neptune. This aspect fell *exactly* on Gudlaugur's ☉/☽ midpoint with Saturn marking that point to the very minute! Thus the whole ♄ = ♇ = ☉/☽ configuration which depicts how seemingly fated or dramatic events become central to Gudlaugur's inner experience receives the clearest message of 'endurance through the sea' at the very moment his boat turned over. Noticing elsewhere how Saturn transits to the ☉/☽ midpoint can coincide with the end of life, Gudlaugur's ordeal in the icy waters is even more remarkable. Such a Saturn transit is much more likely to correlate with lower energy levels, lack of clear purpose or the sort of delays and restrictions in all corners of life that so often mark major Saturn phases. Its natal contact with Pluto in the 16th harmonic may well indicate how Gudlaugur managed some personal, inner reassessment of Saturn's more traditional expression to provide an unshaking control over his deepest resources.

Experience suggests that when someone has a very strong 16th harmonic chart, that is when the 16th harmonic chart itself is full of tense aspects, then the midpoints in the 16th harmonic will say more about the basic energy structures and psychological experiences of that individual than anything else currently available to the consultant astrologer. Transits, too, which are multiples of 22° 30′ exclusively seem to correlate powerfully with events and changes as well as their more commonly used larger multiples. If this comes as a surprise, it is probably due solely to the fact that so little is ever written about using midpoints in this harmonic despite their use in Germany for half a century.

It is worth reminding ourselves that astrologers influenced by the work of Witte have been using 22° 30′ aspects both for 'fine-tuning' predictions and for determining the effects of the outer planets since the 1930s. Theodor Landscheidt has similarly used this aspect, and taken it progressively smaller towards what he calls the 'I Ching Aspect' – 55° 37′ 30″ or 1/64 of the circle. This is employed in the radical chart to locate midpoints in the same manner as the Ebertin school and predictively through the use of 64th harmonic graphic ephemerides. Indeed, in the course of his research into the relationship between solar activity and terrestrial events he has routinely used aspects of the outer planets in the 1024th harmonic producing a wavelength of 20' 46.1". While this may seem just an extremely rarefied example of what is now possible through the use of computers, this is not the case at all. Certain ancient Hindu traditions use even smaller divisions of the circle and would contend that such subdivision towards infinity is the natural expression of cosmic forces. These can be considered identical to the forces or patterns which move outwards in the opposite direction and in Hindu belief divide the evolution of the Universe into the Yugas – and beyond. Seen in these terms, the use of astrological techniques such as the various harmonic sorts is a mirror of this phenomenon and similar to examining the band-width of all possible radiation; a scale on which our familiar, visible light takes up only the smallest fraction. In staying solely with conventional methods of chart analysis we risk suggesting that only what we see in our limited vision counts for anything.

A man who has probably done more than most to expand the limits of human experience is the inventor of LSD, Albert Hofmann. Born in Basle on 11 January 1906 at 2.00 p.m. GMT, he has some appropriate 8th harmonic midpoints including AS = ♂/Ψ, Ψ = ☉/AS and ☿ = ♅/♇. In the 16th harmonic the Ψ = ☉/AS is joined by the Moon and the ☿ = ♅/♇ by the Sun. Hofmann records 4.20 p.m. CET on 19 April 1943 as the time he first ingested the results of his 25th experiment with lysergic acid diethylamide tartrate. At that moment Uranus was aspecting his radical ♂/Ψ midpoint by a multiple of 22° 30' to within *one minute* – crossing exactly as the experience took place! Figure 9.10 shows how Mars, Jupiter and the MC for the moment are *all* picking up the same midpoint with very close orbs. All are 16th harmonic aspects.

Figure 9.10 Transits of Mars, Jupiter, Uranus and the M to the chart of Albert Hofmann, for the moment he first took LSD. Transits are all multiples of 16° and all within 30' of orb.

In examining the basic harmonic charts currently used by astrologers, the 5th, 7th and 9th, one can frequently be struck by the significance of a planet at the midpoint of two others. This is the second 'effect' of midpoints. Here we notice that the planetary energies focused at the midpoint are capable of being modified and given shape by a planet on that point regardless of which harmonic cycle we examine. Our interpretation, however, remains geared to the number in which this aspect occurs and is concerned solely with the direct midpoint.

As we shall explore more fully in Chapter 12, one facet of the 5th harmonic seems to be connected with power, in as much as the 5th harmonic (quintile aspect) depicts the manner in which an individual may seek to impose his or her style or mental grasp upon the world. Not surprisingly, the charts of major Nazis have strong 5th harmonic patterns. While Hitler's is one of the strongest, there are some other interesting observations to be made here. Arch-propagandist Joseph Goebbels has Pluto on the Mercury/Neptune midpoint in his 5th harmonic, suggesting immediately that Pluto will bind together and motivate his ability to communicate ideas to the masses in a power-orientated manner. Indeed, this one midpoint encapsulates much of Goebbels's abilities. It suggests a man whose style and mental abilities are those of the mass communicator. A man whose style is to impose a dream of power, a man who has a natural art of controlling and manipulating ideals, for whom power is an active dream. In watching film of the wildly-gesticulating Goebbels in action, one sees this midpoint at work almost exclusively.

Another top Nazi who was concerned with imposing enduring dreams of power was Speer. Hitler's architect conceived of a rebuilt Germany as a memorial to the promised 1,000-year Reich. Traditional bourgeois design was rejected in favour of huge concrete edifices dominating the landscape; a modern re-working of the symbols of ancient Rome. For someone who chose such images to express his ideas, a $\Psi = \hbar / E$ in the 5th harmonic is remarkably apt. A dream of imposing authority built of steel and concrete; what Speer 'knew' about (the 5th harmonic in action) was how to build an enduring tribute to his dreams of power.

This 5th harmonic – quintile – relationship with one form of

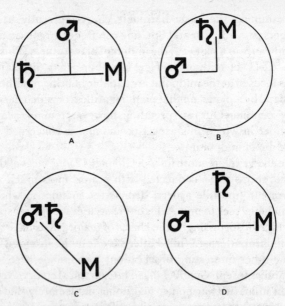

Figure 9.11 Contacts of Mars, Saturn and the M in the 5H charts of Eichmann (a), Goebbels (b), Himmler (c) and Rommel (d).

power is further amplified when we note that Eichmann, Goebbels, Himmler and Rommel *all* had quintile contacts involving Mars, Saturn and the MC (Figure 9.11). We have noted elsewhere how the Mars/Saturn midpoint has been dubbed the 'death axis' as well as being associated sometimes with sadism or killing; here its darkest side has conscious (MC) expression in a political 'style' which glorified the image of the war machine – ♂/♄.

CHAPTER 10

Starting to Use Midpoints

MICHAEL HARDING

The previous chapters should have given an outline of *how* to use midpoints as part of the process of chart interpretation, but there can still remain the problem of where to actually *start*! Some students can find the switch from looking at the familiar round chart to examining a series of glyphs a little daunting, and this may have stopped them from making the leap. In practice we quickly recognize that we are dealing with the same planetary energies in a very similar manner; we want to know how the planets react to each other and what the final results might be. As the message we can get from midpoints can sometimes contradict the immediate impression of the natal chart, we may need to start with the simplest factors first until we gain the necessary experience to work with all the images that the use of midpoints presents us with.

Become familiar with what *COSI* has to tell you. This book is not the last word on the subject, but it does give the foundation upon which to construct your own associations. Robert Hand's *Horoscope Symbols* also gives valuable examples of how planetary pairs might operate together. Start to think in terms of putting planetary energies together *all the time*. Planets do *not* operate in a vacuum, and we first face this when we start to look at the possible meanings of planets in signs. The image we get from looking at a Moon in Aries, for example, is derived in part from putting together key-word associations of lunar qualities and Aries attributes. We ask ourselves how well these two principles might operate together on different levels. Our assessment of what might take place when the Moon moves into Aries emerges from our reflections on what reinforcements or contradictions occur when specific lunar principles operate within an Aries environment. The Moon becomes endowed to some extent with the qualities of the first sign and 'acts out' both the conflicts and the harmonies. We can suggest that in such a case there might be conflicts between the watery, reflective and past-orientated mode of lunar operation when trying to fill the role demanded by the assertive and dynamic Aries energy. We can also recognize that both the Moon and Aries symbolize different facets of birth and creativity and might share at that point great creative potential. The meeting of all pairs of astrological symbols challenges us to experience and reflect upon the dynamic of their interactions. In using midpoints we try to focus on this as closely as possible, moving from the core meaning to explore the rich possibilities that can emerge from the fusion of any two ideas.

In starting to apply these ideas to the natal chart, the first midpoints to look at are those of the Sun and the Moon and the Ascendant and Midheaven, if the time of birth is known with reasonable accuracy. If there *are* planets on either of these points then your view of the chart may alter considerably. Initially you may prefer just to work with these two midpoints, adding in extra information as you become more familiar with their use. These are key points and should be examined as a matter of course in *every* chart, both radically and for transiting or progressed contacts. To miss a planet on one of these degrees can be to miss the whole message of the chart, and many astrologers who otherwise do not use midpoints routinely will always pay attention to what is happening here. If there is a planetary pair within minutes of the Sun/Moon or AS/MC midpoint, you may wish to take these also into consideration and check whether the energies or themes they symbolize function as part of the process as well.

Assuming you have a complete computer print-out of your midpoint trees, the next step might be to look at the closest midpoints to the Sun, Moon and inner planets. If the Moon is conventionally well aspected but also on the ♄/♇ midpoint we would need to pay immediate attention to *that*. What is this Moon/Saturn/Pluto triple conjunction telling you? Are you prepared to ignore the undercurrents that may be behind a façade of emotional ease that, say, a trine to the Moon can *also* endow? A person may express one level of feeling very easily while completely blocking off a deeper, more painful area. Looking at only a few major planetary contacts to the personal planets can give you an enormous advantage over the conventional approach towards assessing aspects. Simply to pick up *one* clear message can radically alter the quality of information you are able to present to your client.

Focus on immediate, obvious messages and stay with them. If someone had Saturn opposing a Sun/Neptune conjunction you are unlikely to omit interpreting it. $\hbar = \odot/\Psi$ can mean much the same thing and needs the same close attention! Stay with symbols that you are familiar with and recognize at once when you see them on the midpoint trees; bring in the interpretation of others as your experience grows. Do not obligate yourself to extract every last ounce of meaning from every midpoint combination you see; no one can do this trick. Look for themes which strongly reinforce or contradict each other; work with the major dynamics these themes suggest to you. Ignore at first anything that seems to offer little help; if it doesn't mean anything then don't use it. Its meaning may emerge during the course of the consultation or it may not. This is exactly the same procedure as using any other method of chart analysis and you should use midpoints in the same way.

Think, or meditate, on this simple process of bringing planetary energies and ideas together. Ask yourself *what* is coming together, *how* is it interacting, *which* issues are being underlined. Major themes are going to show up as you scan the tree structures looking for how the same planets re-express their stories in different phrases. A strong Mercury, for instance, might show up first as bringing together a lot of diverse pairs on its own axis and also by appearing frequently on the axes of the other planets. Simply recognizing that this is taking place is already a clear first step to understanding what that Mercury might be doing, and lessens the chance that you might underestimate its function within that particular chart. As it appears in other trees, so is it turning up in different areas of the psyche, and its presence there deserves to be recognized.

In using midpoints we view the planets from two angles; how they act as a lens through which their own attendant midpoints are brought together and how they in turn modify the structural dynamics of the other planets. It can often be enough at first to note that this is taking place, to recognize the complexity of a particular theme even if its full implications initially remain elusive.

In forecasting work you may wish to add in the Sun/Moon and AS/MC midpoints on the year's graphic ephemeris. The natal importance of these two key points can only be reinforced by the transits or lunations they receive during the course of the year. If you have noted the relevance of a specific, unaspected midpoint in the past then enter this on to the graphic ephemeris as well. It will almost certainly continue to be important in the future.

If you're looking at charts from the point of view of synastry, then it would be as well to stay with major contacts only. The enormous amount of possible interactions can often only be made sense of as part of constructing a case history retrospectively rather than by working from the initial position of two unknown charts. Contacts like A's Pluto to B's ☉/☽ midpoint, however, do deserve to be explored further. Similarly such contacts known to have possible problems where relationships are concerned, such as a personal planet picking up ♂/♆, ♂/♄ or something of that nature, may also warrant noting down. In business partnerships planets highlighting ♂/♃, ♃/♅ and particularly ♃/♇ can stimulate a positive and successful attitude and are important to note.

In the last analysis, skill in using midpoints comes not so much from mastering any complex ideas about wave-forms, but from a familiarity with the basic symbolism of the planets and an ability to extract a diversity of images from their archetypal meaning.

PART TWO

Harmonics

CHAPTER 11

Introducing Harmonics

MICHAEL HARDING

Astrologers are concerned with the nature of time and its measurement. The cycles of heaven have been paced out for centuries, their journeys recorded in celestial longitude along the route of the Sun's apparent motion around our planet. The division of this path has given us the zodiac, the elements, the triplicities and the four cardinal points of the astrological year. In many respects astrology can claim to have been conceived against the backdrop of the major arcs of the celestial circle. While East and West may argue about the starting point, they are united in how this circle may be divided. Our familiar 30° zodiacal segments are like some universal currency whose value is recognized immediately and whose coinage is accepted without question.

Time starts anew for us at 0° of Aries. We measure its motion in terms of how far each planet has moved from this point, and we plot their journeys in two ways. How many multiples of 30° each body has covered gives us the sign that each is in; how far each is from the other tells us which aspects have arisen between them. In each case our dividers are fixedly set at those familiar 30° and all other measures are excluded. Plato's *flowing image of eternity* becomes a series of juddering icons, like a film caught in the gate, in which all sense of continuity and rhythm are lost. All we see are formal structures, rigidly discrete and lost to much of their meaning. Without intention we have created an astrology which disallows a vast spectrum of possibilities, and created within it a quasi-psychology that can describe only what it finds in boxes that are neatly packaged like psychic apparatus on a celestial conveyer belt.

Perhaps there is some necessity to all of this. It could be that we have carefully cultivated the quarters and thirds of our world to make it accessible to measure, encouraging those emerging patterns while warding off the myriad alternative possibilities which otherwise might swamp everything from view, forcing on us the need for painful reassessment of our practice. Our cosmology has become that of the remorseless clock, its gears lurching forward with each trip of the escapement. If we are to create an astrology which moves towards replicating the shifting complexity of human experience, which accepts the odd measure with the even, which provides an image of a cosmos that is *alive* in every fragment of its being, then we are going to have to return to a very old idea indeed; the idea of harmonics.

The core concept of harmonic theory is indeed ancient. It is central to the way in which Hindu astrology has developed, and as that branch of astrology is probably the oldest in the world, there is the possibility that harmonics lies at the very heart of our work, from which everything else has developed, much of it long since ossified into dogma. It is an irony, then, that except for some work done by Ernst Krafft during the 1930s in Switzerland, it was not until the 1950s that the late John Addey independently rediscovered this ignored approach to chart analysis out of his own researches. In examining the aspects between the Sun to Mars and Jupiter in the charts of 970 nonagenarians he noted that this possible indicator of longevity displayed itself through the charts in a *wave-form* that approached and retreated from exactitude; a phenomenon he then observed in many other sets of data. Figure 11.1 shows one such example. It is taken from Addey's *Harmonic*

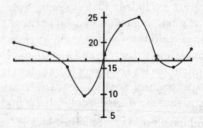

Figure 11.1 The distribution of Sun/Jupiter aspects above and below the average of 16 in the charts of 970 nonagenarians. Note the wave-form pattern with a peak 2° *beyond* exactitude. The tendency to peak 1°–2° after the exact contact is shown in other studies with different planetary pairs.

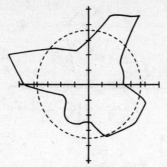

Figure 11.2 This classic Gauquelin distribution pattern of Mars in the charts of 1,485 sports champions is the precursor of hundreds of similar studies demonstrating the wave-like correlation between planet and character trait or occupation.

Anthology and shows the degrees of exactitude of Sun/Jupiter aspects in the charts of nonagenarians.

Similarly the work of Françoise and Michel Gauquelin, which burst on the astrological community in 1955 with their analysis of the distribution of the planet Mars in the charts of 1,485 sports champions, displayed a further wave-form (Figure 11.2) – this time one which rose and fell four times each day. Although this and all subsequent large-scale analysis is statistically orientated, the *patterns* which they produce are relevant to our understanding of the ordinary natal chart, and their implications are in the process of reforming the nature of astrology. So what on earth is going on?

The message we are getting from these research projects is that planetary relationships ebb and flow. They do not switch on and switch off, neither do they leap about from box to box. We are witnessing a shift of position which is reflected in a literal *shift of meaning*. As Mars gets closer to a 'power zone' so does it get more powerful and assertive; as it retreats so it gets weaker and more accommodating.

Finally – and most importantly – the 'power zones' are defined by *number*. Rhythms of two, four and eight contribute to the assertive positions of Mars, rhythms of three to its expression in a muted and more harmonious manner (Figures 11.3 and 11.4). In using harmonics we are looking at how the perceived energy of the

Figure 11.3 The distribution of Mars in the charts of those described as assertive.

planets is shifting according to the number which describes their relationship. To begin to explore the potential of this we shall have to examine these relationships in ways that up to now have been effectively ignored – through the use of aspects which are *not* multiples of 30° – and in doing so we may enrich our work immeasurably. The scope of harmonics is vast. It covers the whole of astrology and its ideas can be applied to any of its problems; as such, an analysis of its methods is beyond the purpose of this book. We shall concentrate only on one application of its principles; as they apply to our understanding of planetary aspects in the birth chart.

In Part One of this book we have already chosen to focus on a

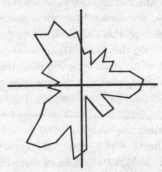

Figure 11.4 The distribution of Mars in the charts of those described as non-assertive. Note the completely different harmonic pattern.

sequence of aspects which are *not* part of the 30° range, the forgotten multiples of the 45° series. Apart from its use in midpoint work, this Keplerian division of the circle has not really been integrated into modern astrology. The semi-square and sesqui-quadrate fit within its framework as uncomfortably as their pronunciation, their meaning almost universally relegated to that of a somewhat insipid square. The use of midpoints should have demonstrated that this is very far from the truth, that when exact these aspects possess enormous power and in many cases should be the first contacts needing scrutiny. We now need to extend this discovery into examining whether or not other, less conventional, aspects *also* possess unique properties which to date have been relegated to astrology's backwaters. Considering that so many of these aspects are even harder to see in the natal chart than some of the 45° series – which is almost certainly why they have been omitted in the past – we first need a mechanism which will allow us to spot these newcomers as quickly and easily as we can see the squares and trines. This is the real function of the *Harmonic Chart*.

Many students in astrology fight shy of using these charts, perhaps seeing them as yet another confusing circle to be examined, or avoid them on the grounds that they 'prefer to stick to the natal chart'. A sound plan indeed; one should never duck confronting this particular map as it's the only one we've got! The harmonic chart is not a substitute for the natal chart, it is not an alternative to the natal chart, neither is it separate from the natal chart. It *is* the natal chart; the natal chart laid out in a way which makes certain aspects immediately recognizable and their interpretation relatively simple. The first point that perhaps needs to be grasped here is that *there is not a specific manner in which charts have to be laid out*. There is only convention, and that convention has not only shifted many times over the centuries, it also fulfils the differing visual needs of various societies. If we explore how we might *now* choose to portray our natal chart we may recognize more quickly the function of its harmonic equivalents.

Hindu astrologers have long recognized that there is more to our birth chart than can be expressed in a single map. It is standard practice for them to set up two charts, the conventional natal chart and what we would call the 9th harmonic chart, though many

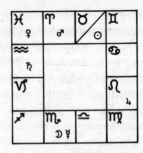

Figure 11.5 The Rasi (radical) and Navamsa (9th harmonic) charts of John Addey. The charts are laid out in the opposite direction to the Western approach, with the Ascendant on the right, indicated by a diagonal line.

others can also be called upon for specific information. Figure 11.5 shows a typical Indian presentation of a Rasi and a Navamsa chart, neither of which include the outer planets. The Hindu astrologer will then interpret these charts according to very specific but often extremely complex tables of rulerships governing both symbolic meaning and time-periods. Hindu astrologers see the birth chart as a series of wave-forms or zodiacs, each with its own meaning and each containing yet another smaller zodiac which contains yet another smaller zodiac until extremely small sections of the chart – aspects of 12' in length – known as the *nardis* can be examined. We shall return to this idea of describing an aspect as either a wave-form or a miniature zodiac later in this chapter.

In the West some astrologers use the Draconic zodiac, or Draco. This is a form of harmonic chart which relates all planets not to 0° Aries but to the Moon's node. In the Draco the actual planetary relationships remain exactly the same – a square is a square in all zodiacs – but the planets will almost certainly change signs and are thus open to new interpretations which are made to some extent from the point of view of the Moon; its node being the phasing or focus point. Similarly Witte and his followers in Germany used many other 'zodiacs' in which planets could be studied in terms of their relationships to the one chart factor – or planet – to which each body was related. Arabic astrologers introduced the use of parts or lots, using an almost identical system for the precise examination of how planets interacted with each other when one of their number – or the Ascendant – was brought into high relief through acting as the focus point of a 'mini-zodiac'. Without going into great detail it is already very clear that astrologers through the ages have recognized that there is no one single way to depict the position of the planets against the ecliptic. In using harmonic charts we are exploring this process further, and perhaps should begin our discoveries by seeing what happens if we temporarily abandon the circle of the zodiac altogether.

The simplest way to depict the 360° of the zodiac is as a straight line; this is also the nearest approximation to what we would actually see were we to stare at one point in the sky for twenty-four hours to witness a complete revolution of the twelve signs. We could enter all the signs into our 'straight line' chart and draw in the Sun, Moon, planets and angles in their correct place, as in Figure 11.6. Such a chart would be technically correct and we could interpret from it, albeit initially with some difficulty until we got used to the layout. We would need to look left and right from each planet to spot the aspects, and may need a measure to help us. One factor, however, would be very easy to spot: the conjunction.

If we were to use this chart for a while we would soon be able to produce a full analysis from its content, which is, after all, exactly the same as in the format we are more familiar with. In fact the Ebertin school has used a 45° version of this 'straight-line' zodiac for synastry purposes and Theodor Landscheidt has experimented with using other harmonic contacts using this form of graphic representation.

It may happen that some heretic astrologer would then decide to turn the straight line into a circle, in an effort more accurately to approximate the circle of the zodiac. In doing so, something would become apparent immediately: in this new circular chart those

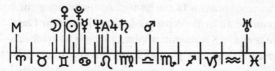

Figure 11.6 John Addey's chart laid out as a straight line.

planets which are in opposition to one another *actually are in opposition*! Furthermore, those planets which are in a triangular relationship to one another actually *are* depicted in a triangular relationship and those deemed to be square are seen to be in a literal 90° square to each other. Whereas the 'straight line' chart allowed us to see only conjunctions at a glance, the circular format allows us to see oppositions, trines and squares with similar ease. Nothing has changed, no tricks have been played and no positions distorted. The data of the planets' positions have simply been entered on to a different format, and one which seduces the eye into spotting specific series of aspects by having 30° intervals inscribed around its circumference. It is not so easy to spot the same two planets in square aspect if those twelve 30° marks are replaced by a pattern which divides the circle by five, seven or nine. Thus our conventional chart form allows us to see the basic geometry of the heavens quite quickly, but biases our perception towards specific planetary relationships.

Harmonic charts do exactly the same thing. The harmonic chart is a chart which allows us to see quite complex planetary patterns very easily. For this to work properly, we need a different chart for each set of aspects. Each chart is calculated in exactly the same manner and drawn up in exactly the same way. The harmonic chart shows us a *particular number in action* and allows us to see how it operates within the birth chart as a whole by literally bringing into aspect all planets that resonate to the nature of that number.

We have already seen in Part One the power of the 8th series of aspects – the 8th harmonic, in fact. This sub-division of the two-series of numbers is associated with will, effort, energy and its expression in the world, and its use in midpoints is a *specific expression* of a harmonic chart in action. The other divisions of the circle – the other aspects – all have their own unique meaning and some of these will be explored more fully in the following chapters.

First we need to set up a harmonic chart and see what is actually going on as we do it. We shall set up a 5th harmonic chart, but the principle is exactly the same whatever number is chosen.

Figure 11.7 shows six planets in a natal chart and except for the Saturn/Pluto opposition there are no obvious aspects. In Figure 11.8 the actual degrees between each planet are indicated and we

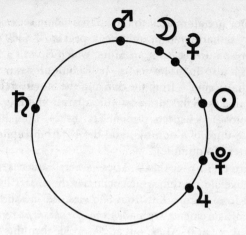

Figure 11.7 Only the Saturn/Pluto opposition is clear, the other planets seem to be laid out randomly.

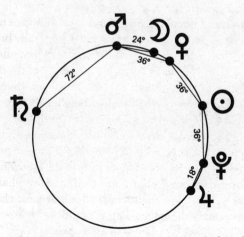

Figure 11.8 Adding in the degrees we see that they are in fact all separated by multiples or divisions of 72°.

see that they are all related to the 5th harmonic series of aspects. The basic 5th harmonic, or quintile, aspect is 72° (360 divided by 5) and here Saturn is 72° from Mars, which is itself 72° from the Sun. Mars is also 36° from Venus – half a quintile away – the same distance that Venus is from the Sun and the Sun from Pluto. This obviously makes Venus also a quintile apart from Pluto. The other two quintile-series aspects present are the 24° from Mars to the Moon (one-third of a quintile) and the 18° from Jupiter to Pluto (one-quarter of a quintile).

In Figure 11.9 we see that 0° Aries – where Saturn is – marks the start of a fivefold rhythm which encircles the chart. This rhythm starts not from Saturn but from 0° Aries. As in the basic natal chart, all measurements are made from – or *phased from* – 0° Aries. If Saturn were *not* at 0° Aries, but at 20° or 30° then this wave-form would start 20° or 30° earlier. Figure 11.10 shows how this wave-form can also be expressed as a complete zodiac in its own right, as the Hindu astrologer would choose to do. There is a complete zodiac, or wave-form, in each of the five divisions of the circle. In this example we can clearly see already that Saturn, Mars and the Sun are all at the start of one of the zodiacs, thus they *must* be each 72° from the other. We cannot yet so readily see what

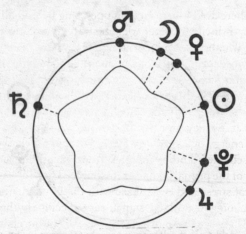

Figure 11.9 A fivefold wave-form connects all planets separated by exact multiples of 72°. Those separated by 36° fall at the trough.

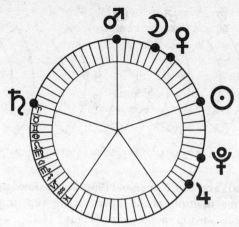

Figure 11.10 Each section of the fivefold division can also be thought of as a complete zodiac in the manner of the Hindu astrologers. Thus a planet falling half-way along this zodiac would be at 0° Libra, and have an 'opposition' relationship with any planets at *any* of the 0° Aries points.

relationships exist between the other planets, but this is about to become plain. In choosing to think of there being the same separate zodiac or cycle in each of the five sectors we are underlining the idea that there are basic principles operating behind all astrological effects; principles which demonstrate the same process in operation, whether we are examining the longest cycles of the outer planets or measuring astrology moment by moment. Here, in the 5th harmonic chart, we are concentrating on the principle of 'fiveness', and how this can be expressed throughout the gamut of its own zodiac in exactly the same way as we view the interactions of the planets as they process through the twelve familiar signs.

It is an energy of a specific wavelength, but an energy that will express itself like all other energies, from start to finish, using the archetype of the primal zodiac as its source. Thus the same precise moments of stress and ease phase with the fundamental zodiacal pattern, echoing its initial design in each specific rhythm.

If we wish to see this more clearly we can cut the chart up, so to speak, and lay each of the five pieces side by side to see at once where common relationships exist (Figure 11.11). Along with

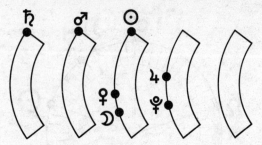

Figure 11.11 The five sections or zodiacs are each a separate cycle.

Saturn, Mars and Sun, Venus and Pluto are *also* lined up – they too must be one multiple of 72° apart. If we superimpose the 5 segments one on top of the other (Figure 11.12), we see quite clearly how the 5th harmonic conjunctions line up. There is only one more step to complete; we need to expand our one-fifth of the circle into a whole once more. This we do in Figure 11.13 and we see the completed 5th harmonic chart. All planets which are multiples of a quintile apart from each other form conjunctions. Those planets which are *half* of a quintile apart form oppositions, those which are one third of a quintile form trines and those which are separated by one quarter of a quintile form squares. In this way

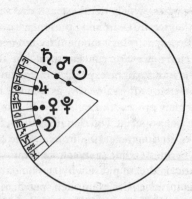

Figure 11.12 Putting the five sections together shows at once how all bodies at similar positions within each section line-up or become conjunct in the 5th harmonic.

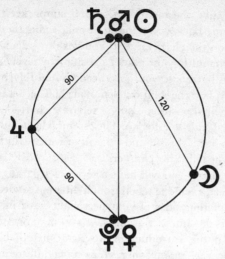

Figure 11.13 Completing the circle, multiplying it by 5 to expand to fit the full 360° is to create the 5th harmonic chart. The planetary relationships are identical to those in Figure 11.7, but here we can see at once what they are.

the basic relationship they hold in the natal chart is maintained *precisely*; all that has happened is that we have laid out the planets so that we can *see* what is going on. We see that in this example the planets are not randomly dispersed around the chart, but are all interconnected and specifically interconnected in a *quintile* manner. Thus their energies will interact with each other in a manner which is characteristic of 'fiveness' – the meaning of the number 5. What this characteristic may prove to be will be explored further in the next chapter.

In the absence of a computer, all that is needed to calculate a 5th harmonic chart is to *multiply* each planet's position by five and then enter the planet in this new position on a separate chart form. This is the mathematical 'shorthand' for bypassing the sequences we have just been examining. For example, if Venus is at 5 ♉ 15 then Venus's position from 0° Aries is 35° and 15'. Multiplied by five this comes to 176° 15' or 26 ♍ 15. This is its 5th harmonic position and is drawn in at 26 ♍ 15 in the 5th harmonic chart. If, after multiplying by five, the answer is *above* 360, simply keep deducting 360° until you are back within the circle once again, then enter this new position on the chart form. If you wish to calculate the 7th harmonic, then multiply the planet's position by seven instead. To calculate each harmonic you only need to multiply by the harmonic number, find the solution (removing 360° as necessary) and then enter the final position, using a separate chart form for each harmonic you decide to draw up. The essential harmonic charts to create are the 5th, 7th, 8th and 9th, all of which will be covered more fully in the following chapters.

With these charts you will have a series of separate pictures of your birth chart, each one taken from a different angle. They will focus in on different sides of your personality and pick out how certain planets are interacting in ways you may previously have overlooked. In the Introduction we suggested that one route towards a clearer, more coherent astrology is to use specific techniques to explore the underlying structure of the birth chart, and not expect one overall method to supply every detail. The use of harmonic charts is a major step towards that goal.

We are trying to establish 'what kind of Mars' someone has; what type of Jupiter they possess, or what type of Pluto possesses *them*. Just as midpoint structures give us valuable information, so in using a sequence of harmonic charts we will quickly see if one or more of the planets is acting as a focus for different types of drives and energies. We shall be looking to see what structures emerge, which planets get pulled most often into the picture and what patterns of behaviour or psychic states are indicated. When we start to put the picture back together again and refer once more to the original natal positions, with their signs and houses, we shall have a much richer experience of the planets we have been observing. We shall know more clearly its particular shape and texture in that chart and how it differs from another, superficially similar moment. The use of harmonic charts will place layers of meaning on particular planets and aspects in a similar way to the patina applied by traditional signs and houses, which can drastically demarcate one body from another.

In using harmonic charts we shall be concentrating first on what planets become *conjunct* in each chart, for those planets are most sensitive to the specific meaning of the aspect that has brought them together. Then we shall look at what other major aspects occur, interpreting them according to the stress or ease of either the hard or soft aspects that connect them one to the other. The maximum orb we shall use in all the harmonic charts is 8°, as this provides a useful base line and translates back to orbs of about 1° to 1.5° in the radical chart, which are reasonably close for major aspects. As in most other areas of astrology there are differing views as to orb size; initially you may prefer to use tighter orbs and focus more directly on the main chart patterns, experimenting with other possibilities as your experience grows. The first thing, however, would be to get a feeling for what each harmonic number means and what an awareness of this number in action brings to your understanding of the chart as a whole. As with all aspects, it is invariably those planets in the closest contact that give the salient features of the chart.

It is unlikely that you will have strong harmonic contacts in each of the three main harmonic charts. This does not imply that inner meaning of these patterns is forever lost to you any more than having nothing in your third house means you are unable to communicate or a lack of a tenanted 7th house denies you relationships for all time. Such omissions more readily suggest that these areas of life are not likely to be so prominent, or such a source of issues, as those parts of your chart rich in planets. As with the patterns in the radical chart, relevant transits can amply make up for any natal shortcomings!

It should be stressed that what follows is not to be taken as the definitive word on the subject, nor should the use of these four main charts be seen as defining the boundaries of harmonic astrology. The use of these lower numbered charts (based on 5, 7, 8 and 9) is a *starting point* for the work of the future and the ideas used to describe their possible manifestation will undoubtedly need amplification in the light of future experience.

CHAPTER 12

Consciousness: The Number 5 and the 5th Harmonic

CHARLES HARVEY

> The key to every man is his thought . . . he has a helm which
> he obeys, which is the idea after which all his facts are
> classified (Ralph Waldo Emerson).

The apple seems intertwined with the meaning of the number 5
and the development of conscious knowledge, and as such can
serve as a useful image for the 5th harmonic and its interpretation.
In the ancient world, and still today, Pythagoreans identified
themselves to each other by cutting an apple across its diameter
and exposing the two halves. If you do this you will find that you
are looking at two perfect pentagons, for the seed pods in the apple
are always arranged in a fivefold symmetry. In Greek mythology
the Golden Apple, like the sun, is used as a symbol of the conscious
mind through which we can rise above, or, if we are not careful,
through which we can cut ourselves off from, the animal innocence
and ignorance of the body. 5 is said to be the 'Number of Man' as a
self-conscious being who takes command of his own destiny. In this
it will be recalled that the most famous apple in history was given
by Eve to Adam. It was the fruit of the tree of the knowledge of
Good and of Evil. In other words it was the fruit of the tree
of choice, of free will, which is both the reward and the penalty of
possessing self-consciousness. This idea of conscious, personal
choice – and the power which comes from such choice – is the nub
of what fiveness is about. It is knowledge that gives us the power to
shape and create our world.

It is appropriately symbolic that one of the greatest abstractions
of science, the postulation of the principle of gravity by Newton,
should have allegedly resulted from the observation of the descent

of an apple. Man's capacity for reflective self-consciousness, by which he is enabled to extract the underlying formal principles from matter, is very decidedly related to the function of fiveness.

But Adam and Eve as the archetypal couple can also be seen as symbolic of another aspect of 5. They represent the conscious coming together of the first female number, 2, with the first male number, 3. Seen in this way 5 was considered by Pythagoras to be the number of marriage, the marriage of form with matter; the union of the idea with the material which embodies that idea.

Man, as an ensouled being, is said to be 'in the blessed station of the midst' because he can, from his perspective of self-consciousness, look both up to Heaven, to the Divine Creative Ideas, and down to Earth, the material world. By so doing he is able to translate one into the other. He may think thoughts, thereby materializing the spiritual and spiritualizing the material. This is the very act of creation: seeing an idea, in the noumenal realm, and embodying it in the material world. As Addey has pointed out, this 'middle' quality of the 5 principle is literally symbolized in the sequence of the first nine numbers when set out in three triads, representing the three primary levels of Spirit, Soul, and Body:

$$1 \quad 2 \quad 3$$
$$4 \quad 5 \quad 6$$
$$7 \quad 8 \quad 9$$

Here we see 5 to be the middle term. We can also see it in the four-faced pyramid where the 5th aspect is seen in both the point of the pyramid and the base, as the fifth surface.

5 has been described as the Number of Man. It can be taken to represent the principle of Soul at work amidst the four elements of Nature. It is likewise related by Addey to the faculty of Mind, in its fullest sense.

As astrologers have increasingly begun to reflect on and investigate the interpretative meaning of the 5th harmonic and the quintile series of aspects, some useful concepts have begun to emerge. John Addey[1] speaks of the 5th harmonic as showing us something about 'our place in the order of art', meaning art in the widest sense as the application of any kind of knowledge or skill. David Hamblin[2] echoes this in relating fiveness to the idea of 'making, arranging, building, constructing, structuring, forming' and to 'the creation of order out of chaos' and 'the search for order and form'. He sees it as intimately related to the way in which we 'structure' ourselves and hence with our 'style', our approach to life. Terry Dwyer specifically relates it to the individual's 'deliberate behaviour' and 'conscious strategy'.

In each of these key phrases we have implicit the idea of choice. In this idea of choice fiveness can be seen to relate to the soul as a soul, as the human prerogative of being able to choose and so become consciously creative, the conscious creator of its own life and the world about it. Such choice, if it is in anyway real, must be based on some kind of knowledge, some kind of knowing. This knowing may be some kind of intellectual knowing or it may be the skilled knowing of the kind that we find with the craftsman who 'knows' his materials, who 'knows what he is doing', even though he has no formal training or paper qualifications. Through such different kinds of knowledge and art we each have special and characteristic skills by which we are able to take command of and shape the world in line with our internal perceptions and priorities.

In relating the 5th harmonic to the word 'art' we do not mean art in the limited sense of the arts of representation and design, such as painting. We mean all those skills by which any knowledge is applied and put to work in the world. Hence the 5th harmonic has as much to do with the Art of Medicine, the Art of Politics, or the Art of Prayer, as with engraving or sculpture. The dominant planets and aspect patterns in the 5H chart will give us a picture of the characteristic way in which individuals will go about their work in the world, and the kind of planetary and dynamic ideas around which they will consciously focus, at some level.

We cannot necessarily tell from the 5H chart the likely occupation of an individual, but we should be able to tell something about the kind of energies which will most engage his or her creative consciousness at different levels. Interestingly there are traditionally said to be five orders of art through which creative ideas are united with materials suitable for their expression. These correspond to the five primary channels or faculties through which we meet the world and handle the information with which we are constantly being bombarded. These five faculties are: the senses, the instincts, the power of estimation, the reason, and the intuition. These can be related to the human faculties and the four primary ideals of the Greeks in a hierarchical picture which reads from bottom to top as follows:

INTUITION	— MYSTICAL FACULTY	— UNITY
REASON	— THE MIND	— TRUTH
VOLITION	— THE WILL	— GOODNESS
AFFECTIONS	— THE HEART	— BEAUTY
SENSES	— THE BODY	— UNITY

We can look at the five orders of art which relate to these five faculties as being a hierarchy which starts from the most material at the level of body and ascends to the most abstract at the level of the mystical faculty. Starting at the level of the senses we are at the level of the body and the development of physical skills which give us all the pragmatic or useful arts, from that of the shoemaker and the gardener to the carpenter and the stone mason. At the level of the heart we have the expressive and rhythmic arts which relate to some aspect of the beautiful, such as music, painting, poetry, sculpture, and so on. At the level of the will we find the ordinative arts such as medicine, law, and statescraft, which tend towards the good. At the level of the mind we find the interpretative arts such as teaching, philosophy, which are concerned with the Truth. Finally we have those few elevative and mystical arts which relate to our large spiritual unity: prayer, meditation and contemplation.

SOME BRIEF CASE STUDIES

It is important that we recognize that the kind of 'knowing' that the 5H relates to is not 'intellectual' in the usual sense of that word, but relates to that larger 'knowing' of the soul by which it contacts and resonates with the phenomenal world through any of its faculties, be it Heart, Mind, Will or the Mystical Faculty. The nature of this 'knowing' is well illustrated by the chart of Lester Piggott.

LESTER PIGGOTT, the world champion jockey, is one of the most remarkable horsemen of all time. He rode over 4,000 winners, was the youngest ever winner of the Derby at only eighteen and a half, and had a total of twenty-eight wins in the classics, more than any jockey ever before. He knows more about thoroughbred horses than any man alive.

Lester's natural affinity for animals showed from an early age when he was first of all obsessed with a pair of cats. His obsession became equine almost from the moment he was given his first New Forest pony at the age of three. By the age of six he was regularly winning races against children twice his age at horse shows. From then on he spent every moment he could riding, riding and riding. It is perhaps significant in relation to his 5H, that the report in *The Times* of his first racecourse win, on 18 August 1948, says that it was 'most intelligently ridden'. He was soon to be recognized for his combination of 'judgement with vigour and courage', as the *Daily Mail*'s Captain Heath put it. As for his style of riding: this has become notorious, and was with him from his 'Boy Wonder' début. Sean Pryor vividly evokes it in his biography, *Lester*: 'The style was all blood and thunder, flailing whip and flashing stirrup. He rode as if the hounds of hell were snapping at his heels . . .'

So much so in fact that by the age of fourteen he was suspended for 'reckless riding' for the first of many times. Depending on the viewpoint, his approach to his racing has been described as 'courageous', 'heroic', 'determined' and 'daring', or 'rash', 'reckless', 'disobedient'. For those who take either view his many accidents, some of them serious, testify to his willingness to push himself to the limit and take risks that other jockeys would not have considered.

What does his 5H have to say? Figure 12.1 shows a close T-square of the ☉ with ☿–♂ and ♃–♆, all brought into high focus by the MC. 'Blood and thunder' is assuredly the personification of ♂–♃, just as the ☿ involvement with the close ☉–90–♂ speaks of 'flailing whip and flashing stirrup'. The 'snapping hounds' again speak of ☿–♂ with ☉ but 'of hell' seems to invoke the close unaspected ♄–♇ conjunction (in Scorpio if you wish to note sign positions!). As we have seen ♄–♇ is a combination renowned for its toughness, tenacity, self-discipline and 'capability to make record efforts of the highest possible order'. It reinforces

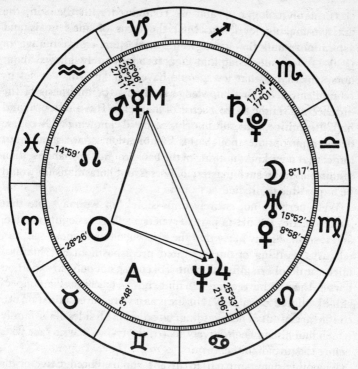

Figure 12.1 The 5H of Lester Piggott, whose courage, daring and 'flailing whip and flashing stirrup' made him the world's greatest ever jockey.

the obsessive and Scorpionic hallmark of Piggott's character as a rider, where his reluctance to relinquish a lead was legendary, and where his recklessness and ruthless determination to win led to repeated suspensions.

We may note that the dominant ☿–♂–M –180–♃ picture is another expression of the very close midpoint picture: M = ♃ = ☿/♂, an illustration of how the deeper significance and area of influence of midpoint structures can so often be read from the harmonics. But turning to the larger picture of the 5H in terms of Piggott's 'place in the order of art' and his likely focus of interest in 'carving out a career', it is difficult to think of a more appropriate pattern. Here we have both the traditional rulers of horses in classical mythology, ♃ and ♆, configured with the Sun, the decision-making level, the MC, the focus of one's goals and aspirations, and the 'riding whip and spurs' and courage of ☿-0-♂. Is it surprising that Piggott so intimately 'knows' about horses in a way that few people have ever known? Yet, let us remind ourselves, his knowledge is almost the antithesis of the 'intellectual' in the narrow sense of that term. It is a practical and highly intuitive, and, ultimately, inspired 'knowing'. Of course deeply appropriate though this combination is, we should not forget that if we knew nothing of the background the manifestation of this picture in such mastery of horses and horsemanship would be impossible to predict.

Well, perhaps not entirely impossible! For we may note that Addey relates the 5H in part to genetics and genetic inheritance, and it seems highly likely that the 5H, when fully understood, can tell us something of our inherited predisposition, our 'natural talents and inborn gifts'. Piggott is of course not only an expert on horses, their pedigrees and breeding, but he has himself an impeccable pedigree for a jockey. His life is as it were the culmination of a confluence of outstanding riding 'blood' from all sides of the family which had already collectively scored thirty-two classic race wins before the turn of the century.

That this dominant pattern is a T-square is indicative of his restless striving to actualize these ideas, the relentless effort 'to become the greatest jockey' and to master his chosen field of study. We might perhaps have also expected a strong focus on communication as well as skill and dexterity with ☿ so much to the fore. Interestingly enough, in the light of Addey's emphasis on the relationship of 5H with the five senses, Piggott is excruciatingly hard of hearing and of speech. With his congenital partially cleft palate he has always tended to restrict himself for the most part to half-uttered monosyllables. Indeed, it has been said of him that his answer to any problem was always to get on a horse and ride. His communication is through actions and example, not words. Another feature of his 5H is the extremely close ♄-0-♇, which is -120-☊ and -60- ♅.

The qualities of self-denial in his personal life have given him a reputation for extreme frugality, meanness and a 'pathological

kink about money'. The latter is perhaps more readily seen in his
8H as ♄–180–☉ and ♀, setting Saturn which closely configures
MC/AS, ♃/AS, ☉/♀ and ☿/☊.

For the 'luck' and 'good fortune' aspect of Piggott's pattern we
have to look to his 7H, Figure 12.2, where the beautifully integrated 'winning' combination ♃–0–♅ dominates the scene with
its –180–M, –120–☉–0–☽ and –60–♄, and testifies to the importance of 'inspiration' to complete real genius. The ☉–120–
♅ could be simply translated as 'I am motivated by the delight of
sudden success.' The MC–180–♃–♅ can be seen as the challenge
to actualize the 'winning breakthrough' and the ☉–60–M and
–60–♄ can be seen to show how this 'winning motivation' became

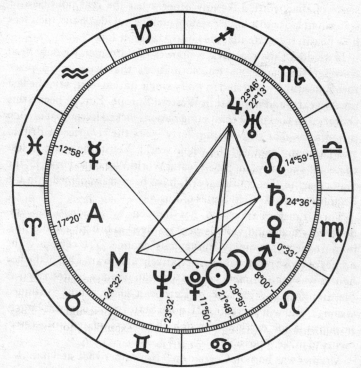

Figure 12.2 The 7H of Lester Piggott, revealing the ♃–♅ tense winning
combination as the central inspiration of his success.

integrated (⊙) into Piggott's very habits (6H) and professional
(♄) 'rhythms of life' (6H) and aspirations (MC).

THE ART OF POLITICS: While artists who shape colours, sounds,
words, clay, or stone are greatly revered in our culture, there is in
general little respect or admiration among people at large for those
individuals whose life is in fact spent moulding and shaping the
very fabric of nations and the lives of their inhabitants. Indeed in
most countries of the world there is a general cynicism about
politicians and those administrators involved in the planning and
organization of national and international life. Few would normally consider such people as 'artists' or give their leading exponents a
place in the pantheon alongside Mozart or Leonardo, Shakespeare
or Michelangelo. Yet in truth great statesmen are artists in the real
sense of that word. Like any other artist the real politician or
statesman looks to a higher vision, an idea, an ideal, and then sees
how he can translate that idea into a tangible form.

If we doubt the real creative power of statesmen we only need
consider the enormous transformations that have taken place
throughout the world and in every single nation over, say, the last
ninety years, and not least in Western Europe. Europe began this
century as a cockpit of competing nations locked in combat of such
proportions that twice within forty years the rivalries of Britain
and Germany engulfed the whole world. Yet in the space of less
than half a century since the Second World War ended in 1945, the
major part of this continent will have been transformed into the
beginnings of a 'United States of Europe'.

This transformation did not happen by accident and undoubtedly many individuals were involved in bringing about this,
in retrospect, seemingly miraculous change. Yet curiously the
names of those responsible are relatively unknown. One of the key
figures was Jean Monnet, a man who can perhaps be described as
the architect and initiator of European unity, whose sustained
vision of, and will to create, a 'United States of Europe' was largely
responsible for carrying through the necessary political agreements to make it possible.

Monnet was born in Cognac on 9 November 1888 at 8 p.m. LT
(birth certificate from Gauquelin). He was never a popular political figure, but was rather a behind-the-scenes organizer, a man of

quite outstanding talents as an economic planner and diplomat. To gain some idea of his stature as a shaper of nations we need to look at some of his achievements. In 1919 at the age of thirty-one he was appointed the first Secretary-General of the League of Nations, the forerunner of the United Nations. Between 1923 and 1938 he worked, as a private adviser, on the economic reconstruction of both Romania and Poland, and on the reorganization of the Chinese railway system. In 1939 when war broke out he was appointed President of the Committee for the Co-ordination of the Allied War Effort and played a leading role in proposing a political Anglo-French alliance. During the war he was sent by Churchill to Washington as a key organizer on the Roosevelt Victory Program. Following the war he was in charge of the French/American lend-lease program, and then in 1946 in drawing up a plan for the total modernization and reconstruction of the French economy, a plan which was adopted on 11 January 1947. He was the originator, and first President, of the European Coal and Steel Community, which was to be the forerunner of the European Community. In 1955 he created, and became President of, the 'Action Committee for the United States of Europe', composed of representatives from all the leading political parties and organizations in Europe. In 1976 the European Community made him a 'citizen of Europe' in honour of his work to create a united Europe.

Looking at Monnet's natal chart (Figure 12.3) we see at once many of the hallmarks of an individual with a powerful will. Mars closely setting in Capricorn depicts the ambitious and determined knight errant, a man with a mission, ready to fight other people's battles, though its seemingly unaspected condition may make us wonder how this will actually be used. The Sun in Scorpio in 5th house −90− ♄ in Leo in 2nd says a lot about sustained, deliberate, individual effort to take a disciplined control of resources and make manifest some personal creative vision. The ☽ in ♒ −120− ♇ is a classic signature of someone who is motivated at an instinctive level by the image of the beauty of the power of either personal or collective transformation and regeneration. (The Moon in Aquarius is certainly apt for his cosmopolitan outlook and echoes H. G. Wells's Moon rising in Aquarius vision of world government.) At a personal level ♄ − ♅ has a great deal to do with the -

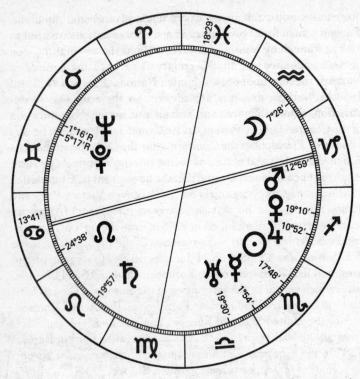

Figure 12.3 The natal chart of Jean Monnet, the politician, economist and architect of European unity.

deliberate exercise of will and the perseverance and the determination to carry through one's plans. In world affairs this ♄–♅ cycle appears to be the driving wheel of the free enterprise economy and is deeply connected with the cycles of industrial development and the harnessing of technology. Here the close ♄–60–♅ indicates someone who can integrate these ideas into the daily rhythms of their life. This major pattern is directly involved in Monnet's personal values by ♀ being in almost exact 60 and 120 to it, while its Yod with the MC, the MC/IC falling on the ♄/♅, indicates that these ideas will be central to the ideals he consciously seeks to cultivate and to his long-term goals and aspirations. While this orthodox approach to the chart obviously reveals much of the picture, nonetheless it cannot as such tell us much about the kind of things on which Monnet, as a creative individual with free will, is likely to choose to focus his potential. For this, harmonic theory and practice tells us that we must turn to his 5H, Figure 12.4. By any standards this is a remarkably strong chart. We see immediately that the seemingly unaspected setting ♂ in the radix is in fact here –0– ☿ –0– ♄ in a close Grand Trine with ♀ and ☽ and –60– ♂. This produces a powerful kite formation with the almost partile ☽–180–♅ as the pivot, denoting a central striving to awaken people from their habitual clannishness and nationalisms

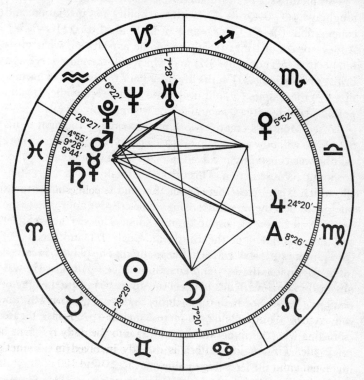

Figure 12.4 The 5H of Jean Monnet, showing the mixture of idealism, toughness, negotiating skills and regenerative power that enabled him to become an awakener and remoulder of nations.

to a larger view. If we take the time of birth as given, the whole of this formation is tightly locked in with the ASC as part of an almost complete Grand Sextile formation, indicating a capacity for highly motivated and unremitting work (6H) for his ideals (3H). Other notable features of this chart are the ☉–90–♇, which is highly characteristic of someone whose mind is focused on grappling with the transforming power of 'the ideas of the time' (♇), and the MC–0–♆ which is –90– ♀, –150–♆, which is very much the signature of the idealistic mind and the individual whose choices in life are dictated by some overriding vision of manifesting an ideal harmony and unity.

This picture is a beautiful mixture of a direct (AS), no-nonsense toughness (♂–0–☿–0–♄), with an ability for mediation and conciliation (☽–♀–☿–♂) and a high idealism (MC–0–♆). Addey speaks of trines in 5th harmonic as showing what gives intellectual (5H) delight (3H) and which will therefore serve as a prime motivation (3H) in the life. Monnet's motivation to harmonize (♀) the peoples (☽) of Europe into a single economic (♄) and political community (☿) could not be written more vividly.

To see Monnet's creative work more vividly in the light of his 5H, if you will now go back to his case history, above, we may note that he was constantly involved in plans and negotiations (☿) for economic reconstruction. This obviously totally befits his ♄–60–♅, which is still close here in the 5H and is here shown to be integrated into the very heart of his whole creative approach to the world. Note how with cosmic appropriateness he was the architect and first President of the European Coal (♄) and Steel (♂) Community (☽), a role which, like many that he played, involved immense diplomatic (♀) and communicative (☿) skills! He was obviously tailor-made for his Secretaryship (☿) of the League of Nations (☽–♀); for his responsibility for reconstructing China's railways, or 'iron roads' (☿–0–♂) as they say in French; for his co-ordination (☿) of the Allied (☽–♀) war effort (♂–♄); for his crucial work on Roosevelt's Victory (♀) Plan and his central involvement in the lend-lease program (☽–☿–♀).

Statesman and Nation: Monnet's crucial post-war plans for the modernization and reconstruction of the French economy are an excellent illustration of the resonance between an artist statesman and his materials. Figure 12.5 shows the chart for the then recently established French IVth Republic, which was in some senses the raw materials with which Monnet had to work. The interaction between the two charts is remarkable. Monnet's 5H Grand Trine/ sextile formation dovetails exactly with the IVth Republilc's fine fan formation of ☉–0–♃–60–☽–120–AS in such a way that the dynamic and pivotal 5H ☽–♅ falls almost exactly on the national Moon stirring up the people, while his 5H ♂–☿–♄ is right on the ASC: a remarkably powerful picture. It also is noteworthy that the Republic's ☉ ♏ –90– ♄ ☊ echoes Monnet's own identical –90– but in degrees which resonate with his 5H pattern rather than with his 1H.

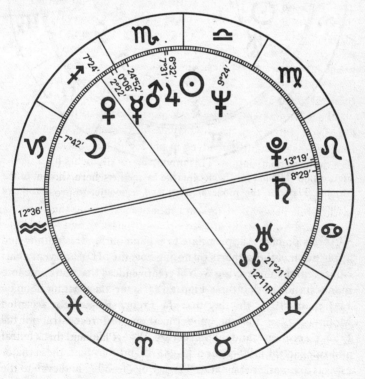

Figure 12.5 The natal chart of the French IVth Republic: the raw materials with which Jean Monnet had to work.

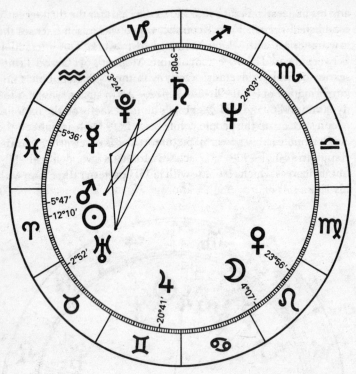

Figure 12.6 The 5H for the acceptance by the French Parliament of the Monnet Plan for the modernization and economic reconstruction of France.

At this point it is appropriate to expand our understanding and application of these charts by noting how the 5H of an event chart can reveal the underlying web of creative ideas that can come into manifestation at that time. Figure 12.6 is the 5H chart for noon on 11 January 1947, the day that the French Parliament accepted Monnet's plan for the modernization and reconstruction of France's economy and infrastructure. We are at once struck by the almost exact ♅–120–♄ and ♅–90–♇ and that both these major aspects are made personal to this day by ♂ and ☿ and even to the hour by the ☽ (though we have not yet been able to ascertain the exact time of the adoption). As we have noted, when considering

Monnet's close natal ♄–60–♅, the ♄–♅ cycle is the one most associated with economic development. This ♄–120–♅ in the 5H perfectly symbolizes a time when people can be motivated (3H) by the idea (5H) of a flourishing economy. The simultaneous ♅–90–♇ likewise relates to what *COSI* describes as 'the process of transformation . . . the creation of new conditions of living'. The –90– in the 5H is indicative of the idea (5H) of meeting this challenge of innovation and reconstruction. The involvement of ☿ and ♂ and even ☽ indicate that these large-scale social processes can be translated into practical decisions, words, and actions at this time.

While this chart is highly appropriate in itself, its fuller significance becomes apparent when we compare it with that of the IVth

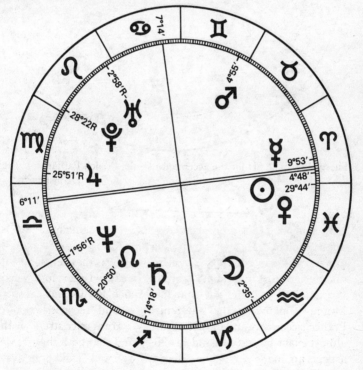

Figure 12.7 The natal chart for the Treaty of Rome, the founding moment of the European Community.

Republic (Figure 12.5) and Monnet's own 5H (Figure 12.4). Here we note that the ☿ at 5⟩(36 which bisects the ♄ –120– ♅ is with the IVth Republic's ASC and Monnet's conjunction of DS–♂–☿ –♄. We may also note that the almost exact –0– of 5H ♃ with the IVth Republic's ♅ and IC and the 45/135 relationship of the ♅–90–♇–☽ with the Republic's MC/IC. The ♅–♇ and possibly ☽ are also tightly involved with Monnet's 5H M/IC and Ψ.

Following the same principles, we can study the chart for the signing of the Treaty of Rome (Figure 12.7), which founded the European Community, in relation to that of Monnet whose vision, work and purposive will were very much at its heart. Here we find the M/IC lying across Monnet's 5H ☽–180–♅, and the AS/DS in

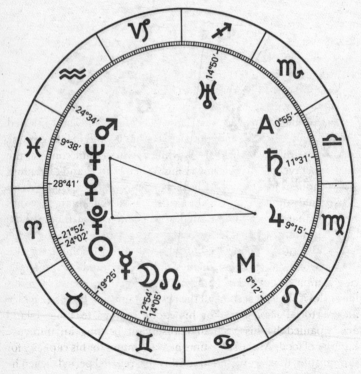

Figure 12.8 The 5H of the Treaty of Rome. This should be compared with Monnet's radix, Figure 12.3, and 5H chart, Figure 12.4 above.

close –90–. At the same time we find that the Treaty's ☽–180–
♅–90–Ψ falls right across Monnet's 5H MC–Ψ, so that there is a
direct interchange of these aspects! Turning to the 5H for the
Treaty (Figure 12.8) we find that the AS is exactly with Monnet's
Grand Trine/sextile while the striking ♃–180–Ψ–45/135–☉,
symbolizing the desire to manifest high ideals (and the cynic might
remark the EEC's deep-rooted 'instability in material things' and
tendency to 'squandering of physical strength'!), is almost exact to
the minute with Monnet's 5H ☿–♄–DS and interlocked with his
major trine/sextile pattern.

   While such detailed study is impossible in most client work, this
type of analysis enables us to see just how infinitely related
mankind, individually and collectively, is with his works of
creation.

   NIKOLAI TESLA: If Piggott illustrates knowing at the level of the
senses and of special talents and skills of a pragmatic kind we can
see Tesla, said by some to be 'the greatest inventive genius of all
time', as representing the intellectual/intuitive pole of 'knowing'.
Looking first at his radical chart (Figure 12.9), we see a strong
paradoxical emphasis on Venus and Mars. We find ☉–0–♀ in
Cancer on the IC with ♀ very close 90–☽ in Libra, and ♀ ruled
Taurus rising. At the same time we see that ☉ and M form a close
T-square with ♂ which is –0–☽, while ♇, which some consider the
'higher octave' of ♂, is closely rising. When both ♀ and ♂ themes
are prominent in a chart this is likely to emphasize sensuality and
sensationalism, a paradoxical mixture of soft self-indulgence and
obsessive hard work. These suggest someone who will tend to be
both charming, sensual, easy-going, with a strong aesthetic sense
and a love of the good life, but who will also be something of a
driven workaholic. These themes do indeed stand out amid the
rich complexity of Tesla's enigmatic personality. He was famous
for his love of being seen in all the best restaurants, for his elegance
and sartorial *savoir-faire*, for his exotic outings to Long Island
accompanied by his Serbian manservant bearing an immense
hamper of food. At the same time he was famous for his capacity for
unremitting hard work and his ability for frenzied periods when he
would barely cease from his labours for days on end, surviving on
the briefest of catnaps. Likewise from the radical chart the closely

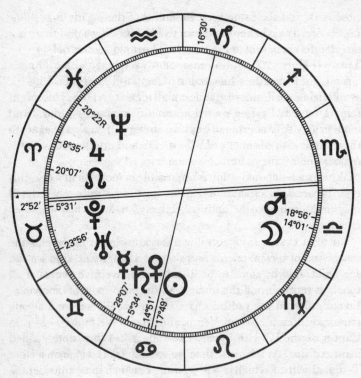

Figure 12.9 The radical chart of 'the modern Prometheus', Nikolai Tesla.

rising Pluto in exact sextile to Saturn, in the 3rd house in a key
Gauquelin position for scientists, is suggestive of someone who is
likely to be preoccupied with 'power' in some form, and with
putting it to work in the world, probably in a scientific way. In
Tesla's case it was quite literally harnessing electrical power which
became his obsessive, and abundantly fruitful, preoccupation, as
he notched up invention after invention, patent after patent.

But if some of the broad issues are clearly shown by an orthodox
reading of the chart, there is a great deal that is not. Tesla has been
described as a 'modern Prometheus' and 'the greatest inventor the
world has ever known'. It was he, not Edison, who harnessed the
alternating current. It was he, not Marconi, who invented radio.
He it was who invented fluorescent lighting, who opened the way

to computers, robotics, satellite communication, and the funda-
mentals of Star Wars beam weaponry. His countless revolutionary
breakthroughs make him one of the truly great pioneers of modern
technology and one of the most remarkable geniuses in history.

This type of Promethean invention is normally associated with
Uranus. Indeed the brilliant American astrologer Dr Rick Tarnas
has suggested that Uranus is a misnomer for this planet and that
we should think of it as Prometheus if we are to understand its real
significance. But where is Uranus-Prometheus in this chart? Even
if we admit that its first house placement gives it some emphasis, it
has only a close −45− to Jupiter, but is otherwise virtually unaspected, apart from a very wide trine to the MC. Midpoints give it
some strength through the picture ☉/☿ = ☿/♂ = ♃ = ♅ =
☿/☊, which shows that it is important to the way in which he
works as a thinking being (☉/☿). This picture is certainly indicative of a breadth of thought and originality. As *COSI* says of
☉/☿ = ♅, it gives 'sudden ideas, inventions, a flair for applied
science and technology'. But these considerations aside, Uranus
would not normally be considered to be an especially key factor in
this chart.

When we turn to Tesla's 5H the picture instantly changes. In
Figure 12.10 we see ♅ −0− ♂ in an almost exact square with
☉−0−♇ with AS and forming a T-square with MC. In addition we
see ♃, Jove 'the Thunderer', joining and amplifying this powerful
picture by being −135− both ♅ and the ☉−♇, such that it is in fact
at the midpoint of the ☉−♇/♅. Here is a graphic picture of Tesla's
'place in the order of art', of what he 'knew' about. Here are his
creative preoccupations. Here is the essence of his style given in
bold, unmistakable brushstrokes. In terms of his 'place in the order
of art', Ebertin gives the sociological correspondences of ♅−♇ as
'pioneers, reformers, explorers, people who are very out of the
ordinary or who are endowed with universal genius'. Ebertin could
have had Tesla in mind when he wrote that, but in fact he certainly
did not, since the central importance of ♅−♇ for Tesla's life only
becomes apparent when looked at through the lens of the 5H chart.

Looking at this chart as depicting Tesla's 'style', and his whole
approach to being in the world, we note that, in addition to the
dominant ☉−♇−♅−♃ pattern, ♀ is exactly −0− AS. As we have

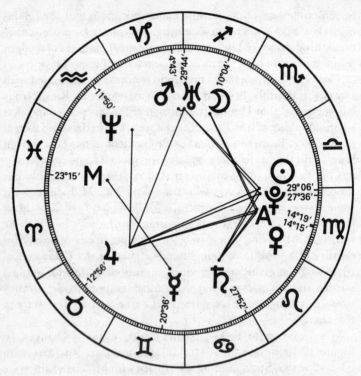

Figure 12.10 Nikolai Tesla's 5H, which reveals something of the mind and manners of 'the greatest inventor the world has ever known'.

seen, Tesla was a highly Venusian individual, with a strongly elegant, aesthetic side, concerned to create a good impression. But most of all, overshadowing the Venus element, his style was dramatic, indeed electric. He delighted in putting on flashy, limelight-grabbing shows to awaken interest in his work. Mark Twain and others were treated to the sight of Tesla surrounded by a halo of darting flame-like electric discharges coming from every part of his body as he sat impassively while 2 million volts played over his body. His obsession with the scientific and aesthetic study of lightning, both natural and of his own creation, led him to produce electric storms which hurled lightning in a twelve-mile arc around his laboratory in Colorado Springs. These he recorded on film and in descriptions which his biographer Margaret Cheney describes as 'detailed, loving, almost erotic in their lingering portrayal of the colours and grandeur'. He created artificial lightning on a scale that has never since been replicated and built generators capable of achieving an electrical potential of 20 million volts decades before anyone else. Could this 'larger than life' Promethean aspect of his life – which combined power ($\odot$, ♅, ♇) and aesthetics (♀) – be more vividly depicted?

Those who wish, like the Hindus, to consider the sign emphasis in these charts may also like to make inferences about Tesla's style and approach from the powerful Virgo stellium. This relates well to his intense perfectionism and especially to his obsessive fear and preoccupation with germs. This was so strong that he would use eighteen clean linen napkins at each meal in polishing all his tableware before eating, and led him to compulsively calculate the cubic capacity of every dish of food before eating. Virgo here may well be a factor, though Tesla's countless phobias must also be strongly related to his classically phobic combination ☿ = ♄/♆ which is within 9′ in the natal chart.

In Tesla we can see the 5H working on all its levels: in terms of mind, style, career, and the kind of choices which he habitually made. In this latter respect his early choice to leave Yugoslavia and abandon his old way of life for the new frontiers of the USA is typically Uranian and Plutonian. His repeated attempts, often temporarily successful, to obtain wealthy patrons are as characteristic of the exact ♀–0–AS as was his tendency to fall out, and go his own way, regardless of the consequences, the moment his plans were in any way thwarted. ♀ and ♅ as dominant formative archetypes do not make comfortable bedfellows!

If the rich paradoxes and final place in the scheme of things of Tesla are only passingly written in a traditional reading of his natal chart, how much less is the essential JANIS JOPLIN written in her horoscope (see Figure 4.1, p. 60). As we saw when looking at her midpoints (p. 61), Joplin's chart 'makes as little sense as did her short life' when considered using orthodox methods. We saw there how her ambition to lead a life of 'superhypermost' was reflected in the presence of Jupiter on her Sun/Moon midpoint. That picture is certainly vitally important in understanding

Joplin's psychology. However looking at her 5H should also tell us about Joplin's 'place in the order of art' (Addey), her 'style' and how she will 'structure' herself (Hamblin), and about her 'deliberate behaviour' and her 'conscious strategy' (Dwyer).

Indeed, turning to Joplin's 5H (Figure 12.11), our understanding of her chart's potential is immediately transformed. The seemingly 'all Saturn' chart becomes at this crucial level extravagantly Jupiterian. Jupiter and Neptune exactly bracket the Ascendant ($\mathrm{2\!\!\!\!\perp/\Psi} = 7\mathrm{\triangle}41$), opposed to the true Node and with the Sun 135° this $\mathrm{2\!\!\!\!\perp}$–AS–Ψ grouping, indicating a central (Sun) need to purposefully (8H) project herself (AS) through rich, extravagant fantasy. In addition we can see that the close Jupiter-180-true

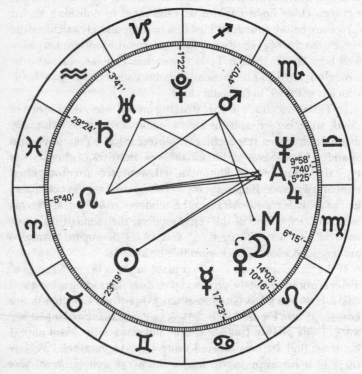

Figure 12.11 Janis Joplin's 5H revealing her 'superhypermost' style. Her radical chart is Figure 4.1 on p. 60.

node forms a double sextile formation with ♂ and ♅, adding a hard, aggressive, 'rhythmic' (6H) drive to this pattern. Pluto, with its potential for single-minded obsession, is also widely involved in this pattern as the apex of a T-square.

SHIRLEY MACLAINE offers us a less dramatic, but nonetheless telling example of the way in which the 5H can put us 'inside the head' of an individual and show us the way they think about the world and the kind of way in which they are likely to choose to lead their life. In showing us a 'person's place in the order of art' as Addey puts it, the 5H is likely to offer important clues as to how a person will choose to carve out a place for herself in the world, and hence the kind of career and interests she is likely to pursue. In the case of Joplin we saw ♃–Ψ rising as indicative of her 'superhypermost' style and approach to the world. It is equally of course indicative of the glamour world of stage and screen and the whole process of creating images and illusions, of pretending (Ψ) to be someone else in order to entertain and amuse (♃). Here in MacLaine's chart (Figure 12.12) we see a very similar picture with a close T-square of ♃–☉–Ψ–☿ which falls right with the angles. If this is highly appropriate for such a charismatic and purposeful (☉) film actress, who has won five Academy Awards, it is equally appropriate for her more recent incarnation as a New Age guru with her books on reincarnation, telepathy, and the psychic dimension of reality. This T-square centred on the ☉–0–AS speaks of her struggle to manifest (90/180) ideals, visions, dreams, insights, and to help to work to make the world a happier and more deeply spiritually aware place. The strong involvement with both ♇ and ♅–☊ in this pattern to form a double kite focused around the ☉–AS gives an additional power and revolutionary fervour to this work.

Like Joplin's chart, this is a classic example of how midpoints and harmonics reinforce each other. MacLaine's solar midpoints read: ♀ = ☽/M = ☽/AS = ☉ = ♇/☊ = Ψ/M = Ψ/AS. The first part of this picture emphasizes the importance for MacLaine of focusing (☉) her life around some form of personal (☽/M = ☽/AS) artistic (♀) expression. The second part of the picture indicates that she will also need to focus herself upon mass-movements or transformative groups and relationships (♇/☊) of

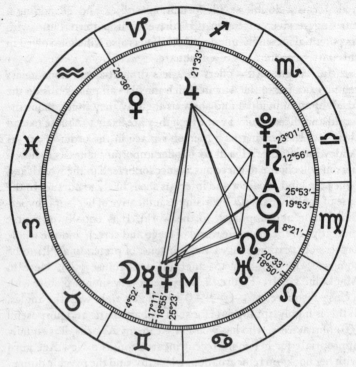

Figure 12.12 The 5H of film actress and New Age aficionado Shirley MacLaine.

some kind, and bring all that relates to Ψ in her world (AS) and thinking (MC) to the centre of her stage. While there is no denying the significance of the ☽–0–Ψ in her natal 12th house as an indication of the importance of the hidden and transcendent dimension of life, we see here in the 5H, as well as in the midpoints, just how central this theme is in her pattern.

MARIE STOPES: Figure 12.13 shows the 5H of the great pioneer fighter for sex education and birth control, Marie Stopes. The *DNB* says of her that she was a 'fearlessly dedicated woman, with a touch of the mystic', 'her arrogant argumentativeness and vanity . . . made co-operation difficult', 'prickly, demanding, stimulating', 'her demonic advocacy of planned parenthood never waned'.

☉–180–♅ on MC/AS is the hallmark of someone whose inner choices constantly direct them towards the original, towards discovery and reform, and in personal terms towards independence and autocracy. And here we should not forget that before she took up her pioneering work in sex education she had already carved out a career for herself as a pioneering scientist. She was the first woman to join the science faculty of Manchester University and as an expert in palaeobotany had made important observations in this area. In personal terms her 'style' was autocratic to the point that both her second husband and her son became alienated from her (she had divorced her first husband).

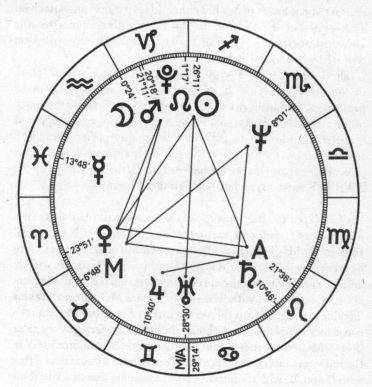

Figure 12.13 The 5H of Marie Stopes, the 'prickly, demanding, stimulating' pioneer fighter for sex education and birth control.

This said, the ☉ here also forms a Grand Trine with AS and ♀, a fact reflected in midpoints by ☉ being within 41′ of ♀/AS. And, despite her undoubted interest in eugenics, there can be no doubt that what motivated her approach to life was her deep desire 'to see woman's lot become a happier one – a pursuit of general happiness which she did not herself attain'. This Grand Trine involving Venus, and the MC–180–Ψ, was very much reflected in the romantic style of her best-selling books, *Married Love*, *Radiant Motherhood*, *Wise Parenthood* and *Enduring Passion*. But this contrasts strongly with the impassioned ♀ in square with the very tight ♂–0–♇ which is also appropriately –0– ☽, which manifested in her as the arrogant and argumentative fighter who in one way or another spent much of her life either attacking or being attacked. The –150– of the ♂–0–♇ to the AS vividly summarizes the awkward aggressive aspect of her style which is commented on repeatedly by those who knew her.

The T-square of M–Ψ–♄ is a hallmark of someone whose 'place in the order of art' is to struggle to 'earth visions' and make practical a 'romantic vision'. In this there was certainly the touch of the mystic. She had seen a vision and could not rest until it was realized. In addition to the romantic quality of her writing on sexual relations for the general public, the main focus of her output in her latter years was poetry such as 'The Bathe', described by the *DNB* as 'a sensuous and rather high-flown verse'.

We have seen (p. 102) how ♂ was a central feature in EMMELINE PANKHURST's midpoint pictures, being at the ☉/☽ midpoint. Here in her 5H (Figure 12.14) we are again able to see that ♂ will be a key factor in her, for it is involved in a tight T-square with ♄ and Ψ, characterizing the sheer toughness, tenacity and idealism of her struggle, and with Ψ is –135– ☉ and MC, integrating this 'idealistic struggle' into the very centre of Emmeline Pankhurst's conscious aspirations and choices in life. Likewise the very close ☽–90–MC, 'the struggle to actualize a feminine consciousness' of the radix remains close here, and is seen to be in a fine Grand Trine with ☿ and ♃, with the latter –180–AS forming a partial kite. This is a beautiful depiction of someone who was so motivated by the desire to articulate women's aspirations and the healthy develop-

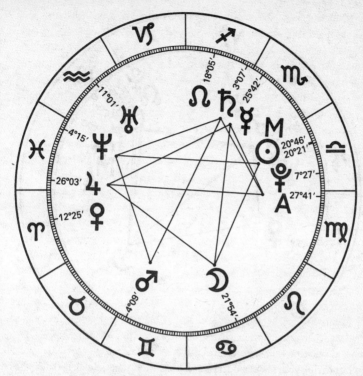

Figure 12.14 Women's Rights campaigner Emmeline Pankhurst's 5H. Some of her main midpoint trees were discussed in Chapter 6.

ment of the women's movement, and who had such a fluent and persuasive style, notably in court ($\, 24 \,$!).

ROBESPIERRE (Figure 12.15), the French revolutionary leader, is described as a martyr or a monster depending on one's perspective. But friends and enemies alike agree that Robespierre's 'style' was totally rigid, honest, uncompromising and unequivocally ruthless. He saw himself as the defender of the people, the 'incorruptible' who was justified in instigating the Reign of Terror, in which hundreds of 'enemies of the State' were executed, for the sake of 'ethical democracy'. In his view 'without Terror, virtue is impotent'. He had leaders of both the moderates and of the 'ultra-revolutionaries' executed as being elements 'destructive to

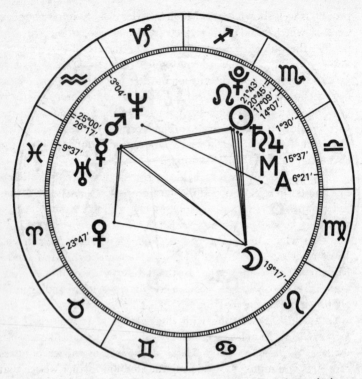

Figure 12.15 Martyr or monster? The 5H of the French revolutionary leader Robespierre, who instigated the Reign of Terror for the sake of 'ethical democracy'.

the revolution'. In the end his violence and sacrilege shocked even the mob. Soon after his theatrical display as chief priest at the 'Festival of the Supreme Being', his attempt to produce a substitute for Christianity, he was in turn denounced and executed.

Much of Robespierre's basic psychology can be read from the moralistic and inflationary effects of Jupiter on the MC in Sagittarius with Pluto, a Pluto which is –90– the rising ruler ♅ and –135– ☉/☽ (cf. Hitler and Mao). The ☉–90–♂–♆, which are –120– the culminating ♃, showing both the spiritual aspirations and the temptation to misuse power in the challenge to exercise the individual will. His personal advocacy of identification with 'the people' is well shown by his Moon in Aries exactly square node in Cancer, which could be translated as 'strong associations with the people, the public, popular causes'. The nature of these associations is vividly shown by the midpoints: ☽ = ☊ = ☿/♃ = ♄/♇ = ☿/♇ = ♄/♅. It was his gift for putting into words what others were feeling, and his oratorical skills and powers of persuasion (= ☿/♃ = ☿/♇), that so readily gained him the ascendancy in the Jacobin club. It was his sheer ruthlessness (= ♄/♇ = ♄/♅) that obtained him his dictatorial power and brought him the encouragement of the Paris mob (☽ = ☊).

With such a vivid picture, in hindsight, from the broad chart and midpoints, an exploration of the harmonic charts may seem rather redundant. Yet turning to Robespierre's 5H we cannot but be struck by how strikingly it reveals the previously invisible web of quintiles which link Saturn, Sun, Node, and Pluto, and indeed Jupiter, all together (in Scorpio!), in a T-square to the Moon and a Mercury-Mars conjunction. In this line-up we can immediately appreciate that Robespierre, as a creative individual and agent of choice, is so tuned that his ☉ –90–♂ and the ♇ = ☉/☽ are spontaneously resonating with the tight ☽ = ☊ pattern. ♇–☊, *COSI* tells us, is 'mass meetings'. ☽–90–♇–☊ sounds like 'mobs', while ☉ = ☽ = ☊ = ♇ sounds like 'a leader or organizer' of 'mass meetings and mobs'. Considering the stellium further we see that the ☉ is closely conjoined the ♄/☊ and ♄/♇ midpoints, indicative of someone who will focus their choices around 'the participation in achievements brought about by large groups or masses of people' and the 'application of force or compulsion' and who may have 'a tendency to violence and a fanatical adherence to one's principles . . .' and indeed someone who may, to quote *COSI*, be 'a martyr'.

While Jupiter had just risen in the maximum Gauquelin position in MARTIN LUTHER KING's natal chart (Figure 12.16), his 5H chart, with its almost exact trine to Ψ, is highly characteristic of a man whose life was motivated by the beauty of an ideal and vision of the larger spiritual unity of mankind and a general love of humanity, it is less obvious why this particular configuration should take a central place in this life. When however we look at his 5H to see just what, as a human soul, he would choose to do with

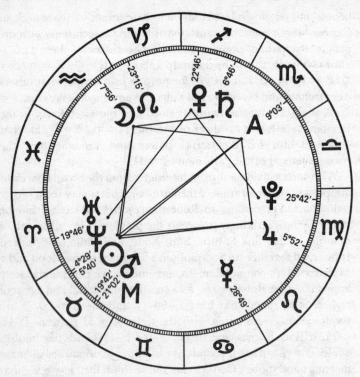

Figure 12.16 The idealistic dream of Martin Luther King stands out here in the ⊙–0–Ψ –120– ♃ of his 5H.

his life, we immediately see that this ♃–Ψ combination is at the very centre of this man's patterning. The ⊙ joins Ψ in exact 120–♃, whilst the ☽ is –90– Ψ, and if his mother was correct in giving 'high noon' as his birth time, then the whole combination is configured closely with the AS. When he said 'I have a dream' he was not being rhetorical. This is clearly the picture of a dreamer and a visionary, a fact expressed equally in the midpoint pictures where we find AS = ☿ = ⊙/Ψ and ☽/AS = ☽/☿ = Ψ and ⊙ = ☽/Ψ. Additional confirmation of the time of birth is perhaps given by ♂–0–MC testifying to the willingness of King to fight for his vision as a real crusader, a warrior priest.

While it is important to recognize that the 5H is not simply telling us about the intellectual qualities of the mind, by the same token it is important to recognize that the 5H can tell us about just such intellectual possibilities. As Hamblin shows, ALBERT EINSTEIN had a powerful 5H (Figure 12.17). We may note that the powers of focused, and often narrow, thought of the natal ☿–0–♄ are here dramatically broadened and given a universal perspective by the –180– to the triple conjunction of ♆–☽–♃. If Einstein's intellect has transformed our view of the universe, it could be said that JAMES DEWEY WATSON (b. 1.23 a.m., 6 April 1928, Chicago, birth certificate), Figure 12.18, in his brilliant work with Francis Crick, has transformed our understanding of the structure of life with his work on unravelling the structure and function of DNA. It is interesting to note that DNA has, appropriately, a fivefold

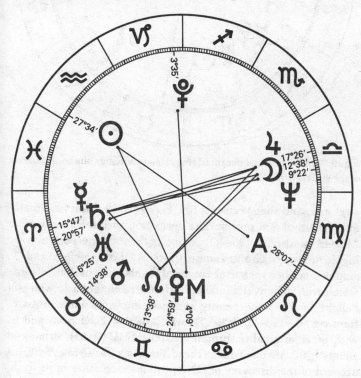

Figure 12.17 The 5H chart of Albert Einstein.

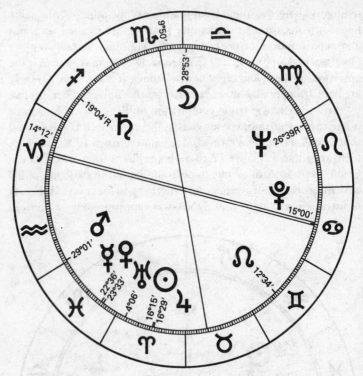

Figure 12.18 The natal chart of James Dewey Watson, the co-discoverer of the structure of DNA.

structure, and that Watson's 5H, Figure 12.19, shows a remarkably beautiful and precise 'kite' formation with the almost exact MC–♅ (and ♆) –180– ♂ acting as the focusing point for the highly motivated Grand Trine of ☉–0–♃ –120– ☿–☽–♀ and ♂. Addey described such trines in the 5H as showing the kind of ideas which will 'delight the intellect'. Here we see someone who will delight in (3H) the beauty of clear, intellectual and incisive thinking (☿–120–♃–120–♂), which they will consciously focus with great originality, insight, purpose (MC–0–♅), drive and energy (♂). Anyone who has read Watson's *The Double Helix*, his account of the discovery of DNA, will also recognize in its fresh, frank, lively and iconoclastic style the zest and vitality of this remarkable 5H. For those interested in exploring sign positions in harmonic charts, it is interesting to note that Watson's Grand Trine falls towards the end of Air signs and that Einstein's ☉–120–♀ (and ♃ by –180–) occupy similar degrees. Not inappropriate for minds that have breathed fresh air into our understanding of the scheme of things!

A study of these diverse examples above will give you something of the flavour of the 5H chart. They illustrate how a very literal translation of the outstanding features and patterns of the 5H chart will immediately focus in on some of the central issues in the individual's life. Where there are strong patterns in this harmonic we can expect that person to be a strong individual, who is highly creative in some appropriate direction, sometimes to the point of

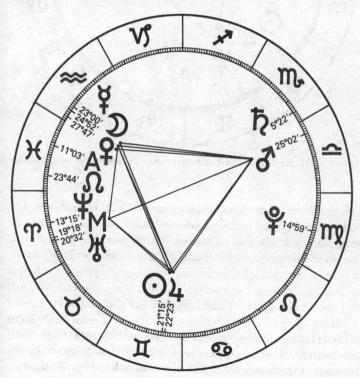

Figure 12.19 The 5H chart of James Dewey Watson.

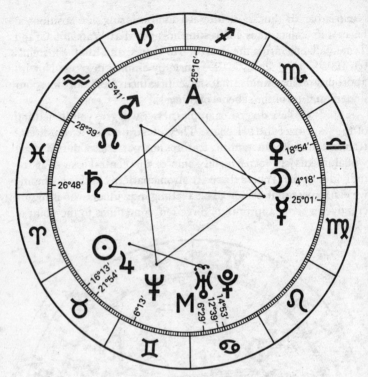

Figure 12.20 The 25H chart of James Dewey Watson.

genius. Where there is no obvious activity in this harmonic, the individual may still be highly creative, but if so it is unlikely to be from this conscious and purposive centre, from their elective will, but will be likely to come from their 7H or some other level.

THE QUINTESSENCE OF THE FIFTH

If the 5H shows us something central about those ideas with which the individual as a purposeful human soul will most readily resonate, and around which he will choose to build his life, then we can see that the 25H, which will highlight the quintile series appearing in the 5H should tell us something about yet deeper levels of 'knowing' and consciousness within the individual.

MAO TSE-TUNG's 5H is shown in Figure 12.21. Apart from the wide ☉–0–♄ and –60–♆ which speaks of an approach to life which is characterized by a certain self-disciplined dedication to actualizing a vision, and the ☊–180–♃, –90–♇ and 120–☿ which encourages a focus of consciousness on issues to do with the regeneration of the masses (♃–♇) and a strong motivation to communicate with others, this could not be considered to be a particularly strong harmonic. Yet when we look at his 25H, Figure 12.22, our perception immediately changes.

Here we see an almost exact Grand Cross of Sun-Moon-Uranus

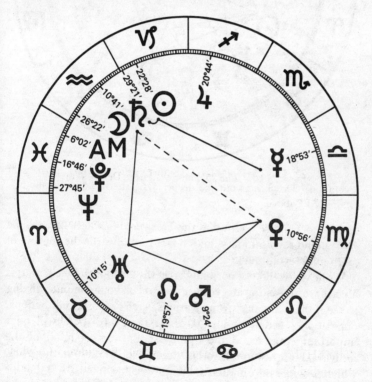

Figure 12.21 The 5H of Mao Tse-tung, which seems to show little of the mind or style of the man. But see 12.22 below.

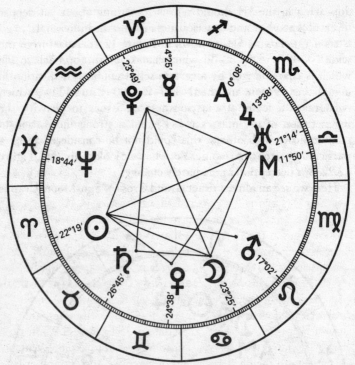

Figure 12.22 The 25H of Mao Tse-tung, who preached 'permanent revolution'. This brings out the deeper 5H pattern hidden in the 5H, Figure 12.21 above.

and Pluto. Can we doubt that the *Thoughts of Chairman Mao* will be radical and revolutionary, and in fact turn towards the concept of 'perpetual revolution'.

While we would not normally erect the 25H for every client, it is always worth casting an eye over the 25H on your computer listing to see if there are any strong features, such as close conjunctions, oppositions, trines, and squares. If there are these will offer important clues as to the 'quintessential' set of mind of the individual in question. Another example of an illuminating 25H, which provides information not readily visible in the 5H, is that for James Watson, Figure 12.20. His remarkable 5H was given above, Figure 12.19. While his 25H is not as impressive in its own right as his 5H, we see that it does reveal some interesting additional information about the qualities of his mind. Notably we see a strong ☿–180–♄, which is, for the birth certificate time given, exactly –90– AS. This adds a depth and concentration to the turn of Watson's mind which was not immediately apparent on the 5H. ☿–♄ is an element we might especially expect to find in someone whose creative mind was so preoccupied with the challenge to discover the structure of DNA and to build an intelligible model of it.

The close Grand Trine of ☽–♂–Ψ reveals yet deeper levels of motivating 'delight'. It is suggestive of the highly imaginative, yet purposeful, qualities of Watson's reveries. Just as in Mao's case 'the idea after which all his facts are classified' focused on a central (☉ and ☽) striving for a permanent revolution (♅–♇), so too here Watson's conscious approach to life (MC) is, as it were, focused not only upon the possibility of awakening to larger possibilities and making discoveries, M–0–♅, as witnessed by the 5H, but is here in the 25H also further focused and intensified by the addition of ♇. As we will see in Chapter 13, Watson has ♄–0–♇, the signature of the 'deeply searching scientist' prominent in his 7H, the picture of what inspires him. Ebertin goes on to note that 'the urge to do research work' and 'the desire to solve difficult problems' is related to ♄/♇–☿. Those who wish to explore Watson's fiveness, and the deeper reaches of his mind, to yet another level, will note with interest that this ♅–0–♇ in his 25H is almost exactly –36– from ☿ and –108– from ♄. This will thus go on to produce a suggestive ♄–♇–0–♅–☿ picture in his 125H!

How finely tuned are the inner recesses of genius. Does this perhaps suggest that Watson, and each one of us, sees just what we are tuned to see? Such methods suggest a whole new dimension to vocational guidance and personnel selection and especially for research scientists!

Much exploration still lies ahead for our full understanding of 5H charts, but we certainly already know enough to say that the number 5, as Kepler foresaw, is of profound significance in understanding the nature of the individual in the scheme of things. As you study these charts you will come to see that to attempt to grasp the essence of an individual without this tool could be said to be tantamount to malpractice.

One feature of the 5H which requires additional emphasis is its relationship with power. Knowledge is power. The knowledge of Good and Evil gives us the power to choose to be consciously destructive in a way that no animal following its instincts can begin to equal. Likewise we know that the magician traditionally stands inside a pentagram when invoking power. But there is also a quality of instability about the Idea of fiveness. This gives it a relationship to the life principle for life is inherently unstable, constantly on the move, enabling a blade of grass to force itself through solid concrete. Indeed as soon as something becomes stable, inert, we take this as a sign of death. Both Daphne Jones and Pamela Crane have pointed out that the underlying structure

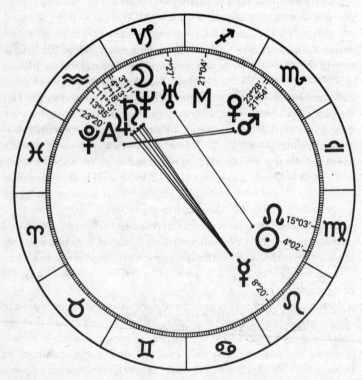

Figure 12.23 The 5H of Adolf Hitler, whose remorselessly purposeful mind dominated Europe for a decade.

of DNA is fivefold. Jones also points out that the asteroid belt, thought by many to be the remains of a shattered planet, is the fifth orbit from the Sun and that this has precise parallels with the fifth shell in atomic structure, which is held to be untenable. The leading Swiss astrologer Dr Hans-Jorg Walter in his as yet untranslated major contribution to the study of harmonics, *Eschluesselte Aspektfiguren* (Encoded Aspect Figures) relates the 5H to the planet Mars. He rightly draws attention to the sheer power, often of a highly destructive kind, that can be present when this harmonic is strong. This is obviously relevant in the case of Mao and Robespierre above, and in the case of Hitler whose 5H (Figure 12.23) opposite is one of the most powerful one is likely to meet. Walter also draws attention to the number of world champion racing drivers, such as Jackie Stewart, who have this harmonic strong and how in addition to the obviously highly dangerous and martial nature of their pursuit they have also often tended to die violently on the track. There can certainly be a quality of sheer purposive energy about the 5H chart, as we can see in characters as different as Hitler, Mozart and Lester Piggott. Perhaps it is that energy and power that comes from constantly being aware of making conscious choices, and which in consequence makes such individuals more aware than most that what they achieve is the result of their own choices: indeed a powerful self-reinforcing feed-back loop!

NOTES

1. John Addey, *Harmonics in Astrology*, L. N. Fowler, 1976; Urania Trust, 1990. This is the authoritative text on the theory of harmonics and should be in every student's library.
2. David Hamblin, *Harmonic Charts*, Aquarian Press, 1983. This is the standard work for the interpretation of harmonic charts and is an invaluable starting point for your chart analysis.

CHAPTER 13

The 7th Harmonic
– Whatever Turns You On

MICHAEL HARDING

THE IDEA OF THE 7TH HARMONIC

The number 7 has long been associated with spiritual or mystical matters. References to its significance abound in biblical and metaphysical texts and as astrologers we recognize the importance of 7 as the number of planets known to the ancients. These were seen as controlling or containing all human affairs and destiny, and this observation was in part reinforced by the seemingly bizarre quotient which results from dividing 'all' (1) by 7 itself. The result, .142857 recurring, has given mathematicians a field day ever since its properties were first discovered thousands of years ago.

For example, each multiplication of that number 142857 by any number from 1 to 6 will produce a number that contains all the same figures in different sequences. Split it into 142 and 857, add the two parts and you get 999. Multiply 142857 by 7 and the result is 999,999. The sequential and cyclic nature of the many permutations of the number 7 have absorbed mathematicians for centuries. Several books and many articles have been written over the years in an attempt to explore these unique patterns and symmetries. Suffice it to say that the image of 7 as a spiritual number with an ability to transcend the commonplace, encompass the whole and mystify us all with its complexity can be borne out by some of the finest mathematical minds the world has seen. In one of his earliest studies John Addey amply demonstrated its place in the spiritual scheme of things with his pioneering research into the fundamental principles underlying astrological phenomena. Using data originally gathered for use as ammunition in the tropical/sidereal argument he showed convincingly that the solar positions of 4,465 clergymen when plotted out in either zodiac showed no inclination to back east or west in the dispute. Instead they displayed a significant 7th harmonic wave-form (see Figure 13.1). Further analysis revealed a second sevenfold wave within each seventh division (the 49th harmonic) reinforcing the image of 7 as the literal prime number of spiritual endeavour, while its sub-harmonics unravelled this same message into increasingly fine threads.

The number 7 has some baffling properties, and when we begin to approach it we must be prepared to recognize that we are dealing with an extremely complex idea which has the potential to both inspire and ensnare. The numinous and the brutal can coincide as enjoyment (3) and matter (4) come together and seek expression in the world as the septile, an aspect that has been re-discovered in recent years as a pattern of major importance in chart interpretation.

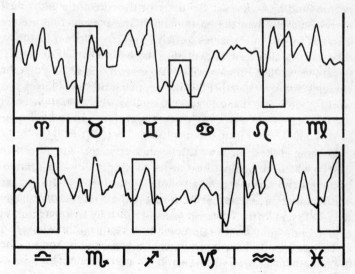

Figure 13.1 The distribution of the solar positions in the charts of 4,465 clergymen show a marked 7th harmonic pattern. For further information see Addey's *Harmonics in Astrology*.

In *Harmonics in Astrology* John Addey does not say a lot about the 7th harmonic in individual charts, but stresses its essentially spiritual and mystical nature. He sees it as having the capacity to bring together seemingly disparate images, to unify and to unite, creating within the individual a receptivity towards inspiration. The importance of the 28th harmonic (4 × 7) for showing the manifestation of this inspiration in the world is noted and David Hamblin has provided many examples of composers with powerful 28th harmonic charts – this is indeed the case with many great creative artists in other fields, as we shall see in Chapters 18 and 19. Hamblin himself sees the 7th as bringing a *romantic* link to planets, making this a powerfully emotional contact with great creative potential. Creativity grows out of the individual's *need* to express this aspect in everyday life. The images created by this contact are seen to inspire and 'turn on' the native, for they are a product of his 'wild, fertile and unpredictable imagination'.[1]

Terry Dwyer sees the 7th as a key chart for understanding the 'ultimate person';[2] it provides an image of the 'spiritually mature person' and he believes it can describe the core of the individual more concisely than the basic natal chart. Inasmuch as we are inspired by our unconscious to strive towards spiritual maturity, this chart is also seen as depicting those ideas which do indeed inspire us. Robert Hand echoes this picture by suggesting that the energies brought together by the septile series are 'not of this world', but warns that an excess of such aspects within the chart can correlate with 'a lack of connection with the physical universe as we know it'.[3]

Looking at these ideas we can begin to construct a picture of an aspect which embodies the images of spirituality, inspiration, profound emotional meaning coupled with the ability to engage our imagination and turn us on. It is perhaps in this latter capacity that we first meet the 7th harmonic and here may be a good time to explore more fully some of the possible mechanisms of fantasy.

To the depth psychologist 'fantasy' does not mean day-dreaming. It does not mean imagining that you win the lottery, have thrilling romantic encounters or get to tell the boss exactly what he can do with his job. Strangely enough, the technical term for such interior imaginings is called 'wishful thinking'. Fantasy is something quite different. It is to a large part unknown to us and describes the *unconscious* imagination which underlies our thoughts, feelings and actions. As such it has a lot to do with the way in which we *believe* the world to be. In this respect it has the potential for being absolutely correct and hopelessly inaccurate at one and the same time. If this sounds confusing then a simple example should clarify things.

Take the well-known case of the Self-Made Man. Typically, he was one of several children brought up strictly in a poor (but honest) home. When telling you about himself he is likely to stress the point that there were not enough shoes to go round, that cold potato was a luxury and that he never had clothes that were not hand-me-downs until he got his first job. The work ethic was firmly instilled and consequently over the years he has become rich and successful. But the internal fantasy he has of life has not changed. No matter how many companies he owns, how many Rolls Royces dot his various driveways, in his heart of hearts he *genuinely* believes that he is still poor and that the rent man is about to come knocking on the door for money that isn't there.

His colleagues may secretly laugh at the fact that their boss saves string, insists that envelopes are used twice, only orders the cheapest meals while entertaining and haggles over ridiculously small amounts when closing a deal. But his identification with harsh early experiences has made him wealthy and the reality of that vision is greater than his perception of what he actually *has*. The world around him continues to be obscured by a cold fog of poverty and he simply *cannot* see what is in front of his eyes. Furthermore, as it is the *fantasy* that he is poor which has contributed so much towards his success, he has a vested interest in maintaining it. At some unconscious level he may fear that by accepting that he is rich he may actually remove his motivation and pull the rug from under his own feet! What had the potential for motivating and inspiring has instead become much like a drug, numbing him to the reality of his existence and sapping his true potential.

Another person, brought up in luxury, will probably have a belief system in which the world is a wonderful place where any problem can be solved with a little money and anything extra can be obtained with slightly more. Such a fantasy would be, for *him*, totally correct. From his inner perspective, the world *is* that way, no matter that a more objective observer could point to untold areas of abject poverty and human degradation.

Similarly, the child who experiences itself as being unwanted and unloved will probably act out, as an adult, whatever fantasies coalesced during the formative years. The world is still seen as cold and rejecting, affection is still regarded with deep distrust and once again fantasy reinforces itself as – inevitably – potential friends and lovers get fed up with being given the cold shoulder and unwittingly collude with the fantasy of rejection by committing yet another act of abandonment. The truth of the 7th harmonic chart is the truth of an *inner reality*, which may or may not get to become imposed upon the world, depending on its nature and the circumstances of life. The strength of this inner reality reminds us again that people *see the world very differently indeed*. We are always inspired by our truth, not our lies, pursuing it in much the same manner as countries that only go to war for 'just causes'. Later analysis may finally convince us that what we held to be true was in fact quite ludicrous, but this is *later*. How we see and experience the world, what we feel and fantasize about it is our truth and remains so until we see our own inner landscape from a changed perspective.

While it may be hard for us to recognize our world-view by introspection – this amalgam of beliefs, inspirations and yearnings does not yield easily to intellectual analysis – we *can* see how we are paradoxically drawn to it in life time and time again through the process of our own projections. Just as our hypothetical Self-Made Man projected his inner image of poverty on to the world until it obliterated the reality of his wealth, so we all project our wishes and beliefs on to the people, organizations and art that surrounds us. Our capacity to project our unconscious on to visual representations has long been known to psychologists, and forms the basis of tests such as the Rorschach ink blots and the various sets of Thematic Apperception cards. Certain outer images seem to resonate within us and cause our immediate identification – or disgust! For projections classically take two very different forms.

The mother who always wanted to be a dancer and now thrusts

her young daughter into ballet school will probably readily acknowledge her projections. Her daughter is, in part, herself and acting out her mother's unfulfilled ambitions. All her daughter's imagined future successes are her mother's lost chances. To what extent this will be harmful to her daughter will depend on how well her mother recognizes what she is doing and – most importantly – whether the little girl actually wants to dance in the first place! What is happening here is Projective Identification – the mother projects her desire to be a dancer on to her daughter while consciously recognizing her own yearnings for stardom. This conscious recognition may not be the case where the projections do not deal with the comparatively refined world of the classical ballet. More often than not, projections are accompanied by denial.

Instead of recognizing a particular desire as being projected, it is more common that this fact is ignored. We do not like to recognize all of our drives and wishes, but they may be too strong to ignore, so 'someone else' has them for us. This is more convenient and avoids the onerous task of doing something about it. Internalized conflicts with introjected parental figures – that is, Saturnine images we have absorbed or been made to learn – can often become projected on to all forms of social authority and everything becomes 'their fault' – again temporarily getting us off the psychic hook and making the world all too easy to blame.

Problems with sexuality and repressed anger can become projected, for instance, on to suitably repressed minority groups who, growing weary of being repressed, finally get to act it out! Never let it be said that fantasy is all in the mind; it is on the streets with the litter and the garbage. It hangs on the walls of art galleries, it fuels the whole of the entertainment industry, it emerges from the mouths of 'rent-a-quote' politicians and through the vapid witterings of television personalities. People who have so little personality of their own that they seem able to exist only through the courtesy of others. Media heroes made in reality from fragments of a myriad housewives who sit and dream. Sportsmen whose exploits on the field deny the tired weight of emerging beer-guts and the growing impotence of their middle-aged fans on the terraces. Should these heroes ever stumble on their way through life, should they ever reveal a predilection for young boys or exotic chemicals, then the true nature of the projections is revealed and they are devoured by their followers as surely as any fallen tribal chief. The projection is absorbed and taken back, and in a very literal sense the former worshippers can feel 'personally betrayed'. They have been; only they did it themselves by denying the truth of their own dreams. Through fear, ignorance or doubt they allowed others to act out their own desires while they sat and watched; voyeurs of their own internal geometry.

When someone is profoundly moved, inspired, turned-on, excited, absorbed, captivated or besotted with some image or ideal then the mechanism of this inner fantasy is probably at work and projections are actively engaged. This is the circle of the 7th harmonic, where the base and the numinous can merge; where the noble cause, the highest ideal and the darkest longing are a septile apart. As astrologers we must approach this chart with respect and caution, and be prepared to acknowledge all the riches it contains; for here we are truly walking with dreams of others.

THE 7TH HARMONIC IN ACTION

Perhaps the most useful way to begin our examination of this number is to look more closely at our ability to project our personal experience of its meaning on to the world. Just as the psychologist can examine this process through interpreting how a series of Rorschach patterns are described, so we can get our first glimpse of what the 7th harmonic means for an individual by that person's taste in art. What inspires or captivates the soul can strikingly reflect the planetary patterns within the native's 7th harmonic chart. The same can be true, by the way, in the native's choice of heroes and heroines. Here the inner pattern is unconsciously projected on to suitable character-types whose behaviour mirrors to some degree the symbolic content of the aspect structure; a process which can create a highly personal mythology. One astrologer, looking at her 7th harmonic chart for the first time, suddenly recognized that its close Sun, Uranus, Pluto T-square exactly fitted a heroine of hers, Marie Stopes, whose revolutionary approach towards social reform through birth control and the liberation of women could scarcely be better described.

In an attempt to explore further this facet of the 7th harmonic, art students at several colleges were requested to give a short description of a painting for which they felt an immediate affinity. The painting was not necessarily to be 'great art', the only requirement was that it should have a real appeal for the subject. Birth data was also requested and only those replies which contained an actual birth time were proceeded with. The reason art students were chosen for the experiment was the assumption that they would have been exposed to a greater variety of works of art and would thus be more likely to have had the opportunity to find a

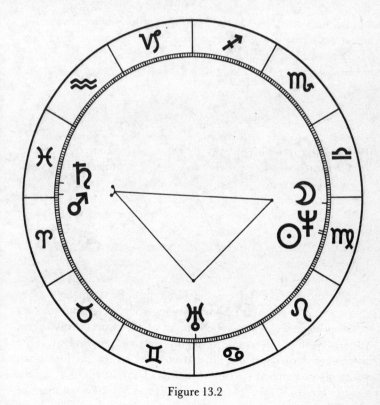

Figure 13.2

pictorial 'soul mate'. As it turned out, one of the first who responded admitted an affinity with a picture in his local pub and thus amply demonstrated that beauty is not just in the eye of the beholder, but also lies wherever that eye might happen to fall!

Figure 13.2 is the 7th harmonic in question, which contains a powerful Mars/Saturn conjunction in opposition to the Moon and both square to Uranus, with a disconnected Sun/Neptune in very close conjunction. Its owner describes his favourite painting as being '. . . a picture in our local pub of an old movie actor' (there's Mars/Saturn and Sun/Neptune in one go!) '. . . I like it because it has amazing bright, vivid colours' (Mars/Moon/Uranus T-square). 'The expression is weird' (that T-square again; to be inspired or turned on by the unusual). 'There's a very abstract

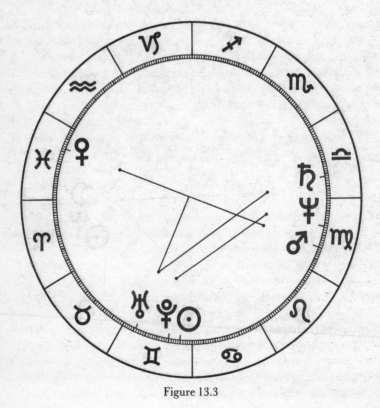

Figure 13.3

backdrop of breaking waves and he's wearing a top hat and scarf. It's a mixture of unrelated themes combined with a feeling of hallucinogenic alertness and immediacy.' The attraction of the different themes, the conservative (Mars/Saturn) old man in an old-fashioned top hat, the breaking waves and references to hallucinogenics in a pub (Sun/Neptune) and the overall attractiveness of disconnected images (the major T-square) are clearly spelled out in this chart in very simple, basic astrology.

Figure 13.3 describes the choice of another student '. . . a very large painting with washes of intense colour rubbed into the canvas. Deep reds and blacks. Emerging rectangles form shapes suggestive to me of windows and surrounded by the paintings allows me to look 'out' into the colour and be enclosed within it. Deep and moving. I would like to own a series of these paintings in different rooms to enter appropriately depending on how I was feeling.'

The obvious enjoyment of the rich, red and luxurious quality of the paintings referred to (Mark Rothko's, in fact), coupled with the desire to be enclosed or surrounded by them, strongly suggests the symbolism of the Sun/Pluto conjunction, square to Neptune. Being inspired by the image of 'losing the self' in some way is classic of a solar contact to these two planets and the obviously implied fantasy of wealth – being able to have a house-full of them, each for different moods – is another facet of the same contact. The physical quality of the shapes themselves ('colour rubbed into the canvas') is suggestive of the Saturn trine Uranus; the traditional and the modern coming together to produce a classic, simple rectangular shape. Where Saturn comes into the picture in the 7th harmonic there is often an emphasis on simple craft or the classical skills of the traditional artist. Someone able to work with his hands and express the fruits of experience with sure confidence.

Figure 13.4 with its Mercury conjunct Saturn describes a similar affinity '. . . the figure of the woman is classically perfect and beautiful and shows simple, subtle emotions. After looking at the picture in depth the figure is full of drama' (Moon trine Pluto!) 'showing a strong mix of different emotions . . . the setting and costume of the woman is rich, luxurious and dramatically stylized.' If a triple conjunction of Sun, Uranus and Pluto in the 7th doesn't

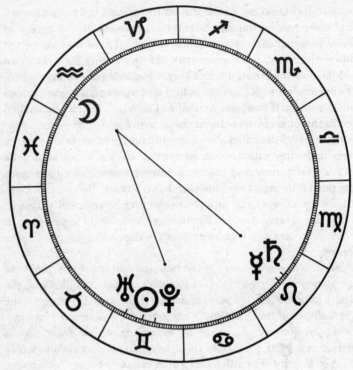

Figure 13.4

provoke a desire for rich drama in a highly stylized manner then little else could! The writer continues '. . . I would like to own this painting because of its strong atmosphere of beauty and luxury and also it would not become uninteresting.' The implication here is that the student might get easily bored with an ordinary scene, again just what one would expect from a Sun/Uranus contact here – needing some constant form of stimulation or being unable to accept the ordinary for long. The use of the word 'luxury' echoes the feelings expressed in connection with Figure 13.3 and emphasizes their similar Sun/Pluto conjunctions.

Another strongly Pluto chart is Figure 13.5, but it is the Mercury/Ascendant and Mars/Uranus which are first described. 'What I like is the quality of the line, which is scratchy, rough and instant – what people describe as naive children's drawings, but I find these words offensive.' A Mars/Uranus in the 7th harmonic *would* be turned on by the instant action and a Mercury/Ascendant *would* empathize with children. The two feelings are brought together by the writer as clearly as the aspects on the chart. Now the Jupiter/Pluto comes in: 'From these paintings I gain strength. I am not alone. They have power, I am pulled in, head over heels, feeling it in my stomach.' Again, as in Figure 13.3, the Pluto contact is expressed as provoking the desire to be swallowed up into something larger, some greater emotional experience. The word 'power' also crops up again. The writer is clearly inspired by the powerful; well, he would be, wouldn't he?

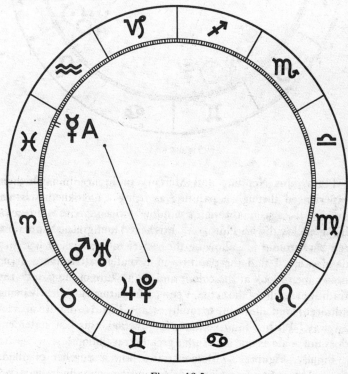

Figure 13.5

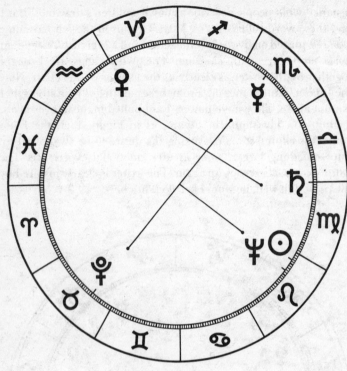

Figure 13.6

Pluto joins Neptune and Mercury in Figure 13.6 which is experienced through a painting as being '. . . immediately seductive . . . a scene through a window' (once more that image of being enclosed with Pluto) '. . . bright red and green shapes on a red background . . . allowing the viewer to form his or her own daydreams. I find the painting immediately attractive . . . [it] draws me to look at the colour and the texture of the paint' (the traditional skills of the artist, Venus trine Saturn, are clearly being admired) 'and allows me to totally escape. I tend to daydream a lot anyway.' With a Sun/Neptune conjunction, this last statement does not come as one of nature's greatest revelations!

Finally, Figure 13.7 demonstrates how a number of major themes identified in a Caravaggio painting echo the basic struc-

tures of the observer's 7th harmonic chart. Two powerful oppositions, Mars to Jupiter and Venus to Neptune, cut across the
chart. Pluto is brought into the pattern by T-square and Mercury
joins a Saturn/Uranus conjunction by square. Looking at this one
would expect issues of sexuality and energy (Mars/Jupiter), art
and beauty in some powerful form (Venus, Neptune, Pluto) and
the original use of traditional images (Mercury to Saturn/Uranus)
to dominate. These are the images which could be expected to
inspire and illuminate the native and propel her to identify with
their expression in the world. The very title of the painting chosen
is appropriate: *Profane Love*. The T-square of Venus to Neptune
and Pluto is neatly summed up. Although, as we shall see, there is
an interesting slip here.

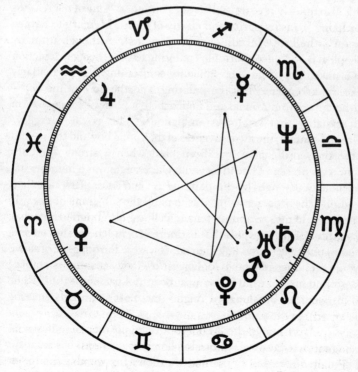

Figure 13.7

The student has called the painting *Profane Love*, though this is not the correct title. The painting depicts an Amor, or cupid figure, and is actually called *Amor Victorious* – implying the victory of love. This, of course, is spot-on for the Mars/Jupiter opposition, especially as the painting makes it clear that the love in question is temporal rather than divine. Just how well the student was able to tune into or resonate with the underlying image of the painting is indicated by the art historian Giorgio Bonsanti: '. . . One is bewildered by this painting, by the absolute freedom that the subject actually enjoys.'[4] Which is, of course, Mars/Jupiter to the last letter!

While the image of freedom is clearly a major source of inspiration for the student, there is much more going on in her 7th harmonic chart than just the opposition of Mars and Jupiter, and this also quickly reveals itself as she continues: 'One of my reasons for liking [it] is its purity and clarity of form' (Mercury to Saturn again – the love of traditional proportions). 'Although to many people it is an "uncomfortable" painting to view, being a depiction of a naked boy, I have no difficulty confronting it. I particularly like the arrangement of the painting, and the pose of the boy – although confrontational and unabashed, it possesses a naive form of sexuality that is almost ambiguous.' This is the Mercury/Uranus contact, the attractiveness of the young boy and the second time the word 'naive' has been used when a strong Mercury contact is present. 'The theory that Caravaggio was a homosexual is lent a lot of weight by this painting . . . and if this is the case then I admire the artist for being able to paint the subject as he does. It possesses, to me, an almost defiant feeling – an "I don't care what they think of me" attitude that I admire very much. It is unconventional, unabashed and unashamed. If it were the opposite of this I would feel uncomfortable looking at it – coy sexuality is embarrassing to me . . . what is the most beautiful passage – the feather of his wing tip brushing his thigh – the most stunningly sensual movement in the painting.'

Not surprisingly, the Mars/Jupiter opposition manifests as being attracted towards direct and honest expressions of sexuality. The tone of the description clearly shows the writer's desire for forthright expression in all things physical. She admires Caravaggio's honesty for painting a cupid in an unashamedly erotic pose and implies that it might be partly due to Caravaggio's supposed homosexuality. If so, then this expression of the artist's decision to confront the world with his sexuality is applauded for its directness, as one would expect from a Mars/Jupiter opposition. The sexual ambiguity of the cupid is also commented upon. Uranus trine Venus and square Mercury could indicate the writer's preoccupation with this image; finding inspiration in all that was young, beautiful and unusual.

This, of course, begs the question as to what extent sexual orientation can be deduced from the chart. Lee Lehman and others in America have undertaken a number of research projects in this area, with mixed results. It would seem unlikely that any one, simple factor would give the answer here; indeed the results of virtually all research in all areas of astrology suggest that simplistic solutions will not be found. As far as the 7th harmonic is concerned, what one may be able to derive from it is an *image* of what may be attractive, and obviously sexual relationships are one area in which the attractive is sought. In Chapter 18, which is a case study of the writer James Joyce, we can look more closely at how *his* 7th harmonic certainly reflects his sexual preoccupations and we shall see in a moment how this is also true for another well-known writer, but it would be wrong to generalize at this point.

Figure 13.8 is that of a woman who had a history of relationships with physically violent men, in which alcohol sometimes played a part. The Mars/Saturn opposition *can* be expressed as seeking some form of sexual confrontation. The clash with authority, so often a feature of Mars/Saturn contacts, does have a tinge of sado-masochism about it, especially if the 'authority' sought is known to be violent. The opposition itself would suggest a striving to bring form to the libido, to make practical use of energy, to be a workaholic perhaps, and to be inspired by decisive action. In Part One the Mars/Saturn contact was discussed at some length and the 'killer-instinct' quality it can have was noted; the ability to act swiftly and decisively. It also connects with the image of the sculptor, chipping away at stone and its association with hard work and crafts in general is strong. The woman in question was a potter for part of her life and expressed a liking for the knives and

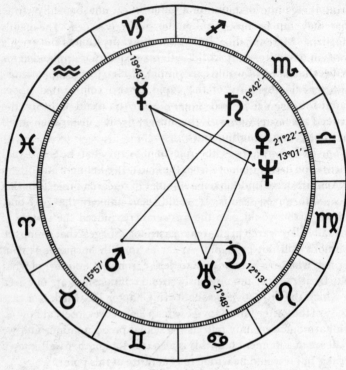

Figure 13.8

tools in her father's workshop, admiring their simplicity and usefulness.

The problems in the chart are not so much the Mars/Saturn itself, but the same Mercury/Venus/Uranus contacts noted in the chart of the student who admired Caravaggio, together with the Mars square Moon. The probable need for different and unusual relationships, being turned on by the unconventional, coupled with the possible expression of the Moon/Mars as a need for constant emotional stimulation and a tendency towards impulsive action, can lead to problematic relationships for anyone. The addition of the Mars/Saturn could then suggest a tendency to choose some authoritarian figure who may provoke these reactions. This, of course, is the opposition at work; the strong need to bring things into manifestation, to get them out into the open so that they can be brought together and reconciled. The highly idealizing Mercury square Neptune always runs a risk of further confusing issues, and the whole chart suggests such contradictory drives that *all* relationships are probably going to be difficult until sufficient life experience has been absorbed to allow the woman better to recognize her true inner needs. As it happened, she later worked in a hostel for battered women and took a very active role in an alternative feminist commune – being inspired to work with women who are angry as the result of physical abuse by brutal men is almost a description of this chart in shorthand.

As with any other chart, the energies brought together in the 7th harmonic can operate on a number of levels, and this can clearly be

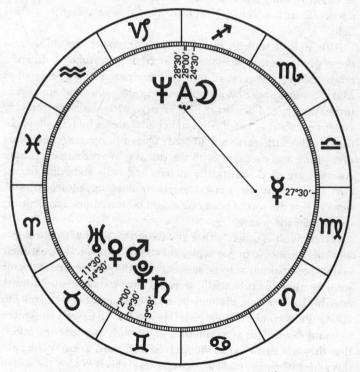

Figure 13.9 The 7th harmonic chart of Lewis Carroll.

seen in the 7th harmonic chart for Lewis Carroll (Figure 13.9), the author of *Alice in Wonderland*. At the first level the Moon/Neptune/ Ascendant describes his religious beliefs – he was a priest by calling. Obviously the same conjunction indicates a love of fantasy, art and imagination; exactly the sort of daydreams that might have gone into producing the images in his two famous books. In them, references to hallucinogenic drugs abound – yet a further mani- festation of strong Neptune contacts. He wrote about a little girl (the same Neptune/Moon, now square to Mercury) – a very active little girl who liked riddles and word-plays; another classic Moon/ Mercury contact. He was a lover of photography; one more direct hit for Neptune's artistic inspiration! But it is here that the chart takes a different turn. He particularly liked photographing young, naked girls. Now one starts to look at the rest of this chart, and in particular at the Venus/Uranus conjunction in a slightly altered light.

Although there is no record of any impropriety resulting from these photographic sessions, the need for unusual or different relationships is suggested, and the very powerful conjunction of Mars, Saturn and Pluto amplifies an ambiguous and somewhat brutal message. Their trine to Mercury partly describes the very violent events that befell Alice in her adventures underground. In the bowels of the earth a mad (red) Queen rampages, controlling everything and everyone with the threat of immediate execution. Animals are used sadistically as bats and balls and Alice herself goes through a variety of extremely unpleasant physical contor- tions in just the sort of book one would *not* recommend as bedtime reading for the young!

Candidly, it is unlikely that any parent familiar with astrology, and this harmonic in particular, would be happy to entrust their young ones to photographic sessions with the good reverend doctor were he alive today. In fact, were he alive today he would quite possibly be in prison; his interest in children did not extend only to taking photographs of nude girls. He was known to send penknives to young boys of his acquaintance suggesting, in a covering letter, that they use them to cut themselves, and learn to enjoy the pain this activity brings . . . At an extreme level this is exactly the sort of fantasy a Mars/Saturn/Pluto conjunction in the 7th harmonic can induce, but there are alternatives. Indeed Lewis Carroll was obviously expressing this energy in creating the dark world of Wonderland, and that it should have proved to be such an enduring country is equally symbolic of the energies which fuelled its creation.

Not only fictional countries can be created. Mao Tse-tung's 7th harmonic chart (Figure 13.10) reveals his fantasy of becoming a revolutionary leader and political reformer which led to the actual total reconstruction of the world's largest and most populated country. If Mao's ☉/☽ axis (see pp. 62–5) told us a great deal about his capacity for the ruthless regeneration and transformation of the base, ugly, and inordinate in his homeland, his 7H depicts the guiding fantasies that carried him forward in this

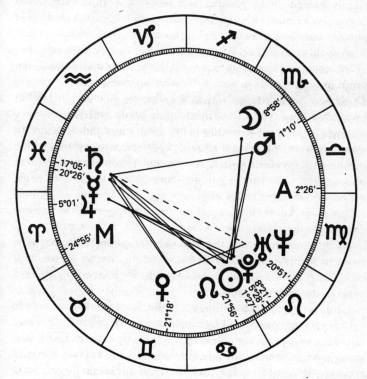

Figure 13.10 The 7th harmonic chart of Mao Tse-tung.

endeavour. Here in his 7H we see a formidable triple conjunction of ☉–0–♇–0–♅ in close –120–♃ and –90– ♂–☽. ♄ weighs into this pattern with its double –135– with ☉ and ♂.

If the time as given is taken as exact, the ☉–♅ is –60– AS and ♃ opposed it. In addition to this closely integrated picture we may note that the ♄ is in close –0–☿, –120–☊, –90–♀ and –150–♆. What is that about? As we noted in Chapter 4, Mao was a poet and philosopher and someone who was 'astonishingly meticulous about details of duty', but the *Encyclopaedia Britannica* entry on Mao tells us specifically that he was 'inspired by reading China's history and the romances of heroes and brigands'. The heroes and brigands of Chinese history were certainly of a ☉–♅–♇ –120–♃ disposition and 'reading history' is certainly ☿–♄, but Mao was clearly turned on by reading and study to a quite exceptional degree. As a result, although he was from a poor peasant family, his parents somehow managed to borrow money from friends so that Mao could go to school. While the other peasant children were out in the fields working from dawn till dusk, Mao would spend the same time propped up with a book in intense study. Later, the *Encyclopaedia* tells us, 'he was to spend every moment in Hunan provincial library at Changsha reading books and newspapers', studying to become a revolutionary leader and politician. Mao was, as it were, following a sustained pattern of inspiration which combined the violent radical revolutionary with the student and philosopher. Could these guiding fantasies and inspiration of his life be shown more graphically?

But as we know, inspiration does not simply take the form of dominant guiding fantasies. As we have seen, to those so disposed by their harmonic tuning, inspiration is something which seems to strike suddenly, unasked, from outside of the normal processes of consciousness, lifting the mind into extraordinary insights and penetrating understanding.

John Addey commented that '. . . the charts of creative people very often seem devoid of anything noteworthy unless the 5th and 7th series of aspects are observed'.[5] Creativity can obviously take many forms; the very attitude of mind (5H) towards a particular task can elevate it from the banal to the divine, as many Zen texts remind us. Yet inspiration is not always about poetry and music;

it is also about mathematics, chemical structures, computer algorithms, better mousetraps and quantum mechanics.

In a classic study by Nick Kollerstrom and Mike O'Neill[6] of the charts of scientists and inventors whose discoveries arrived in a flash of inspiration, they noted that in the charts of fourteen major scientists, from Brahe and Galileo to Einstein and Watson, an excess of septiles abound. Indeed there are 45% more septiles and 30% more quintiles than chance allows. Furthermore, in the charts for eighteen moments of major scientific discoveries – which the researchers named *Eureka Moments* – the excess of septiles over chance was 50%!

If we take the case of Alexander Fleming and his discovery of penicillin, we notice some striking examples of how 7th harmonic transits on the day of discovery are telling us something extremely important about the different phases of planetary cycles. Seen in this light, we are reminded that we should no longer look at transits as 'events which just happen' but as resonant points in an expanding arc of possibilities.

Figure 13.11 shows the relationship between transiting planets and radical planets on the day Fleming realized that certain bacteria had the potential to destroy infectious organisms. We notice at once that Fleming was born some weeks before a Saturn/Neptune conjunction – two planets which together often relate to work with hospitals – and closer inspection would reveal that Neptune is on the Sun/Moon midpoint. As is so often the case with people born close to a major conjunction, the various phases of the cycle between those planets can mark important turning points in their lives. One thinks here of John Lennon, who was born and died within days of a Jupiter/Saturn conjunction.

In Fleming's case his own 7th harmonic patterns clearly resonate with the septile phases of the transiting bodies. On the day of his discovery the Sun was 1/7th from his Ascendant and Uranus 2/7th from it – and thus obviously triseptile to each other. Saturn was 3/7th from Neptune while transiting Neptune was 2/7th from its radical position – putting the two transiting bodies 2/7th apart. The node was septile Mercury and the Moon septile the south node – and all these aspects are under one degree in orb!

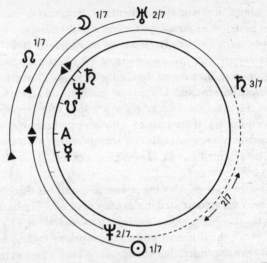

Figure 13.11 7th harmonic transits to the chart of Alexander Fleming for the discovery of penicillin. Only those factors in Fleming's chart that are receiving transits have been included, for the sake of clarity. Note how the Sun and Uranus and Saturn and Neptune are *also* forming 7th harmonic patterns to each other, making this a day of powerful septile energy.

A 7th harmonic graphic ephemeris (Figure 13.12) shows this at once – though it does not include the transiting Moon for reasons of clarity – and points to this as a time of major importance for someone open to the possibility of being inspired by the principles of Saturn and Neptune – such as a medical researcher! That the inspiration came suddenly and 'by accident' is implicit in the Sun/Uranus contact to the Ascendant.

With such a powerful 7th harmonic pattern in the sky for the moment of discovery on 3 September 1928, it is very interesting to note what else was going on around the world at that time. The *Daily Telegraph* informs us that on 1 September the League of Nations was setting up a special commission to investigate the problems of world-wide drug trafficking. In Belfast the White Star Line, perhaps hoping no one would remember the *Titanic*, announced the laying-down of the keel for the world's largest ocean liner at Harland & Woolf's shipyard. On 4 September the TUC

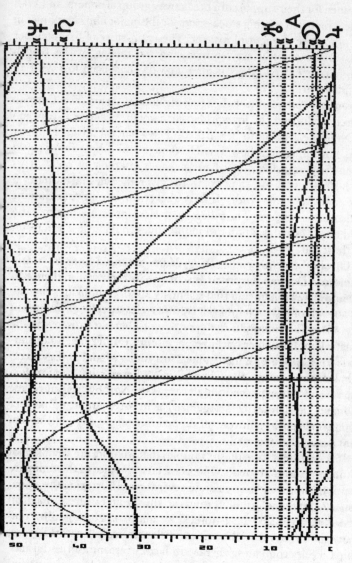

Figure 13.12 The discovery of penicillin as seen on a 7th harmonic graphic ephemeris.

played Saturn by expelling the Neptune-ruled National Union of Seamen for their support of a breakaway group of miners, and Wall Street reported soaring stock prices for the major film companies in an otherwise uneventful market. The main story of 6 September was of a memorial service following the raising of the British submarine *L55* two days before. The *L55* had been lost with all hands in 1919.

On 8 September the League of Nations heard the German Foreign Minister call for world disarmament – a classic expression of Neptune seeking to be earthed. The French Foreign Minister was not impressed, however. He thought the whole thing was a sham and said Germany had 'a whole reservoir of men' at its disposal – a very apt choice of words given the celestial patterns at the time. In Simla, India, a huge racket concerning fake quinine pills was uncovered. The pills were useless for combating malaria and a spokesman said up to 4 million lives could be lost as a result of the fraud.

On 12 September the *Daily Mirror* reported that a certain Professor Donnan surprised his British Association audience in Glasgow by announcing that scientists might be able to create life as a result of research into cell culture – clearly cell culture was in the air at the time! On the very day of Fleming's discovery the Australian Parliament rejected a motion calling for American-style Prohibition by a handsome 2 to 1 majority and an Egyptian, Ishak Helmy, swam the Channel in 23 hours and 40 minutes – the second longest time it had ever taken. Not to miss out on the moment, Welsh farmers organized a massive round-up of over 250,000 sheep which were all dipped in a single day! The sheep, that is, not the farmers.

It is very clear from these examples that what we are seeing is not a random series of events. The planetary energies of the times are coming across loud and clear, in several cases mirroring the actual aspects for good or ill. Fraud in the drug business, medical research, organized drug-trafficking, control of alcohol, film company shares, sunken submarines, misleading calls for world peace, ships' keels, combating disease in farm livestock and endurance swimming are all basic Saturn/Neptune issues. Such moments and discoveries are not random, isolated events, as Kollerstrom and

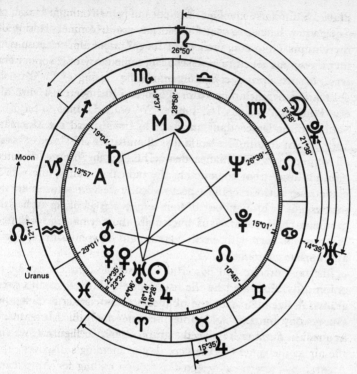

Figure 13.13 The discovery of DNA. Only the septile aspects in Watson's chart have been included. Note the equivalent of a 'grand cross' and the multiplicity of septile aspects by transit.

O'Neill's research amply demonstrates. They are clear indications that the various phases of planetary cycles bring with them distinctive and recognizable manifestations at all levels of life, from the trivial to the tragic.

Another typical case demonstrating the significance of the 7th harmonic is that of James Watson (Figure 13.13), the co-discoverer of DNA. Watson has some striking septile aspects, including the equivalent of a Grand Cross, which ties in the Moon to Saturn, Pluto and Uranus. Ebertin associates such Saturn/Pluto contacts with the image of the dedicated researcher, here *inspired* by the prospect of such labour. It is also pertinent that Uranus and

Pluto are similarly involved. The idea of 'genetic engineering', of using a new science to transform society is one likely expression of the Uranus/Pluto conjunctions of 1966/7. Here we see those two themes coming together in the chart of someone whose work could result in such a prospect coming into being.

Transiting septile aspects also abound for the moment of discovery. Pluto to Watson's IC, Jupiter to Venus, Uranus to Saturn, Saturn to the Descendant, the node to Uranus and the Moon to both Saturn and the Descendant – all multiples of 51° 25' 42" and all with orbs of less than a degree! Transiting Uranus is only minutes away from conjuncting the radical Pluto. As these two planets are in close septile aspect radically we have some image of what might be brought out at their conjunction; looking at the 7th harmonic chart would tell us much more about 'what kind of Pluto' Watson was born with, hence what might come to fruition at an appropriate conjunction.

Just how precise and powerful such septile contacts can be is graphically illustrated by the use of one of Mike O'Neill's programs, designed to plot the abundance and strength of septile aspects day by day. As septiles become closer in orb or more frequent in number, so does the graph climb. In Figure 13.14 we

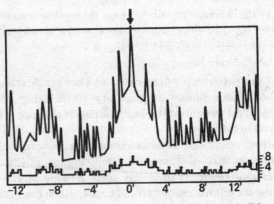

Figure 13.14 Mike O'Neill's 'harmogram', showing the build up of 7th harmonic aspects in the twenty-four days surrounding the discovery of penicillin. The discovery took place at the moment of greatest intensity.

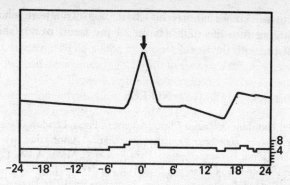

Figure 13.15 The discovery of the laser. A harmogram covering forty-eight hours shows how the discovery arrived at the moment of maximum septile activity.

see the period around the moment for the discovery of penicillin. The arrow marks the day of discovery – at the very peak of the graph! Similarly in Figure 13.15 the moment for the invention of the laser occurs at the day of maximum septile intensity.

The inspirational and motivating dynamic of the 7th harmonic is a powerful one indeed; its importance must be recognized and its message integrated into the daily work of all counselling astrologers. Clients with strong 7th harmonic patterns must be put in touch *sensitively* with the energy latent in that particular wavelength. To be conscious of its potential and to be able to utilize it is to accept the responsibility for ourselves in the same spirit as that which led to Freud's famous dictum *where Id was, there shall Ego be*.

Without striving to achieve such a personal awareness of the 7th harmonic we risk experiencing only its capacity to take over or temporarily control us through the mechanisms we have already discussed. There is little doubt that this is the factor that has given the more traditional meaning of *fated* to the septile series, and with some good reason. If we do not make an effort to come to terms with, and express *creatively*, what is in our 7th harmonic chart then we risk its operating without our conscious awareness and enmeshing us in needlessly complex situations as we act out the planetary archetypes without recognizing what they are really trying to say. If we ignore this chart, then we ignore what we are bringing into life each day in all the facets of our shifting relationship with the world.

NOTES

1. David Hamblin, *Harmonic Charts*, Aquarian Press, London, 1983.
2. Terry Dwyer, *Harmonics Newsletter*, Astrological Association.
3. Robert Hand, *Horoscope Symbols*, Para Research, Mass., USA, 1981.
4. Giorgio Bonsanti, *Caravaggio*, Frederick Muller, 1984, p. 44.
5. John Addey, *Harmonics in Astrology*, L. N. Fowler, 1976; Urania Trust, 1990.
6. Nick Kollerstrom and Mike O'Neill, *The Eureka Effect*, privately published, 1988, by the Urania Trust.

CHAPTER 14

The 9th Harmonic

CHARLES HARVEY

By a life in conformity with the Ideal a light as from a fire is enkindled in the Soul and there itself nourishes itself (Plato).

The world is not painted or adorned, but is from the beginning beautiful, and God has not made some beautiful things, but Beauty is the creator of the universe (Ralph Waldo Emerson).

Every being entering into the ineffable sanctuary of its own nature, finds there a symbol of the Father of all (Proclus, *Theology of Plato*).

By the spreading of his simple essence, the Master useful vessels makes, which with wise administration bless all beings impartially (*Tao Te King*).

Joy could be defined as the manifest sign that we are fulfilling our ideal purpose . . . (Piero Ferrucci).

Be here Now.

Follow your bliss.

The above quotations are an attempt to evoke some of the essential qualities of the number 9 and the ideas which are embodied in the 9th harmonic.

Of all the charts we can study the 9th harmonic can undoubtedly give us some of the most profound insights into the essence of a moment. Yet what it has to reveal to us is an aspect of life and of the psyche which the Western mind finds it difficult to recognize and articulate. While the implications and significance of the 4H, 5H and 7H charts can be readily seen once we have grasped the meanings of the numbers involved, the 9H is more elusive. This is apparent from the seeming contradictions in the literature on the subject of the 9th harmonic and the relative lack of discussion of it by Western astrologers, as compared to the ubiquitous use of the 9th, the Navamsa chart in Hindu astrology.

The Navamsa chart, which is geometrically identical to the 9H, is considered in the Hindu tradition to reveal the fruits of the radical chart. Addey shows us that 'fruits' here represent 'the fruit of the pursuit of particular ideals'. He suggests that the 9th harmonic represents 'the ideal to be realized'. Hamblin does not wholly accept Addey's ideas and points out that the ideal or purpose towards which a person is striving, and the products of his life's work, are often more clearly seen in one of the other harmonic charts. He suggests that the key idea of the 9th harmonic revolves around the idea of joy, happiness and that peace which comes from accepting one's place in the scheme of the cosmos.

Hamblin brings out the heart of the issue when he says '9 is perhaps the most truly powerful of the numbers that we have considered, even though its power is essentially non-assertive.' This idea of non-assertive power is the crux. In the West we are so used to thinking about power in terms of the will and 'doing' things, that the idea that there is a deep power which flows from simply being truly oneself is somehow alien. What does it mean? Hamblin gives us another window on this dimension when he suggests that in the 9th harmonic we 'accept the world for what it is'. Addey and Hamblin may not be all that far apart, for Addey is in fact suggesting that the 9th harmonic represents those ideals, those ideas to be realized, those very images which move and motivate us to their pursuit and unfoldment. In this sense the 9th harmonic is showing us that which we may become if we are true to our simple essence, but not the means by which we arrive at that state.

As Addey points out, this inner image which draws us to it is what the Greeks called the 'entelechy' of a thing. It is the image of the oak tree which informs the acorn. It is that higher vision of ourselves which draws us, that inner image of what we in essence are and into which we grow effortlessly if we can but see it, yet which we must strive after if we have only partial sight. It represents that perspective of our life which allows Wu-Wei, that non-striving, through which comes clarity of vision and adherence to our inner truth. It is who we can become if we 'follow our bliss'. We could in fact say that the 9th harmonic is that pattern of ideas which should serve to guide all others. If we can once be what we are at this level then all the other levels will automatically serve this entelechy . . . they will fall into place.

Here it has to be said we are touching on very profound issues as to what it is to be alive and to be a human being living in space and time. Each one of us potentially is, yet without aspiration and effort of some kind we cannot unfold our potential being, we cannot discover the person 'who we already are', as Jung so succinctly put it. The relationship between being and becoming and the relative importance of each in East and West is reflected in their respective astrologies.

It can be argued that here in the West, the high point of astrological understanding lies in the German schools of Witte, Ebertin, and their followers. As we have seen, the nub of their work focuses around their insights as to the importance of the hard aspects in the chart, the divisions of the circle by 2, 4, 8, 16, etc., as the means for identifying what in a chart will manifest and produce characteristic events and behaviour in this world. And since all of us, except the most truly philosophical and enlightened, tend to see the world around us through the filter of our particular time and place and culture, it is hardly surprising that these insights about what will 'manifest' and 'actualize' have come from the heart of the Western materialist tradition: Germany, home of Marx, of reductionist physics, of the Protestant work ethic, of the ability to 'get to grips' with matter and to 'master it' and 'to make something of one's life'.

This emphasis on the volitional aspect of man, on 'getting on our bikes', on achievement, on our outwardly manifest behaviour, on choice, on 'making' a living, on 'doing' and striving, on being ambitious, is second nature to us. We tend in the West to feel uncomfortable, indeed indignant and even disgusted, at Eastern cultures who do not spontaneously see the exercise of the will as the pre-eminent prerogative of man. 'How can they live in such squalor?' 'Why don't they do something about it?' is our spontaneous reaction to the sight of the living conditions of more traditional cultures.

On the other hand there is equally something which many Westerners find seductively attractive about the traditional Eastern outlook. The emphasis on the inner life, on being, on the non-judgemental playing of one's own part, on a laissez-faire approach to problems that are not one's own immediate concern, the living for the moment, the calm confidence that the Justice of the Infinite One is Absolute, Eternal, and Perfect. This 'be here now' approach suddenly puts all the busy-busy striving and rushing and doing of the Western approach into perspective.

When we examine Hindu astrology we find that the predominant emphasis is upon the numbers 9 and 27, i.e. 3 × 3, and 3 × 3 × 3, upon the Navamsa chart, and the twenty-seven lunar mansions. This emphasis seems to reflect the Indian emphasis upon the inner life of the individual, upon the vital being and essence, and the idea that whatever we do should be done for the sake of the Highest. In the words of Sri Krishna in the Bhagavad Gita: 'Whatsoever thou doest, whatsoever thou enjoyest, whatsoever thou givest, whatsoever thou engages in austerity, do thou that as an offering unto Me.' And: 'Actions affect not Me, neither in Me is there desire for action's fruit: he who knows Me thus, is not bound by works.'

In fact the 9H is not at first glance the most obvious kind of thing to boost the nation's GNP or keep one's bank manager sleeping happily at night. The 9th harmonic seems to be very much about our vital Being and those ideas and ideals which will preoccupy us. It is about those ideals and issues which the individual or entity will embody not by any act of will, but by simply being who they are, by 'following their bliss'. The 9H may or may not contain elements of striving, of knowing, of inspiration, but it certainly contains something of the essential 'light' of our life. This chart represents, as it were, what we are when we are present to ourselves . . . When we are consciously engaged in this dimension of our self we are in touch with our life, with our deepest motivation, with that which gives us the greatest joy, with our *raison d'être*, our entelechy, our lodestar, our guiding light. By reading this chart as representing those ideals that delight, and hence move and motivate, the soul, we may glimpse something of the individual's final goal.

These are some of the main ideas that are depicted in the 9H chart and the kind of information that it can yield. We are conscious that this is not by any means a total picture, and that much more lies tantalizingly beneath the surface. We end this chapter with a consideration of 9 in tradition and myth. Those who still feel dissatisfied with their understanding of this principle and who would prefer to soak themselves further in the meaning of the number 9 before proceeding should turn to p. 281 for some further considerations on its meaning.

SOME SUGGESTIVE EXAMPLES OF THE 9TH HARMONIC

TERESA OF AVILA: If the 9H reflects the image of one's ideals and the fruit of the pursuit of those particular ideals, then it would seem appropriate that we start with an individual whose life was guided by the highest of all ideals: the pure love and service of God. Teresa of Avila is by any standards a most remarkable individual, and she is generally reckoned to be one of the greatest mystics, in the true sense of that term, being someone with her head in Heaven and her feet firmly planted on the earth. She was simultaneously an individual who attained to great personal inner serenity and vision and who became one of the acknowledged masters of the art of prayer, meditation, and contemplation, while at the same time being an immensely practical woman who almost single-handedly carried through one of the greatest reforms in the history of the Christian church.

Born on 28 March 1515 (New Style) at 5 a.m. in Avila, Teresa came from an ancient and noble Spanish family who had played a courageous part in defending the frontiers of Christian Spain against the incursions of Islam. This family tradition of courage was to find its expression in Teresa in her life of battle, against incessant opposition, for the reform of the Carmelite Order which was at this time in danger of complete degeneration. Although she was forty before she conceived of the idea of a reformed rule, by the time of her death at sixty-seven she had established many founda-tions both for friars and nuns and her reform had been officially recognized. Paralleling this outward 'fruit' of her pursuit of her

ideals was her inner mystical life, which experience she summarized for the use of her nuns in *The Way of Perfection* and *The Interior
Castle*, while she gave a vivid account of her travels, difficulties and
triumphs of her work of reform in *The Foundations*.

This reforming zeal arose out of an inner perception of the way of
the perfect life. This mystic insight was the consequence of her
deep love and devotion and sustained periods of prayer, meditation, contemplation, and the continuous Practice of the Presence
of God.

In Teresa's natal chart, Figure 14.1, we are immediately struck
by her Venus rising in Pisces in close square to MC in Sagittarius
conjunct Pluto, which is –120–Uranus in the 1st in Aries. If the
♀–0–AS in ♓ is traditionally an indication of universal love and
compassion, the MC–0–♇ in ♐, 120–♅ is most certainly the

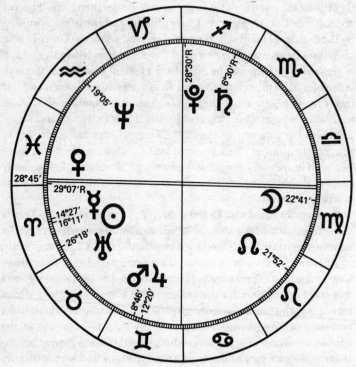

Figure 14.1 The natal chart of St Teresa of Avila.

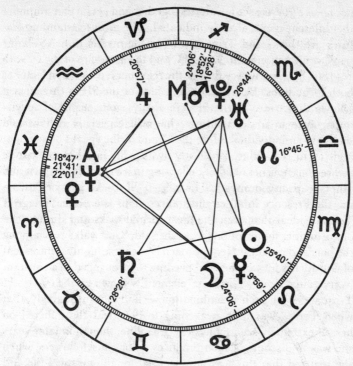

Figure 14.2 Teresa of Avila's 9H reveals the qualities of her *raison d'être* as mystic and reformer.

hallmark of someone whose life may focus around radical reforms of a moral or spiritual nature. The possibility that religious issues and conflicts will be a major focus of the life is shown by the ♂–0–♃ in the 3rd –180– ♄ in ♐ on the 9th cusp. The overall drive, enthusiasm, and initiative is well shown by the ☉–0–☿ in ♈ in the 1st and the general emphasis on Fire in the chart. Certainly this picture is fully in accord with the life, and when we find in addition the all-important ☉/☽ = ♆ = ☽/☿ = ♃/♅, the picture of a highly sensitive individual who has a profound awareness of her own thought processes and who is preoccupied by spiritual reform, ♆ = ♃/♅, becomes vivid indeed.

So what can we expect to learn from the 9H? If we treat this chart, Figure 14.2, as a map of Teresa's 'mission', as an 'image' of her *raison d'être*, we see how it ties together and yet further amplifies the different issues already indicated. The most outstanding features are the Grand Trine involving the mystic love AS–Ψ–♀ triple conjunction with ☽ and ♅, and the T-square of the ☉ with ♄ –180– ♅. Here we see that ♅ the reformer is a common factor to both formations. Because the root idea of the 9H is threeness it follows that trines in the 9H are always going to be of special importance in understanding what will especially delight and motivate an individual. Here the Grand Trine speaks of a delight and joy in remaining constantly awake, ♅, in a higher state of aware consciousness and of delighting in awakening her own and others' capacity for mystical love, ♀–0–Ψ–0–AS and for Practising the Presence in all circumstances. This is a perfect image of Teresa's ideal that even the most menial tasks and duties were opportunities for devotion for, as she said, 'God walks even among the pots and pipkins.' Her approach is of course highly reminiscent of Gurdjieff's idea of the Soul needing to be engaged in a constant 'war against sleep'. This 'war' element is shown by the ☉–♄–♅ T-square. With such a combination we find, not surprisingly, that when Teresa was first awakening to her ideal she inflicted on herself extremely severe physical discipline, though in later years she was to discourage such practices among her followers, when she realized that this was not essential for the mystical life and could be extremely harmful. We may further note that this highly motivated Grand Trine is in part focused and channelled through the close involvement of ♃ –60–AS–Ψ–♀ and –180–☽. As always sextiles tend to indicate those activities which can be made regular and habitual, and this picture is beautifully symbolic of the rhythms (60) of religious (♃ and Ψ) devotion (♀) in the world (AS).

This first Grand Trine pattern inclines the mind to an alert (♅) but more inner and passive joy and delight in the religious life. By contrast, the T-square of the ☉ with the ♄ –180– ♅ graphically depicts the effort of will for the attainment of enlightenment. In addition, this T-square shows how Teresa's awakened mind focused on the image of reforming the old and degenerate ways of her Order (♄), and on the need to grapple with problems regardless of the consequences. Again, as we have seen, this T-square, and the square of ♂–0–♇ to her Ψ–♀ (and AS if the time is precise), can also be seen as what she describes as eighteen years of strife and contention 'which arose out of my attempt to reconcile God and the world', years when she often doubted the truth of her own revelations and visions. Again this image evokes the ultimate reconciliation of these doubts through her moment of enlightenment, when she was conscious of overwhelming contrition and devotion and the desire to resign her will utterly to the will of God, the ideal that in doing God's will and conforming to order, ♄, is the only free will, ♅, an insight that countless mystics have experienced down the ages. This is of course the peace and joy of acceptance which Hamblin relates to this harmonic.

MAO TSE-TUNG, whose midpoint structures we discussed on p. 62 and 7H on p. 243, was an entirely different kind of reformer, but like Saint Teresa he harboured images of conforming the individual will to the larger will, which in his case meant the State, and himself as the personification of the State. Like Teresa his 9H (Figure 14.3) shows a close ♄–180–♅ which forms a general T-square with the ☉. While the T-square is not as close in this case, we see that the radical ☽–90–♅ was so close that it has been brought over to form a general Grand Cross. This pattern is further galvanized by the fact that ♇ here is –45–☉ and still on the ☉/♅ midpoint as it is in the radix. This ♇ is close –120–☊–☿ and –60–♂ integrating the 'comrades-in-arms and -in-thought' of the ♂–180–☊–☿ (and if the time is precise with the MC/IC).

As always in the 9H, trines are vitally important in showing the deeper motivating ideals, that which will delight the heart and evoke the image of highest beauty. Here *COSI* comments on ♇–☊ as relating to 'the common destiny of a large mass of people' and 'the wish to become a public figure or to exercise an influence upon the people . . .' while ☿–♇ is 'the art of persuasion . . . intellectual triumph over others . . . a convincing speaker, the power to influence the public or the masses . . . the attainment of public recognition'. If we put together these 'motivating' pictures with the will-orientated Grand Cross, we can vividly see that Mao's guiding image and ideas to be realized were of enthusing his comrades in thought and arms in the struggle to overthrow the old, to radically transform the structures of the State and to strive for, Grand Cross,

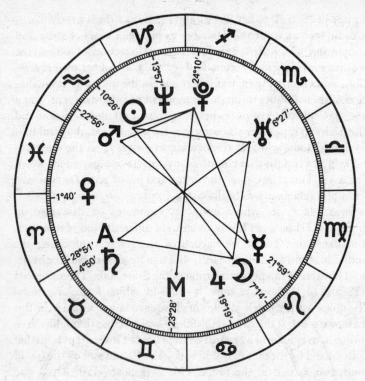

Figure 14.3 Mao Tse-tung's 9H.

a state of 'permanent revolution' of constant alertness, ever awake to those forces of reaction which might stifle it. While we saw much of this picture emerging from Mao's midpoint structures, here we can recognize that it is deeply connected with his guiding image in life, in those ideals that were drawing him onward and informing his place in the scheme of things. Paradoxically, as with Teresa, this ideal Mao has the concept of 'struggle' embodied within it. The very act of striving to manifest is part of the larger purpose.

MARGARET THATCHER has a very strong ♄ and ♅ picture in her chart, e.g. her ☉ is on the ♄/♅ midpoint and she has a very exact ♄–180–♅ in her 7H, but these are not present in her 9H (Figure 14.4), perhaps indicating that though she is a radical reformer and is 'turned on' by undertaking the challenge of such fundamental reform, nonetheless revolution is not, as such, part of her over-riding guiding image. What is, is the continuing presence of the ♃–180–♇, which, if her birth time is precise, is here shown to fall across the AS, and is, in any case, joined by Neptune and by a powerful double –135– to each end from the almost exact ☉–90–♂. (♂ is only weakly –45– ♆ and ♇ but almost exactly –45– their midpoint.) This integrated pattern speaks volumes about her ideal of the fighter, who struggles to 'make something of himself' and to obtain the power of self-reliance. *COSI* says of ♃–♇ that it relates to 'the striving for the development of power', in all senses of that word, and to 'an appreciation of the need for social or religious regeneration, a brilliant gift for organization . . .' This theme of course runs through all her first 9 harmonics, and is

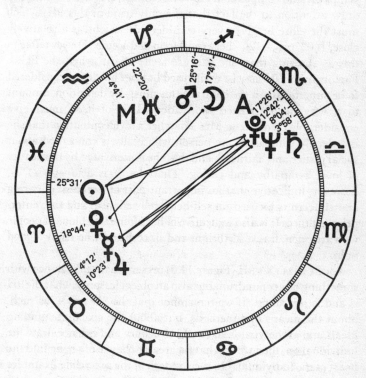

Figure 14.4 Margaret Thatcher's 9H.

immediately coupled into her lunar level in the radix, but it is only here in the 9H that we see it directly integrated with the ☉ and the very close ♂–45–Ψ carried over from the radix, so that it is coupled to her formidable 'visionary' will. This gives her, as it were, an ideal to be realized of the 'crusader' and 'fighter for a cause'.

Another strong feature of this chart is the almost exact ☿–180–♄, which if the time is precise is also –90– MC, indicative of a guiding image which is focused upon the ideal of clear, consistent thinking, and a desire to be logical and thorough in her principles. Her opponents might interpret this as a propensity to hold facts as more important than feelings, to placing the god of narrow-minded logic and doctrine over the higher virtues of sympathy and compassion. However, the astrologer would have to draw attention to the fact that the only trine in this 9H, which must therefore be given very considerable weight, is a relatively close, 1° 03' orb, –120– between Moon and Venus. Dwyer refers to this as showing that 'she can use facile charm when she likes'. Factors in the 9H may be easily used but can hardly be considered to be superficial; on the contrary this must, by definition, amount to a very deeply rooted motivation. This of itself must give considerable credence to Mrs Thatcher's own contention that she is a deeply compassionate person who really is concerned about social justice and 'fairness', and that she is motivated by the beauty of love, sympathy and caring. That the ☽ is also –0– ♂ is, however, indicative that an important part of her ideal of caring and concern is focused on self-help, self-reliance, and the 'enterprise' culture. It is also indicative of her often stated love of people who are open, frank, forthright and sincere and who enjoy a good fight.

ADOLF HITLER's 9H (Figure 14.5) presents us at first glance with something of a conundrum but also an object lesson in what the 9H is and is not about. If we remember that the 9H is not, as such, about the means and methods, but about the goals, the guiding ideals and archetypal images whose beauty and essence draw the individual on, then we will have a greater chance of seeing into the heart of the individual. On the strength of the preceding examples we might have expected to find a much greater involvement of the

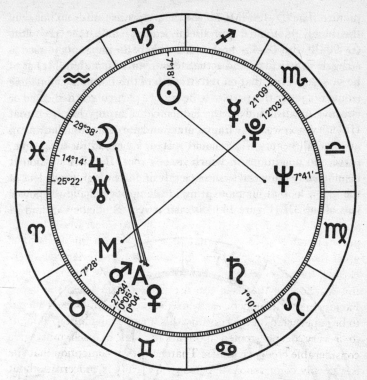

Figure 14.5 Adolf Hitler's 9H – an object lesson in what the 9H is and is not about.

outer planets in tight integration, but though there are some such features they are relatively weak. Here the dominant feature is the ♀–0–♂ with the AS, with the ☽ in close –90– to the conjunction. The ideal of unity, of the struggle to unify the German people through military means, springs to mind. His repeated insistence on his love for the people and his vision of Germany as a place of joy and happiness suddenly makes more sense. The Jupiter trine Pluto, on the MC/IC axis, if the time is precise, speaks of someone with a deep desire for the enjoyment of power and the motivation to regenerate the masses. The ♂–60–♅, which is still in orbs of its natal –135–♇, forms a practical link with this profoundly trans-formative and revolutionary energy and helps integrate it into the picture. The ☉–120–MC, if the time is precise, adds an image of the highly motivated purposeful leader, while the very close ☉–90–Ψ with ☿ –45– both ends speaks of the image of the need to struggle to articulate and actualize a dream of some kind. It has to be said, however, that on the strength of this harmonic alone one would not judge this pattern to be one of a particularly dedicated or effective idealist. Indeed the judgement of history has been that Hitler's vision was very fragmentary and particular and lacking in any overall beauty which could sustain it beyond the local time, place and conditions in which it took root. If Hitler's vision is insufficiently universal to show clearly under the high power lens of the 9H, a look at his motivating ideals through the lower power lens of the 3H (Figure 14.6) is instructive. (Students will find in

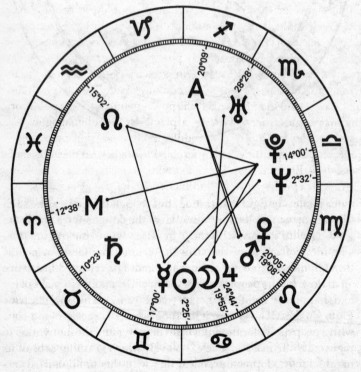

Figure 14.6 Adolf Hitler's 3H, revealing some of his primary motivations.

many cases that the 3H chart is a more obviously accessible picture of what delights, moves, and motivates an individual.)

Here we see an 'arrowhead' formation with the Grand Trine of ☿–☊–♇ (cf. MAO's 9H) and ♇–180–MC forming the shaft and making this formation personal to this precise time of birth. Trines in the 3H or 9H are always of primary importance and a Grand Trine will always indicate principles that will be of central importance in understanding the deeper motivation and guiding light and life of an individual. Of ♇/☊ Ebertin (who, we should note, certainly did not know of the striking importance of this pattern in Hitler's chart since there was no recognized aspect of any kind between ♇ and ☊ when Ebertin was compiling *COSI*), says, 'the common destiny of a large mass of people . . . the urge to seek contacts or associations with many people, the wish to become a public figure or to exercise an influence upon other people'. He gives the sociological correspondence as 'crowds or large groups of people, mass meetings'. Of ☿–♇ Ebertin says: 'The art of persuasion . . . restless thinking, good powers of observation, a quick grasp of every situation, an amazingly sharp criticism, intellectual triumph over others, slyness or cunning, crafty subtlety, diplomacy . . . a convincing speaker, the power to influence the public or the masses, a critic, a writer – a plagiarist or a demagogue . . . persons who are guilty of fraudulent representation or misrepresentation in speaking or writing . . .' Putting all three together, of ♇/☊ = ☿ Ebertin says, '. . . the ability to exercise a compelling and magnetically powerful influence upon the community at large'. Of the combination ☊ = ☿/♇, Ebertin says: 'The desire to be a spokesman of the community, to dominate others intellectually.' While interestingly of ♇ = ☿/☊, the only midpoint contact between these factors which Ebertin would have found by conventional methods, *COSI* gives 'The desire to be intellectually superior', which is in fact the least telling of these pictures.

When we see the above picture mounted on the shaft of the ♇–180–MC we can see that these issues will be pivotal to the whole process of 'the shaping of the individuality' and in making manifest (180) Hitler's (♇–MC) 'desire to become important, the growth and development of strength. The power to attain success in life, the ability to organize, prudence, vision, authority.' We can see that in the pursuit of these ideals he may manifest (MC–180 –♇), '. . . Foolhardiness and daring, licentiousness. The abuse of power, anti-social conduct. The tendency to create feelings of resistance and vindictiveness in people . . . The attainment of recognition and power . . . The likelihood of sudden ruin through the misuse of power . . .' Of these characteristics only 'licentiousness' is off the mark.

The other tight trine in this chart of the ♀–0–♂ with AS has been dealt with when we were discussing the 9H above, but we can see it here more immediately as a motivating energy, the delight in ♂–AS, 'a fighting spirit' and in 'the tendency to force one's own will upon others, the ability to lead or guide others resolutely . . . the forceful attainment of success . . .' and in ♀–AS a reminder of that other primary motivation which gave him 'artistic inclinations . . . a sense for a beautiful and even artistically furnished environment'.

The wider ♃–120–♅ adds to the picture of someone who is deeply motivated to be an expansive revolutionary and 'adventurer' and who delights in 'a quick grasp of every situation'.

If the 3H here reveals what we can immediately recognize about Hitler's inner dynamic more vividly than his 9H, it is nonetheless probably true to say that the compulsive strength of the man appears to have been rooted much more in his openness to the compelling dark inspirations of his 7H, and in the formidable quality of his will and initial aspiration which are so vividly shown in his 4H, 8H and 16H series (see p. 289 ff.) and in his 12H and 24H, and his remarkable will as revealed in his 5H.

JAMES HILLMAN, Figure 14.7 (birth data not available for publication), a former Director of Studies at the Jung Institute in Zurich, is one of the most important and influential psychologists in the area of depth psychology today. He is in the vanguard of those fighting for a 'revisioning, a fundamental shift of perspective out of the soulless predicament we call modern consciousness'. As befits someone born with the richly intuitive and imaginative picture of an exact ☉–0–☽ in Aries exactly sextile/trine a close ♃–180–♆, he is perhaps most famous for his concern to return soul and the subjective reality of the experience of being to the centre of psychology. Indeed he describes himself as an 'imaginal

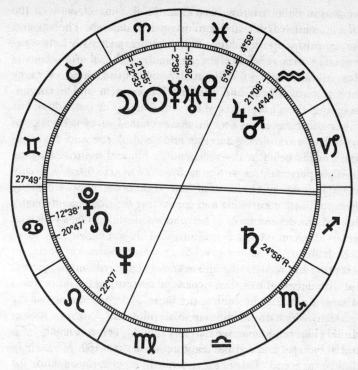

Figure 14.7 The radical chart of James Hillman, the outstanding psychologist and author of *Revisioning Psychology*. The ASC could be into the first degrees of Cancer.

psychologist'. His constant affirmation is that we are souls rather than that we have a soul. He is the great portrayer of the vital reality of the inner life, of the Gods and the myths we enact. He sees the work of psychology as to 'revivify our relations with the world around us' and to encourage an inner meeting with 'our individual fragmentation, our many rooms and many voices'. With true ☽–♃–♆ he seeks to 'further the imagination to show all its bright forms' and to release psychology from what he sees as its repressive preoccupation with making the rich autonomous inner diversity subservient to consciousness and will.

Hillman's ♅ –90– AS and –0– ☉/M encourages this desire to 'revision', to bring about 'a fundamental shift of perspective', to break down the 'narrow biases' and stultifying tyranny of the predominance of 'self' and 'ego' in modern depth psychology and the unhealthy preoccupation of psychotherapists with consciousness and the 'integration of the personality'. This ♅–AS picture is also characteristic of Hillman's radical questioning of every psychological system simply because it is a system, and his emphasis on the direct experience of the individual as an individual. His most radical stance has been his attack on the Cartesian division of the universe into living subjects and dead objects and the exposition of his belief in the independent life and livingness of the multiple personalities within each one of us. His work is deeply rooted in Jung's but he forcefully rejects the preoccupation of many therapists with controlling and connecting the rich inner diversity through the development of will and intellect, a process which he sees as all too often depersonalizing and 'de-souling'.

In Hillman we have a psychology which focuses on being, on accepting and recognizing and acknowledging without judgement but with delight the endless riches and diversity of the inner world of soul. Anima is the centre, the *raison d'être*, the essence of the entelechy which draws Hillman to his fulfilment. When we look at his 9H (Figure 14.8) we see that this brings together not only ☉ ☽ and ♆ but also ♇ in a grand conjunction in exact 180 ☿, with ♀ in 60/120 each end. This is a dramatically appropriate picture for someone who says of himself 'anima is my root metaphor', 'my work has always been anima based, from *Emotion* (1960) to *Betrayal* and the Psyche/Eros tale as the myth of analysis, on to soul-making', and more recently, the focus on the aesthetic imagination and the soul of the world, *anima mundi*. Here we see vividly depicted the prototypic ideal of someone whose life as a depth psychologist, ☿–♇, revolves around the concept of bringing to awareness and acknowledging the reality of the 'personifications' of the endlessly rich inner world of soul (♇–☽–♆). His work *Anima* (1985), 'An Anatomy of a Personified Notion', is an exhaustive annotated commentary on the concept of anima in Jung's writing. In its preface he says:

> . . . isn't devotion to anima the calling of psychology? So another deep-seated reason for this book is to provide ground-

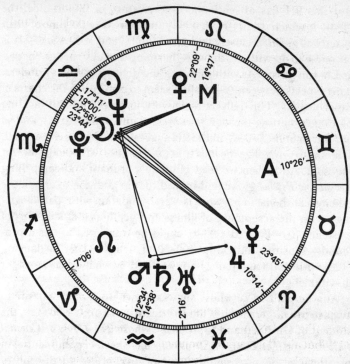

Figure 14.8 James Hillman's 9H whose life and work is focused upon bringing greater awareness of the rich inner world of the soul. Angles should be treated with caution.

ing for the vision of soul in psychology, so that psychology doesn't abandon itself to the archetypal perspectives of the Child and developmentalism or the Mother and material causalism. The vision of soul convinces; it is a seduction into psychological faith, a faith in images and the thought of the heart, into an animation of the world. Anima attaches and involves. She makes us fall into love. We cannot remain the detached observer looking through a lens. In fact, she probably doesn't partake in optical metaphors at all. Instead, she is continually weaving, sewing, and enchanting consciousness into passionate attachments away from the vantage point of perspective.

But this 9H has at least one other feature of importance: the ♂-0-♄ which is 120 ⊙-Ψ, 60 ♃, and, if we take the time of birth exactly as given, is closely with the MC/IC and 120-AS. ♂-♄ is of course to do with death, with 'harming and destructive energy' as Ebertin puts it. As with surgeons and dentists and lens grinders, hard aspects between ♂-♄ often seem to come up in the charts of psychologists. This reflects their work in grappling and tackling blockages, cutting through to repressed and painful areas, and so on. But to find ♂-0-♄ in the 9H suggests something else as well. It seems to symbolize the idea that ♂-♄ issues will be lodestars for this soul. And when we read Hillman's brilliant and compelling *Revisioning Psychology* we find indeed that in addition to anima the other great theme in his work is a preoccupation with 'pathologizing', with the acceptance of illness and death as a crucial part of existence. ⊙-Ψ -120- ♂-♄ could be translated as 'As a profoundly sensitive individual (⊙-Ψ) I delight (120) in dancing (120) with death and pain. I am vitalized by what others consider de-vitalizing.'

Another individual whose life was drawn upward by a desire to awaken to a larger vision of life and death was RODNEY COLLIN, the student of Gurdjieff and Ouspensky whose *The Theory of Celestial Influences* and *The Theory of Eternal Life* have been very influential in broadening the philosophical perspective of twentieth-century astrology. He was born on 26 April 1909 at 9 a.m. in Brighton. His 9H chart (Figure 14.9) shows a remarkable 'mystic rectangle' formation involving Ψ-180-♇ and ♂-180-♅. ♂ is also -135-♄, which is -180-⊙, while ☿ is -90- the ♂-♅. Collin's 9H self-image resonated totally to the Gurdjieff-Ouspensky doctrine that man is a house wired for electricity but not normally plugged into the mains. He saw that 'only extraordinary efforts count' in the 'war against sleep' and the awakening from our habitual somnolence which keeps us from our true spiritual potential. Collin's sister-in-law Joyce Collin-Smith gives a vivid portrait of this exceptionally tall, mild and amiable (☽-♃-♀) aspirant in *Call No Man Master*. She describes how his pursuit of awakening (♅-Ψ-♇) through his driving will (♂-♅) led him to work himself to total exhaustion in pursuit of the 'Work'. He would go on marathons of endurance, sometimes walking for several days in the

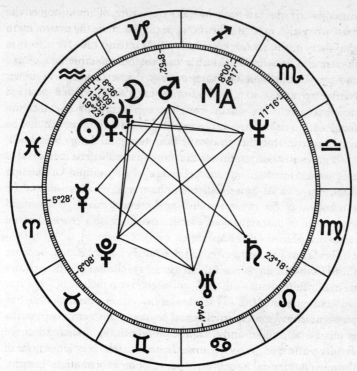

Figure 14.9 The 9H of Gurdjieff and Ouspensky's pupil Rodney Collin, author of *The Theory of Celestial Influences*.

full heat of the Mexican sun without water or rest, pushing himself to the absolute limit.

Collin was a man who was determined to do something with his life. Apart from his influential writings he wanted to establish a spiritual centre in Mexico and to use his enormous energy and dedication to actively help improve the lot of the world. He bought an old hacienda high in the hills twenty miles from Mexico City and while his wife established a health clinic to alleviate the suffering of the local people, he, with the help of local peasants, began the construction of a planetarium temple hewn out of the rock. This was made up of two interlinking circular rooms, the Sun chamber and the Moon chamber, around both of which was a passageway adorned with mosaics depicting the development of man from the first life forms to perfected man. The two main chambers of the temple were to lead up into an area for a lecture theatre and floor for ritual dance and another chamber for Collin's enormous collection of esoteric books. The project was never completed, as at 3.15 p.m. EST on 3 May 1956 Collin fell, perhaps deliberately, to his death from the tower of Cuzco cathedral, tempted, Joyce Collin-Smith suggests, by his own maxim that 'The way towards unity lies in escape from time . . .' Those who know his books will know that these are more than sufficient memorial to a remarkable man, but in the image of the temple Collin was building, with its Sun and Moon chambers, its mosaics, and its symbolism of the evolution and perfection of man, we see vivid expression of that remarkable stellium of $\math$D$-0-\math234-0-\mathQ-\odot$ in the Aquarius phase of this harmonic.

This is not surprising, for, as John Addey has indicated, because the 9H shows many of the salient features of the image which draws us to our fulfilment, so the 9H will often give a picture of what it is we create in our life. This may show either externally in our physical, emotional, or intellectual creations or internally in terms of our life and philosophy. With Collin both types of creation are vividly portrayed. We turn now to someone who is no doubt one of the most influential figures on the development of modern thought: CARL GUSTAV JUNG. His concepts of Individuation and of the Collective Unconscious have become central to a great deal of New Age thought. Something of a guru figure in psychological circles, his influence has spread out into many areas of art and literature where his work has served to reintroduce the transcendental element into the Western psyche. Those who feel uncomfortable with orthodox spiritual studies of the world's great religions have found through Jung's work a personal and intellectually acceptable path by which they can be 'bound back' (the meaning of the Latin word *religio*) to the deep mysterious processes of the Gods, who when reintroduced as the Archetypes of the Collective Unconscious appear to present a more acceptable and reasonable face for twentieth-century man. Jung's 9H, Figure 14.10, shows how his very close natal $\odot-90-\Psi$ continues in orbs and is linked into a strikingly appropriate Grand Cross with $\math24-\mathP$ and $\math⚥$. $\math24$ can in

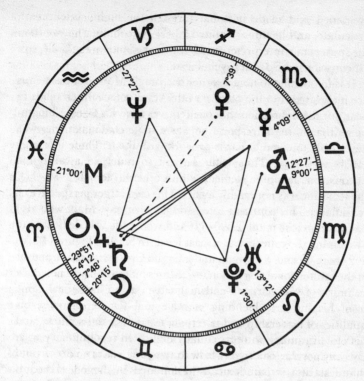

Figure 14.10 The 9H of Carl Gustav Jung, who sought spiritual integration and individuation and has become a guru figure for many.

some respects be considered even more the principle of wholeness and integration than the Sun, which more obviously represents individuation. ⊙–O–♃ speaks volumes about a man who was motivated by the quest for spiritual integration, and who, albeit unconsciously, took on the role of spiritual guide and prophet. This is a picture of the individual who is motivated to actualize and make manifest (90/180) a penetrating integration and expression of the individual and collective depths. Ebertin says of ♅–♇ that it relates to 'The Supernatural . . . an intensified and purified soul-life . . . an inclination to delve into unusual and supernatural phenomena, a love of mysticism, self-knowledge . . .' When this is combined and made personal through the highly intellectual, articulate, and health-orientated ☉–♃–☿ combination we have the spokesman, interpreter, and integrator of and for the Collective Unconscious, the depth psychologist.

It is interesting to note that neither Jung's Moon nor his Venus are integrated into the picture at this level, a fact which tends to bear out the impression that one receives from his franker biographers that in many respects he was a male chauvinist who was never able to come to terms or work with the feminine in a very satisfactory way. Thus while he did so much to awaken the unconscious feminine element within others (radical ☽–90–♅), the feminine was not readily a part of his own larger perspective or self-image. This contrasts interestingly with, say, Mao, who also had a very close natal ☽–90–♅, and whose life was dedicated to awakening the collective at a mass level. In his 9H (Figure 14.3, p. 262) both ☉ and ☽ form up in the Grand Cross with the ♄ and ♅ of the 'professional revolutionary'. Mao's biographers all note how so much of his charisma and magnetism as an individual came from his intimate blending of male and female energies, his qualities of leadership and poetry, of toughness and softness, and his close intimacy with his equally dedicated revolutionary wife. By contrast the 'oak tree' which draws Jung's acorn into life and manifestation is paradoxically dominated by Logos. His ideal self-image is a conscious intellectual and spiritual one (☉–☿–♃). His voluminous *Collected Works* (☉–☿–♃) and his development of Freud's 'talking cure' (☉–☿–♃) as an instrument for the exploration of the deep mysteries are his fruits.

If the number 3 is related to Life, then the number 9 as 3 × 3 is in some sense the triple unfolded essence of Life. In this century one theologian, philosopher and practical idealist stands out above all others for his 'reverence for life'. This phrase emerged 'unforeseen and unsought' into the mind of ALBERT SCHWEITZER deep in the tropical jungle of French Equatorial Africa, as he reflected on the core of his philosophy. As he expressed it in his autobiography *Out of My Life and Thought*:

> Affirmation of life is the spiritual act by which man ceases to live unreflectively and begins to devote himself to life with

reverence in order to raise it to its true value. To affirm life is to deepen, to make more inward and to exalt the will to live . . .

The 9H of Schweitzer (Figure 14.11) must therefore be of special interest. To understand it more fully we should remind ourselves that Schweitzer was one of the outstanding idealists of this century. He was a great medical missionary, scholar, theologian, philosopher, Bach scholar and interpreter, organist and authority on organ building, who obtained doctorates in medicine and surgery, theology, philosophy and music. He won the Nobel Peace Prize in 1952 for his efforts on behalf of 'the Brotherhood of Nations', and

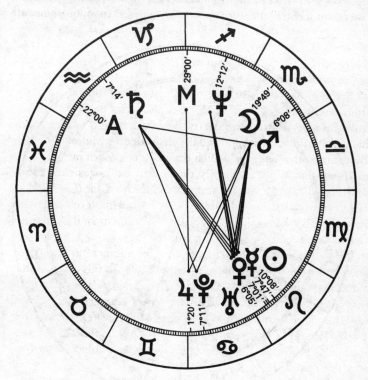

Figure 14.11 The 9H of Albert Schweitzer, philosopher, theologian, musician, medical missionary and practical idealist, whose key idea was 'reverence for life'.

specifically for his decades of devoted work at his tropical hospital in Lambaréné, Gabon, which he built and ran with his wife, primarily with income from his organ concerts, lectures, and writings. There he helped heal some of the earth's most neglected and destitute people. Schweitzer was born in Kayserberg, Alsace at 23.50 LMT, 14 January 1875 (Figure 14.12), the eldest son of a Lutheran pastor, and seems to have held from the outset the view he expressed on receiving the Nobel Prize: 'You don't live in a world all alone. Your brothers are here too.'

The radical chart already shows us the intellectual and idealistic strivings for concrete achievement of ☉–0–☿ in Capricorn –90– ☊–☽–♆ in Aries in the 7th house. This speaks volumes about the need to centre the life upon the manifestation of some all-

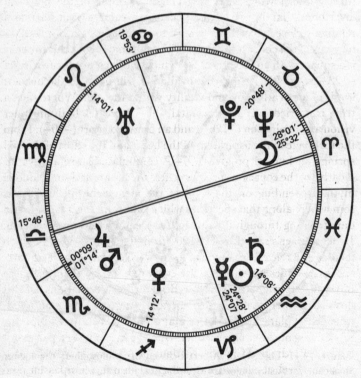

Figure 14.12 Albert Schweitzer's radical chart.

consuming dream or vision. This is an innately sensitive and compassionate combination, yet one which by its Earth-Fire mix is going to be something of a steamroller or bulldozer. This need for action and a driven, self-punishing, and potentially dangerous and destructive approach to life is also highlighted by the almost exact T-square of ♄–♂–♅, which is so close that it remains in tight orbs throughout all of his first thirty-two harmonics. His natural sympathy for others is shown well by the Libra Ascendant with the ☊–☽–♆ setting and the ruling Venus in the 3rd house of 'brothers', one of Schweitzer's constant themes.

When we turn to the 9H we see that the dynamic and driven T-square joins the ☉–0–☿, which is likewise very closely joined by ♀. At the same time we see that the ☉–90–♆ of the radix has been turned into a trine. This is a classic example of the powerful 'overtones' that the orb of an aspect can give. Here what starts as a relatively close orb of 3° 33′ is seen to be generating a close –120– in terms of the chart's 'nineness'. (The optimal orb for this to occur is a square with an orb of +3° 20′ which will then produce an exact –120– in the 9H.) Any trine in the 9H will point to the deepest levels of motivating joy and vitality within the soul. Where such a trine is carried over from a natal –90– it creates both an inner vision and aspiration (–120–) and an outward effort (–90–). From the marriage of the aspiration of the heart and the effort of the will springs all human progress. ☉–♆ combinations are always indicative of the conscious need to centre the life around some kind of myth. Depending on the level of the ideals, the life will focus somewhere along that spectrum which runs from sheer fantasy and daydreaming through dreams to transcendent and mystic vision. In Schweitzer's case this 9H –120– from ♆ to ☉–♀–☿–♅, which focuses and releases so much of the powerful drive of the T-square, speaks volumes about his acute sensitivity on all planes. At the physical, Schweitzer would redesign the foundations of his hospital rather than disturb an ants' nest. At an emotional-intellectual plane he was both a major Bach scholar and a supreme interpreter of the music of Bach (the ♄–♅ composer par excellence, according to the observations of Michael Harding). At a spiritual level he was an individual of supreme compassion and deep mystical insight.

It is easy to idealize an idealist, but it would be untrue to say that Schweitzer did not express the negative side of his T-square. Apart from his choice of living in some of the most inhospitable conditions on the planet, he was not always the easiest person to get on with. He was very driven, and could be extremely tough and forceful when confronted with opposition. But the possibility that the guiding light, the lodestar and *raison d'être* of all his efforts could be a supreme sensitivity at all levels and a 'reverence for life' is clearly shown in this chart, which brings together the disparate elements of tough and tender into a dynamic and integrated whole.

Of course other people must have been born very close to this time with very similar charts. They did not become Schweitzers, at least not as far as we know, on the same scale or in the same manner. This 9H does not tell us that this is Albert Schweitzer, but it does tell us the kind of inner vision that such a person could have. As John Addey has pointed out, the Hindus also use the 9H to judge the marriage partner. This is on the basis that ideally our marriage partner will be in some important sense a reflection of our ideals. For some born at the same time as Schweitzer the qualities of this chart might find themselves entirely reflected in 'the other' in their life.

If in these examples we have focused primarily on conscious idealists, this is not to suggest that a strong 9H is a sure passport to canonization. But it must be the case that the more aware we are of the inner 'vision of the soul', that image, that entelechy which draws us to it if we will but let it through, the more idealistic we must become. But even in the relatively unselfconscious the 9H will still express itself in terms of the level of the individual. Here it is important never to lose sight of the fact that the level or levels at which a chart will predominantly express itself during a life must to a great extent be dependent first upon the family background, genetic inheritance, education, society and all the other qualities of time, place and condition surrounding the individual. Second, and even more significantly, the level at which we express our potential must be dependent upon the level at which we habitually energize our life. The individual who lives his life almost entirely at the level of the body and the senses will respond to the same formative ideas in a very different manner from the individual who spends a significant part of each day in prayer, meditation, and contemplation. A good education, inspiring teachers, colleagues and friends, uplifting family and social mores, and the deliberate cultivation of ideals through devotion to the highest Goodness, Truth, Beauty, and Unity, all have a vital part to play in making the ideas of the 9H actual. An Ideal is an Idea to be realized. In the 9H we may glimpse something of the 'fruit of the tree', the fruit of the pursuit of the Ideas portrayed therein, the fruit of 'following our bliss'.

FURTHER CONSIDERATIONS ON
THE NUMBER 9

As we will explore further in Chapter 15, the number 3 is related to form and the formal cause of things, and to the heart aspect of the soul, as opposed to 4 which relates to matter and the will. Threeness in any chart shows that which delights us, that which enlivens us, that to which we aspire for the joy that it brings. It is in musical terms, as Hamblin so delightfully puts it, the 3/4 time of the waltz compared to the 4/4 of the march.

Indeed, as we saw in the case of Hitler, if we want to have a clear picture of what motivates a person, what 'moves' them, and 'gets them going', a look at their 3rd harmonic chart will usually be highly instructive, and especially if we note any trine aspects in the 3rd, which can often vividly depict an individual's most immediate aspirations, and what delights their heart, eye, mind and taste. Indeed for general counselling purposes there is a good case for examining the 3rd harmonic rather than the 9H in that it seems to give a less deeply ingrained, but often more immediately accessible, picture of the guiding ideals and images shown in the 9H. In this respect the 3H can show the kind of people to whom we will be attracted quite as vividly as the 9H, which is in Hindu astrology traditionally related to showing the qualities which will be ideally looked for in one's partner.

Looking at 9 (3^2) as 3 raised to a higher power, we can see it as the original Trinity of Love, Life, and Light, each themselves unfolded into their triple aspects. This relates to the Pythagorean description of 9 as 'utter perfection', as wholeness and completeness, and it may be as well to remind ourselves of just how profoundly 9 is entwined in the sacred myths and legends of the world.

Myth recounts that the Norse god Odin hung upside down from the World Tree for nine days and nights before he was able to bend down and take up the magical runes which brought inner knowledge and the gift of prophecy. The association of the number 9 with initiation, wisdom and spiritual knowledge is widespread. In the Eleusinian mysteries of Greece the initiation process lasted nine days. The Hydra, symbolic of wisdom, with which Hercules fought, had nine heads. In the Arthurian legend Merlin had nine bards and King Arthur battled for nine days and nights with an enchanted pig, which can be seen as symbolic of man's lower nature or alternatively as representing battling with the limits of the mind.[1] The mythical North European cat of wisdom had nine tails.

In the Welsh *Mabinogion* the goddess Cerridwen, who lives, significantly, in 'the Land Under Waves', has a Cauldron warmed by the breath of nine maidens in which she boils science and inspiration for her ugly son till 'three drops of the grace of inspiration' are yielded.[2] These nine maidens of course exactly parallel Apollo's nine muses whose divine wisdom embraces the past and the future as well as the present, and who were considered to be the inspiring powers and source of all human wisdom.

In the kabbalistic Tree of Life, the divine model for the Universe and Man, the ten Sefirot, the ten prime attributes of the Creator, can be seen as a nine suspended from the One, or as ten with identity between the first and the last. For the aspirant of the spiritual path there are often said to be nine stages. These are reflected in the nine Beatitudes of the Sermon on the Mount, the means by which we may ascend to enlightenment. These have their counterpart in the Nine Woes in St Matthew 23, which indicate the stages of descent and destruction. In the Tarot the ninth trump is the Hermit, a card related to self-transformation through withdrawing from the outer world in order to awaken the inner self. Gurdjieff saw the Enneagram, the ninefold division of the circle, with its sevenfold inner process, as mirroring the whole of life. (This inter-relationship of the 7 and the 9 is an aspect of number symbolism that deserves far more space than we can give it here. But it is obviously apparent that there must be a close connection between those ideals that inspire us and those ideals that motivate us. Where, because of chart geometries, there is a ready connection between the 7H and 9H positions, the planetary ideas involved will be likely to be of paramount importance in the life.)

Nine lies at the very heart of the Western tradition of numbers, for Pythagoras states that there are only nine numbers, and everything, both cosmic and divine, unfolds from its root idea, its innermost potentiality, to its outermost expression, its actualized perfection, through nine stages. Thus nine is as it were the culmination of the whole process of manifestation and creation. It is the point at which an idea becomes 'new born'. This is obviously seen in the fact that the normal period of gestation is nine months (but ten lunar months). And here we have the interesting fact that in most European languages the word nine and new are closely related, e.g. in German we have *neun* = 9 and *neu* = new; in French *neuf* = 9 and *neuf* = new; in Spanish *nueve* = 9 and *nuevo* = new.

This idea of new in relation to the 9H as our ideal pattern brings to mind St Paul's Epistle to the Romans, xii, 2: 'Be not conformed to this world; but be ye transformed by the renewing of your mind, that ye may prove what is that good and acceptable and perfect Will of God.'

From this perspective the 9H may be seen as a template for the 'renewing of our mind'. By turning to this higher image, our entelechy, our particular aspect of Archetypal Man, the Christos, we can bypass the distortions of our particular time, place, and condition and be 'reborn' into our potential wholeness and perfection.

Hamblin relates the 9H to the 'pleasure of pleasure', to joy, happiness and peace, and planets linked in the 9H show in what respect a person can spread joy and happiness to those around them, and be at peace with himself and with the world. Dwyer, following his study of Addey, Hamblin, Hand, Seymour-Smith, Williamsen, and others, gives for his key concept for the 9H the word Acceptance. To this he adds the subsidiary ideas of 'facility; happiness; humility; inertia; line of least resistance'. Presumably the latter phrase is intended in its higher sense as used by Robert Fritz.

In attempting to get to grips with the root archetypes of the numbers we have to recognize that we are having to translate into relatively localized and parochial terms the profound principles and ideas which form the Cosmos and its consciousness. On that scale almost anything we say about these numbers must inevitably seem somewhat banal. By the same token any idea associated with one of these first numbers must be seen to relate to a fundamental principle in life.

In 'being here now' all of our past, present, and future are as one . . . and as such we may see them enfolded. Wholeness and the implicit order are at once apparent. Thus the relationship to prophecy, to the muses, who draw upon the eternal Truth rather than the temporal.

In any hierarchy it is the King who is both ruler and servant . . . In this sense the 9H tells us the picture to be painted, the 'sweet repose of so great a happiness' which because it is our 'goal' can only draw us onward with all the power of that image which turns acorn into oak.

If this is so then we can see that the seer, who sees, is a 9H type because this is the level at which the final outcome is self-evident. If that is what we 'are' then no amount of beating about the bush will alter it . . . the acorn must eventually become an oak tree however much it may be distracted by other things en route.

NOTES

1. I am indebted to Tim Addey for pointing out this alternative interpretation.
2. In another version of the myth the cauldron has a nut-tree growing over it. The ninth nut to fall into the cauldron is the nut of wisdom.

CHAPTER 15

The Harmonics of Manifestation

CHARLES HARVEY

Most astrologers probably feel more confident interpreting the hard aspects in a chart than the soft one. While oneness relates to the idea of subjective wholeness and potentiality, twoness represents that division through which all potential becomes actualized, for all growth is through division. The simplest expression of this can be seen in the fact that each one of us started our physical existence as a single fertilized cell. That single cell, that wholeness, contained subjectively within itself all the information necessary for our final manifestation. It was only when that unity divided into first two, then four, then eight, and so on, that the cell's potentiality became actualized. So it is with the hard aspects. They represent the process by which our subjective potential becomes objectively manifested.

In seeing twoness as related to the process of objectification it is also helpful to think of the idea of 'the Opposition' as it is used in Western parliamentary democracies. The wholeness and unity of the typical monolithic one-party states may promise much but their level of productivity, both economically and culturally, is notoriously sterile and uncreative. With the coming of the idea of Government and Opposition we see the introduction of a creative dynamic which demands that the performance of those in power is constantly being scrutinized, and hence objectified by those 'in opposition'.

The numbers 2, 4, 8, 16 and so on can be seen then to represent ever deeper levels of objectification and manifestation, as the original unific Idea, represented symbolically by the conjunction aspect, moves out into the realms of duality and manifestation. The concrete, manifest qualities of this series of aspects is evident when it comes to interpreting a chart, for most astrologers will be much more confident in describing 'what it's like' to have for example ☉–90–♂ than ☉–120–♂. The ideas associated with the square are so much more tangible, clear cut, and visible to Western perceptions.

Likewise we know that in forecasting we are more likely to expect something 'to happen' to us when we have hard angle progressions and transits than soft angle ones. As we have seen, Ebertin and the cosmobiological school have focused on the 8th, 16th, and even deeper levels of two-based harmonics in developing their observations of what will manifest in a chart in terms of behaviour and events.

Psychologically we could say that the aspects and harmonics based on two and its derivatives are related to the faculty of Will. While the 3/4 time of the waltz, in David Hamblin's analogy, can be seen to awaken our hearts and aspirations, and turn us towards the ideal of what the Greeks named the Beautiful, by contrast the fourness of the 4/4 time of the march can be seen to relate strongly to the will, to manifestation, to the ideal of the Good. The typical march invokes in us strength, it encourages us to believe that we can do more than we had thought possible. It stiffens our resolve and impels us to action, 'to do or die'. The hard aspects based on 2, 4, 8 have been characterized by Arroyo as 'challenging'. They certainly represent those ideas within us which are demanding to be made manifest, to be actualized, through an effort of the will. When we examine those harmonic charts based on this series of numbers we are looking at maps of the way in which the individual, or event, is likely to impact upon the world. To distinguish between the different levels of twoness is not always easy, for they have much in common. However, at each level certain additional qualities and refinements seem to occur. A brief summary of what major aspect patterns in the different two-based harmonic charts are showing us follows. These ideas can equally be applied to the understanding of aspects in the natal chart.

2nd and oppositions in any chart = inherent polarities within the individual; those ideas which show the greatest potentiality for manifestation; the characteristic qualities of the first outward impulse to manifest.

4th and squares in any chart = the characteristic kind of efforts that we choose to make and which constantly challenge us; those ideas which we try 'to get to grips with' and 'to make happen' and 'make manifest' in our life.

8th and semi-squares and sesquiquadrates = those ideas which we can purposefully and productively pursue; fruitful efforts; built-in skills and behaviour patterns. The 'goods' delivered; the manifest destiny.

16th and 22.5 series aspects = the full manifestation in the material world coupled with its effect; the impact of the products of the moment, the individual, on the outer world.

It will be seen that as we proceed through this series, the qualities involved become more and more definite and concrete. We move from the impulse and tension of 2 with its possibility of oscillation between ideas, to the compulsive efforts and challenges of 4, to the productive activities and behaviour patterns of 8, and to the actual impact of all these levels of manifestation of 16. We could say that each chart in the series represents an ever deeper level of the individual's will. Where charts at deeper levels continue to show close oppositions, squares and 45/135 aspects, this is indicative that we are dealing with someone who is likely to make a deep impact on the world.

In theory we can continue ever deeper in our pursuit of the twoness of a moment, and it is interesting to note that the 6th power of 2 is 64, the number of hexagrams in the I Ching. The I Ching is said to express the complete pattern of 'the rhythms of life'. John Addey indicated that the number 6, which is 2×3, represents the objective expression (2) of Life (3), or 'the rhythms of life' and hence to health, which is dependent on the uninterrupted rhythms of the body, cf. the health connotations of Virgo, the 6th sign, and the 6th house.

It could be argued then that the 'I Ching aspect', as it has been called by Theodor Landscheidt, of 5° 37.5', and the 64th harmonic represent some kind of ground bass to manifestation in the physical world.

It is also worth considering that with twoness in addition to the fundamental polarities of positive and negative, male and female, yang and yin, we also have the idea of cause and effect. Thus oppositions and squares are often said among 'esoteric' astrologers to relate to karma. We can see that these aspects will certainly show us where the individual's will is going to be most challenged and most engaged in getting to grips with the world, and hence where they will be putting out and receiving the consequences of those actions. The Greeks saw the number 8 as relating to Justice in that it can be seen to represent the four Aristotelian levels of cause (Final, Efficient, Formal, and Material), linked together with their effects, i.e. the final consequence and outworking of being and acting in the world. From this we can see that it is but a small step to the concept that what happens to us is the result of who we are and how we manifest our being. 'Character is destiny' and as Jung put it 'What we cannot accept of ourself comes back to us as Fate.' In terms of mundane astrology we can see why these charts, and their related midpoint structures, often speak volumes about what is being manifested or actualized at any specific moment of space-time.

To sum up then, we are suggesting that twoness and the 2nd, 4th, 8th and subsequent harmonic charts relate to the idea of objectification, to manifestation, to the faculty of will and to the kind of ideas with which we are likely to have to get to grips and make decisions about during life, and which can be most productive for us. These charts show us the kind of 'goods' we have to deliver during this life, and the characteristic way in which we will exert ourselves to actualize these 'goods'.

It has been said that each one of us is constantly moving to that place in the scheme of things which we are creating for ourselves. In this sense these charts (together with the 5th harmonic) in describing, to a great extent, the actions and effects of the will are describing 'what we may become' as the result of our best efforts.

Adolf Hitler's chart is an excellent illustration of many of the harmonics. His particular power, as he himself realized, was in his rare combination of mind, motivation, vision and will. His 3rd and 9th, 5th and 7th tell us much about his inner motivations and ideals, his set of mind, and the visions that inspired him. His two-based harmonics, of which the 4th, 8th, and 16th are given in Figures 15.1 – 15.3 illustrate vividly the sheer will-power, and will to power, of the man. The 4th harmonic (Figure 15.1) reveals a powerful kite formation involving the very close ♅–180–♇ as the axis, precisely bisecting an almost exact ☉–90–♃. This is a

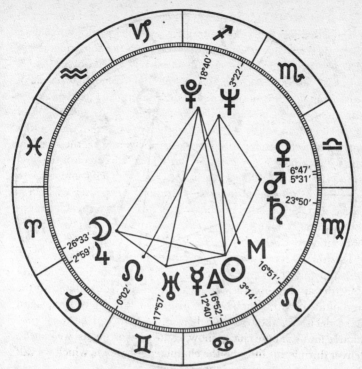

Figure 15.1 Adolf Hitler's 4H. Note the powerful kite formation involving Uranus, Pluto, Sun and Jupiter.

remarkably powerful combination, showing the enormous drive to actualize individual ambition and advancement in life (☉–90–♃), focused round revolutionary and reformatory activities, and immense untiring effort (♅–♇). One glance at this chart and any picture we may have had of the man as a relatively Venusian and easy-going Libra rising, Sun Taurus, Moon–0– Jupiter artist, must inevitably be given an entirely different perspective. This man will need to be doing radical things on a large scale. The close ☉–120–♆, –60–☊, –60–♀–♂, does however indicate that there will be a strongly idealistic and visionary motivation, and a certain passionate drive to the way in which he will go about exerting his will, and manifesting his destiny.

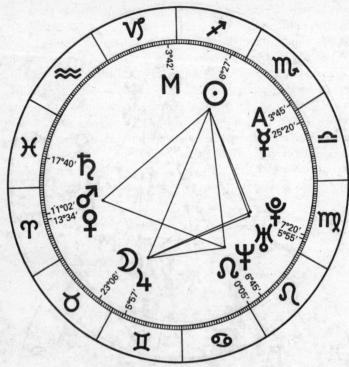

Figure 15.2 Adolf Hitler's 8H. Note the T-square of Sun/Jupiter with Uranus/Pluto joined by a Sun/Mars/Neptune Grand Trine.

Magnifying the twoness of this pattern, we see that in Figure 15.2, the 8H, the underlying aspect patterns are so close that we still have a remarkably tight T-square interaction of ♅–♇ with ☉ and ♃, while ☉–♂–♆ form a Grand Trine (reflecting *inter alia* that the delights of military strategy and sneak attacks may well motivate the development of this man's will and activities). The ♅–♇–☉–♃ T-square can be seen to represent very deep levels of will-power and effort directed towards the manifestation of personal power and the compulsion to bring about radical changes in the world, and 'the collapse of the old order of things and the construction of the new', to quote *COSI*. When hard aspects are this close we are looking at a determination to manifest the ideas involved (☉–♃–♅–♇), which seems to go down into the very 'structure of the world'.

We see this, and the consequences of it, in the 16H (Figure 15.3), where Hitler's impact upon the world is shown as ☉–0–♃ (still less than 1° orb, representing a natal orb of less than 8′) –180–♅ –♇, and only 18′ from the exact ♅/♇ midpoint. Could a picture better describe a man capable of stating that he would 'either rule the world or go down in flames with it'? Those who want to take signs into consideration will note the appropriate Leo-Aquarius polarity involved in this struggle to objectify a social revolution through individual power and dictatorship. Note how even after multiplying the radical positions by 16 the ♃–180–♅ is still only

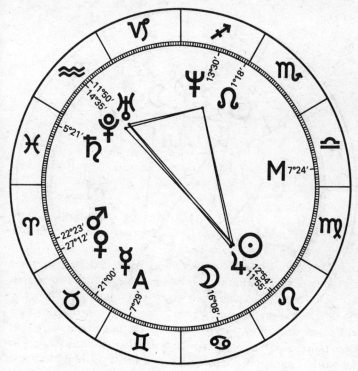

Figure 15.3 Adolf Hitler's 16H, representing his likely impact upon the world.

5′ from exact, indicating that this must have been within 20″ of arc at birth (these positions were calculated by computer working to .1′ accuracy). We may also note here, and in the 8H, how closely Ψ continues to be involved in this picture. The Sun moves almost 16° per day in the 16H chart. Thus the Sun's involvement here to this degree of precision with ♃, ♅, Ψ, and ♇ is something that was possible only for little more than three hours on that day.

Such a pattern might of course be considered to be a coincidence. But we in fact find, for example, examining the charts of other 'great dictators', that such ☉ involvement with outer planets is the norm, and, especially, tight hard aspects of ☉–♅, which seems to be the predominant hallmark of the autocrat, i.e.

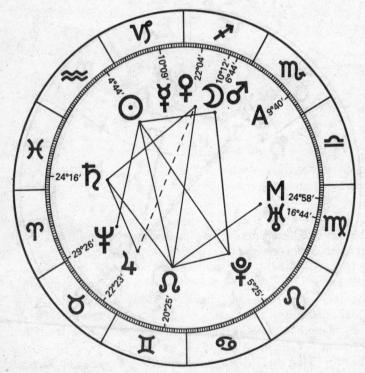

Figure 15.4 Catherine the Great's 16H. Compare with Figures 15.2 and 15.3 above, and 15.5 opposite.

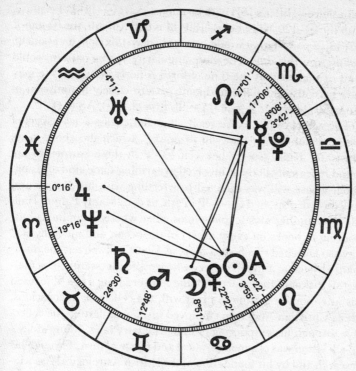

Figure 15.5 Napoleon's 16H. Compare the Sun, Uranus, Jupiter pattern with Hitler's 16H, Figure 15.3 above.

the 'self-ruled', and/or of ☉–♇, which of course Ebertin relates to 'the striving for power, the craving for rulership'.

Close ☉–♅ hard aspects appear in the 8H and 16H charts of Mussolini, Franco, Tito, and in the chart of our own autocratic Winston Churchill, and of 'le roi soleil', Louis XIV. Frederick the Great (24 Jan 1712, 11.30 a.m. LT, Berlin), had ☉–90–♇, –60–♆, and –135–♃ in 16H, Catherine the Great (2 May 1729, 2.30 a.m. LT, Stettin, Figure 15.4) had ☉–180–♇ and –60–♂ in the 16H. That other would-be conqueror of Europe and Russia, Napoleon Bonaparte's 16H (for 15 August 1769, 11 a.m. Ajaccio, Source Barbault) is shown in Figure 15.5. Here we see a precise variation on Hitler's 16H with an almost exact ☉–♅–♇ T-square, with the ☉–120–♃. The ☉–180–♅ is only 16′ orb, the ☉–90–♇ just 13′, a pattern that would have only been this close for about 25 minutes on this day. The close angularity of this pattern would tend to suggest that the time of birth is fairly accurate. We may note here also the natal midpoint pattern closely reminiscent of Hitler: ☿/♃ = ☉/☽ = ♃/M = ♆/♇ = ♅ = ☉/AS = ♂/♇.

The will of course expresses itself in actualizing every aspect of life, and not just in the 'will to power', which the above cases illustrate. Tight aspects between ☉–♆ in these harmonics are found repeatedly in those involved in earthing some kind of vision. Jung, whose will was directed to wrestling with his dreams and collective depths, had ☉–0–♆ in 4th, as does Manly Palmer Hall, the outstanding mystic and philosopher whose voluminous outpouring of books on every aspect of the occult and metaphysical have so enriched this field. Likewise Albert Schweitzer, the musician, physician, and missionary who worked incessantly to actualize his vision of the 'sanctity of life'. Where Jung's ☉–♆ focused his attention on getting to grips with the collective unconscious, Hans Christian Andersen employed his in manifesting the collective through his outpouring of immortal fairy tales. John Addey's ☉–♆ vision was of a metaphysical and mystical turn. Through his research and by his foundation of the British Astrological Association and the Urania Trust he produced concrete evidence and enduring channels for a previously nebulous study.

Normally in evaluating this will aspect of the individual we can either look at the 4H, as Hamblin ably suggests and illustrates in *Harmonic Charts*, or we can move up to the 8H which can give us an even tighter picture of the kind of area in which the individual's efforts are likely to be applied. If you use a computer print-out that lists harmonics charts in batches, it is very useful to have it run out, say, the first thirty-two harmonics. In that way you can run your eye quickly over the 2, 4, 8, 16 series and can note the way patterns are shaping up, and then draw up the one which shows the sharpest focus. Clearly any pairs of planets that stay in close hard aspect contact throughout the series will be of considerable importance and will give strong indications of the kind of ideas with which the individual will be grappling and seeking to make manifest. Close trines in these charts will show what ideas will motivate the individual to take action and to exert themselves.

PUTTING TOGETHER HEART AND WILL

It has been said that all progress comes about through a combination of aspiration and effort. When we see someone making changes in their life we immediately know that something must have motivated them to exercise their will. Thus when we see a teenager whose room is normally a bedlam of discarded clothes, half-read books, assorted unspooled cassettes, coffee cups, and general detritus, actually at work with a vacuum cleaner on a visible carpet, we know that probably someone has caught his fancy. As the French say, 'Cherchez la femme.' Some aspect of the Beautiful has touched his heart and in so doing has motivated him to activate his will to do something about his physical world, perhaps even to the extent of getting a part-time job to fund this new interest.

As we have seen, in harmonic terms we are motivated by threeness, by the trines, and we are impelled to action by the squares. The product of aspiration (3) and effort (4) is 3×4 or 4×3 which is 12. Thus the 12H can be seen to represent the earthing of our aspirations in the mundane world, and goes a long way to explaining why traditional astrology has always placed such emphasis on twelvefold divisions. As a blend of aspiration and effort, the 12H chart, and the closely related 24H, will tell us a great deal about the characteristic way in which we are able to marry these two crucial aspects of the psyche. As has long been observed, the individual with an opposition or square which is relieved by a planet in trine/sextile to each end of the opposition, or in trine/semi-sextile to one of the planets in square, is someone who seems to be able to put these hard aspects to dynamic and creative use. This is of course because in the 12H these planets will all come together. (A less powerful version of this combination is seen in the 6H, $2 \times 3 = 6$, which Addey relates 'to the rhythms of life and work'. This harmonic can be useful in assessing the characteristic approach to work, and also seems to have some bearing on the health patterns of the individual.)

Figures 15.6 and 15.7 show the 12H and 24H of Adolf Hitler. Here we see even more vividly the way in which this master of manipulating the collective unconscious has all three collective planets, plus Jupiter, configured with the Sun. In the 24H we see that these all fall closely with both MC and AS, tending to confirm the view that the time of birth as recorded (6.30 p.m., 20 April 1889, Braunau, Austria) is probably almost exactly right. If we were interpreting the 12H or 24H from scratch we might say that it represented the characteristic way in which we integrate our heart

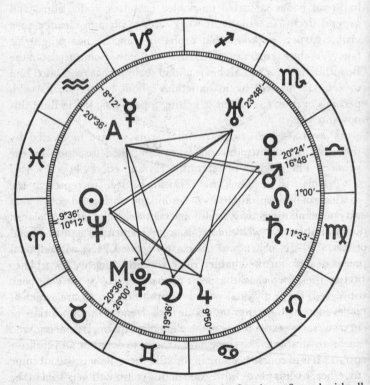

Figure 15.6 Adolf Hitler's 12H in which the Sun is configured with all three collective planets plus Jupiter.

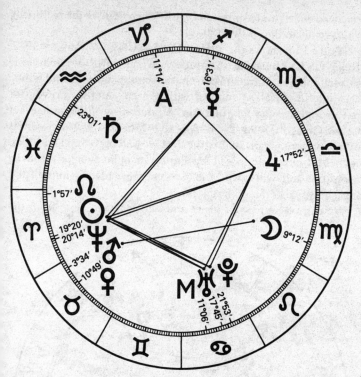

Figure 15.7 Adolf Hitler's 24H.

and will, and so actualize our aspirations. In other words the dominant planetary pictures in these charts will show those types of ideas which will enable us to progress and to unfold our potential and 'follow our bliss' as a Buddhist might put it. The 12H, as 3 × 4, will show the balance between effort and aspiration, the 24H, as 3 × 8, weights the picture towards the will and what we may be motivated (3) to produce (8). Here with Hitler's 24H we see a man who is motivated to actualize and manifest (−180− and −90−) a grand or grandiose vision (☉–Ψ) of collective revolution and regeneration, and who will probably be able to get it out into the world (connection with the angles). As with the 16H, the closeness of the aspect picture suggests that this pattern of aspiration and effort will be extremely deep-rooted and sustained by ever

renewed efforts and aspirations, with ☿ here joining the picture by
−120−/−60 to the ☉−Ψ−180−♃.

Figure 15.8 shows the 12H of Cassius Clay (17 January 1942,
18.35 CST, Louisville, Kentucky), which gives a remarkable
picture of the aspiration to personal success, popularity and public
acclaim (♃−MC−☾) coupled with a deep, intense 'striving for
power and craving for rulership' produced by the almost exact
Grand Cross of ☉−90−♇−90−AS−180−MC−♃−☾. The closeness
of this pattern means that in the 24H we find both Sun and Moon
with MC exactly opposed by Pluto, an indication of the deep
aspiration and 'will to win' and to regenerate and to lift himself and
his fellow blacks out of the ghetto.

We can of course put heart and will together more from the

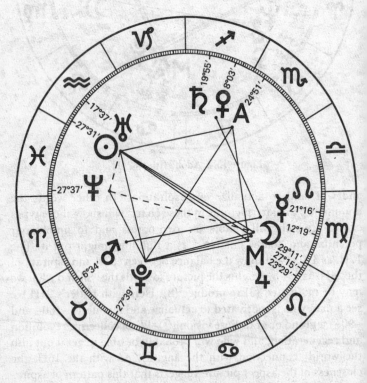

Figure 15.8 Cassius Clay's 12H.

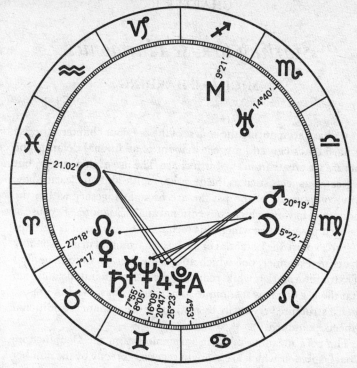

Figure 15.9 Margaret Thatcher's 18H. Note the Sun, Mars, Jupiter, Neptune, Pluto T-square.

perspective of the ideals and aspirations. In that case we would look at the $9 \times 2 = 18$ and $9 \times 4 = 36$, which would be seen as showing the characteristic way in which an individual actualizes (2) and makes manifest (4) their ideals (9). While Margaret Thatcher does not have a ☉–♅ or ☉–♇ contact in her 2, 4, 8, 16 series (though she does have a ♃–♅–♇–♆ in 16H), Figure 15.9 shows her 18H with its ☉–♂–♃–♆–♇ T-square, a vivid depiction of a forceful idealist who focuses herself around manifesting regenerative power. The ☽–☿–♄–M picture equally shows the narrower and more cautious and conservative side to the characteristic way in which she goes about actualizing her ideals and aspirations.

CHAPTER 16

Starting to Use Harmonics

MICHAEL HARDING

As we have seen during the course of the previous chapters, the use of harmonics can add a great amount of additional detail to the picture we create from the birth chart. The use of such major, but neglected aspects such as the quintile, septile and novile can show how components of the psyche are brought together within the individual in ways which conventional analysis ignores. Because of the rich possibilities which this technique opens up, it is perhaps best to explore the potential of the basic harmonics in a reasonably structured manner; one which allows the user maximum amount of extra information while reducing the risk of an initial confusion that the use of a new technique sometimes brings. We can impose such a structure very easily by restricting the amount of additional aspects examined.

The core meaning of each harmonic lies in the Conjunction. That is, planets which are brought together directly by the number of the harmonic resonate the most strongly to it, carrying its message most clearly. The planets which come to opposition, trine or square within the same chart modulate the core meaning because the nature of their own relationship one with the other has also to be taken into account. For this reason you may initially prefer to begin using harmonics by concentrating on the Conjunction and using this aspect alone for your first interpretation. David Hamblin's book *Harmonic Charts* is possibly the best source of information on interpretations for *all* the individual aspects within each of the major harmonics; it is a must for all serious students.

Assuming the chart you are using *has* such a Conjunction, this alone can give you a considerable amount of insight into the manner in which the two – or more – planets operate. Exploring these images with the client will also begin to open up the natal chart *and* the harmonic one. If there are indeed further aspects within the harmonic, you may well hear the client refer to them by the specific use of language or the information he gives regarding life experiences. If you feel confident, you can then pursue these directions using the additional aspect structures as a guide. If you still feel uncertain about their meaning then simply make notes of your observations and go over the charts again after the session.

Possibly the main purpose of offering astrological insights to a client is in order to impart *useful* information in a reasonably coherent manner. It is legitimate to explore some uncertain or confusing avenues as well; much can emerge from travelling these less trodden paths. It is *not* on, however, to try out a variety of techniques in a haphazard manner hoping that one of them might just work! This is not counselling, it is desperation, and it is very often the result of not getting to grips with the astrology of the situation. When you begin to use harmonics you greatly expand the reservoir of information you have to impart and at the same time get a greater clarity as to the areas of life where it is likely to apply. This in turn will open up the consultation to more possibilities and you must be prepared for this eventuality. This can be particularly true in the use of the 7th harmonic.

As we have seen, inspiration and fantasy are extremely powerful, though often unconscious motivators; we cannot move into this area unless we are competent to handle the issues that might emerge from its exploration. By limiting our initial use of harmonic charts to the (clearer) meaning of the Conjunction alone we can take account of our level of experience. Once you have got the feel of a particular number, and it is as clear to you as your sense of number 3 or 4, then you can expand your use of the chart with greater confidence to extract some of the dynamics that might lie behind it.

As you start to use harmonics so will you begin to re-think the whole way in which you approach the interpretation of the radical chart. You will have noticed that familiar aspects regularly throw up oddities, as if unrecognized symbolism is masquerading behind them. Someone with a tough square, for example, announces that she has a natural affinity with, and enjoyment of, the energies being brought together in such a brusque manner. Another's trine seems to show in practice not an easy, accepting attitude towards the planets concerned, but an almost mystical, compulsive relationship with them. Again and again we see how fragments of quite separate experiences cluster near our familiar turning points. We are at first perhaps tempted to suggest that this is just how some individuals get to experience their charts, that there must be some other factor at work, some gremlin that astrologers as yet know nothing about. The truth is much more simple, and harmonics will show you how to reach towards it. The answer almost certainly lies in the way we use orbs.

Most astrologers will allow an orb of 8° for a trine, even 10° if both lights are involved, but taking such wide sweeps allows the trine to hide within itself a multitude of possibilities which can emerge with unexpected examples of itself during the consultation. Close to the exact 120° aspect lie several very important points. 126°, for instance, is a *square* in the 5th harmonic. 115° 43' is a *square* in the 7th and 128° 43' is an opposition in the 7th. Although the energies of the planets separated by the trine are always going to be pulled into play, clearly their dynamics are going to be very different depending in which part of the accepted orb they lie.

The same effect takes place within the accepted orb of the square. 96° is a trine in the 5th harmonic, 85° 43' is a trine in the 7th harmonic and 93° 20' a trine in the 9th harmonic. Within the range of the radical opposition we see this effect once again. 171° 26' is a trine in the 7th harmonic as is 188° 34', and 186° 40' is a trine in the 9th harmonic. Again, these all fall within orbs used by many astrologers and it is clear that a whole range of very subtle human experiences are being lumped together with very little thought. The harmonic aspects clustering around the square, for instance, all demand their own recognition, and while it is probably true that the very nature of the 4th harmonic wave will tend to produce a basic tension of some kind between two planets 96° or 85° 43' apart, we can no longer say that these two particular aspects are 'both squares', for they simply are not. It is probable that most of the arguments regarding the applying and separating 'effects' of the same aspect may well be resolved by a deeper understanding of the many *different* aspects which are in reality coming into play in the same arena. Those astrologers who use harmonics are going to be the first to observe this phenomenon, and their craft will benefit from it immeasurably.

Getting used to using harmonic charts as a routine part of chart analysis, getting familiar with the ideas their number suggests, and maintaining case histories of those examples which most clearly show these dynamics in action will revolutionize astrology. As more coherent observations can be made of exactly *how* a specific wavelength was experienced or presented, out of the spectrum of all its possibilities, so will we begin to see much more clearly and more accurately the individual geometry of personality.

PART THREE

*Astro*Carto*Graphy*

CHAPTER 17

*Astro*Carto*Graphy*

MICHAEL HARDING AND CHARLES HARVEY

Astro*Carto*Graphy is perhaps one of the most challenging of modern astrological techniques. It not only opens up a whole new vista of interpretative, predictive and even therapeutic possibilities, it also confronts many preconceptions head-on and forces us to re-appraise how we believe astrology may function in the world. While this is far from being a bad thing, it does mean that it may take a long time before the implications of Astro*Carto*Graphy are fully recognized even if the technique is of itself quite straightforward.

Astro*Carto*Graphy is based on a traditional astrological tool – the relocation chart. This is a chart set for any place other than the actual place of birth, using the same birth time but – obviously – different geographical co-ordinates. The resulting chart tells the native what his or her chart would have been like had birth taken place in that particular place. Because the chart is set for the same birth time the planets will always be in exactly the same zodiacal position, only the angles and houses will be different. The chart can then be interpreted in the light of these mundane changes.

The idea behind setting up such a chart lies in the belief that if one travels to a different place one's internal 'birth chart', that blueprint of the birth moment that each individual somehow embodies, is in some way sensitive to the geographical shift. If one moves to a place where Saturn would have been on the MC should birth have taken place there, then some quality of actually having a radical Saturn conjunct the MC would come into the life of the native if he remained there. Relocation charts are erected to see how proposed moves alter the diurnal dynamics of the chart and their subsequent expression in the world.

Anyone who has worked with relocation charts can have little doubt that they are extremely revealing, especially where planets become angular. It is this phenomenon of angularity that Jim Lewis set out to explore with Astro*Carto*Graphy, a technique which had only sporadically been used by others previously. A computer calculates each place on earth where each planet would be on the Ascendant, Descendant, MC or IC for the moment of birth and plots these points on a map. Because the MC and IC are created entirely by the rotation of the earth – the intersection of the plane of the meridian with the ecliptic – the lines indicating these potential contacts for each planet run from pole to pole and so appear vertical on a Mercator projection. The Ascendant and Descendant, however, are created by both the rotation of the earth *and* a shifting of latitude. Consequently the lines on the Mercator map depicting potential contact points are a mix of a straight line and the circle described by the rotating earth. They emerge as a wave-form running from south to north, and then back to south as they track the moving intersection of the plane of the horizon and the plane of the ecliptic. Recourse to a Table of Houses which lists Ascendants for several latitudes will quickly illustrate how the rising degree for the same moment alters in a regular manner as different degrees of latitude are examined. There remains one other important point to be made.

Astrologers have paid very little attention to the significance of a planet's celestial latitude. It is important to recognize that the Astro*Carto*Graphy map takes celestial latitude into account and thus depicts things as they are, relative to the earth. Planets are shown where they really are rising, culminating, setting or anti-culminating. This is an important point to bear in mind as there can be some difference between the two possibilities. An ordinary birth chart drawn up for a particular town where a planet appears to be angular shows in fact where the planet's ecliptic degree was on one of the four angles. On an Astro*Carto*Graphy map that planet's line may be some distance away; it was there, however, when the planet was itself on the angle. As the ordinary chart calculation program does not (and indeed generally cannot) allow for latitude, it is important to recognize this crucial difference.

The Astro*Carto*Graphy chart depicts all those points on the surface of the earth where angularity exists at a specific moment of time. As we look at an Astro*Carto*Graphy map we are seeing all those places where Mercury really was rising, where Pluto really was culminating, where Saturn really was setting all over the world at one specific moment of time. This is powerful stuff because it offers a balance against our past insistence on ignoring a very important question: how do we relate to the planet on which we are born?

The moment of birth anchors us to both time and space; we are defined by the double matrix of heaven and earth. Up to now, astrology has been almost exclusively concerned with analysing the significance of that moment of time. The moment of space has been virtually ignored. Astro*Carto*Graphy shows us how we relate to the earth as a whole whether or not we are conscious of it. That is, it echoes in space our more familiar relationship with the planetary cycles. Our chart is in a continual spatial relationship with the earth which mirrors its synchrony with the planets. In fact, Astro*Carto*Graphy also gives us a glimpse of something much beyond that, as we shall see later in this chapter.

The moment of birth somehow defines for us a very specific relationship with the whole earth in exactly the same manner as it defines some form of internal harmony with the skies. We can chart our relationship with the planets through the pages of an ephemeris; our relationship with the earth is shown in the Astro-*Carto*Graphy map. How telling that may be can be judged from Figure 17.1, which is part of the Astro*Carto*Graphy for John F.

Figure 17.1 Pluto on the Midheaven at Dallas in the chart of John F. Kennedy.

Kennedy. At the moment he was born, Pluto was culminating at Dallas. In other words, we begin now to introduce quite a new idea into astrological practice. Kennedy can be described as having a Pluto in Cancer, a Pluto in the 9th house and a Pluto in Dallas. The 'Pluto in Dallas' is as much an accurate description of him as using the previous two, more familiar, methods of measurement and identification. In many respects it fits our memory of him more sharply than anything else.

Looking at the map one will see, of course, that Kennedy must also have Pluto culminating at every point along the 96° meridian, so what is so special about Dallas? By itself, the answer has to be 'nothing' (but there *is* actually something more, as we shall see shortly). Looking at only a single factor, we would have also to say that there is similarly nothing particularly special about Pluto in Cancer – everyone in the world for about twenty years will have had that placement. Similarly, there is nothing remarkable about having Pluto in the 9th house; that is the lot of about one twelfth of the world's population at any one time. As we mentioned in the introduction, measurement in any one plane, be it space, time or geography will only show you the relationship between the thing measured and the method of measuring. The meaning of it lies in understanding what each different technique has to offer and the goal of the astrologer should be a synthesis of that information. Astro*Carto*Graphy has barely begun to reveal its language.

In Kennedy's case, Astro*Carto*Graphy focuses our attention on Pluto's relationship with Dallas in exactly the same way that his birth chart draws us into examining its meaning in Cancer and in the 9th house. If we regard the more familiar methods of depicting Pluto's permanent fixtures in his life as being a correct approach, then Astro*Carto*Graphy strongly suggests that we also have a permanent relationship with various parts of the world *at all times*. This idea may take a while to be fully absorbed, but there is no getting away from it. Furthermore, this relationship between the individual and various clearly-defined areas of the world can come into sharp relief in at least two ways: we can go to it, or it can come to us.

There are many examples of people travelling to parts of the world where their planets are angular and meeting the energy symbolized by that encounter in a direct and quite unambiguous manner. Alternatively, just as we have long recognized that parts of the birth chart tend to get projected on to others, so do Astro*Carto*Graphic contacts also seem to be at times expressed by individuals who embody the psychological essence symbolized by the angularity in their own circumstances. A person with Uranus running through a certain town may come into contact with someone from there who acts the part of Uranus for a while. The encounter may be shocking, exciting or life-altering in some way. Letters from a place where the native's Neptune hovers on the horizon may get inexplicably lost. Head office may be where Saturn marks the MC line or a relationship may be formed with someone whose Venus line runs through the native's place of birth. These are all basic astrological connections, ordinarily quite invisible. They exist beneath the surface of the birth chart like nerves beneath the skin and require another dimension of measurement to be clearly described.

When we hear them, they are unmistakable echoes of their celestial origins.

'My experience in Minneapolis . . . was much more inner for me – with much Plutonic upheaval, Saturnine hardship and Piscean solitude,'writes a woman with a 12th house Scorpio Sun of her experiences in a city where Pluto is on the Ascendant and Saturn on the IC. Contacts with these two planets frequently bring with them the need to face the hard realities of life, to get down to work and confront issues head-on. Ebertin writes simply 'hard labour' for this as a midpoint combination, and this is also particularly apt here as the writer continues: '. . . work and graduate school were hard struggles – I learned about independence (alone, female, new city in different harsh weather, new work responsibilities). I established for myself that I could work in a professional position, I observed myself feeling "as hard as stone" and like an immovable force. I dealt with authority and competition issues. My perfect symbol for Minneapolis was trudging through deep snow – life was hard, hard, hard. I'm still recovering from what Minneapolis did to me. I don't understand what happened there . . . I feel in the aftermath, as though my head was split open so that I'm open to universal energies . . . I am also infinitely more serious.'

What is so striking about the writer's choice of phrasing is that although she was familiar with her chart, the description was written *before* she understood the significance of what Astro*Carto*Graphy had to say about its geographic expression. Even though the experience of having both Saturn and Pluto brought to her front doorstep like a permanent transit was clearly an exhausting one, it was also ultimately rewarding. 'My intuition sharpened, I had beautiful inner experiences, started interpreting astrological charts, went on long trips like pilgrimages to beautiful wilderness areas. I had a deep relationship with a therapist.'

The Saturn theme occurs again in how another woman reacted to that planet on the IC in Los Angeles. 'I was there three weeks and was so sure that I wanted to leave right away it was almost laughable! I was never so turned-off a place in my life! "Terrible" was hardly the word. I did my best anyway and requested a transfer back to the east after three months.'

When Saturn is coupled with Neptune life can also be difficult. Such transits can bring doubts and confusions, a need to reassess spiritual goals or confront unrealistic dreams and face reality. A student attending college when such an Astro*Carto*Graphy crossing took place reports that he found his time there 'a point in my life of great disillusionment, spiritual extremism and impracticality'. In moving to another town 'under the Mercury line I got married, fathered a child and enrolled at the Art Institute . . . The symbolism of Mercury evolved here in my artwork.' Here Mercury, the ruler of hand/eye co-ordination and graphic skills, is brought to the surface as the native moves to that point where it was angular at the moment of his birth, reinforcing the image that such contacts are a unique form of terrestrial transits.

An angular Mars in the birth chart often correlates with arguments and conflicts – sometimes even fights – until the native learns to express this fiery energy creatively and constructively. This can be equally true Astro*Carto*Graphically, as one man with Mars on the Descendant relates when being caught speeding while literally driving over this contact point: 'I was ripped off of all my money by the cops in order to be let on my way.' Later in life at a town where Mars was once more on the Descendant the same man was arrested for possession of a small quantity of marijuana and subsequently run over by a car in the same location. This is angularity with a vengeance! Fortunately he also benefited from other contacts. He experienced the results of successful studies under a double Jupiter/MC, Venus/Descendant crossing, a place from which he also successfully avoided being drafted into the army.

We have commented elsewhere that Jupiter by no means always plays the part of the benefic, but in Astro*Carto*Graphy it would appear that here it more readily lives up to its traditional role dispensing good fortune, knowledge and honours. John Addey had Jupiter running through Bombay and within hours of his arrival was awarded an honorary Doctorate of Astrology by the Minister of Education – an event which made the number two slot of that night's television news!

Venus and Jupiter together can result in a strong sense of wellbeing and enjoyment when they meet at a particular location. 'I felt a wonderful warmth of place and told a friend I wanted to walk around the town and speak with some of the shopkeepers. This is quite unlike my very reserved self,' reports a man who drove into a small town which marked the connection of his Venus and Jupiter lines. 'It was a happy place for me. I returned there ten years later and felt the same.' Rome, however, was different for him. There Saturn crossed the city and he felt 'compelled to leave there after only fourteen hours, most of which were spent in my hotel room'. Saturn also crossed Buffalo, New York, and here the unexpected death of a relative cut short an intended one-month visit to that city. The negative effect was felt so strongly that 'I didn't even stay for the funeral and left after five days.'

In India, however, Neptune rose at a village where the same man's spiritual leader lived. 'I love it because I am completely anonymous and feel akin to the Indian culture, yet retain my privacy. I am not expected to be anything at all except "the foreigner".' Neptune's rulership of spirituality and community are clearly evident here, just as Saturn and Jupiter previously. Astro-*Carto*Graphy can also show clearly where something can 'come to us' and pin-point its location in the world. A woman living on the East Coast of America with Uranus transiting her Ascendant writes: 'I find myself listening to more, writing more articles and publicity for bands out of Northern Ireland and Scotland where according to your map I have Uranus on the Descendant.' This is quite remarkable, and if similar examples continue to occur then we shall be forced to re-evaluate how we interpret such major transits. We can no longer think of them as being related only to ourselves in an isolated manner, but perhaps recognize that such transits actually connect us in some way to various parts of the world. The angle or the planet then would no longer be seen as somehow just part of ourselves, some internal touchstone to the cycles of the heavens, but as an almost literal connection to those places on the surface of the earth with which we have a resonant affinity.

One particularly dramatic example comes from a woman who has $P = \odot / \mathbb{D}$ natally and thus could be expected to have a natural affinity with that planet. The symbolism is so striking that we are forced again to recognize how powerful is this unexplored region of astrology. We have to come back to that image of the symbol of a planet somehow embedding itself in the surface of the earth, as much part of the landscape as it is a part of the natal chart. This almost literal transposition of glyph to globe demands its own language; for a start we can perhaps use one of James Joyce's words: *geoglyphy*.

Joyce coined this word to describe how he blended the symbolism of the human form into the landscape. We are doing something very similar and can rightly speak of a planet's geoglyphy as the physical expression in the world of its role in the geometry of birth. In this next example, a woman's experience of her Pluto's geoglyphy focuses in Istanbul, where the planet is on the MC.

'The first visit was a clandestine adventure, which involved much scheming and duplicity to prevent our parents finding out, as we assumed, doubtlessly correctly, that they would put a stop to it. We wanted to go there because it was the most exotic place we could think of to lose our virginities, and also because we'd been told it could not be done. The former part actually fell through as we only held out as far as the Red Cow in Dover, which was in a way a pity as we had managed relatively chastely for the previous year. Going to Istanbul I met a French mercenary called Gerard, on the back of a lorry, and later became engaged to him – to the consternation of my friend. Gerard later tried to sell me to a Turk and I only got out of it by making a scene in a restaurant and slipping off in the confusion. We slept out in one of the main parks, which was a trifle foolish, as we nearly got ourselves murdered. The problem was solved by Gerard pulling a knife and being horribly threatening. The details are a bit blurred.

'I tried illegal substances for the first time in a rather sleazy night-club and also nearly got lynched for dancing and playing a guitar on the beach. I had long blonde hair then and wore a bikini and was taken for a whore. We had to be rescued by boat. It was also the first and last time in my life that I tried shoplifting. I got caught, and if the shopkeeper hadn't been a decent chap I'd probably still be rotting in a Turkish jail minus hands. I still have nightmares about that. The second time I was there wasn't so dramatic. I experienced my first orgasm and was involved in a drugs raid in my hotel. The man I was with – not the same one as the previous year – was rather devious and has since made rather a lot of money.

'As a matter of fact my Jupiter/MC line goes through eastern Australia. I was at primary school there when I was eleven, but had to be moved to high school because I was so far ahead of the others. I can't remember the details but I took some sort of academic test and came well ahead of everyone else, including seventeen- and eighteen-year-olds. My Neptune/MC line runs through Colombo, which I always describe to anyone who will listen as the nearest place to Paradise on this earth.'

In mundane astrology Astro*Carto*Graphy is equally revealing. Country can be compared to country, leader to leader and business to business. The focus points of ingresses and lunations stand out in the world quite vividly. The slow march of eclipses clearly show presence around the globe while the major cycles of the planets can be quickly related to where their aspects lie across the land. Astro*Carto*Graphy is a powerful tool for our understanding of history and its projection into the future.

The other important phenomenon which Astro*Carto*Graphy allows us to explore is the paran. The paran – short for paranatellon – is the simultaneous crossing of both the MC and the

Ascendant by two planets. Unless an individual is actually born with one planet conjunct the MC and one conjunct the Ascendant (a configuration called a mundane square whatever aspect exists between the two bodies), the potential for an exact paran can be hard to spot. To calculate the possibility of such a contact requires taking into consideration the planets' oblique ascension relative to the place of birth. This, of course, is just what the Astro* Carto*Graphy program is built to do. Such double crossings can be particularly powerful in the birth chart and are traditionally viewed in two ways. If there is the potential for the existence of a paran then as the earth rotates under the two planets there will come a moment when they become angular; in other words the moving angles will pick up the planets as a type of transit shortly after birth. Similarly, directing the planets or the angles might produce a paran by direction during the course of the individual's life. This simultaneous locking-in to the energy of two bodies which are the same angle apart as that which separates the MC from the Ascendant is obviously a moment tense with possibilities. Astro*Carto*Graphy can relate such moments to the whole earth.

When two 'planet lines' cross on an Astro*Carto*Graphy map this indicates that a paran exists at that geographical latitude. Thus as the earth rotates during the day the energy of that crossing may well be felt along the whole of that degree of latitude. This might be particularly important when slow-moving planets in hard aspect to one another are picking out such a parallel. Thus, while the individual Astro*Carto*Graphy map is calculated for a particular moment in time – generally birth – it is well worth seeing if such crossings take place at latitudes relevant to the individual concerned, for the planets *would* have become angular at that degree some time during the course of the birth day. The fact of one specific parallel of latitude receiving a powerful transit for twenty-four or more hours has great implications for those who believe that astrology may offer valuable clues to why specific moments in history occurred in the location they did. The moments of major planetary phases becoming exact seem to lay down patterns of energy upon the surface of the earth; patterns which wait to be triggered by subsequent transits and lunations, sometimes with great drama.

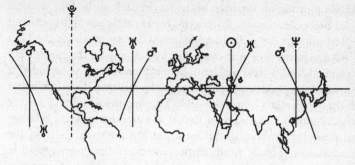

Figure 17.2 Mars/Uranus, Sun/Uranus and Mars/Neptune lines all crossing at the Dallas latitude in the chart of John F. Kennedy.

Figure 17.2 shows a striking series of parans for President Kennedy – Mars MC/Uranus Dsc, Mars Dsc/Uranus IC, Sun IC/Uranus Asc and Mars Asc/Neptune IC – all lined up *along the latitude of Dallas*. Such Mars/Uranus/Neptune energies tied in with the solar (self) symbol have long been associated with violence, treachery and plotting. Witte identified one manifestation of ♂/♅/♆ as 'attempted assassination'. Combining these paran symbols with Kennedy's Pluto on the MC geographically locates the focus of their energy. We are no longer looking to see Pluto's energy possibly being expressed *anywhere* along the 96° meridian; we would probably look exclusively to Dallas.

ACGs – Astro*Carto*Graphy maps – are of especial value to the astrologer who works for the business or political community or who is in any way involved in having to make national or international forecasts. Using normal astrological methods one would have to recast the charts of major cycles, ingresses and lunations for every major capital and area of the world. As a result few astrologers could normally contemplate undertaking such work. But by using ACGs it becomes possible to assess the likely impact of any particular cycle in a few moments, and to see whether during the course of the year, or any other cycle, any particular area is under especial pressures.

A ready-made research tool of special value here is the annual *Source Book of Mundane Maps* published by ACG originator Jim Lewis, which has been appearing since 1979. Each year these give

ACGs plotting on the map of the world each of the four tropical solar ingresses, the four sidereal ingresses, and each of the new and full Moons for the year. In addition ACGs are given for the 1775 USA Declaration of War chart, for the UK and for the current US President and Vice-President. Beneath each map is included a listing of the planets' zodiacal longitude, latitude, declination and Right Ascension. Since the 1988 edition, drawn charts set for Washington DC for each of the ACGs are also given. These are valuable for evaluating the total pattern for each chart in the normal way. This is vitally important to do, because we need to know 'what kind' of Uranus is rising through London. If Uranus is square Mars on the ♄/♇ midpoint we can expect very different Uranian 'surprises' than if the Uranus was trine Mars on the ☉/♃ midpoint.

Various examples of the uses of such ingress and lunation charts are given in *Mundane Astrology* by Baigent, Campion, and Harvey. For instance they demonstrate how the ACG for the Aries ingress of 1945 (Figure 17.3) clearly shows the differing fates of the main protagonists as the Second World War drew to a close. Thus ♃ is seen to be on the M at rejoicing London, ♀ is on the IC for victorious Moscow, while Ψ (which was close −90−♄) is on the M down through Berlin and Rome, marking the final dissolution of the Axis powers, while ♇ (on ♅/Ψ) is on the IC at Tokyo, marking the country on the earth which was to reap the whirlwind of the release of atomic energy. Washington shows ♄ (−90−Ψ) on the M, seemingly inappropriate until we remember that only twenty-three days after this ingress the much beloved President Roosevelt was to suddenly die.

Not all such ACGs of ingresses are quite so vividly instructive, but, when considered in relation to the overall planetary patterns of the time, they can usually be relied upon to focus on some of the main areas that will come into the spotlight in subsequent months. The same goes for ACGs of the twice-monthly lunations, which will often reveal the topical areas of news. Thus, as we write, the war in the Persian Gulf has been heating up with the US Navy's tragic shooting down of an Iranian airliner at 6.54 a.m. on 3 July. The preceding full Moon of 29 June 1988 (Figure 17.4) shows the highly dangerous combination of ♄−0−♅ on the M crossing ♂ on

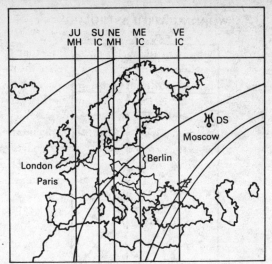

Figure 17.3a The 1945 Aries ingress placed Jupiter on the MC right through London and close to Paris. Venus, the traditional planet of victory, is on the IC for Moscow, while Berlin has Neptune on the MC and Uranus on the DS.

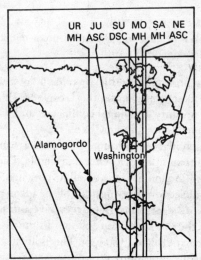

Figure 17.3b The 1945 Aries ingress placed Moon conjunct Saturn on the MC through Washington DC square Neptune AS. Just twenty-three days later President Roosevelt, 'father of the nation' since 1933, died suddenly. Note how Uranus is on the MC right through Alamogordo, where the first atomic bomb was exploded on 18 July.

Figure 17.3c The 1945 Aries ingress shows Pluto exactly on the IC through Tokyo. It is conjunct the Uranus/Neptune midpoint. Uranus on the AS passes through north Japan.

the AS in close proximity to this area. We may note that that ♂ was at 22♓59 exactly triggering the US ♂–90–♆, that nation's propensity for military and naval confusions and disasters, which we have examined more fully in Chapter 8.

But while such ingress and lunation charts are important, they are only specific examples of a general principle. The charts for the beginning, conjunction phase, of all cycles are important for studying the subsequent outworkings of the ideas represented by that cycle. In *Mundane Astrology* Harvey gives an example of the importance of the ♂–♇ cycle in relation to the violent release of energy, sudden explosions, and so on. This is illustrated by the case of the spontaneous explosion of the oil tanker *Betelgeuse* off Bantry Bay in January 1979. He shows that the chart for the moment of the explosion, which occurred as Mars came –90– ♇, was intimately connected to the chart for the ♂–♇ conjunction of the previous August, as well as to the chart for the preceding Capricorn ingress.

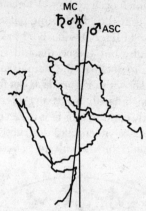

Figure 17.4 Full Moon on 29 June 1988, and the Saturn/Uranus conjunction on the MC and Mars on the AS crossing in the Persian Gulf.

At the time of writing (1988) the world's worst spontaneous gas explosion occurred at the Piper Alpha field in the North Sea, killing 166 people. It happened at 21.31 BST on 6 July 1988, at 58N29, 00E17. Could the danger of this catastrophic explosion have been foreseen? Figure 17.5 shows a section of the ACG for the preceding

Figure 17.5 The Mars/Pluto conjunction of 11/12/87 at 12.24 GMT has Uranus on the MC and the Moon on the DS crossing exactly over the Piper Alpha oilfield.

♂–♇ conjunction, which occurred on 11 December 1987 at 12.24 p.m. It will be seen that the ♅ MC line passes exactly through Piper Alpha. Why the ♅ line? Obviously ♅ has to do with sudden explosions of all kinds, but to see the full significance of this placement we need to look at the actual map for this ♂–♇ conjunction. This is shown in Figure 17.6, set for the Piper Alpha field. It is a chart which hardly needs any interpretation, for here we find that the exactly culminating ♅ is in fact exactly –45– to the ♂–♇. A closer and more violent and destructive combination on this Meridian it would be difficult to envisage. Indeed if, as

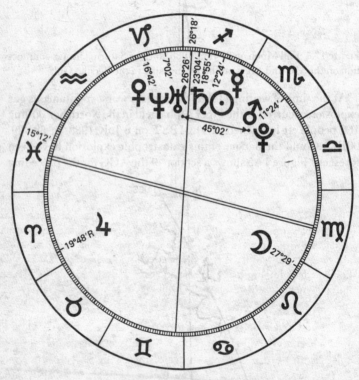

Figure 17.6 The chart for the Mars/Pluto conjunction of 11 December 87 set for the location of Piper Alpha. Note how the conjunction is only 2′ from an exact 45° to the culminating Uranus. This highly volatile axis was being triggered by Mars at the time of the disaster.

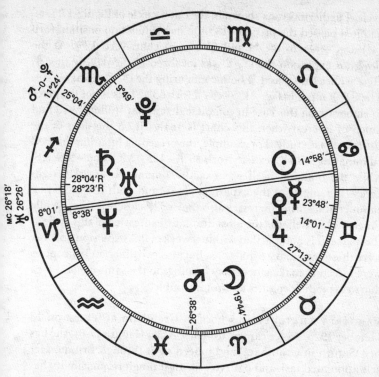

Figure 17.7 The first explosion, 6 July 1988 at 21.31 hrs. This occurred as Mars moves from semisquare Pluto to square Uranus setting up an exact resonance with the Mars/Pluto square Uranus/MC shown in Figure 17.6 above. Note how Mars is just 14′ from sesquiquadrate its conjunction point with Pluto and just 12′ from squaring Uranus/MC of the Mars/Pluto moment. Outer positions are from Figure 17.6.

suggested in *Mundane Astrology*, a 'World Astrology Watch' were in force, there is no doubt that Piper Alpha would have been placed on alert for the duration of this cycle, and particularly at this time.

Why was this particular *time* in the cycle so critical? In the *Betelgeuse* chart it was noted how the explosion happened just after ♂ had formed the –90– (orb 59′), 'manifesting' phase of the cycle. In the Piper disaster (chart Figure 17.7) we see that ♂ has just recently formed (orb 1° 49′) the –135–, 'manifesting' phase of the cycle. Furthermore, as shown in the outer circle of Figure 17.7, ♂ had just passed the precise −135− to its conjunction position (orb 14′) and −90− to the M and ♅ of that chart (orb 12′). At the *Betelgeuse* explosion the ♂−♇ was localized to the day by the ☉. Here we see the ☉ and ☽ both configuring the ♂/♇ mp at 18♑14. The ☉/☽ mp is in fact −135− ♂/♇ (orb 53′). This is not the place to elaborate on this case in complete detail, but students will find much of interest when this chart is analysed on the lines of the *Betelgeuse* case study. For example, the preceding lunation shows ♇ culminating with ♂ exactly (orb 30′), −135− MC, and −90− AS, while the lunation itself was exactly conjunct ♆ at 8♑16 right across the angles of the explosion chart, and both the preceding summer and spring ingresses also showed ♆ closely setting. While Piper Alpha itself was the most dramatic expression of this cycle at this place, it is notable that within a week of this explosion not only were there secondary explosions, but also two different helicopters were forced to make emergency landings in the same general area due to exploding engines and rotor trouble.

MARGARET THATCHER was born in Grantham at 9 a.m. on 13 October 1925. As we can see from her ACG (Figure 17.8), she has her 'Saturn in Grantham' and indeed right through Britain. Her self-appointed task and path to growth through responsibility lies on her doorstep, through personal effort, through tackling the problems of her world, her environment. At the same time she has Moon in Britain, indicating that this is where her capacity for caring and for popular concerns lies. It is not perhaps without significance that the Moon and Saturn intersect most closely through Scotland, Wales and the North, the very areas where she faces the most serious problems and where her policies of cutting out dead (♄) work (☽) and encouraging self-reliance (Moon-Saturn) and self-discipline have hit hardest in terms of unemployment and brought her her greatest challenges and unpopularity.

Looking a little further to the West we see that she has her ☽−0−♆ through Ireland, and that it then passes down through Gibraltar. Indeed the ☽/♆ midpoint is almost exactly on the MC through Belfast, Dublin and Gibraltar. These are the areas where she is constantly confronted with the Neptunian with the

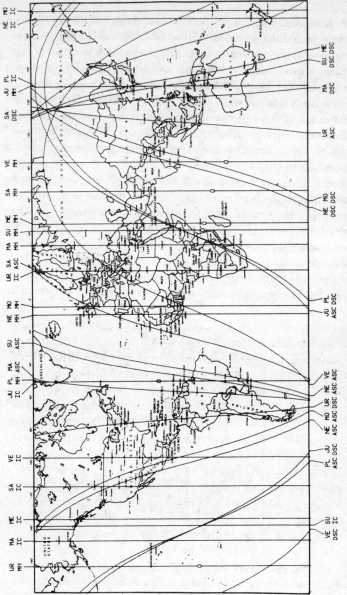

Figure 17.8 Astro*Carto*Graphy map for Margaret Thatcher.

subversive elements of society, and at the same time with allegations of hidden agendas, with confusions and deceptions and issues involving the secret security forces which constantly arise to remind her of her weaknesses, and which can 'run loose' and undermine her best laid Saturnine plans. It is notable that the most serious internal crisis of her career to date – which led to the resignation of two senior ministers – centred around the Westland helicopter company. Its activities are based in Yeovil, Somerset, close to her Moon line and very close to the precise latitude where Saturn crosses her ☽ – ♆.

But if Thatcher faces many of her problems on home territory she manages to shine elsewhere. It was the Russians who first named her the 'Iron Lady', and turning to Moscow we see that indeed her wide ☉–0–♂ brackets the MC there. There her reputation (MC) for toughness (♂) was given world recognition (MC). Moscow has always been where Thatcher has perceived the danger and the challenge which has motivated her to take a tough, almost militaristic approach to East/West relations. Yet, what do

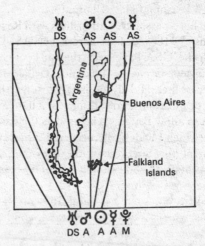

Figure 17.9 A section of Margaret Thatcher's ACG showing how Mars and the Sun were exactly rising through the Falklands at the moment she was born. Note how Mars passes through Buenos Aires while her Uranus DS line also passes through Argentina.

we also see here? Thatcher's $♀$ on the AS is well within orbs at Moscow. And behold when she visited Moscow she became the nation's sweetheart, and is perceived as having a highly charismatic intimacy with Gorbachev. She is hailed as the catalyst ($♀$) of the Reagan/Gorbachev summits and arms ($♂$) agreements ($♀$). Her glamorous relationships with Moscow and the Russian people ($♀$–$♂$ and $♀$–$☉$) at the run up to the 1987 UK General Election are said to have been an important factor in Thatcher's election victory ($♀$). The Iron ($♂$) Lady ($♀$) indeed!

But where the full force of Margaret Thatcher's $☉$–$♂$ will obviously shine to the utmost in a personal sense is where it is rising. And where else should that be but the Falklands, with $♂$ exactly on the Ascendant through Buenos Aires, not the person for Argentina to pick a fight with! 'Born with Sun-Mars in the Falklands' says a great deal of what many would see as the high spot to date of her career. And note that we also find close by Thatcher's capacity to upset and fall out with and unsettle other people, and perhaps in some sense also free them, her $♅$ on the DS line also falls through Argentina . . . That same line then passes on and up through Washington and Toronto.

While Thatcher's personal relationships with Reagan have been very close (his $☽$–180–$♃$ falls across her AS–DS), her relationships with the USA have been the cause of continuing controversy and upsets: Grenada, Falklands, Cruise missiles, Libya. In the latter case her $♅$ IC line is right down through Libya, reminding us of the almost fatal drama of Thatcher's agreement with the USA to allow Britain to be used as the base for bombing that country (which incidentally occurred almost exactly at the Saturn return of the Suez crisis, the previous occasion when sudden joint military action resulted in Britain being condemned by much of the world community).

Not surprisingly for such a natural autocrat, Thatcher has a strong Uranus which is just as central to understanding her complex character as her rising Saturn or her $♂$ = MC/AS. Her $♅$ is –180–$☉$/$☽$ and is –180–$♂$/M = $☉$/$Ψ$ = $♄$/$Ω$ = AS/$Ω$ = $♀$/P, as well as being –90–$♀$/$♃$ and 45–$☽$/$♃$ = $☽$/P. This is a powerful, but mixed message of sudden self-assertion ($♂$/M, $☽$/P) and fortunate forcefulness ($♀$/$♃$, $☽$/$♃$) and magnetism ($♀$/P)

combined with sudden sabotage ($\odot/\Psi$), upsets and separations ($\hbar/\Omega$, AS/Ω).

This was the message of the Libyan affair. It came to meet her in London with the Libyan Embassy siege and the subsequent breaking of diplomatic relations. In Toronto with ♅ on DS it confronted her through the 'other'. As the Argentine had suddenly invaded 'her' territory, so in Toronto a knife-wielding madman attempted to assassinate her. Following the ♅–IC line further south we note that it passes right through Cape Town. Thatcher's autocratic and almost unilateral stand within the Commonwealth against sanctions against South Africa, and the subsequent ructions this has caused, becomes more intelligible in the light of this place, together with her strongly power-oriented ♃–♇ AS/DS lines which can also be seen running right through South Africa. This latter placement is highly indicative of her involvement in the final settlement in Zimbabwe where ♂ MC and ♃–♇ AS/DS cross, and of her interest in helping resolve Mozambique's continuing civil war in this region. It may well augur a future powerful role in helping further remodel (♅ and ♃–♇) this region.

Staying with ♅, we may note that on the other side of the world Thatcher's ♅ ascends through Indonesia where she made unguarded and highly controversial remarks about the British trade union movement, while further north it passes up through Hong Kong and China where she physically fell down soon after making controversial remarks about the colony over which she was later obliged to make a rare U-Turn.

But if Margaret Thatcher's natal ACG can tell us a great deal about her personal relationship to, and impact upon, the world, we can also use this same basic approach to study the relationship between the individual and the state of the larger cosmic dance into which they are born. For in the same way that we can only fully understand the *Betelgeuse* or *Piper Alpha* disasters in relation to the ♂–♇ cycle in which they occurred, so too the significance of our own personal natal chart can only be fully understood when it is related to the larger cycles in which it occurs. The events and circumstances with which we find ourselves involved are not simply the product of the moment of their occurrence. This web of unfolding events called Life arises out of the interaction of that myriad of cosmic cycles, great and small, which is forever unfolding the enfolded order of Eternity. Put simply, if we want to understand Margaret Thatcher's 'appointment with destiny' at 9 a.m. on 13 October 1925 we need to relate her natal birth chart to the charts for the major cycles preceding her birth. From the interaction between these patterns we can begin to gauge something of the kind of role that Thatcher, given her position, will be likely to play in unfolding the ideas represented by those cycles.

To express this in another way, we know from studies of the ACGs for lunations, eclipses, and ingresses that the lines of planetary angularity in such maps remain sensitive long after the actual moment for which they are set. Such maps establish a pattern, a matrix, which remains sensitive to subsequent transits. Thus, for example, the longitude on the Earth at which Uranus was on the MC at the Capricorn ingress will carry that Uranian potential for many months afterwards. Depending on other factors, along that longitude we can expect to see sudden unexpected events, upsets, possibly changes of government, even earthquakes. Indeed theoretically we can say that the Uranus position at the beginning of any annual cycle will remain sensitive throughout the life of that cycle. (This idea in relationship to world events has been discussed in some detail in Chapters 9 and 10 of *Mundane Astrology* by Baigent, Campion and Harvey. In that work some examples are also given of the way in which the individual birth chart can be seen to be related to the charts of major cycles.)

In theory, to fully understand the part we each are here to play we would need to study the relationship between our natal chart and the chart for the conjunction phase of each pre-natal cycle. In practice we can simplify things by saying that in general we will each tend to be most closely related to the cycles of those planets which are most prominent and closely aspected in our natal chart.

Returning to Thatcher's chart (Figure 17.10), with its closely rising Saturn, we can see that she is obviously going to be very closely tuned to those cycles involving Saturn. In particular, being born at the outgoing –60– phase of the ♃–♄ cycle, her life is likely to be particularly related to the practical working (–60–) expression and application (–60–) of ♃–♄ ideas. Note how this is phrased! We are saying that Thatcher's life will be involved in helping to express the idea of the ♃–♄ cycle, not that the cycle will give importance to Thatcher, though this prominence may be a consequence of the role she has to play in helping to unfold history. For at this level of analysis we are looking at the role of the individual within the collective wholeness and larger purposes of things. Indeed to a medieval astrologer who saw Jupiter and Saturn as the Great Chronocrators, the Great Markers of Time, which unfold society and civilization, this outgoing ♃–60–♄ would have been seen as the hallmark of someone who would 'make their mark' on their society, and be able to play a significant role in the work of the Creator.

To understand Thatcher's role in this creative process we can look at the chart for the seed moment of this ♃–♄ cycle in relation to her own birth chart. The conjunction took place on 10 September 1921 at about 4.14 a.m., i.e. four years and one month prior to Margaret Thatcher's birth. Theoretically we can say that this chart contains the seed ideas that Margaret Thatcher's ♃–60–♄ phase will work out (6H), and will embody into the rhythms of her life (6H) and consciousness. Because these two planets move relatively slowly we cannot be absolutely certain of the precise time of the exact conjunction. Raphael's gives it as 4.15 p.m. and the American ephemeris, based on more recent orbital elements, gives it as 4.14 p.m., for which we have set the chart (Figure 17.9). The angles given are for Thatcher's place of birth, Grantham, for we want to assess in what way her particular moment of birth connects with and expresses the cycle.

This chart symbolizes, among other things, the cycle of 'social structuring' into which Thatcher was born. Such cycles have two levels of expression. First they have a 'contemporary' life, which unfolds during the course of the cycle itself, which in this case would have lasted until the next ♃–0–♄ in 1940/41. Second, but no less important, they have a 'generational' life, which will express itself through all the millions of people, those cells of consciousness, born during the course of the cycle. These people both individually and collectively 'embody' and give continuing living expression to the significance of the cycle long after it has been completed in temporal terms.

In 'contemporary' terms this ♃–0–♄ cycle, which began at

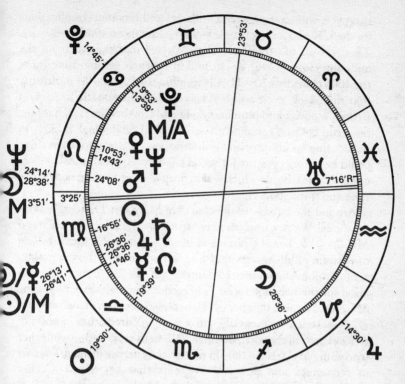

Figure 17.10 The Jupiter/Saturn conjunction of 10 September 1921 set for Grantham, Mrs Thatcher's birthplace. Her natal positions are shown on the outside.

26♍36, closely –90– the galactic centre, covered the period from the great 'boom' period of the 'roaring twenties', and reached it full at the –180– in 1931 at the depth of the world economic depression and social austerity. Perhaps the most striking features about the general pattern of the chart are the –90– of ☽ to the conjunction and the close –45– to it from ♀; the ♇ (exactly with the 1066 and UK chart MC/IC and ☉ axes) in close –45–♂ and 120–♅; the ☽–135–♆. When set for London/Grantham we see the conjunction is brought strongly to the fore by being almost exactly –120– MC from the 2nd house, indicating that the 'social structuring' of this cycle will have profound financial and economic implications for the UK and for her people (–90– ☽ exactly on 1066 ♅–90–☽). This was all too tragically true. We see that the AS is on the midpoint of the ♀–45–♃–♄, and ♅ is nearly setting. In terms of the 1066 chart this AS–♅ falls right on the ♇–180–♃, indicating that this ♃–♄ cycle will be likely to have a dramatic impact on Britain's 'power and plutocracy'. The MC of the chart localizes the powerful ♇ 45–♂, an indication of a social cycle which is likely to be focusing on military and militant social issues, and when there could be strong pressure for social changes. All in all this ♃–0–♄ cycle was clearly one which would deeply affect Britain, both at the time and through its children.

Around the outside of the chart are Margaret Thatcher's natal positions. We are immediately struck by the fact that her natal MC–0–☿/♇, her aspirations in life as a 'successful speaker' who can 'attain public recognition' and 'influence the public' is exactly conjunct the AS, while her all-important ♃–180–♇, her 'appreciation for the need for social . . . regeneration' falls exactly on the MC/AS. We note that her ☉/M, her 'goal or object of life', and her ☽/☿, herself as a 'mentally active woman', are within minutes of the exact conjunction with the 2nd house ♃–0–♄, while her 'revolutionary' ☉/☽–180–♅ falls exactly across the 2nd/8th axis of economics and finances! We note that her ♆–45–♂, her 'inspired action', is exactly locked in with the very tight ♂–45–♇ –45–MC pattern. Additionally note that her ☉ is exactly 9′ from the ☊ of this chart while her ☽ is –120– the ♃–♄ ☽ to the minute! Looking at this synastry we cannot but recognize that there will be a very deep resonance between Margaret Thatcher's life and goals and this cycle of 'government' and 'social structuring'.

While few individuals can have the impact on national affairs of a determined prime minister, an examination of the natal chart of any individual in relationship to the relevant preceding cycles would seem to be an important factor in such matters as vocational guidance and an understanding of the individual's place in the larger scheme of things.

Please note that Astro*Carto*Graphy is a registered Trade Mark.

PART FOUR

Case Histories

CHAPTER 18

James Joyce

MICHAEL HARDING

> Imagine the twelve deaferend dubbawls of whowl
> abovebeugled contonuation through regeneration of the urut-
> teration of the word in pregross (*Finnegans Wake, p. 284*).

One of the most important creative artists of the twentieth century
was the Irish writer James Joyce. His two major works, *Ulysses* and
Finnegans Wake, have been described respectively as the ultimate
novel and the ultimate use of the English language.

What characterizes these two books is their richness and complexity. Puns, word-plays and multiple-meanings all abound in
writing that may at first glance seem chaotic but is in fact as
carefully crafted as the Book of Kells and – in the case of many
passages in *Ulysses* – actually timed with a stopwatch for very
specific literary effects. Joyce discarded nothing; myths, legends,
psychologies, theologies, conversations, railway time tables, high
mass and pigs' gruntings all have their place and all emerge and
re-emerge with brilliant literary choreography. In fact it is precisely this ability to blur all conventional boundaries and juxtapose
incongruent images to produce strikingly original insights into
how the human mind and emotions operate that inevitably links
his name with that of Freud and Jung. Joyce was certainly familiar
with the ideas of psychoanalysis ('the children were yung and
easily freudened'), and met Jung on several occasions, but the
work of the two doctors palled besides that of the Italian philosopher Giambattista Vico. 'I don't believe in any science, but my
imagination grows when I read Vico as it doesn't when I read
Freud or Jung,' he confided to a biographer.[1] To understand some
of the themes and images in Joyce's life it could be useful first to
have an outline of how Vico saw the world, as this view had great
appeal for Joyce.

Giambattista Vico lived from 1688 to 1744. In the course of his life he created a complex philosophy which attempted to bring together the history of the physical world with the development of language and the political and spiritual growth of the human race. He saw the evolution of human consciousness as a cyclic phenomenon, forever returning to its point of arrival, but with the potential then to experience a rebirth at a higher level. These cycles towards change he termed *ricorsos*; the point at which everything comes back to itself as it spirals towards the divine. All things which emerge in time may *look* new, but are in fact re-workings of basic principles or ideas taking on new guises for different ages. Similarly, Joyce's constructions go through such metamorphoses innumerable times, and it is the hunt for each new facet of his imaginings which provides so much of the enjoyment for his readers. Vico's theories of cycles and language development embody two of Joyce's main artistic concerns.

While Vico may have given Joyce the intellectual and philosophical matrix in which he could create his own dance of time, there are other equally compelling reasons why Joyce was drawn towards the Italian philosopher which reveal even more the writer's particular preoccupations. Both he and Vico had a morbid dread of thunderstorms, and near to the Joyce family home in Dublin was a Vico Road. Joyce did *not* believe in coincidences! In fact he was an obsessive recorder of all such synchronicities, a deeply superstitious man forever on the watch for omens and a great believer in the significance of particular dates. Both *Ulysses* and *Finnegans Wake* were published on his birthday which, not surprisingly with his Moon in Leo, he felt was a particularly important event for the world at large.

When we come to approach the chart of James Joyce (Figure 18.1) we should see in it some of the qualities that his genius possessed; a brilliant academic mind, orientated towards mystical/psychological philosophy with an extremely inventive bent. There is also the capacity to speak a multitude of languages, the ability to recognize similarities in seemingly disparate images and the capacity to use ruthlessly the emotions of others.

Few writers have cannibalized the lives of those around them so meticulously and often so cruelly as Joyce. To open your mouth

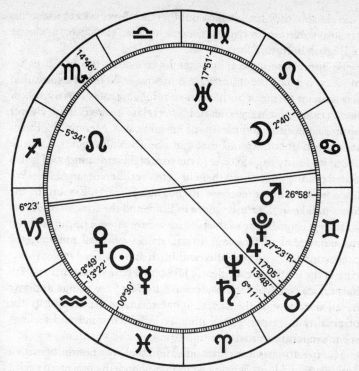

Figure 18.1 James Joyce's natal chart.

around him was to invite the risk of seeing your intimacies in print, with clear and unambiguous attribution. He was well known for loitering at the edge of drinking parties, waiting for the whisky-confessions to start and then scuttling off into the lavatory to write them down. His use of others extended even to demanding that his wife should write down her sexual fantasies, her feelings about all her bodily functions as well as her dreams for Joyce's use and analysis. Their one time apart was bridged by Joyce's deliberately pornographic letters – many still unpublished even in these more open times – aimed at bullying her into replying in kind. The tone of many of them is hard, anally preoccupied and full of sexually ambiguous longings. Nevertheless, Nora remained for him 'my wild flower of the hedges . . . my dark-blue rain-drenched flower'.

And the day they first walked out together Joyce was to use as his greatest tribute of love; it was the day he chose to change the course of English literature forever.

To appreciate more fully what Joyce's chart has to tell us we must go beyond the immediate Sun square Neptune aspect that sets a major theme of his life and start looking more closely at how the various planetary energies interrelate to give us a clearer impression of the complexity of his genius. A Mercury in Pisces says much about a mind that can absorb philosophies but little about its ability to go at once to the core of their meaning and spin a dozen erudite puns about them in as many different languages. We learn how the mind receives, but not how it reacts. Expanding the focus to take in the close square to Pluto and the trine to Mars, we start to get something of the picture we are after. The quick reply, the enjoyment of language in an almost physical manner, the preoccupation with sexuality and birth and the need to get to the core of the matter are all clearly laid out. These strong 3rd and 4th harmonics construct the basic wave-forms of the zodiac and give us an overview of the chart. What seems to be missing is the originality of response; the manner in which mind and feelings seem to operate as one.

Missing also is some clear indication that we are dealing with a highly original human being who single-handedly produced such a wealth of new literary material that at the time of writing (1989) over 9,000 separate academic papers and dissertations have been filed on his work. No other modern writer has attracted a fraction of this attention. Where then is Joyce as *he* depicted himself, as Stephen Dedalus, the hero taking flight to reach the Gods?

If we turn to the midpoints in question (Figure 18.2) we get to the heart of the matter at once. On the Mercury tree there is the sign of the jester, $\mathgroup \yen = \mathcal{D}/\mathcal{O}' = \odot/\mathrm{H\!\!\!I} = \mathrm{H\!\!\!I}/M$, the immediate emotional/intellectual reaction to everything; the scavenger/trickster figure who can pun in several languages and on many levels at the same time about the most learned of subjects and slip in 'where the bus stops, there shop I' as a quick afterthought. This is the *conscious awareness* ($\yen = \mathrm{H\!\!\!I}/M$) of his originality, the need to use it to further himself, to project himself towards his chosen future (MC). Here is the need to be highly original in artistic and

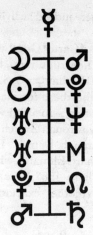

Figure 18.2 James Joyce's Mercury tree.

religious matters ($\mathord{\smash{\text{☿}}} = \text{♅}/\text{Ψ}$) as well as the urge to be what he modestly called 'the conscience of his race'. Ebertin describes the $\mathord{\smash{\text{☿}}} = \text{♇}/\text{☊}$ as describing an urge to 'dominate other people intellectually or mentally' and 'having the ability to exercise compelling and magnetically powerful influences over the community at large'. This is Dedalus on the wings of his own making, challenging the gods with his audacity as he flies towards the light.

On this tree is also the image of Joyce stealing the housekeeping money, often having to move home several times in a month to escape creditors or avoid landlords (fleeing two lodgings on the same day was the record here). There is also Joyce afflicted with failing eyesight ($\mathord{\smash{\text{☿}}} = \text{♂}/\text{♄}$) and in constant pain from glaucoma and its attendant operations. Finally there is in same combination the ruthless user of language, the man who bullied Norah with his sexually explicit letters, so often expressing the sadism of Mars/Saturn. Though, as we shall see, what makes this contact so particularly powerful is that in Joyce's 7th harmonic this Mars/Saturn contact becomes a conjunction. All that we are missing is something that would make Mercury absolutely central to everything, a structure like $\mathord{\smash{\text{☿}}} = \text{AS}/\text{M}$. But a Dublin birth did not give him this; to get such a combination he would have had to have been born in, say, Trieste . . . where indeed he lived when he wrote some of his finest work.

If we look at Joyce's Astro*Carto*Graphy map (Figure 18.3) we also find that his Venus line runs right through Trieste, with Mercury close enough to make that $\u263f = AS/MC$ aspect. Both also run through Rome – another base for many years in which he manifested the creative writing associated with these two planets. His Pluto line runs exactly through Zurich, where he died, while Neptune runs straight through Detroit. Detroit? This was the birthplace of Professor Richard Ellmann, who made Joyce his life's work and, until his death in 1987, was the world's foremost authority on the writer. Another exact contact in America is

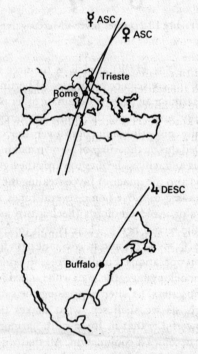

Figure 18.3 ACG for James Joyce. Note how Mercury crosses through Trieste and Venus through Rome. Jupiter crossing through Buffalo, New York, marks a major world centre for Joyce studies.

Jupiter running through Buffalo, New York. This is the home of the State University of New York's collection of Joyce papers, arguably one of the most extensive in the world, making this one of the world centres for Joyce studies.

Returning to his midpoints, we can see how they bring together the basic energy, growth and inspirational factors in his chart along with his conscious goals, the MC (Figure 18.4).

Two things strike us simultaneously when we first look at this extremely complex tree: first we are dealing here with someone quite unusual, and second there's simply far too much going on to make sense of at one sitting! But we *can* see at a glance that the energies of the Sun, Mars, Jupiter, Neptune and the MC all come together and interact in one way or another with each other and that the midpoints they activate are related to the work of a creative writer. They depict a man who draws heavily on mythic, powerful and emotional images and the midpoint structure ends with $\u263F/\u0127$ – the need to formalize language or communication in some way. Putting it all into words, in fact. Transits to this cluster of planets and their attendant midpoints marked major points in Joyce's life and creative works.

Those who know Joyce's work will recognize how the powerful Neptune, both acting as a focusing planet ($\Psi = \odot/M = \mathbb{D}/\mathrm{P}$) and also strong by midpoint aspect ($\odot = \mathbb{D}/\Psi = \Psi/M$), reflects the continual references to water, to the idealized all-powerful woman from whom all life comes; in fact the anima figure Anna Livia Plurabelle from *Finnegans Wake*. The concatenation of languages in the name 'Plurabelle' symbolizes the containment of all beauty in one woman, who is also the waters of Dublin's river Liffey and the waters of the world, the women of the world, everywhere. The idealizing of Woman, the need to create an image to worship, probably lay behind his choice to set *Ulysses* on 16 June 1904 – the day he first walked out with Nora Barnacle.

While it can take a little practice to put such a complex, interlocking tree structure together, we can at least look at how some of its other components say very specific things about Joyce, which can also be applicable to the charts of others. For a start, the $\odot$, σ, Ψ and MC sharing so many of the same midpoints – no matter what they are – should give us some image of 'idealistic

Figure 18.4 The interlocking midpoints to Joyce's Sun, Mars, Jupiter and Neptune bring an enormous focus of creative energy together culminating in ☿/♄ – the professional writer.

'ambition', of the ego being identified with some vision and with the energy to strive towards realizing it.

Without the Neptune the image could be quite different. The Neptune is particularly powerful, being configured with ⊙/M and ☽/♇; here is someone whose emotional and home life could be chaotic and changeable. He could be wildly romantic (Ψ = ♀/♃) or seek the affection of idealized women. Nora was clearly one of those; like Goethe he saw no attraction in a woman who came near his intellectual equal, choosing instead a barely educated chambermaid who never developed the slightest interest in his work and hardly read any of it.

The tree structure ends with Jupiter; the end result is some form of growth. Artistic growth that requires much research and labour −♃ = ♄/♇ = ♀/♇. The 'controlled expansion' of words or ideas, ♃ = ☿/♄ with attendant optimism and pessimism as to its outcome. Probably this factor also says something about Joyce's litigious behaviour. There can be something pompous and conservative when Jupiter and Saturn come together, and despite a Bohemian, drunken life in which he awoke in many gutters or brothels, the need to be seen as a man of some means and elegance was strong. Writs were issued at the drop of a hat if he felt his honour had been impugned, though nothing was learned from the costly failure of such ill-conceived suits. No doubt the strong Neptune/MC configuration – *also* = ♀/♃ – contributed towards a view of himself and his financial resources that the rest of the world didn't always share. Not surprisingly, the Ψ = ♀/♃ contact also mysteriously brought money *into* his life as well, as we shall examine later.

JOYCE'S HARMONIC CHARTS

In looking at Joyce's harmonic charts we shall be paying particular attention to those aspects which emphasize specific themes; for it is these which lay down patterns within the individual's life and give us the clearest understanding of what is actually going on. These themes will almost certainly be created by those aspect structures which are *closest in orb* in any particular harmonic. The idea that the closest aspect most accurately defines the dynamic operating between the planets concerned is hardly a new one. In using harmonic charts we must always keep in mind the harmonic number of the chart we are examining, this being the major modifier of that dynamic. A conjunction always remains a conjunction and a trine stays a trine, but our interpretation of what they are bringing together, what they are telling us about the nature of what is being expressed, can vary enormously from number to number. This is particularly true of the harmonic conjunction, for in the radical chart the conjunction does not have a specific 'meaning'.

What defines the radical conjunction most accurately are the planets themselves, and how well they are likely to operate together. The conjunction in the harmonic chart most accurately defines the core meaning of the number which brings the planets together (all other close contacts other than the conjunction within a particular harmonic chart are in fact *sub-harmonics* of that number), thus a Sun/Uranus conjunction in the 5th harmonic will be seen in quite a different light from a Sun/Uranus in the 7th, and this is obviously also true of other contacts. As it is quite possible for the same planets to form close contacts with others in a number of different harmonic charts it is very important to be clear as to what one is looking at, to avoid the phenomenon of seeing all and everything in any particular chart – and thus perpetuating a common astrological habit!

For example, a radical chart may have Saturn quintile to the Sun which in turn is septile to Uranus. In both the 5th and 7th harmonic charts we will see displayed different images of the solar principle in the form of conjunctions. In the 5th we shall see a style which suggests the need to structure self-expression in some manner, perhaps the need to appear businesslike or conservative or to create only within clearly-defined boundaries. In the 7th harmonic, however, we catch a glimpse of a person turned on by the originality of Self. Now the chart depicts a person inspired by highly individualistic actions, a free-ranging spirit, hating petty restrictions. We must not mix these two images but must *synthesize* them. We cannot drag in the septile to Uranus while looking at the quintile to Saturn. In the 5th harmonic chart the septile to Uranus is a disconnected, possibly irrelevant aspect. In the 7th harmonic chart it is the conjunction with Uranus which dominates; the quintile to Saturn now appears unattached and unimportant. We can bring these two images together by suggesting that perhaps we are looking at someone who might be a highly original entrepreneur hiding behind a rather dull grey suit. Someone who looks like just another businessman until we hear the plans and the ideas that inspire him.

Each harmonic chart looks at a particular idea and gives us a specific view of an individual which we can start to bring together out of our own experience as astrologers. We do this in exactly the same way as we synthesize basic planetary relationships. We may learn a lot from studying the interaction of Saturn and Uranus, but Saturn is not Uranus and Uranus is certainly not Saturn!

When we start to apply these ideas to Joyce's 5th harmonic chart (Figure 18.5) we note that only hard aspects exist – the creative style is stressful and arises out of a need to take up the challenge of art. The Moon/Mars opposition is the closest to exactitude and of particular importance, as we have already noticed the $\mathaccent"27E \varrho = \mathcal{D}/\mathcal{O}$ in Joyce's midpoints. This opposition in the 5th harmonic often goes with a boisterous sense of humour; Hamblin refers to the slapstick quality of this relationship, and obviously we could expect some physicality with Mars being involved. Thus the Moon opposition Mars would suggest a striving to bring together immediate emotional responses with some form of action *in a 5th harmonic manner*; that is primarily mental and stylized. Knowing that Mercury *also* brings these planets together we must immediately recognize that the emphasis towards mental functions and reactions is going to be greater than towards a purely physical response. The humour indicated will almost certainly be of the mind rather than the body; Charlie Chaplin gives way to Mort Sahl. If we had a client with this configuration and to date he had failed in his chosen ambition to be a humorous performer and was seeking our advice as how best to pursue his career, we could see very clear evidence that he might have far better success as a comedy *writer* – thus what may appear to be astrological hairsplitting can in fact tip the balance towards locating extremely valuable information.

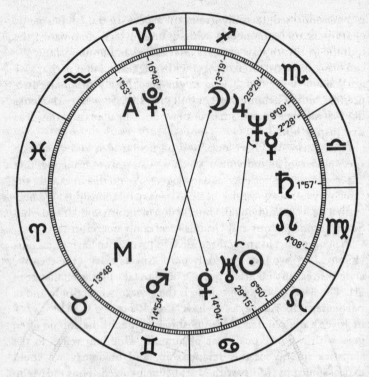

Figure 18.5 James Joyce's 5th harmonic.

The next opposition, Venus to Pluto, does not exist so closely in other harmonics. It is unique to the 5th and it does underline further our previous observation of Joyce as a man deeply concerned with the power of the feminine and in particular with the ability of women to bear children. Seeing this pattern now we can substitute 'obsessed' for 'concerned' – again, a very important distinction. Many people are interested in creative activity, only a minority are obsessed by it. The need to create a style of art which is transformative is also clearly depicted there. Considering that Joyce actually went the whole hog and transformed the art-form itself, this is not a totally inappropriate observation!

He did it with great originality (Sun/Uranus conjunction) and

with words (Sun/Uranus square to Mercury). Once more the
contacts we had noticed on his Mercury tree (☿ = ☉/♅) come to
mind as the Sun/Uranus theme is repeated again, further emphasizing the essentially cerebral nature of Joyce's originality.
Although it is only when we get to the higher numbered harmonics
that we can see just how striking this planetary relationship
actually is.

In the 7th harmonic chart (Figure 18.6) the Mercury/Sun/
Uranus contact becomes part of a kite formation along the
Uranus/node axis – the originality is to be shared, it has to go out
into the world. In this Grand Trine we can see the shape of a man
inspired by the principle of experiencing his own individuality and
sharing it with others; a man turned on by his own mind. We also

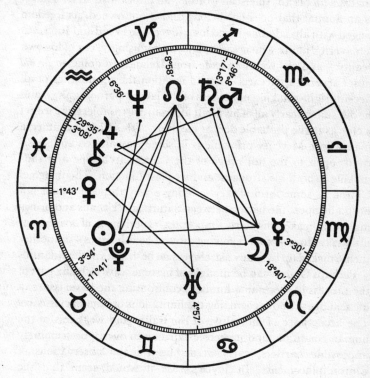

Figure 18.6 James Joyce's 7th harmonic.

see for the first time how Chiron comes into the picture along with Jupiter to expand that image of originality and add another dimension to Joyce's use of the Mercury function. The Jupiter/Chiron conjunction of itself exists in the radical chart and consequently describes quite a long period of time; it is the contact with Mercury which demands our closer attention.

Zane Stein, Zip Dobbyns, Al H. Morrison and Erminie Lantero among others in America, and Eve Jackson and Melanie Reinhart in England have been pursuing detailed observations as to the possible workings of this planetoid. The connotations of 'maverick' and similar images pointing to the peculiar within the individual are now well known and seem in this case particularly apt. In her book *Chiron and the Healing Journey*, Melanie Reinhart reminds us that *maverick* is an American word for an unbranded steer. Thus it is an animal that does not belong and is not owned, its freedom tinged with abandonment and loss. Joyce, like Freud and Jung, *was* a maverick figure who created, uncompromisingly, out of his own reality – and always as an exile from Ireland. In doing so he *did* upset several applecarts – not to mention the sensibilities of all decent, right-thinking upholders of the law on pornography – and he did suffer nearly all of his adult life from eye trouble. Here we get a clue as to the probable deeper meaning of this Chiron contact; a man whose Mercury principle is in some way altered and sensitized, open to the full range of the Chiron archetype and thus making it both his strongest and weakest function. The image of Chiron as some form of 'key' offering a way through a door not normally open, mediating between Saturn and Uranus and bringing in its wake singularly important experiences of a confrontational nature – often revolving around health issues – is another theme picked up by many astrologers on both sides of the Atlantic.

Perhaps Chiron can be thought of in some ways as being part of the process of 'becoming human', confronting the basic issues of life and death and recognizing the limitations of human existence. The acceptance of mortality, of the frailty and weakness of the human condition, and its heroic capacity to overcome seemingly impossible barriers, carry across from many observations of Chiron placements. In Joyce's case it would seem that the price of experiencing the enormous breadth of the Mercury principle was precisely that: its *loss* is part of the spectrum of its experience.

Forever the noter of omens and portents, Joyce himself saw clear parallels between his own, at times, near blindness and the blindness of Homer – the original chronicler of the deeds of Ulysses. He also recognized how both the bastions of law and order and the literary establishment saw him as a literal 'eyesore' – a punning image he made much of and clearly identified with as one would expect from someone with this in a 7th harmonic contact.

The real power of the Mercury/Chiron contact which brings out the ambiguity of this planetoid's capacity to confront the individual with his weakest link lies in how Joyce's failing eyesight actually contributed to his originality as a writer – for he concentrated on the *sounds* of words. Thus his language *always* contained the ripple of poetry and innumerable passages of his work only make complete sense when read aloud – and with the appropriate accent. Focusing on the sounds, smells and tastes all around him gave Joyce a phenomenal ability to describe the totality of a situation from a fraction of its parts. Hemingway recalls an anecdote whereby Joyce refused the offer of a hunting trip with the American writer on the grounds that he would never be able to see the lion, much less shoot it. Nora replied that this would not be necessary – just for Joyce to touch the beast would tell him all he needed to know of the animal's behaviour. His obsessional recording of every detail and observation, of trying to achieve a totally accurate record of everything and everyone he came into contact with, was a hedge against the ever-present fear that he might wake up one morning to find himself totally blind.

The Mercury/Chiron contact in Joyce's 7th harmonic chart forces us again to look at the manner in which we interpret this number; do we *really* say that he was inspired by the fear of blindness? As blindness is only one of a myriad of possibilities this contact could bring, such an interpretation would be as wrong as it is bizarre. What seems much more likely is that Joyce was inspired or turned on by the idea of opening himself to the totality of the Mercury archetype, to make it as personal and idiosyncratic as possible and to grasp at its essence come what may. In doing so he seemed to pay the price that the gods extract for the crime of *hubris*;

the principle that earned him human immortality failed him most.

Carl Jung was another who was prepared to open himself to the wider reaches of the mind, coming perilously close to insanity at times in his struggle to come to grips with the dark symbols of the collective. As Joyce followed his image of Dedalus so Jung followed his *daimons* as they led him through almost shamanic experiences towards the last unexplored continent of the mind. Jung also had his same Mercury/Chiron opposition in his 7th harmonic (Figure 18.7); in fact the synastry of the two men is quite striking and will be examined later in this chapter.

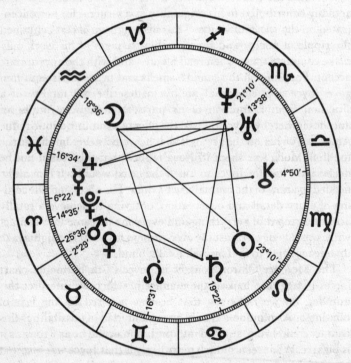

Figure 18.7 Jung's 7th harmonic. Note the Sun/Moon opposition square to Uranus and Neptune, as the natal squares come together. Virtually all of Jung's work is concerned with bringing together opposing psychic energies through insights into dreams!

Two other strong patterns exist in Joyce's 7th harmonic, the Mars/Saturn conjunction and the Venus/Uranus square. Seeing Mars and Saturn together reminds us that we have seen this combination before, on the Mercury midpoint tree, so this is another reinforcement as well as a reminder that the energy needs to be used – it exists in both the 7th and 8th harmonic. The fantasy has to be brought into the world, it has to be put to use. We have said quite a lot about Mars/Saturn contacts already, so it should be sufficient only to point out how this works together with the Venus/Uranus, as both should operate at the same level, being part of the same harmonic.

Joyce saw himself as a master craftsman with words, the 'old Artificer'; clearly this was an image which inspired him and with which he identified, and equally clearly this describes one aspect of Mars/Saturn. His preoccupation with sexual guilt is another, and this also brings in the Venus/Uranus square. While Joyce remained emotionally faithful to Nora, he was not exactly sexually constant and was drawn to sudden encounters which generated their share of guilt and remorse. Without foundation he questions Norah's fidelity, even to the point of occasionally doubting the parentage of his son Giorgio. He has Leopold Bloom similarly doubting Molly's behaviour (though in the fictional case there was good cause) and brings these two 7th harmonic contacts together in the *Circe* episode of *Ulysses* when he describes Leopold Bloom's visit to a brothel.

In the brothel Bloom fantasizes that he is being put on trial for a whole variety of quite implausible sexual practices. He is mocked and humiliated over Molly's adultery, is forced to confess to sado-masochistic behaviour and homosexuality and is whipped as a punishment. He then imagines himself as a great military leader receiving homage and tribute as a result of his victories and a huge statue is built in his honour. In the midst of all this reverie he also talks of a talisman he keeps to ward off rheumatism – a classic Mars/Saturn illness amid a welter of similarly apt occurrences!

A scene like this takes place in *Finnegans Wake* when the sleeping landlord dreams that he is also accused of sexual crimes, including incest (Venus/Uranus) which is enacted in a park made notorious as a result of its being the scene of a multiple murder

(Mars/Saturn). These images of sexual violence, real or implied, underscore many passages in both novels and Joyce also uses the stereotype of the cuckolded husband as a poor, downtrodden victim-figure; the unfortunate male made impotent by circumstances.

While all of this is very much part of the symbolic language of a Mars/Saturn contact, so too is Joyce's total dedication to his life as a writer and his methodical and hypercritical approach to all his work. But there is one very particular manner in which his $\male = \male/\saturn$ operates which evidences how truly powerful such planetary contacts are when repeated in different wave-forms, and this is Joyce's attitude to Fate.

We noted in Chapter 13 how the septile aspect is traditionally associated with fated and inevitable events and suggested some of the reasons why this might be so. In Joyce's case his superstitions were extremely fatalistic and invariably included *death* – the ultimate Mars/Saturn expression. A surprisingly large number of his acquaintances committed suicide, and he often felt it was something to do with their coming into contact with him and his work; he saw his *writing* as in some way being responsible. In a letter he confides:

> The word *scorching* has a peculiar significance for my superstitious mind not so much because of any quality or merit in the writing itself as for the fact that the progress of the book is in fact like the progress of some sandblast. As soon as I mention or include any person in it I hear of his or her death or departure or misfortune: and each successive episode, dealing with some province of artistic culture . . . leaves behind it a burned up field.[2]

The images for $\male = \male/\saturn$ here are quite amazing: *scorching, sandblast, death, misfortune, artistic culture, a burned up field* and all as a result of his writing! This one contact alone, repeated in two harmonics, is a major theme running through the writer's life, providing him with his alter-ego Dedalus (who, like Christa MacAuliffe with the same $\male = \male/\saturn$ combination, also risked death in flight) as well as the ability to make his own language an enduring part of English literature.

If we track these main contacts through those charts which resonate to the 7th harmonic, the 14th, 21st and 28th amongst them (Figures 18.8–18.10), we see other images of how Joyce's creative fantasy manifests. In the 14th harmonic Mercury joins the Chiron/Jupiter conjunction and Mars trines Neptune – the creative dreamer in action. Looking at the 21st harmonic chart we should see how the principle of enjoyment (3) and inspiration (7) work together: they produce a very powerful map. An almost exact Sun/Mercury conjunction opposes Chiron and Uranus while Saturn sextiles one and trines the other. This 'relieved opposition' is one of the most powerful and creative of aspects; the basic tension of the 2nd harmonic gives tremendous energy while the 3rd and 6th harmonic bring enjoyment and the facility to make use of

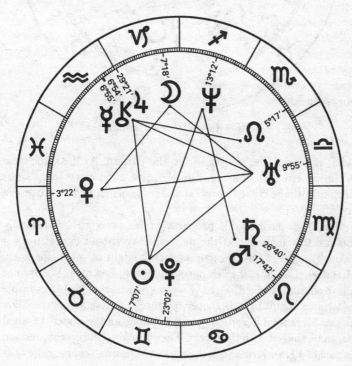

Figure 18.8 James Joyce's 14th harmonic.

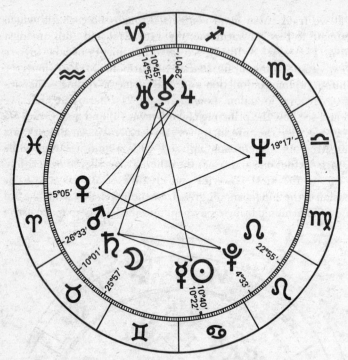

Figure 18.9 James Joyce's 21st harmonic.

what potential lies caught within the pattern. At the same time
Venus is trine to Pluto and underscores once more Joyce's obsession with the creative process and transformation as a process in
art.

The 28th harmonic is probably as far as we can realistically
pursue this sequence at the moment. We should expect from it
some glimpse of how the 7th harmonic might be most effectively
manifested as 28 is the 7th harmonic multiplied by 4. We are not
disappointed! Indeed, we have within it an almost classic example
of what is meant by a 'planetary picture'. Cutting across the chart
is the Mercury/Chiron conjunction opposing the node; the ideal
has to be shared with the world. The Mercury/Chiron conjunction
is part of a grand trine with the Sun and Uranus – echoing the ☿ =
☉/♅ structure in Joyce's midpoints and re-emphasizing the

importance of Joyce as the highly original, iconoclastic thinker. Two close squares mirror one another on two sides of the Grand Trine, Mars and Venus and Jupiter and Neptune. The effort depicted here is of a purposeful striving to bring together the basic principles of male and female while manifesting some cosmic vision.

As very little work has been done with higher-numbered harmonics it could be unwise to take this chart further. Its strength and importance lie primarily in demonstrating how, from basic principles, one would expect a consummately successful creative writer to have a very powerful 28th harmonic pattern describing some of the major ideas of his life. These clearly *are* there within the

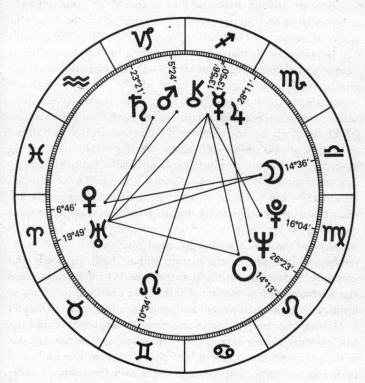

Figure 18.10 James Joyce's 28th harmonic.

chart and in a manner which underlines both the joy and the effort of his life. Furthermore, we can see in this chart a specific example of how astrology is almost certainly going to develop in the future. Higher numbered harmonics can bring together planetary energies in a highly idiosyncratic manner using simple relationships. If we learn how to recognize and interpret these interactions we shall start to create a blueprint of the psyche that becomes more defined as we track the numbers that bring it into being.

Joyce's strength as a creative genius lies not in his close Sun square Neptune (important though that obviously is), as this factor repeats twice each year and does *not* produce biannual equivalents of *Finnegans Wake*! Neither can one focus on the important natal Mercury in Pisces or the Jupiter trine Uranus, close and contributory though it is; the first is shared by approximately one-twelfth of the human race and the second will be in orb for weeks. We must push beyond the basic three- and fourfold cosmology and long-lasting planetary relationships towards that which is unique and uncommon. What we are *really* seeing in this chart is a glimpse of how a large number of Joyce's radical factors are resonating to the number 7 and its sub-harmonics. When these same factors are also vibrating to other harmonics, such as the ☉/♅ and ♂/♄ already mentioned (and there are quite a number of others), then a unique resonance is being created. We are no longer trying to find simplistic explanations by cutting astrology into conveniently large chunks of zodiac – much like the Sun sign forecasters – but trying to arrive at an understanding of how key planets are operating one with the other and thus come to see more clearly 'what type of Mercury' we are dealing with; what kind of mind, what measure of man, what final harmony.

Using this approach the picture will be built up slowly and certainly, and it will continue to surprise us. Where, for instance, is the Mercury/Venus contact that Ebertin observed as being so applicable to creative writers and which we discussed in Chapter 5? We scan our midpoint trees and scour our aspectarians in vain, but it is clearly there nevertheless. Joyce was born on the only day of the year when the nodes of Mercury, Venus *and* Pluto all stood on the same degree! The message might have been slipped under the door rather than coming through the mail slot, but it is just as much to the point; how better to describe a powerful and transformative writer who happened to pick just the right day of the year to start off. But there's a little more to this; planetary nodes return to virtually the same position each year. No wonder Joyce was so attached to his birthday as the ideal launch date for his books. What better day to transform English literature!

BLOOMSDAY AND THE MAKING OF *ULYSSES*

On 16 June 1904 Joyce first walked out with Nora Barnacle and subsequently the two left Ireland for a life together on the Continent. The day of their meeting was the day Joyce celebrated in *Ulysses*. The book begins at exactly 8 a.m. and describes about eighteen hours in the life of Dublin, seen mainly through the eyes of three of its citizens, Stephen Dedalus, and Molly and Leopold Bloom. As the three of them go about the normal duties of the day their observations, thoughts, fantasies and imaginations make up the flowing tapestry of the book. Interwoven are a myriad other themes centred around images of the homecoming (Ulysses' return from the wars), the many conflicts between father and son, sexual doubts and betrayals – real and imaginary – and discussions on such eternal issues as the creative process, sex and birth, the true meaning of religion and our duty as humans. It was Joyce's aim to create an epic tribute to the toils and tribulations of everyman in a manner which would allow him also to draw together as many of the ambiguous threads of existence as he could manage and play as many tricks on his reader as he could get away with. Thus when Joyce describes Leopold Bloom pacing the streets of Dublin while beset with doubts as to his wife's faithfulness, the streets he walks down are itemized; if we trace them on a map of the city we see that his path describes a huge question-mark!

True to both Freud and Vico, images emerge and re-emerge in a free-associative manner; the reader has to recall what images go with each previously-used expression and in what context it was first employed to get the fullest meaning from its current expression. While it has a very precise starting point, the story continually shifts levels and perspectives like the analysis of a dream or the hunt for the deepest meaning of a symbol within the human psyche. Its eighteen chapters are each in part the start of a new cycle; a new perspective of events in a different style but each re-expressing both that which has gone before while laying clues for all that which is to follow.

The publication of *Ulysses* was the major literary event of this century and 'Bloomsday' is celebrated annually by Joycean enthusiasts with a walk around Dublin re-tracing the steps of the major characters. If a man so leaves his mark on the life of one day, that day must surely have left its mark upon him. Looking at the midpoints captured by Joyce's Venus/Saturn square (the traditional significators of binding love), we see the imprint of no less than five transiting bodies (Figure 18.11).

Within a mere 3° the focus of energy around Joyce's ☉/☽ midpoint is considerable; and with Venus, Mars and Pluto all on his ☽/♀ midpoint how could he have avoided falling in love! The fact that this personal love was later to be translated for the world

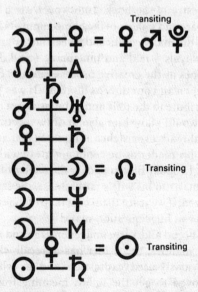

Figure 18.11 Joyce's transits to his radical Venus and Saturn for 'Bloomsday' – 16 June 1904.

to see is clearly marked by the exact t$\Omega = \odot/\mathcal{D}$, the connection between the world at large and his own most intimate feelings. On the 45° graphic ephemeris (Figure 18.12) this period shows up immediately and would have caught our attention at once had we been engaged on writing a forecast for Joyce for that year, doubly so as the eclipse new Moon taking place the day before occurred on Joyce's $\sigma/\mathbb{H}$ and $\mathcal{Q}/\hbar$ midpoint. In Chapter 3 we commented on the importance of the actual midpoints picked up by lunations as giving a feel for the nature of the coming days and this is a typical example: sudden love which becomes permanent.

It has often been pointed out that one person's synastry with another is experienced as something like a transit. It is as if each is permanently triggering the other's chart with perpetually stationary planets. A full comparison of Joyce's and Nora's charts should add much to our picture; unfortunately this is not possible. Nora Barnacle's exact date of birth is not known; she was born on either 21 or 22 March 1884 and no attempt will be made here to suggest the more likely day. Her Saturn conjunct Joyce's node speaks again eloquently of the binding nature of their relationship, as does her Mars conjunct his Moon suggest its passionate intensity. Her Neptune falling on his $\mathcal{Q}/\mathcal{Q}$ midpoint illustrated what we know to be true – that she was the inspiration for his writing of all women and the image of the Feminine that flowed through Dublin 'past Howth Castle and Environs' to merge at last with the sea.

While these contacts are interesting enough in themselves, there is one which is quite remarkable, the contact between her Jupiter and Joyce's Mercury/Uranus midpoint. Nora has almost exact Jupiter/node square and so this midpoint will obviously pick up both aspects. For a writer known to create in a highly idiosyncratic and irrational manner, this constant stimulation of his $\mathcal{Q}/\mathbb{H}$ principle is powerful indeed. Historian after historian has questioned what a Trinity-educated man saw in the barely literate chambermaid and why it was he needed her constant presence to create – they were separated only once during Joyce's life. While it would be facile to suggest that this one contact says it all, it certainly conveys much of it and presents the clearest possible image of an energy which stimulated Joyce's mental processes. More than that, it is the very point that was transited by Jupiter on

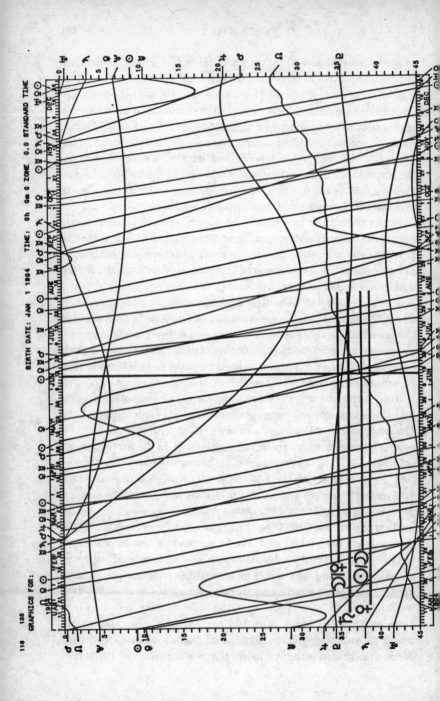

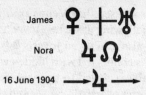

Figure 18.13 James Joyce's Mercury/Uranus midpoint, conjunct to Nora Barnacle's Jupiter/node contact is transited by Jupiter on 16 June 1904.

16 June 1904 (Figure 18.13). Nora had on that day a transiting Jupiter square Jupiter within half a degree and thus both her radical Jupiter/node aspect and Joyce's natal ☿/♅ midpoint were brought fully into play. So did Nora surprise him on 16 June? She did indeed, but those who want the graphic details had better get themselves a good biography!

A year to the day after that first meeting Joyce wrote to his brother Stanislaus (who was to die on Bloomsday 1955) that he had finished the first chapter of *Ulysses*, but the book was not completed and published until 2 February 1922. A little over a year later, on 4 May 1923, and with Jupiter on the ☉/Ψ/M midpoint cluster, he began *Finnegans Wake*.

During the intervening years a daughter, Lucia, was born (26 July 1909) to James and Nora, and in April 1932 Lucia had the first of the psychotic episodes which were to leave her permanently institutionalized. In a vain attempt at a cure, Joyce took Lucia to see Jung. Though the Swiss psychologist could offer no hope for the girl, the two men met on a number of occasions and their brief relationship offers an insight into Jung's own psychology and provides an interesting perspective on synastry.

On 27 February 1918 Joyce had received a letter from a Zurich bank informing him that a wealthy benefactor had taken an interest in his work and was awarding him a monthly grant. We noted earlier that Joyce's ♂ = Ψ = ♀/♃ should have something to do with mysterious gifts or unexpected good fortune and so it

Figure 18.12 The graphic ephemeris for Bloomsday shows the clear focus of energy around the middle of June.

comes as no surprise to see that Venus *exactly* crosses that natal ♀/♃ midpoint the following day when Joyce actually attended the bank. Mercury was also exactly on Joyce's ♇ = ♀/♅, which is not bad for surprise news connected with hidden wealth. The benefactor's identity was later revealed to be the American heiress Edith Rockefeller, a supporter of artistic causes and then in analysis with Jung.

When Joyce finally met Edith Rockefeller she strongly suggested that he enter into analysis with Jung as well – she was willing to pay – but Joyce would have none of it. On 1 October 1919 his allowance was summarily cut off (transiting Jupiter being on Joyce's ♀/♃ midpoint this time, and as that midpoint is also configured with ♅/AS the unexpected result of that combination shouldn't be too unexpected!). It was never quite clear *why* this happened, but in an interview Jung gave for Patricia Hutchin's book *James Joyce's World* he describes how he pressed Edith Rockefeller – still in analysis with him – to terminate a grant she had made to a young painter (who was *also* in analysis with Jung!) and this she did. Jung clearly recognized that she may have done the same to Joyce, but not told him – very remiss of his analysand! What *Jung* did not tell Ms Hutchin was that there was another person also in receipt of substantial endowment from the heiress – a certain Dr Carl Jung of Zurich.[3]

When *Ulysses* was translated into German, Jung wrote that it was an example of the schizophrenic mind at work and that the book could be read as easily backward as forward. While it would certainly take quite a number of close readings to even begin to extract what *Ulysses* has to offer, it is of itself quite a simple story following an obvious time-frame; to suggest that the same sense could be made of it by reading it backwards is utter nonsense and by this deliberate rudeness much is revealed of Jung's attitude towards Joyce – whom he had as yet not actually met.

When they did meet, in 1934, in connection with Lucia's possible treatment, Jung was to write that Joyce was a latent schizophrenic who controlled his condition by excessive drinking. For a doctor to imply that schizophrenia can be controlled by a heavy intake of alcohol when there was ample evidence that it causes the condition to deteriorate is odd indeed. According to

Jung, Lucia was Joyce's *anima inspiratrix* whom Joyce was utterly reliant on. As *Ulysses* was half finished before Lucia was born and published by the time she was twelve, she was clearly a remarkably precocious *anima*, whoever she belonged to. Perhaps Jung was projecting his own relationship with Toni Wolff on to the father and daughter – for there is no doubt that Wolff played that *anima* role for Jung. There is also no doubt that Joyce felt a great responsibility for Lucia's condition and had an unusually close relationship with her (♀/♅ in the 7th harmonic). But Jung insisted that Joyce was unable to have her certified for fear of admitting his own latent psychosis. Anyone who has read Jung will recognize that he could detect the vibrations of a latent psychosis nearly as quickly as Freud could play hunt the penis – so what on earth was really going on?

Jung has an almost exact Sun/Neptune square. Joyce has an almost exact Sun/Neptune square. Lucia doesn't; but her Sun is almost exactly on Joyce's Moon which is also on Jung's Sun – which are all square to Freud's Pluto . . . While the Sun/Neptune squares of the two men make it plain to see why the subject of alcohol should provoke such confusion – and possible deception over the issue of who gets what money – there is something else lurking on the back boiler. Jung has clearly taken against Joyce even before he ever met him, attacking his work in a manner which almost suggests jealousy. This puzzled Joyce. 'Why is Jung so rude to me?' he asked. 'There can be only one explanation – translate your name into German,' replied his publisher. If you do, you get Freud; Joyce liked that one and put it in a book.

James Joyce died on 13 January 1941 at 1.15 a.m. GMT in Zurich,[4] following an operation to treat a perforated ulcer. Saturn was on his Sun/Moon midpoint, the Ascendant for his death was conjunct his Saturn and the Midheaven on his Saturn/Pluto midpoint. It was the time of the full Moon – not favourable for any stomach operation – which became exact later that day. The previous full Moon (on 14 December at 19.38 GMT) was at 22 ♊ 42, hitting within 20′ the same zodiacal degree that had been eclipsed by the new Moon the day before Joyce first walked out with Nora Barnacle. One of Vico's cycles had finally run its full course, and with transiting Pluto exact to the minute on his Mercury/Ascendant midpoint, Dedalus took his final flight.

NOTES

1. To Tom Kristen, quoted in Richard Ellmann, *James Joyce*, Oxford University Press, 1982 edn, p. 693.
2. James Joyce, *Selected Letters* (ed. Richard Ellmann), Faber & Faber,. 1976.
3. Richard Ellmann, *James Joyce*.
4. ibid., p. 741, from hospital records.

CHAPTER 19

Zelda Fitzgerald

MICHAEL HARDING

Zelda Sayre was born at 5.40 a.m. on 24 July 1900 in Montgomery, Alabama, the 6th of 9 children. Her father was a lawyer, strict and aloof and an archetypal Saturn figure. He was ultimately to become a judge and thenceforth be known as 'judge Sayre' even by his wife at home. Her mother seemed to be slightly at odds with the prevailing traditional Southern mores, being regarded as 'sensitive' and 'artistic' by her neighbours, though by all accounts equipped with an acerbic tongue and a stock of petty snobberies. Although they had a good social position, the Judge's ever-present fear of debts ensured that none of the girls had a particularly pampered upbringing, much as Zelda seemed to aspire to it. Photographs of her as a teenager depict almost a caricature of a Southern belle, languidly posed in summer dresses with her lips carefully stencilled into a pout. At the age of eighteen she met Scott Fitzgerald when he was stationed in a nearby town. She fell in love with him almost at once, and after an engagement which was at one time called off by Zelda, they married in New York on 3 April 1920.

The success of Scott's first novel catapulted them both into the public eye from the start. It was a gaze they both eagerly sought and a vanity they easily indulged. Throughout the twenties, with its jazz, speakeasies and glittering occasions, Scott's accounts of their wild behaviour chronicled the age. For over ten years they travelled extensively throughout Europe and America, criss-crossing the lives of the rich and famous, while all the time running up an emotional bar bill that inevitably each had to meet, Scott ending up as an alcoholic hack writer in Hollywood, unable to fully regain the stature of his earlier work, and Zelda as a permanently institutionalized schizophrenic, shrouded in her own failed dreams.

Zelda is generally depicted as an appendage to Scott. A woman with much artistic ambition but little talent; someone who wanted to write, to paint, to dance but always with too little skill, too thinly spread and applied far too late. Scott needed a butterfly on his arm, one that he could indulge and control, and she willingly fluttered into place. Zelda's ultimate inability to distance her own personality from his, to develop whatever she could from her own resources, played a large part in her final emotional collapse.

What is not at first so clear is the part that Scott also played in that descent, and how his needs as a creative writer sapped Zelda's own strengths and talents. There is no doubt that Scott loved Zelda very much and her decline into madness tormented him unbearably; there is also little doubt that his own overwhelming need to stay ahead of every game as a writer devoured whatever emerging talents Zelda possessed. Theirs was the love affair of the Jazz Age and its boozy syncopation was a part of them. While the markets crashed and the dole queues lengthened, Scott and Zelda danced on. Fêted by Europe's literati, sought after by the popular American press, they waltzed together into immortality while in their own slow silence they stepped into private oblivion.

If such a relationship captured the imagination of a whole generation then their synastry should equally engage our immediate attention, but it does not. There is something half-hearted about the conventional astrological approach to the relationship of Scott and Zelda. There are no Moons conjunct Suns, no Venus trine Mars, no clear signatures of their electric, compulsive involvement. In fact there are absolutely no classical aspects of romantic synastry whatsoever.

Using the traditional approach (Figure 19.1) we have a conjunction of Zelda's Mars with Scott's own Mars/Neptune conjunction, which lies across Scott's nodal axis. This contact says much about their sporadic fights and furious rows, and gives us an image of the glamour and the drinking, but little else. It picks up very nicely a typical remark of Zelda's when she described herself as an adolescent caring only for two things – boys and swimming. However, this does not take us far down the road and if one attempted to write a synastry report on this contact alone it could quickly turn into a work of fiction.

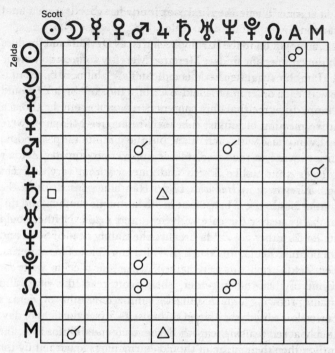

Figure 19.1 Synastry between Scott and Zelda Fitzgerald. Note the lack of traditional aspects between the couple.

The Sun trine Saturn contact says something about the enduring potential of their relationship – and they certainly did find their separations hard to take – but overall we are given very little to explore. Such contacts can occur randomly with any selection of two charts and anyone doubting that should take a few from the file and try it. We need something much more, something that leaps off the page, if the astrology is to match the reality of their relationship. There is nothing remarkable here, nothing larger than life which parallels all that we know of their turbulent life together. We also need to see how Scott could so dominate and devour Zelda, leaving her at his mercy and unable to fight back despite the strength of her own chart. It is almost as if that Mars/Mars contact tells us about the fire that consumed them, but nothing of how or why it started, where the wind took it or what gave it such a fatal attraction.

If one moves on to the harmonic charts, as David Hamblin does with the couple, one finds a Mercury/Mercury conjunction in the 5th. Hamblin suggests that this indicates an 'ability to communicate with each other in style and to write in the same style'. I would be happy to agree that this conjunction says something about a creative meeting of minds, that their respective Mercuries were literally in phase with each other, but the jump to their supposed ability to write in the same style is a hard one to make; Zelda's writing is quite unlike Scott's and emerged from very different needs. Elsewhere in *Harmonic Charts* Hamblin reminds us of the potential for obsessive behaviour in 5th harmonic contacts and this is probably nearer the case with Scott and Zelda. Neither could quite let the other go; Zelda because she simply needed Scott and Scott because Zelda provided him with a large part of his material. When Zelda tried to assert herself, when she tried to write *her* account of their life together, then Scott reacted swiftly and brutally, allowing only a suitably sanitized version of Zelda's experience – edited and altered by himself – to see the light of day. This is backed up by their 5th harmonic Venus/Pluto trine; the creative/obsessive nature of the 5th harmonic is amplified by the creative/obsessive nature of the Venus/Pluto contact, and here we have matters dealing specifically with the manipulation of art and feelings. There can be a devouring need in any Pluto contact and we see something of the 'desire to create and relate together' and the inability to separate coupled with an underlying issue of domination and control. But again, we are only looking at two contacts and in an harmonic which is in itself somewhat detached from the basic energies of a human relationship.

The harmonic that is traditionally used for synastry – but only in sidereal Hindu astrology – is the 9th. In *Harmonic Charts* Hamblin quickly picks up the strong Mercury/Venus and Moon/Venus contacts this chart reveals (Figure 19.2). We have seen elsewhere how important this Mercury/Venus contact can be in the creative process, and here we see it again coupled with the emotional needs of the planets repeated in further contacts such as Jupiter conjunct Mars, Neptune trine the Moon and Mercury opposition Pluto.

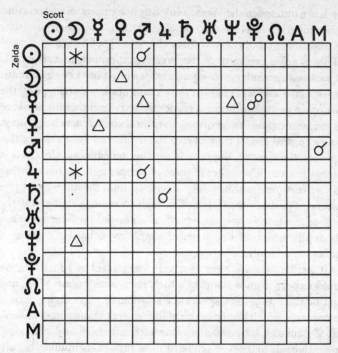

Figure 19.2 The 9th harmonic synastry between Scott and Zelda reveals powerful ties.

These are strong contacts, but in jumping traditions – and zodiacs – we risk overlooking a number of very important facts about the way in which the 9th harmonic chart, the Navamsa, is actually used in the East.

Like all Hindu astrology it is tied directly into what we in the West would describe as a very fatalistic tradition which allows virtually no room at all for free will. Although the final planetary positions of the 9th harmonic chart and the Navamsa are identical, they are calculated in a very different manner which underlines heavily the philosophy the Hindu astrologer takes towards the meaning of each zodiacal degree – something which is effectively missing from the Western approach. Furthermore, the Hindu analysis of the Navamsa synastry concentrates on house positions, which are unused in the West, while applying rules for aspects and their strengths which find no parallel at all outside their originating tradition.

This is not a criticism of the Western approach to harmonics, but rather a reminder once again that we must be very clear about the strengths and weakness of the techniques we are using and the reasons we use them. There is no doubt that there are some striking 9th harmonic (and 9th harmonic to radical) contacts to be found in many couples' charts if one takes the trouble to fully explore this approach to synastry. But how to use this information effectively is another matter. The issues of 'joy', of one person's ability to bring that quality to another's life, seems to underlie many of these contacts. Similarly the Hindu idea of the Navamsa as showing the 'fruit of the tree' – the end result of a person's self-expression – echoes the image of one partner supplying a basic meaning or fulfilment for another.

Altogether, we are here at a very deep level of Ideal – as we would expect from a number which is created from 3 × 3 – and meeting the intangible aspects of a relationship that many couples never reach, much less have the ability to articulate. As far as Scott and Zelda are concerned, both the traditional and the more innovative approaches to synastry show little of their wild, 'beautiful and damned' relationship that abounded with an energy we have yet to locate. Yet it must be there for it indubitably manifested – and manifesting is the key word.

To look at the core dynamics of any relationship we need to examine its basic energies, in other words those aspects that are multiples of two. If we look at the 8th harmonic aspects (Figure 19.3), all the multiples of 45° and their attendant midpoints, we can see at once how powerfully the couple must have experienced each other.

Immediately we see that the 'minor' aspect of 135° brings Scott's Uranus on to Zelda's Moon/Venus conjunction and all their attendant midpoints. This is a very powerful contact, striking her at the most basic feeling level. All that is bold, new, brash, stimulating, shocking and exciting is embodied by Scott. He contains the capacity to both awaken and alienate her, to draw out her truth and to negate her reactions. He circles her like a

Scott Zelda

☉ = ☽/♆

☽ = A/M (Your feelings are with me here and now)

☿ = ♂/♃

♀ = ♀/A

♂☌♆ = ♄/☊ = ☿/M = A/M

♃ = ♂/A = ♆/A

♅ = 135° ♀☽

♇ = ♇/☊ = ♂/♅

☊ = ♅/A = ♇/M

Figure 19.3 Scott's and Zelda's midpoint synastry reveals powerful Sun/Moon contacts including Scott's Moon on Zelda's AS/M.

permanent transit, continually challenging her feelings and charging her batteries. As Zelda *already* has ☽ = ♅/M = ☉/♅, ♅ = ☽/AS and ♀ = ♅/AS natally, these energies are *already* strong within her, and her natal Uranus/node conjunction further spells out the type of relationships she might be drawn towards. Scott could have become a sort of walking overdose and the embodiment of the natal ☽ = ☉/♅ that Zelda would strive to express or experience at a feeling level. Zelda seems to be geared from the start to need the experience of the new via the male principle (☽ = ☉/♅), to express the excitement of this experience of it in everyday life (♀ = ♅/AS) and to incorporate her reactions to it as she strives to achieve personal awareness and status in the world (☽ = ♅/M). The strength of the ♀ = ♅/AS is further amplified by the fact that she *also* has ♅ = ♀/AS and AS = ♀/♅. As with

Christa MacAuliffe's ☿/♂/♄ triple repeat, the ♀/♅ principle is almost like a signature to the events in her life. Her one attempt to break away from Scott's emotional hold over her took place in June 1924 when she had a very brief affair – with a wild, dashing aviator who wooed her by barrel-rolling his light aircraft over their villa! Interestingly, that took place when transiting Uranus was on the ♄/☊ midpoint so strongly hit by Scott's Mars/Neptune conjunction – shattering some of his illusions at the same time.

The contact of Scott's node with Zelda's ♇/M and ♅/AS midpoints re-emphasizes the transformative and Uranian quality their relationship could bring about. Scott's Pluto expands the 'shared destiny' so often attached to the ♇/☊ midpoint – particularly true in this case as the other Plutonian issues of money and manipulation figured so strongly in the excesses of their life together. ♇ = ♂/♅ aptly captures the 'force, violent interventions and Higher Power' Ebertin attributes to this contact, while ♄ = ☉/♃ = ☽/♆ tells us much of Scott's ability to control her self-expression in a variety of ways. ☉/♃ is very much a point of personal energy. It can be thought of as a focal point for issues of health, joy, personal philosophy and creativity. Saturn can lay a particularly cold hand here, and even more so on the next midpoint, ☽/♆.

As we shall see in a moment, Zelda's Saturn/Moon/Neptune contacts in her own chart embody the other side of her powerful lunar midpoint tree. They represent the reflective, solitary and deeply vulnerable side of her personality not immediately evident behind the frantic search for excitement and stimulation that her lunar responses demanded. Scott's Saturn here probably compounds the negative, withdrawing quality such a contact can induce as the most receptive feeling nature (☽/♆) confronts the discipline and fears of the past – her own father, Judge Sayre, included. Ebertin is particularly bleak about this contact, attributing to it 'pessimism, hopelessness and despair, pathological states of depression and the tendency to feel inhibited, frustrated or paralysed'. While this description was true of Zelda for much of her life, it is in part due to the many individual patterns in her own chart which are amplified by this contact with Scott's. However, the simple meaning of their synastry when seen through the use of midpoints *does* add a level of detail otherwise unavailable and *does* identify the main arena in which Saturn manifests. The fact that Scott's own Sun also triggers the same ☽/♆ midpoint *to the minute* only adds weight to this observation.

This other side of Zelda is graphically portrayed on her Mercury axis, Figure 19.4. While the Moon obviously embodies her emotional history and the manner of its current expression, Mercury will tell us a lot about the manner in which her mind operates. The aspects are powerful indeed, and pull together disparate energies.

♀/♇, ☽/♂ and ♀/♂ are brought together by Mercury, Saturn and Neptune. In other words, her mind could tend to interact continually with her compulsive need to relate and express her sensuality, with her spontaneous self-expression as a creative woman (☽/♂) and her basic social/sexual relationship with others (♀/♂). But it is a Mercury that is also configured with the polar opposites of experience – Saturn and Neptune.

The focus of this dichotomy is of course the ☿ = ♄/♆, about which Ebertin has to say 'inhibitions in thinking, an inclination always to think the worst, a nervous disease'. In fact, along with ♂/♄, ♄/♆ is a major midpoint for consideration in problems of health – physical or psychological. Here it is associated with all symptoms or diseases which are hard to identify or diagnose. Phobias, depressions, chronic conditions and energy-sapping illnesses all correlate with ♄/♆. On a sociological level, epidemics, plagues and all experiences of 'mass suffering' reflect

Figure 19.4 Zelda's Mercury tree.

the wider implications of this combination. It does not, of itself, correlate with schizophrenia, although a $\Psi = \hbar/\Psi$ *could* indicate some form of mental suffering – more likely depression and confusion. In many respects the bouts of eczema from which Zelda periodically suffered more concisely pin-point the $\Psi = \hbar/\Psi$ operating on the psychosomatic level – and give us a remarkable insight into how midpoints can define very exactly the symbolic expression of a disease.

Zelda's eczema was sporadic, although it tended to correlate with her hospital admissions. During one spell in hospital her psychiatrist attempted to cure the condition using hypnosis, with dramatic results. Zelda was put into a trance for thirteen hours and on awakening found herself almost completely free of the disease. Furthermore, she had reached an insight into why she believed her skin reacted in that manner. To quote her biographer directly: 'When she felt normal and realized the danger in her conjugal conflicts the eczema appeared. It came, she thought, as a sort of warning device. Her behaviour toward Scott vacillated between being loving and being nasty. She was impulsively affectionate at moments when Scott least expected it, yet might turn on him as he responded to her affection.'

Saturn is the traditional ruler of all boundaries, skin included. With $\Psi = \hbar/\Psi$ we could expect a nervous, hard-to-define skin condition, perhaps allied to the kind of confusions Neptune can often bring. That the condition erupts as a direct result of a tension between affection and assertion describes the $\Q/\P$, $\Q/\mathcal{O}$ and $\mathcal{D}/\mathcal{O}$ conflicts at their clearest. Zelda's Mercury ties them in to the $\hbar/\Psi$ in a sequence which accurately depicts the events unfolding as she describes. She has a conflict of feelings towards Scott, she wants to be nice but needs to express her own emotions. Scott only sees her need to relate as sexual and when he picks up on that cue she turns nasty. She is too dominated by the Saturn principle (Judge Sayre et al.) to act directly and so defines her boundaries with her skin and mysteriously becomes unattractive with a disfiguring condition. The hypnotic cure took place during September 1930, with Saturn stationary direct within 1.5° of her Moon and Pluto crossing her Ψ/Ψ midpoint!

This triple contact of Mercury, Saturn and Neptune along with

♀/♇ and ☽/♂ in particular should also say a lot about the way she could use her mind creatively and what images it would naturally seek to express in the world. Looking at these structures we can begin to see within them traces of half-forgotten dreams, intangible memories that repeat obsessively just beneath the level of consciousness, continually stirring the emotions, galvanizing the senses – a restive anger contained beneath a slow decay.

The creative core of this is the ☽/♂ midpoint. This is the point where Zelda's femininity and energy can meet and the intensely emotional expression of her (Cancer) Moon couples with the forcefulness of Mars seeking immediate release. Mercury here gives a strong mental component – obviously suggesting writing as one possible expression – but also pointing out how her thinking process will almost certainly be very considerably influenced by her moods and shifting energies. Neptune on the same point opens it to the universe; *all* can come in, *all* needs to be expressed. The Moon is suddenly no longer personal but universal and open to everything – and then there is Saturn. Saturn demanding that all of this be made sense of, be put into shape and have a value that the world can understand and judiciously consider before passing its inevitable verdict. This – almost certainly – is again the mark of Judge Sayre, of whom Zelda wrote: 'The Judge became, with their matured perceptions, a retributory organ, an inexorable fate, the force of law, order and established discipline. Youth and age: a hydraulic funicular, and age, having less waters of conviction in its carriage, insistent on equalizing the ballast of youth . . . [Zelda] came to realize that the bones of her father could indicate only her limitations.'[1]

In reading this paragraph it is hard to keep in mind that its author was not consciously using astrological symbolism! The words could come from one of a dozen textbooks on Saturn and balancing the weight of that planet against images of water can only conjure up again the aspects of her Mercury in action as she wrote *Save Me the Waltz*. This 220-page book was produced in a frenzied burst of activity over a six-week period while she was recovering in a clinic from a schizophrenic episode. As we shall see later, its writing was to mark a major period of estrangement from

Scott as he first retreated from its contents and then battled against them.

In looking at Zelda's creativity so far we have noted how the contacts between Saturn, Neptune and Mercury have underscored the events and images in her life time after time. The two outer planets have contributed much of their symbolism and many of the problems latent in such a difficult dual contact. But these are all midpoint contacts in the 8th harmonic; we would expect them to operate in such a manner, pulling planetary energy together for expression in the world. If we see how the same planets may interact in another harmonic we find a clear example of a point made in Chapter 6 on why some midpoints are more potent than others.

In Zelda's radical chart Neptune lies extremely close to the midpoints of ♀/♇, ☽/♂ and ♀/♂. Consequently in many harmonics it will continue to remain on these same midpoints until they gradually drift out of orb. In the 8th harmonic Saturn and Mercury are pulled into the picture as we have already discussed. In the 5th harmonic (Figure 19.5) Neptune still remains at the midpoint of all three pairs but the ☽/♂ aspect is now a close square. Thus we have also to consider the Moon/Mars as a striving towards the *creative style* symbolized by these two planets – an immediate gutsy response to the world, like a comedienne. In Figure 19.5 we can see that Mars is also square to Jupiter – the freedom theme again – as well as to Venus once more. Mercury opposes this triple conjunction – making the communication of ideas, philosophies and feelings a central creative issue and one that should surely manifest as the majority of these same contacts are found on the midpoint structures. Thus our understanding of the basic 8th harmonic configurations is considerably enhanced by recognizing in the 5th harmonic the creative potential of the ☽/♂ and the ♂/♀; we can be much more certain of *how* they will operate. It is probably this presence of Neptune in many lower-numbered harmonics which blurs the immediacy of these contacts, making them harder to express with the clarity she might choose. Insomuch as the 5th harmonic also represents the marriage of 2 and 3 – the marriage of the male and female – it can also give us vivid images of the marriage of the individual. Moon, Mercury and

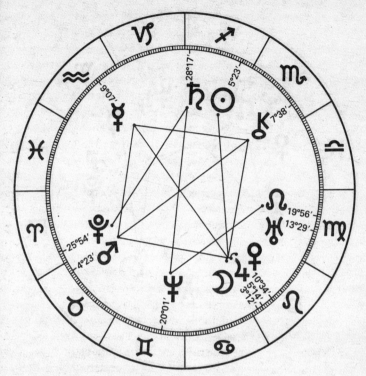

Figure 19.5 Zelda's 5th harmonic.

Mars aspects have for long been correlated with sudden journeys taken on the spur of the moment, and the Fitzgeralds' marriage spread itself frenetically across two continents with little concern for the ordinary rhythms of life. The Neptune at the midpoint of ☽/♂ reminds us of how much a part alcohol played in the relationship with its ensuing health problems, for Zelda almost as much as Scott. Ebertin gives for Ψ = ☽/♂ 'diseased procreative organs' as a medical correlation for this combination. Zelda was only able to bear one child, despite operations and treatment for infertility – possibly the result of an abortion she had in March 1922.

In Zelda's 7th harmonic chart (Figure 19.6) we again find some strong patterns pulling in planets we have already examined and, in the main, underlining our previous observations. A Venus trine

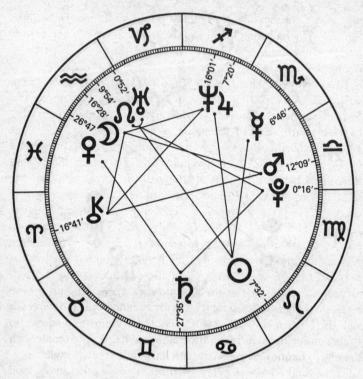

Figure 19.6 Zelda's 7th harmonic.

Saturn further reinforces the Saturn theme by suggesting she
would be inspired or turned-on by disciplined structure, by the
love of the old, by an identification with traditional values. Negatively, there could be a love of lost causes and being what Hamblin
describes as a 'romantic pessimist'. The Sun opposition to the
Uranus/Node and in a very close trine to Jupiter all point to the
goal of freedom. These two different sets of values inhabit her like
uneasy tenants and between them there is the desire for the joyful
expression of the physical in the Moon/Mars trine. This is Zelda
the dancer, inspired by an emotional response towards action like a
call to arms. It could be thought of as the happy, creative woman
with the Venus trine Saturn as the disciplined artistic performer
striving for recognition and perfection. The Sun trine Jupiter is

also a strong indication of a need for public adulation. In both the 5th and 7th harmonics Sun or Moon contacts with the actor's planet often indicate a desire to occupy centre-stage either in manner or fantasy.

It was only after her breakdown in 1930 that Zelda did a lot of writing, which was often the product of her own inner ferment, and Scott describes the process very clearly with Zelda slipping between the 5th and 7th harmonic as her creative style becomes swamped by emerging energy and her subsequent need to control it. In a letter to Zelda's psychiatrist, Scott writes that Zelda alternated between periods of intense self-expression when she indulged in an exaggeration of her physical and mental powers (very clearly the 5H Moon/Jupiter/Venus conjunction opposite Mercury and square to Mars), and periods of 'Conservatism, almost Victorianism, dread of extremes or excesses . . . One of the reasons for gravitating towards the first state is that her work is perhaps best in the passage from the conservative to the self-expressive phase, just before and after it crosses the line . . . the equivalent of creative excitement in an integrated person.'[2] Which sounds like her 7H Saturn so closely trine Venus and square to Pluto coming in as the inspiration of those images try to come with the more chaotic and expansive 5th harmonic creative style.

The actual *content* of Zelda's writing is, not surprisingly, best described by her Mercury/Saturn/Neptune contacts. These points play such a part in her life and their energies symbolize so much of what happened to her that it is almost inevitable to see their images in what she re-creates of her experience. The dreamy, hallucinogenic quality of Mercury/Neptune melds with the starker, harder Mercury/Saturn images leading to highly formalized imaginations presented in an over-blown (5H Moon conjunct Jupiter opposite Mercury) style:

The New York rivers dangled lights along the banks like lanterns on a wire; the Long Island marshes stretched the twilight to a blue Campagna. Glimmering buildings hazed the sky in a luminous patchwork quilt. Bits of philosophy, odds and ends of acumen, the ragged ends of vision suicided in the sentimental dusk.[3]

The evident Moon/Jupiter conjunction in the 5th harmonic, square to Mars, is a particularly important contact as it comes up again in other guises. Zelda has the combination ♂ = ☽/♃ in the 8th harmonic, and to examine further how this basic energy might manifest we should look more closely at her Mars tree.

At a Mars level (Figure 19.7), which would best illustrate her self-assertion, she has a structure which locks in to both Pluto and the MC, making that one particular midpoint – ☽/♃ – particularly strong. Ebertin is uncharacteristically cheerful about this combination. From such multiple contacts we get a picture of 'a healthy love relationship, a striving for success (♂). The desire to start a great enterprise, and extraordinary and unusual striving for possessions and wealth (♇). Popularity, confidence, the happy wife and mother (MC).' Although, as a generalization, he does give 'disadvantages through squandering and wastefulness' as a possible negative expression of the ☽/♃ principle.

In the first midpoint combination on the Mars structure, ♂ = ♅/♆ provides an image of Zelda's personal energy tied into two powerful areas of the unconscious. It contacts both the erratic, impetuous Uranian archetype and the self-negating and idealizing Neptune. Uranus here demands self-realization, living life at the

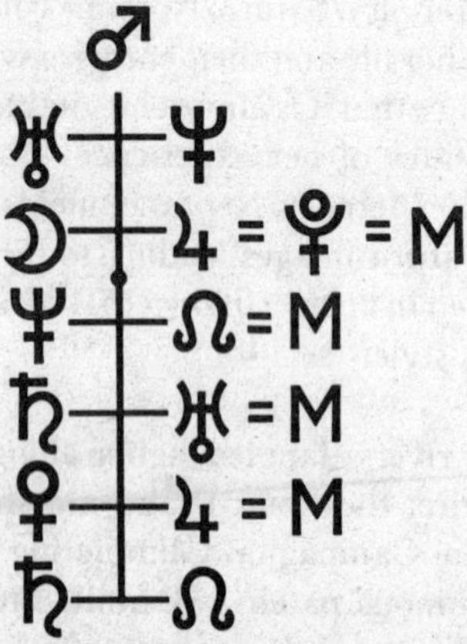

Figure 19.7 Zelda's Mars tree.

very edge and existing totally in the Now, a contact so often seeming to pull the native into situations in which such experiences cut through their lives again and again. Coupled with this there is also the ♂/Ψ need to *lose* self-will and merge with a much higher and less defined awareness. Ebertin interprets this triple contact as indicating 'a lack of stamina, instability, inspirations. Misdirected energy, the state of lameness or paralysis, also of sadness.'

After the ☽/♃ contact comes Ψ/☊ – in other words, Neptune again. This time connected to the world at large through the process of relationships. The implication is that Zelda's will and sexuality could be drawn towards Neptunian relationships, contacts in which circumstances or personalities encountered could make it hard for her to put her own needs and wishes across with the forcefulness they might deserve. This certainly describes much of her life with Scott, but also her continued attraction towards the whole world of art. She painted, wrote and danced, and for a large part of her life mixed almost exclusively in artistic circles – or in asylums.

♂ = ♄/♅, which follows next, can be a tough one, and is redolent of inner stress. The need for discipline and the need for freedom coexist; the individual lives like a spring under tension, awaiting the moment of release. This can come as an explosion of anger or a burst of activity that stretches experience to the limits. It can also describe the powerful, lyrical movements of the dance. ♄/♅ can be a combination that focuses our expression of rhythm. Coupled with the Sun, Moon, Mercury or the angles it is a common combination in the charts of astrologers, mathematicians or anyone involved with issue of pattern recognition or harmonics. Mars here would suggest that the concern with rhythm is more physical, such as a dancer or drummer. This contact undoubtedly contributed much to Zelda's obsession with the ballet as well as constantly keying her into some basic source of nervous energy.

Following on with ♀/♃ brings a clearly 'artistic' aspect into play. There is also the enjoyment of the good things in life, a need for luxury and expansiveness in social relationships coupled with a desire for physical indulgence. It brings a tangible, almost Taurean quality into life and emphasizes the pleasure art can bring. Finally, ♂ = ♄/☊ suggests that the end result of the effort and enjoyment is some form of sadness or separation. Ebertin defines $\sigma = \hbar/\Omega$ as 'the desire to gain release from emotional depression, suffering through others. Enforced separation or bereavement within the family.'

With Zelda's extremely strong Saturn contacts by midpoint and in her harmonic charts this aspect is something to be closely examined, for she is more likely than most to experience the 'shared loss' image that the $\hbar/\Omega$ connection can bring. The final contact on a midpoint tree can often describe how the particular planetary energy eventually gets to be expressed, as discussed more fully in Chapter 2. In Zelda's case she clearly needs to experience some form of separateness, but by no means does this have to be through failure or in the isolation of an asylum. The structure suggests that she needs to express her energy in a controlled and disciplined manner; that the 'end-product' of whatever she chooses to do has to live up to high demands or rigorous scrutiny. The questions one would hypothetically put to Zelda would be to try and elicit *whose* demands are being experienced internally and precisely *what* value judgements are being made.

Attempts to live up to unreasonable parental demands invariably end in failure – indeed, failure is often one of the main goals of a life lived out under such acquired obligations – and so it would be the job of the astrologer to help the client discover what his or her own authentic standards really are. There is no ducking such a strong Saturn, and in this particular position the issue of self-judgement is bound to figure strongly, but it should be a genuine and realistic *self*-assessment, not the blind application of past rules.

With the approach of her Saturn return Zelda resumed the ballet lessons she had taken as a child, determined to achieve a level of professional competence and demonstrate to Scott that she had her own talents and could mould her own career. The dance obsessed and dominated her; in *Save Me the Waltz* she describes her lessons during the summer of 1929 through the eyes of her heroine, Alabama Beggs, and the $\sigma = \hbar/\mathbb{H}$ comes stridently through:

Alabama passionately hated her inability to discipline her own [body]. Learning how to manage it was like playing a desperate game with herself. She said 'My body and I', and took herself for an awful beating: that was how it was done. Some of the dancers worked with a bath towel around their necks. It was so hot under the burning roof that they needed something to absorb the sweat. Sometimes the mirror swam in red heat waves if Alabama's lesson came at the hour when the direct sun fell on the glass overhead.[4]

Through the remainder of 1929 and into 1930 she continued her practice; the 45° aspect then existing between Neptune and Pluto sliding on and off her ☉/☽ midpoint as the planets echoed her dance with their retrogradations. On 23 September 1929 she was offered a solo dancing part in the opera *Aida*. Inexplicably she rejected this chance to demonstrate an independent status. Transiting Jupiter was on her ☉/M midpoint, focusing on the issue of her professional advancement, but now Saturn was on her ☉/☽ and there it struck the stronger chord. She continued with her ballet lessons despite pleas from Scott that they were clearly undermining her health. Her manner became strange and disconnected and on 23 April, with Mars exactly triggering her ☿/♄/Ψ structures and the current Saturn/Uranus square lying across her ☿/♅ midpoint, she was admitted to a sanatorium. She discharged herself after a few days and returned to the dance. On 22 May, hallucinating and exhausted, she was re-admitted to hospital with transiting ♂ = radical ☿/Ψ, transiting ♃ = radical AS/MC, transiting ♅ = radical ♂/AS = ♇/AS and, most powerful of all, transiting ♇ on the ☉/☽. For her remaining eighteen years she was never to free herself for long from the confines of asylums.

When the extent of Zelda's condition became apparent, Scott took her back to America to a house he had bought on the outskirts of Baltimore. Zelda lived there intermittently, spending much of her time in a nearby institution. Scott was now working on an account of Zelda's breakdown, *Tender is the Night*, casting himself as a therapist and adding a fictional childhood rape to Zelda's past. He may have been influenced here by the memory of his first visit to the Sayre household. Zelda apparently teased her father so much that in a fury Judge Sayre picked up a carving knife and chased her round the room with it. Just as we noted in Chapter 6 how midpoints to the solar axis can sometimes provide us with

clues as to how the father appeared, so Zelda's ☉ = M = ♂/♇
gives some image of authority and rage. Interestingly, rape *is*
associated with this midpoint . . .

Apart from those two amendments, the book is probably quite
an accurate account of much of their relationship, especially
bearing in mind that many of Zelda's personal letters to Scott
appear in marginally altered form – as do the actual case-notes
from one of her psychiatric assessments. Scott was drinking heavily
and having difficulties structuring the book when, to his horror and
rage, Zelda submitted a manuscript of her own to his publishers.

Save Me the Waltz was written in six weeks during January and
February 1932 while Zelda was in the institution. Transiting Pluto
was on her ☿/Ψ midpoint and Saturn on her ☿/♀ as she dredged
up her own past and put form to it. Just as James Joyce had an
extremely powerful nodal contact (on his Sun/Moon midpoint) for
the day he chose for *Ulysses*, so the node was crossing one of the
most sensitive parts of Zelda's chart – the Mercury/Neptune/
Saturn complex – and Neptune repeating the same image by also
transiting her ☿/♄ midpoint while she wrote.

The first Scott knew of the book was when Maxwell Perkins, his
editor, sent him a copy; his reaction was swift and furious. He
wrote to the clinic on 14 March demanding why he had not been
told what Zelda was writing and making clear that he would do
everything he could to stop publication in its current form. His
objections to the novel were a mixture of reasonable anger (Zelda
had foolishly purloined Scott's hero from *This Side of Paradise*),
vanity (Zelda was far too indiscreet about Scott's drunken behaviour), and straightforward projection; he claimed Zelda was
plagiarizing 'his' material. The material in question being Zelda's
life.

Scott was quite unambiguous about this last point. It was for *him*
to re-create her insanity in fiction, not her. What happened to her
belonged to him because he was a professional writer and she was
not. She was trying to make him a laughing-stock and wreck his
career. The issue of how others may have reacted to *his* previous
portrayals of Zelda was not mentioned, neither was anything said
about Scott's inserting an incestuous rape into Zelda's childhood.
In the end, a compromise was reached. Zelda allowed Scott to edit

the book substantially and agreed not to write anything which encroached on 'his' territory without permission. *Save Me the Waltz* was published in October 1932 to mainly hostile reviews. Zelda's contract stipulated that the first $5,000 of her royalties should be used to settle Scott's debts with the publisher.

There are a number of positions one can take in trying to find reasons for Scott's proprietorial attitude towards Zelda. But whatever social attitudes need to be taken into consideration there also remains one remarkably powerful astrological observation: Scott's 5th harmonic chart (Figure 19.8) has Venus and Saturn forming the same trine aspect that they do in Zelda's 7th. If Zelda was turned on or inspired by the images symbolized by these planets – and much of her life would suggest that she *was* – then perhaps at

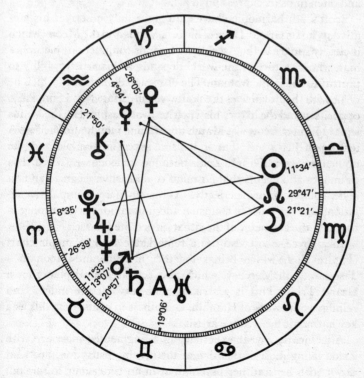

Figure 19.8 Scott's 5th harmonic.

one level Scott genuinely believed that his was the ideal style in which their manifestation should be presented.

In working with clients in a counselling situation, it has long been noted that many chart issues are dealt with by projection. Typical of this would be an inner planet/outer planet opposition in which the energies symbolized by the outer planet are not recognized, and appear to come from 'others'. The Sun/Pluto woman seemingly always attracted towards manipulative or brutal men, the Moon/Uranus man inexplicably meeting a string of reckless or castrating women. Strong patterns in harmonic charts can sometimes work in a similar manner. They are all aspect structures and can be recognized or denied in exactly the same way. Indeed, as we have seen in Chapter 13, the 7th harmonic is frequently projected and often finds its expression in art.

Scott's 5th harmonic chart quite uncannily describes his creative style. Its Grand Trine of Saturn, Venus and the Moon (which is closely square to the Ascendant/Uranus conjunction) pictures a man whose stature in the world depends on his artistic ability to portray an unstable woman. The obsessional manner in which he dealt with their own lives is equally well illustrated by a Sun/Pluto opposition and the luxury to which he always aspired by the Venus square Jupiter. Scott was always attracted to money and success. A feature of his art is that it is *about* successful people and the opulence of their lives. In Zelda he found someone who was drawn to images and events that *his* mind could easily recognize and *his* style could capture perfectly. As in so many compulsive relationships the sense of collusion and mutual identity is strong; in this case the geometry of the situation is quite precise.

Like Joyce, Scott also has a remarkable 28th harmonic chart (Figure 19.9) which brings together his Sun and Moon in a T-square with Mercury, which also acts as a focal planet for a Grand Trine. This is a striking planetary picture indeed and reinforces the work of Hamblin and others in confirming this as a key harmonic for creative artists.

After nearly a year experiencing a fragmented marriage with Zelda living most of the time at the nearby institution, Scott sat down with her and her psychiatrist in an endeavour to sort out their respective needs. At Scott's insistence a stenographer was

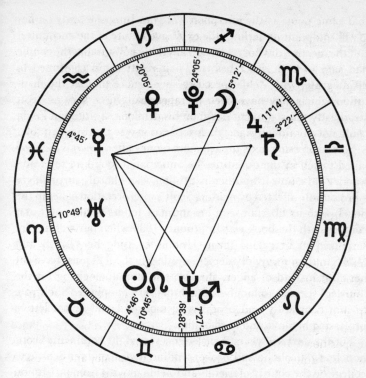

Figure 19.9 Scott's 28th harmonic.

present and Zelda's biographer, Nancy Milford, later had access to a typescript of the afternoon. The meeting began at 2.30 p.m. on 28 May 1933 and Scott's fears about Zelda writing another novel quickly emerged. Scott is scathing of her attempts, calling her a third-rate writer, a third-rate dancer. In Scott's eyes at least part of their situation was clear: he had supported her all along and everything that had happened to Zelda was 'all my material. None of it is your material.'[5] Faced with the possibility of permanent separation from Scott, Zelda tacitly agreed not to use anything that Scott wanted for *Tender is the Night*.

Experiencing such anger over the issues of her writing, it is hardly surprising that Zelda's ☿/♀ midpoint was triggered by both Mars and Uranus during the day, with the Moon crossing that same point as the afternoon wore on. Jupiter exactly on her ♂/♅ midpoint underlines the explosive nature of the encounter. But the meeting did not really add anything new to what the couple had said to each other before. Their relationship continued to disintegrate, with Zelda forced to spend more time at the institution which may have been therapeutically necessary as Scott steadfastly refused to cut down on his drinking, a situation Zelda could not emotionally face; their separation was almost inevitable.

Scott's pressing need to earn more money after *Tender is the Night* failed to sell in the quantities he anticipated took him to Hollywood. Zelda, now in another institution, was – hardly surprisingly – profoundly affected by reading Scott's interpretation of her in the novel, with its liberal use of her intimate letters to him. Her first contact with the book was in January 1934 when parts of it were serialized in magazine form. Uranus crossing her ☽/AS and ♀/AS midpoints vividly depict how deeply the text must have cut her. But instead of anger, she wrote to him apologizing for the 'burden' she was to him, wishing him every happiness. She wrote to him constantly and obsessively; mournful and abject letters professing her love and need of him.

For the next few years their letters crossed the continent; Scott, hopelessly alcoholic and broke, sending their daughter Scottie to college on the charity of friends and Zelda moving from institution to institution, developing religious mania and for a period of time moving back to Montgomery where the family home had declined with her own fortunes. Once the best part of town, their street had now decayed into rooming houses and noise. The inner, self-abnegating fantasy of her 7th harmonic took over more and more of her life, its Saturn trine Venus expressing clearly David Hamblin's suggestion for this aspect: 'Romantically moved by the idea of suffering, hardship and devotion to duty: a belief in love attained through tribulation: seeing beauty in whatever is sad, tragic, expressive of earthly tribulations: a romantic pessimist.' She flirted with fascism, attracted to its order and discipline and mimeographed religious tracts for her friends. On 22 December 1940 she received a phone call: Scott was dead.

In looking at some of the basic patterns in Zelda's chart we noted earlier the importance of her Moon and Jupiter. They are conjunct in her 5th harmonic and in the 8th their midpoint picks up the MC, Mars and Pluto. Pluto crossed that midpoint on the day she was told that Scott had died, repeating its natal placement and marking the last stage of her life.

After the posthumous publication of Scott's unfinished novel *The Last Tycoon* Zelda started to write again. Her planned book *Caesar's Things* was never completed; it is a rambling and incoherent record of an inner world into which she continued to retreat as the years passed. By 1948 she was once more in an institution.

Looking at Zelda's chart for that year one date would have stuck out immediately: 10 March. In the evening of that day there was a New Moon almost exactly square to Uranus configured within a degree of her AS/MC midpoint. Saturn was within 25′ of an exact square of the node and lying on her sensitive D/Ψ midpoint. At about midnight part of the hospital burst into flames, engulfing one of the women's wards where it raged uncontrollably.

During the course of her life Zelda had often used the image of the salamander to describe her own experiences of descent into madness, identifying with the reptile's mythical qualities to survive fire and be cleansed by it. But mythic powers were not hers, and Zelda Fitzgerald died that night along with eight others, later to be identified only by a charred slipper.

NOTES

1. Zelda Fitzgerald, *Save Me the Waltz*, Penguin, 1987, p. 17.
2. Nancy Milford, *Zelda*, Avon Books, 1970, p. 325.
3. *Save Me the Waltz*, p. 70.
4. ibid., p. 139.
5. *Zelda*, p. 327.

CHAPTER 20

Practice Makes Perfect: A Case Study

CHARLES HARVEY

The only bit I can't do is put it all together (student lament).

Like a child learning to read, when you start to look at charts for the first time you begin by recognizing individual words and phrases, but making out the larger meaning of complete sentences, paragraphs and chapters is another matter. Even if you are already fluent in reading a chart using other methods, learning to assimilate and integrate the new types of information produced by harmonics and midpoints does require considerable practice, and the development of what at first will be unfamiliar perspectives. This is closely analogous to the new skills that the doctor has to develop when first working with X-rays, brain scans, or ultrasound. Images which at first seem incomprehensible, with practice soon become indispensable information. In this chapter we will be giving ourselves practice by working through an example chart, looking at ways in which you can learn to recognize crucial factors, and how you can put together the main strands of information that are highlighted by these methods of analysis. We will be looking at some of the ways in which you can present the material within a coherent framework, so that it will be directly useful to the client.

Different clients require different things from the astrologer. But, for whatever purpose you are preparing it, an astrological analysis, be it of a man, a country, a company, a question, or an idea, the purpose of our analysis is to throw as much light as you can on the subject under consideration. Your job as an astrologer is to help to bring as much insight as possible to the underlying dynamics of the particular moment in time being charted and to make informed and intelligent conjectures about it.

In the case of an analysis for an individual, your objective should be to help the subject to see himself and his particular psychological emphasis and biases, motives and potential, and to become aware of the present position and circumstances, more clearly. Such clarity can come only from your own clarity of insight.

If your analysis does not help to throw light on the client's situation then it has failed. It may even do worse. It may fog the question, confuse the client. It may draw red herrings across the path, and instil half-formed fears. In this respect we should always listen to our inner wisdom. Do not use what you do not understand. If when you use harmonics and midpoints you can only see a blur of indigestible information, then you are only likely to induce dyspepsia in your clients if you attempt to use this material. Practise on your own chart and the charts of people whose life and psychology are well known to you until these methods are as familiar as the more traditional elements in your vocabulary. Astrological skills are no different from any others. It is only with constant practice and constant stretching of our repertoire that we can become truly fluent instrumentalists.

In this respect it has to be recognized that the well-tried methods of traditional astrology, in which most students, in the English-speaking world at any rate, begin their training, have a purity and simplicity which can serve us well, provided we recognize their limitations. Planets, traditional aspects, houses, signs, can tell us a great deal about an individual and something of their broad psychology. These factors will often, though not always, sound out the main themes in the life. Angular planets always make themselves felt. The closest aspects in the chart are always of significance. A strong house emphasis is seldom without significance. A strong emphasis on a sign, and especially the Sun sign, will almost always permeate and pervade the whole character and value system of an individual who has begun to live at any kind of purposeful and conscious level.

But while this is often the case, we know that there are also many charts where many of the important issues and deeper harmonies and resonances in the individual's life do not seem to be self-evidently written on the chart, and can only be justified by the tortured *post hoc* wrestlings of those who talk about astrology rather than practise it. Though frequently used as a textbook example, it must be seriously doubted whether many traditional students of astrology, asked for vocational guidance by young Adolf Hitler, would have contradicted his wish to become an architect and artist. How many would have suggested that instead he might consider developing his gifts of leadership and histrionics and think about becoming a political revolutionary or a theatrical impresario? What traditional astrologer would note any special ability in this chart for tapping into and mobilizing the deepest forces of the collective? But if, as we would contend, the traditional approach to Hitler's chart does not reveal such potential then the astrologer not only cannot draw attention to it, but, even more importantly, he cannot suggest a spectrum of alternative ways in which the kind of energies present in Hitler's chart might be used.

In studying the following example chart our objective will be to see how each approach, ancient and modern, contributes to building up a mosaic of the whole. You may care to make your own notes on the chart, the midpoints, and the harmonics, before reading further. This is excellent practice. If you want to do this, the radical chart is given in Figure 20.1, the midpoint structures are set out in Figure 20.2, and the various harmonic charts follow as Figures 20.3–20.6.

THE ART OF SYNTHESIS

The 'art of synthesis' is often seen as the ultimate achievement in astrological skills. But in fact 'synthesis' as usually understood is probably a somewhat misleading term. For while it is highly desirable that we know how to put all the information we have extracted from the chart into one interrelated picture, we need to be clear that this resulting picture will not necessarily look particularly coherent or homogeneous or 'synthesized' in any common sense of the term. Most people are complex, not simple; multi-faceted and contradictory, not single-minded and clear-cut. The chart can show us those contradictions and different facets but it cannot through some magic formula give us an 'accurate' and definitive answer as to 'what a person is really like'. What a person is 'really like' depends to a great extent upon your perspective.

Just as two skilled biographers using the same material can come to quite contrary views about their subject, so too different astrologers studying the same chart will bring their own viewpoints to bear. Likewise two different people with essentially the same natal chart may express it with very different emphasis, as so often happens with twins.

There is no foolproof way of evaluating whether someone's $\odot$–180–σ is stronger than their $\mathbb{D}$–120–$\mathbb{Q}$, and whether they will be more forceful and self-assertive than considerate, gentle and caring. But it is possible to say that if these two very different facets do exist in a particular chart their contradictory natures will have certain possible consequences. In short an absolute synthesis of the chart is impossible because human beings simply are not homogeneous. Dennis Nielsen, the multiple killer, was full of fine sentiments and capable of being kind and thoughtful. The East End mobster Kray twins, who mercilessly tortured their enemies, were considered good-hearted philanthropists by many in their patch. The great Tibetan mystic and sage Milarepa was originally a notorious bandit. People change during their life, showing and developing different facets of their potential at different times. We are all capable of changing our attitudes quite dramatically when confronted by different people and situations. As we have seen, all of the many models of the psyche state explicitly or implicitly that even the most wise and well developed of individuals are not homogeneous, totally integrated individuals. As Walt Whitman puts it in his *Song of Myself*:

> Do I contradict myself?
> Very well then I contradict myself,
> (I am large, I contain multitudes.)

Since this condition is not unique to Walt Whitman, but is true of all of us, to a lesser or greater extent, it will probably be a waste of time if, in preparing an analysis or for a consultation, you rack your brains trying to work out how different facets of the client's personality will work together. They may very well not work together. They may not even be on speaking terms, or indeed even fully acknowledge each other's existence. In short, to spend any great time wrestling to 'synthesize' is often a futile exercise, for you may be attempting to do what the client still has not done over several decades.

Conversely, it is very useful in considering a chart to recognize that we are each in some sense multiple personalities consisting of different sub-personalities, which will get along with each other or not according to their natures and the possibilities open for their expression. The chart which is both strongly Martial and strongly Neptunian may find unconnected expressions for each energy: sport and boozing, heavy rock music and drugs; or it may synthesize them through clandestine terrorism, or through becoming a warrior priest, or a Douglas Bader raising funds for limbless servicemen.

The various semi-autonomous 'gods' within us each have their own needs and gifts and each their own natural dynamic with the others. We are each a theatre with a wide range of characters waiting in the wings or already on stage, each with their own particular lines, each eager to have their say. But all is not chaotic, and here it should be noted that there are certain psychological principles that can help us in understanding the implications of any particular combination of characters. Of particular importance is the principle of psychological balance which gives rise to the concept of the Shadow.

The principle states that whatever is most consciously emphasized at any time will imply an equivalent repression of its opposite. Where reasonable, logical characters hold centre-stage, emotional and irrational figures may well hold sway in the shadows back-stage. Where an inspirational and idealistic figure takes the leading role, sensualists and money-grubbers may be waiting to trip him up stage-left, as the American evangelist movement has of late had cause to note. The excessively civilized and well ordered Saturnine hero may have particular problems if he has strongly Uranian and Neptunian figures in his supporting cast, as stockbroker Paul Gauguin exemplifies.

Within our own life we recognize themes and patterns and dynamics which endlessly seem to recur. If we begin to listen a plot begins to emerge. With conscious awareness and effort, with therapy and training, and by locating and mapping such themes in our chart, we may even gradually learn to direct the characters in our drama to deliver their lines to better purpose as part of a larger plot. If we do not do so, we can be assured that these characters will simply continue to play their parts as best they can.

With this image in mind, the first thing to remember in preparing a report, or consultation, for a client is that it is usually a useful start when producing a play to get a picture of the characters involved. So present your client with an outline of the cast of characters in the client's play, as you see them, stating their outstanding characteristics and attitudes, their likely lines and the spectrum of their potentialities. When this is done you can then go on to suggest which characters may work most effectively together, which may need greater mutual understanding, and which perhaps need to be introduced to each other. Having established the main list of dramatis personae, the contradictions, paradoxes, light and shade that you think it may be particularly useful to consider will become evident.

A BLIND CASE STUDY

Doing a 'blind analysis' for a client is not normally encouraged these days, as it is now recognized that cultural and family background, education, genetic inheritance, sex, and so on, have important parts to play in shaping the particulars of the way in which the astrological potential will express itself. Yet from the point of view of studying astrology the blind analysis is an invaluable, indeed indispensable, tool. It focuses our attention on principles and potentials, and helps to ensure that we are really getting to grips with the astrology of the case rather than matching assorted chart significators to known facts. We will therefore say no more at present about this individual than that he was born in New York City on 23 March 1901, at 7.35 a.m. He lived a full life and died in England on 29 February 1980. The object of this exercise is not in any way to guess who this person was (he will be unknown to most readers), or what he did, but to see what the astrology tells us about the kind of ideas that were likely to be expressed through his life and psyche.

Before exploring the evidence of the midpoints and harmonics, let us examine his chart systematically from an orthodox viewpoint. You may care to study this chart and make notes of your own before proceeding further. The natal chart is shown in Figure 20.1. The first outstanding features of the chart are that the Moon, Jupiter and Saturn are all angular in Earth signs in the Gauquelin zones with the Moon–AS in close trine to the Jupiter-Saturn conjunction. This paradoxical combination speaks at once of the imagination of the poet, Moon rising, the rigour and intellectual discipline of the scientist, Saturn culminating, and the benevolent

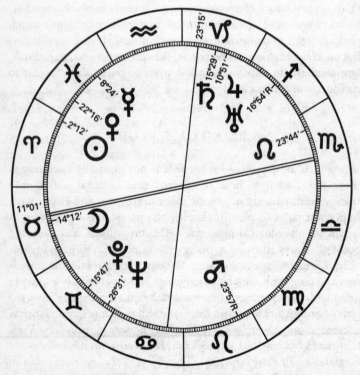

Figure 20.1 Example chart: it is suggested that you make your own notes on this before proceeding with the text.

good nature of the successful leader and philanthropist, Jupiter culminating in exact –120– AS and also 120–☽.

The predominance of Earth in the chart suggests great practicality and a desire to get to grips with the tangible concrete world. With the angular Saturn this is very much the hallmark of the classic scientific temperament, the doubting Thomas who only believes in that which he can see, touch and taste. The ♃–0–♄ in ♑ is likewise indicative of a highly practical, hard-working, constructive, and solidly ambitious approach to the world. With an emphasis on the sensible there will also be an emphasis on the sensual, and with ☽–0–AS ♉ –120– ♃–♄ we would expect a touch of the *bon viveur*, the gourmet, and a delight in the best of the good things of this world. Indeed ☽–♄ aspects, with their propensity to be 'professional' mothers, are often found in the charts of restaurateurs. The close ☽–120–♄, however, also indicates that there will be a delight (3H) in emotional self-control and in being in command of oneself. It is indicative of a strong sense of responsibility and is highly characteristic of someone in the caring professions, who take their maternal duties towards others seriously, and who will be motivated (3H) by a concern for the welfare of others. Likewise ♃–120–AS and ☽ shows someone who delights in benevolence and in creating a sense of well-being in those with whom they come into contact. The ☽–0–AS suggests someone for whom the mother and the feminine will be of considerable importance. This desire in some way to look after others is further emphasized by AS ruler ♀ in ♓ exactly on 12th cusp (Placidus), in close –60– MC and –120–☊, but also –90–♆, a pattern which speaks both of a great capacity for altruistic love and affection and of the aspiration to form close personal relationships with others, though not without the danger of self-deception and a tendency to seek spiritual fulfilment through the partner. This deeply sensitive Venus position is, like the ☽–0–AS in ♉, also indicative of a deep response to music and the arts, a facet in deep contrast with the practical, factual, thrust of the outer orientation of the MC and AS levels of the chart.

We receive further confirmation of this very different picture when we turn to the solar level. Here the ☉–♈ in 12th –90– ♆ speaks of a classic intuitive type, someone of great delicacy of perception and creative sensitivity who will be at home with flights of the imagination and in probing into the unknown. This contrasts strongly with the down-to-earth, 'sensible', material 'realism' of the outward orientation. We must suspect that this hard-headed approach to the world may tend to screen out or interfere with the spontaneous flow of the less testable and more intuitive realities to which ☉–♈ in 12th House –90–♆ would naturally gravitate. (Or should we say levitate?) In one way or another there is a paradox here.

While the strong Earth element, and especially the AS and ☽ in ♉, suggest a certain dogged determination based on inflexibility, this must be in part mollified by the fact that it is the changeable Moon which rises which can produce a restlessness and wander-lust which militates against the pure complacent inertia sometimes associated with this sign. In addition the AS–60–☿–60–♃ is indicative of a quick, vivid, lively mind and large inquiring intellect which enjoys the exchange of stimulating ideas and discussion, and a natural ability to communicate and teach. The almost exact ♂–90–☊ is likewise indicative of someone who will find it difficult to sit around idle for long, but will need to be up and off and putting a great deal of drive and energy into collaborative effort and teamwork, be it through work or sport or some other passion.

In the broad pattern of the chart we cannot but notice the ♅–180–♇, but apart from its very wide –90– ☿ and ♀ and the ♇–150–♄, it does not, from a traditional viewpoint, appear to be in any way integrated. This suggests that, despite the seemingly cautious and conservative tone of the broad sweep of the chart, there will be periods in the life when sudden drastic changes and transformations will be required or take place in the life.

Much else could be said about the implications of the above key patterns, and you may well want to add your own comments and deductions. But with this broad background, and your own observations, let us now explore the chart in greater detail through a general consideration of the midpoint structures and harmonics.

The Evidence of the Midpoint Pictures

What do the midpoints have to tell us? Let us remind ourselves that the planetary pictures based on the division of the circle by 2, 4, 8 and 16 have a great deal to do with the unfoldment and development of the will aspect of the individual. The midpoint pictures will tell us a great deal about those aspects of this individual's psychological patterns which will be most likely to manifest in the world in terms of behaviour, activities, and events.

Examining the planetary pictures as a whole (Figure 20.2), we will want to pay special attention to those factors involving combinations of the personal points. Here we see immediately that the all-important $\odot/\mathbb{D}$ is closely occupied by both Mercury and the MC, which are in an almost exact $-45-$. We also note that the MC/AS is closely squared by the generational $\mathcopyright-180-\mathbf{P}$, making this powerful, impersonal energy, relatively personal and central to the character. Likewise we find Ψ is brought into prominence by its configuration with $\mathbb{D}/AS$, which further highlights the $\Psi-90-\odot/\varphi$.

Looking at the broad brushstrokes of our own analysis above we immediately note (and note that it is immediate!) that neither the central importance of Mercury nor the personal involvement of the $\mathcopyright-\mathbf{P}$ in this chart stand out with anything like this clarity. Likewise the Ψ pictures highlight and draw together a pattern which is far less clear cut to the normal gaze. We may also note immediately that each of these midpoint combinations is in its own way in strong contradiction to this surface picture of relative repose and inertia indicated by the strong Earth and $\mathcal{4}-0-\hbar$ element in the chart.

Having identified these key planetary pictures we can then explore them to see what else they tell us about the way in which this person will tend to manifest his life. The picture $\varphi = M = \varphi/\Omega = \varphi/\sigma = \odot/\mathbb{D}$ indicates someone who will focus his life around everything Mercurial, from travel, to language, to communication in every guise. It will encourage versatility, ingenuity, a quick inquisitive spirit, and a strongly restless and constantly inquiring approach to life. Indeed, we would have to say that this individual will come into his own and feel most whole and integrated when in some sense he is engaged in Mercurial pursuits, when travelling, talking, living by his wits and wit, when joking, interpreting, acting as a go-between, as a telephone line, as a translator of ideas and

```
                                        MIDPOINTS IN HARMONIC No.  8
23 MAR 1901    7:35 AM    ZONE= 5    40 N 43    74 W 0    NEW YORK CITY
PLACIDUS CUSPS:    2nd 10 GE 14    3rd 2 CA 9    5th 18 LE 1    6th 22 VI 50
Weighting:  FIRE 6    EARTH 11    AIR 2    WATER 5
                 CARDINAL 8    FIXED 9    MUTABLE 7
ORBS 2 DEGS. AND 1.5 DEGS.          Calculated at:  10:10:18 on 26 JUL 1989
------------------------------------------------------------------------

    SO       2  AR 12        MO      14 TA 12          NN      23 SC 44
SA--|-PL   0  AR 38      SO--|-VE  27 PI 14        VE--|-MC  22 AQ 44
ME--|-MC  15 AQ 48      JU--|-PL  28 PI 19        SO--|-SA  23 AQ 50
SA--|-UR   1  CP 11      JU--|-UR  28 SG 52          |=MA    23 LE 56
VE--|-JU  16 AQ 33      SO--|-NE  14 TA 21        ME--|-AS   9  AR 39
NN--|-AS  17 AQ 19      SA--|-PL   0  AR 38        NE--|-MC   9  AR 52
MA--|-AS   2  CA 25      ME--|-MC  15 AQ 48
JU--|-NE   3  AR 41      SA--|-UR   1  CP 11          AS      10 TA 55
VE--|-SA  18 AQ 52                               SO--|-PL   8  TA 59
MO--|-NN  18 AQ 58          VE      22 PI 16        VE--|-NE   9  TA 23
MO--|-MA   4  CA 4       NE--|-PL  21 GE 9         SO--|-UR   9  AQ 33
                        UR--|-NE  21 VI 42        ME--|-JU   9  AQ 37
    ME       8  PI 24     NN--|-MC  23 SG 28         -|=NE    26 GE 31
VE--|-NN  23 CP 0       MA--|-MC   8  SC 34        ME--|-SA  11 AQ 56
VE--|-MA   8  GE 6                                SO--|-VE  27 PI 14
SO===MO   23 AR 12          JU      10 CP 50
 -|=MC    23 CP 12      ME--|-AS   9  AR 39          MC      23 CP 12
                        NE--|-MC   9  AR 52        SO===AS  21 AR 33
    MA      23 LE 56     MO--|-ME  11 AR 18        VE--|-NN  23 CP 0
VE--|-MC  22 AQ 44                               VE--|-MA   8  GE 6
  |=NN    23 SC 44          UR      16 SG 54        SO===MO  23 AR 12
SO--|-SA  23 AQ 50       |=PL      15 GE 47         -|=ME     8  PI 24
ME--|-AS   9  AR 39      AS===MC   17 PI 4         NE--|-NN  10 VI 7
NE--|-MC   9  AR 52      JU--|-NN  17 SG 17
                        MA--|-JU   2  SC 23
    SA      15 CP 29     ME--|-NE   2  TA 27
MO--|-PL  29 TA 59
MO--|-UR   0  PI 33          PL      15 GE 47
ME--|-NN  16 CP 4       MO--|-SA  14 PI 50
ME--|-MA   1  GE 10      ME--|-VE  15 PI 20
VE--|-AS  16 AR 35       -|=UR     16 SG 54
                        AS===MC   17 PI 4
    NE      26 GE 31
 |=AS      10 TA 55
ME--|-SA  11 AQ 56
SO--|-VE  27 PI 14
MO===AS   12 TA 33
```

Figure 20.2 The midpoint structures for the example chart as presented
by the AstroCalc software. It is suggested you study this and note which
trees are likely to be of especial importance. The chart factors on the trees
are shown by their two-letter abbreviations: MC = Midheaven; AS =
Ascendant; SO = Sun; MO = Moon; ME = Mercury; VE = Venus; MA
= Mars; JV = Jupiter; SA = Saturn; UR = Uranus; NE = Neptune; PL
= Pluto; NN = Moon's north node. The double lines linking factors
highlight those combinations which involve two personal points, e.g.
Sun/Moon.

emotions, when speaking his mind and following through his own train of thought and developing his own philosophy.

There is here a quality of the eternal youth who must be constantly moving on, never quite able to commit himself to any one career or project for longer than it holds real stimulation, and constantly delighting in the new. With $\memory{} = M$ in $\venus/\Omega = \venus/\mars$ we see that there will be a tendency to be mentally preoccupied and to want to talk about relationships, to form close love relationships, and relationships with creative artists and people with deep feelings and passionate personal convictions. There will also be the desire to communicate strong personal feelings in some way, be it through love poems, or music or art.

The central importance of the $\uranus$–180–$\pluto$ then needs to be explored. Let us remind ourselves that the MC/AS point represents where our axes of being (AS) and becoming (MC) interact. Pictures involved with this point will say something crucial about the characteristic way in which we build and develop our life as a unique individual living in space (AS) and time (MC). MC/AS = $\uranus = \pluto = \mercury/\venus = \jupiter/\Omega = \mars/\jupiter = \mercury/\neptune$ shows someone for whom radical issues will be central, someone who is capable of turning things on their head, of making radical new discoveries, of being a revolutionary in some sense, and who will be capable of going through dramatic changes of perspective, sudden bridge burning, and starting his life over again from scratch if necessary. With $\mercury/\venus$ we might expect both a strongly inventive and mathematical streak, and also intense creative and artistic interests. The involvement of $\mars/\jupiter$ and $\jupiter/\Omega$ is indicative of the possibility of sudden successes and breakthroughs, while the $\mercury/\neptune$ speaks of spontaneous flashes of insight, inspiration and imagination.

The third key picture, $\neptune = \mercury/\saturn = \sun/\venus = \moon/AS$, is one which combines the possibility of intense sensitivity and the desire to translate transcendent perceptions into concrete terms, or morbid fantasy. It brings longings for travel and distant places. It speaks of the quest for the ideal relationship, and the danger of unrealistic and overly idealized emotional expectations. As we have seen, this combination gives immediate focus on the otherwise relatively weak $\sun$–90–$\neptune$ and $\venus$–90–$\neptune$. From this picture we can deduce that however much the Earth/Saturn element in this chart may demand order and evidence and ambition, this combination speaks of lofty aspiration, profound delicacy of perception and inner spiritual yearnings. These could manifest through some kind of personal imaginative creativity such as music, poetry, or photography, and/or through relationships and projections on to the females in his life, but manifest they must.

Having homed in on those factors which stand as pivotal links between the personal points, it is always important to study the planetary pictures of the personal points themselves. The placement and condition of the Sun in any chart shows the ideas around which the person, as a conscious individual, will focus his life, and the characteristic way in which he will make his decisions. Often a reading of the story told by the sequence of the solar midpoints will give us a graphic picture of the essential features of the individual's journey in life, a story which will be re-expressed on varying timescales from the daily round to that of the whole career. Here the solar axis, (Figure 20.2) is extremely active, containing no less than seven midpoints. This mass of information may seem rather overwhelming to the beginner but it can be broken down into digestible chunks in several ways.

One of the most effective approaches is to look at the sequence of midpoints as chapters in a story. It is useful to jot down notes on each combination (you may like to make your own here):

☉ – This individual's life will focus on and revolve around issues concerned with:
= ♄/♇ extreme, dedicated, self-discipline and self-denial, immense personal efforts, secluded, precise, painstaking, thorough, scientific work.
= ☿/M developing one's own philosophy, pursuing one's own interests and communicating one's own ideas to others.
= ♄/♅ developing will-power, endurance through overcoming obstacles and tests of strength; linking together old and new; shaking up old ideas.
= ♀/♃ generosity, warm-heartedness, kindness, enjoyment of pleasure and giving pleasure.
= ☊/AS individual, personal, contacts with others.

= ♂/AS self-assertion, excitement, challenge, love of competition and a good fight.

= ♃/Ψ idealism, philanthropy, delight in creating beautiful art, music; material and metaphysical speculation; extending horizons.

= ♄/♀ self-control, emotional inhibitions and isolation, reserve; professional involvement in artistic and cultural matters.

As a story we see our hero first focusing on tough, challenging goals (♄/♇), which involve the development of his own personal expression (☿/M) and which will allow him to develop his will-power (♄/♅). However, following the hardship and ordeals, there is then a need to relax, to enjoy the good things of life with zest, spontaneity and generosity (♀/♃), and to make personal friendships (☊/AS) and perhaps to enjoy the cut and thrust of competitive games and the will to win (♂/AS). This leads on to an idealistic, altruistic, and even mystical phase in which personal achievements are sublimated to larger ends. This finally leads back full circle to a certain emotional detachment and isolation (♄/♀).

Looked at in broad terms we can see that this planetary picture shows three midpoints involving Saturn, two involving Jupiter and two involving Venus. Here then is someone who is capable of being very tough both on himself and on the world: ♄/♇, ♄/♅, ♄/♀, and yet at the same time warm, loving and altruistic: ♀/♃, ♃/Ψ. We may ask ourselves what kind of images such a mix conjures up? A tough businessman and philanthropic socialite? A Friar Tuck monastic, aesthetic, hard fighting, bon viveur? A nature-loving hermit, scientist/artist, and environmentalist? A Wild West gold bug, gambler, womanizer, and lone ranger who disappears between times back into the hills? Allowing images to form in this way around the combinations and sequences will enable you to feel and see the kinds of energies which this individual is constantly working with from his centre.

Paradoxes are always valuable to explore both in terms of spontaneous imagery and through systematic, structural analysis of the sequence of ideas involved. When they occur as they do here around the Sun, we certainly need to be aware that the central thesis of the life is likely to be shot through with deep contrasts and even splits. The life simply may not provide any easy 'synthesis'.

Here we must acknowledge that the tough, uncompromising Saturn combinations can produce a hard ruthlessness which may mix awkwardly with that most open, warm-hearted and generous of combinations, ♀/♃, of which Ebertin says: 'a man permeated by the joy of love . . . kindness, goodwill towards others . . .' Likewise if ♄/♇ can produce a certain self-punishing harshness, ♃/♆ by contrast is the hallmark of the idealist who has an all-encompassing love and compassion for mankind individually and collectively, but who is also capable of wearing rose-tinted spectacles, and is likely to be prone to gamble and speculate.

Relating this solar picture back to the overall balance of the chart, we may note that it serves to integrate into the centre of the life both sides of the dominant ♃–0–♄ and also the powerful, inventive and transformative energies of the long-term ♅–180–♇. This will encourage a steady, ambitious and constructive focus to the life (♃–♄), while at the same time leading to periods of dramatic change and transformation and Phoenix-like rising from the ashes of burnt bridges (♅–♇).

Turning from this conscious level of self-organization to the more instinctive picture focused around the Moon, we have the tree shown in Figure 20.2. The Moon is always important in every chart, but here it is doubly so because of its proximity to the Ascendant. So we can expect the feminine, unconscious, instinctive, aspect of the life to be very strong, with the mother and other female figures playing an important role in his world. Our notes on this might read as follows:

☽ The habitual and instinctive response to life, and the unconscious assumptions about life focus upon:
= ♃/♇ a natural ambition and the tendency to 'think big' and to be able to plan and organize on a large scale; the desire for both self and social improvement; the desire to develop personal power, be it material, intellectual, or spiritual . . . a natural understanding of others and the ability to persuade others; strong natural powers of regeneration.
= ♃/♅ a spontaneous optimism and insight into the larger issues; innovative, inventive, with a gift for serendipity and 'falling on one's feet'.

= ⊙/Ψ a deep sensitivity and openness to the feelings of others; possible moodiness, psychic gifts; attraction to either idealistic and highly sensitive women, or to weak, dependent and sickly types.
= ♄/♇ emotional self-control and self-isolation; difficulties in expressing one's deepest feelings.

This is a simpler and almost reversed image of the solar picture and shows a spontaneous sense of optimism and expansiveness, followed by an instinct to withdraw and suppress the feelings. The ♃ pictures reinforce the angular Jupiter–120–AS and the ⊙ = ♀/♃ and ♃/Ψ. This will encourage a levity and spontaneity which the strongly Earth/Saturn structure tends to curb. The paradox here between the vital optimism and self-confidence of ♃/♇ and ♃/♅ and the possibly overly sensitive and potentially undermining qualities of ⊙/Ψ and self-repressive qualities of ♄/♇ is a stark one. ⊙/Ψ = ☽ can produce self-delusions and subsequent disillusionments and disappointments, especially in emotional issues. The harsh ♄/♇ tendency to cut oneself off from one's feelings reinforces the image of someone who may at times suffer emotional disappointment and alienation through his high degree of emotional susceptibility.

We have already covered the MC axis in dealing with ☿, because of the almost exact –45– ☿–MC, so that the information there will be equally related to our understanding of this man's goals and aspirations in life. As the time of birth is known with some accuracy, we can note that this is indicative of someone whose goals and aspirations in life will in some sense be mercurial and multifaceted and that he will not be content with only one string to his bow. Turning to the AS axis we find that its pictures combine a useful synthesis of some of the paradoxes already noted. Here we see an approach to the world which focuses on:

= ⊙/♇ a strong desire for personal power, be it physical, mental or spiritual, and an ability to be extremely tough with himself and with others if necessary to achieve his ends, yet by contrast with
= ♀/Ψ a great receptivity and sensitivity to beauty in all its forms with an emphasis on good taste, coupled with a romantic, dreamy,

and highly idealistic view of the world which seeks the ideal relationship; while again there is

$= \odot / \text{♅}$ a need for personal freedom and space and originality, innovation and change; a self-willed desire to pursue his own goals regardless of any opposition, with

$= \text{☿} / \text{♃}$ a persuasive, open, and intelligent approach to the world, thriving on extending and communicating knowledge and

$= \text{☿} / \text{♄}$ logical, systematic thinking; but also with the need to retire into himself and think things through away from the madding crowd.

From this picture we can deduce that as a personality we are here dealing with a man who can switch between tough, even ruthless self-assertion and a romantic dreaminess; who can be highly gregarious and yet equally retreat into himself and seek the solitude of his own company. It is a picture of a man of action and clear intellect who is also capable of being deeply touched by deep emotion, and of evoking deep feelings in others.

It would be possible to examine the other planetary pictures in a similar way, and this would certainly be appropriate if we wanted to look at any particular facet of his life or psychology in greater detail, but for purposes of this general analysis focusing on the pictures surrounding the personal points will give us the most essential information.

Summary of the midpoint evidence: We have restricted our observations to those pictures which directly involve the four personal points. We see from this analysis that the midpoints have in part confirmed the larger overall picture painted by traditional methods. They have, however, shown up other important themes which were relatively invisible to the unaided eye, notably the central importance of ☿, $\text{♅} - \text{♇}$ and ♆ in the chart. These pictures also reveal that at both solar and lunar levels we have here an individual who is likely to be both extremely hard, tough, tense and emotionally self-disciplined, concerned at some level to 'prove himself' and endure, while at the same time being someone who can exude great charm, and warmth and generosity and be highly communicative.

In practice we have seen that this seeming complexity of

information can be presented to the client both analytically and in terms of images and stories. When this is done one finds that, almost invariably, the client will come back with his own vivid, complementary set of images and experiences. These actual expressions in the life can then be explored and discussed in relation to the whole spectrum of possibilities which these planetary pictures present.

The Evidence of the Harmonics

Let us now look at the individual harmonics to tell us something about some of the specific dimensions of this man's character. As the time of birth, 7.35 a.m., was recorded with a reasonable degree of accuracy, an accuracy borne out by life events, we are happily in a position to be able to include information derived from the angles in these charts.

Looking first at the 5H (Figure 20.3) to tell us something of this man's elective will and the style and approach to life that he is likely to have developed, we find an obviously powerful picture. The first feature that strikes us is the remarkable kite-formation with ♅–0–AS and –180– MC as the central axis, and the AS forming a Grand Trine with ♀–0–♃ and ☊. This is in sharp contrast to the first impression of the radix with its strongly Earth, ♄–♃ and lunar qualities, which give the impression of someone who is likely to come over as something of an arch-Conservative.

The 5H is telling us that Uranian qualities such as a love of freedom, independence, rebellion against arbitrary authority, stubbornness, and that freedom of thinking and acting which is often labelled eccentricity, will be to the fore. An enthusiasm for the new and original, for inventions, and for generally shaking up the status quo and the complacent are unequivocally indicated. Such a position is obviously characteristic of an attraction to astrology and new and original approaches to life. What we can be certain of is that these Uranian characteristics will be important in the way in which he meets and thinks about the world. At the same time the close ♃–0–♃ –120– to the exactly rising ♅ confirm the importance of the warmth and generosity of the approach to life. The almost exact ♃ –120– ♅ also speaks of a delight in intellectual discovery and adventure, and a strong touch of serendipity and the

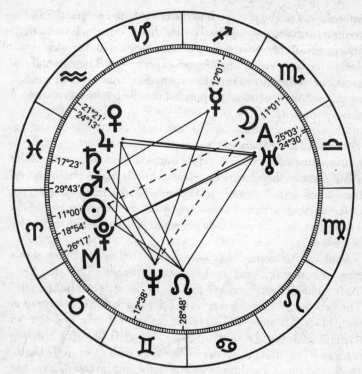

Figure 20.3 5H chart: What does this chart tell us about this man's basic approach to the world and his general style?

ability to see and seize opportunities. With the ☊ this forms a Grand Trine which is likely to give natural organizing gifts and the ability to get on with others.

Additional strong features are the wide triple conjunction of ☉–0–♇–0–MC, which is drawn together by the fact that ♇ is very closely on the midpoint of ☉/M = 18♈38. The ☉ here is also seen to be the relieving –120–/–60– to the very close ☿–180–♆. Any strong ☉–♇ contact is likely to indicate the desire to develop one's own personal powers, be they physical, mental or spiritual. Hamblin says of this combination that it will develop 'self-punishing styles of behaviour: working relentlessly: denying expression of the more carefree sides of the personality'. It can also encourage a probing and research-minded approach to the world, a desire to get to grips with deep and hidden issues, be it through inner work or through research and exploration in the outer world. It is indicative of someone who can 'eliminate and regenerate' and when necessary transform his approach to life. This position reiterates the personal importance of the ♅–♇ generational factor for this man. The ☉ –120–/–60– ☿–♆ is indicative of a delight and a need to get to grips with the intuitive, the poetic and the intangible. Here is clearly someone who is very much 'his own man', whose choices in life will be dictated by his own perceptions and experience of how things are rather than what the world thinks.

If the 5H was remarkably powerful, the 7H (Figure 20.4) is

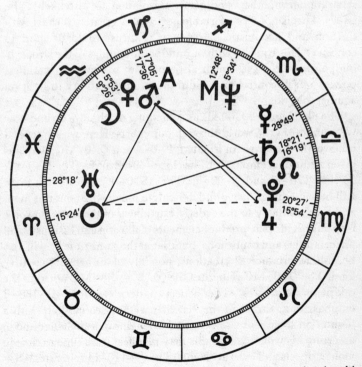

Figure 20.4 7H chart: What kinds of things are likely to inspire this individual and 'turn him on'?

almost equally so. Here the picture is dominated by a very close T-square of ♂–0–AS with the ☉ and ☊–0–♄. The ☉ is further integrated into the picture by a close –150– ♃ and –120– ⛢. Compared with the normal natal chart which shows the ☉ in Aries hidden away in the 12th in a wide square with ♆, and with seemingly no other major aspects, here we find someone who is going to be turned on in a very deep and central way by any kind of personal challenge or struggle, who will find his imagination captured by doing battle against obstacles. If this person centres himself in the intangible and hidden world of the 12th house, then he is certainly not going to be happy or inspired by a quiet life. This pattern speaks of struggle, challenge and activity as being the *raison d'être*, the heart of the personal myth. The ♄–☊ implies that separation from others and personal isolation are also likely to be issues. This is not a comfortable position! A greater contrast with the soft and hedonistic ☽ rising in Taurus would be hard to conceive! This concurs with our midpoint findings of the strong ♄ midpoints to the ☉, which also speak of the need to manifest powers of self-control and endurance and the ability to fight on against the odds.

The 8H (Figure 20.5) tells us something of what we do and how we manifest in the world through our efforts. Here we see several noteworthy patterns: an isolated ♆–0–AS; a ☿–0–MC, which is given additional emphasis by its close –60– ♇ and –120– ☊–0–♂; ☉ close 120–♅ and ☽–90–♃. The AS–0–♆ suggests that there will be something elusive and difficult to pin down about this man, and that, contrary to the orderly Earthiness of the radix, in some respects his life may produce elements of illusion and disillusion, of uncertainties and confusions, but that at the same time he will also be able to produce ♆ creations, possibly of an artistic, creative kind. The ☿–0–MC reiterates the ☉/☽ = ☿ = MC noted in the midpoint structures. The aspect pattern with ♂–☊–180–♇ emphasizes again, as in the 7H, that we are dealing here with a 'fighter' in some sense, someone who delights in a challenge and in asserting his will, but that this may manifest from time to time in violent upsets and even accidents. The ☉–120–♅ reiterates AS = ☉/♅, and that this is an individual with great will-power and independence of action, indeed someone who will delight in doing

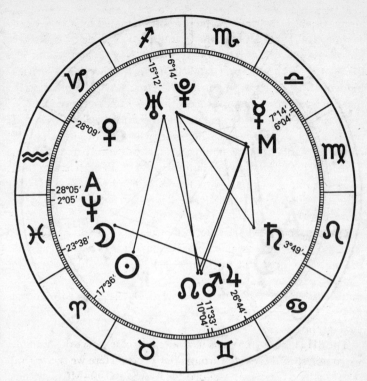

Figure 20.5 8H chart: What is this man likely to produce and manifest in the world through his own efforts?

his own thing in his own way with force and vigour and originality. The ☽–90–♃ highlights the radix ☽–120–♃ and is indicative that that motivating *largeness* and openness and generosity of response to the world runs very deep, and that it is one which is not simply aspiring to kindness and benevolence but that it is constantly striving to manifest goodness, and imitate Providence. Likewise it can also indicate the need to grapple with legal, religious, and marital conflicts and difficulties and problems brought about through the over-extension of resources.

The 9H, Figure 20.6, shows ♃ in close –0– AS; a T-square of ☊ with ☽–180–♂; a ♄–90–♇; and a Grand Trine of ☿–♀–♄. Since this is the 9H the trines must be given some additional emphasis as

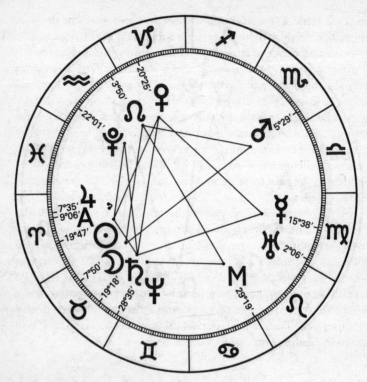

Figure 20.6 9H chart: What are likely to be the ideals and aspirations?

these will tend to show the focus for kinds of ideals and aspirations which will be held especially dear. ♃–0–AS obviously indicates someone who will be drawn by the large, the benevolent and the providential. It suggests a spontaneously religious sense or at least an inner joy in being able to give to others in a philanthropic way, encouraging others, opening up and developing new possibilities. The Grand Trine suggests that some kind of intellectual beauty and order, such as is found in geometry and mathematics, or in the pure music of Bach or Mozart, will serve as guides to his aspiration. The T-square of ☊ with ☽–♂ speaks of a need for openness and frankness and vitality in relationships and the attraction of women who possess such qualities. The ♄–90–♇ mediated by the ☉ is again suggestive of the alchemist, the challenge of becoming in some sense a 'magician or adept' who can transform the base metal of life's most demanding tests and challenges into the gold of courage and personal triumph over hardship and deprivation.

Brief summary of the evidence from the harmonics: The harmonics reveal a highly original, independent, self-willed but extremely warm and generous individual (5H); who will be inspired by extremes of hardship and challenge, and the delights of physical effort (7H), who will have a strongly mercurial, independent, yet also dreamy and romantic nature, who will tend to meet and to create challenges and fights in his life (8H), and who will be motivated by ideals of generosity and intellectual beauty and openness (9H).

The chart as a whole is now far broader and deeper. Both the midpoints and the harmonics have revealed someone who is far more individual and independent than first impressions would indicate. The mixture of scientist (♄) and artist (☽, ♀) remains but another very tough, driven, side also emerges, as does an equally strong emphasis on a personal warmth and generosity of being. The need to get to grips with Neptunian issues is also emphasized. The central importance of mercurial issues is a crucially healing one.

THE ACTUAL CASE HISTORY

The subject of this analysis, on being asked by the writer how he would like to be introduced at a meeting to show a film he had made about the Maya of Central America, said that a suitable thumbnail sketch would be:

> ex-Cavalryman
> ex-polo player
> ex-archaeologist
> ex-celestial navigator
> ex-husband
> Explorer

An enormous wealth of dry and often anarchistic humour was one of the abiding characteristics of Giles Healey, who was, among his many roles, a renowned Mayan archaeologist and explorer. Before looking at his life and career a few words about his family background would be appropriate. Giles's paternal grandfather had been a very successful coach builder who lived in an enormous house in Cornwall, NY. His son, Giles's father, a successful antique dealer, is described as having been a very self-centred and sadistic man who never did anything for anyone. While in Paris he got into a brawl and accidentally killed a man. To escape prosecution he fled to North Africa and joined the French Foreign Legion. There he met Giles's mother, a very sweet French girl whose family were from Lyon, but who had been brought up in North Africa. A measure of the contentious nature of Giles's father is that at one point he actually sued his own father for alienating the affections of Giles's mother! Giles himself did not appear to have any negative feelings for his father, but admitted that at no time in his life had his father ever given either him or his brother a single present.

Giles's fine education was provided by his grandfather. He was educated as a young man in France and Germany and then attended Choate Preparatory School; he went on to graduate from Yale University in 1924 with a degree in chemistry. This was not Giles's own choice. He had himself (shades of all that Earth!) wanted to become a geologist, but was forced to take chemistry by his grandfather. What was of his choice was his study of the violin, for which he not only had a natural gift, but at which he excelled to the extent of becoming for a while the concert-master of the New Haven Philharmonic Orchestra. Any thoughts of pursuing this love seriously were dashed, however, when, with typical courage, while separating two dogs in a dog fight the tip of his left little finger was bitten off. His other gift from his family background was that he spoke perfect French and had as much a European as an American outlook.

Giles was a man of great paradoxes and many parts. He was at once the pillar of the establishment, able, and at times even wanting, to observe social conventions to the T, yet not caring a damn what anyone thought. A conservative out of the top draw, yet an out-and-out maverick. A large, solid man of slow, dry wit yet with a razor-sharp and highly mercurial intellect and disposition; capable of enormous self-discipline and self-denial, yet capable of being the bon viveur and hedonist with a gourmet's appreciation of good food and wine; an immensely practical man who built his house with his own hands out of railway sleepers, yet a great dreamer with deep yearnings for the sublime; at once methodical and yet a great improviser with no time for petty restraints; both a very private man and yet a compulsive communicator who thrived and came into his own ($\mathrm{\male} = \odot/\mathbb{D}$) through daily correspondence and phone calls with a wide range of people; frugal yet the soul of generosity; kindness itself yet an implacable opponent; a peace-loving dreamer who thrived on challenge and adventure; a Bohemian law unto himself yet at home among the polo-playing *crème de la crème*; capable of great friendships right across the political spectrum; proud of the tea in his Bostonian ancestors' boots, yet an immense anglophile and one of life's natural aristo-crats; a man who did not give a damn about conventions yet who would insist to the last, with irritation or wry humour, depending on the mood of the moment, that you did not put your knife in the jam-pot or point at people. His railway sleeper home on the heights of Big Sur, and its various outposts on the estate, were at once a delightfully mad chaos of seemingly endless children, grand-children, visitors, dogs, cats, turkeys (one named Thanksgiving and one Christmas), and other animals. Books, papers, news-papers, records spread higgledy-piggledy with the people and animals in this totally lived in and welcoming space, yet at the same time it was the repository for priceless antiques, which he could not see were unsuitable for the location (though he did keep some of the finer items in store along with his Hispano-Suiza). In similar vein he was a man who would buy really superb clothes, the very height of elegance, and would then stuff them into an old duffel bag when he was going away.

Giles was a large man in manner and outlook, with immediate charm, humour, warmth, and good breeding, a pillar of the establishment, a member of the Explorers' Club, the Chemists' Club, the Yale Club, the National Geographic Society, and the Carnegie Institute. Yet even on slight acquaintance one became aware of someone who was an individual through and through, a born outsider, who had little patience with convention or ortho-doxy, someone who was wholly himself. He was a man who, albeit with finesse, said what he meant with clarity and certainty, a man who was totally devoid of any superficiality, phoniness or hypocrisy. In this respect his 5H with its ♅–0–AS and its Grand Trine with ☊ and ♀–0–♃ speaks volumes, and not least for the generosity of the man, who was forever encouraging and supporting individuals with original and innovative ideas, not least in astrology. In that area he was not only deeply read and a devoted student but he also gave invaluable behind-the-scenes support to the Astrological Association and to John Addey, helping with the publishing costs of the USA edition of *Harmonics in Astrology*, and doing everything he could in a quiet way to encourage whatever would raise the standards and level of education and research. As a past President of the USA Institute of Navigation and an expert in celestial navigation he clearly got a considerable kick out of his support for such an outcast area of study.

Turning to some of the main threads of Giles's life, it has already been noted that he was an outstanding explorer and archaeologist. For someone 'whose place in the order of art' (5H) is depicted by ♅ exactly configuring both AS and MC and 120–♃, with ☉–0–♇–0 –MC, this is not entirely inappropriate! So equally his love affair with the gruelling challenge and hardship of the equatorial jungle and tropical forests is a classic expression of his 7H with its exact ♂–0–AS in T-square to ☉–0–☊–♄ and a close 120–♃–♇, surely the hallmark of a man who is inspired by the role of 'intrepid explorer'. His exploring days began when he went as a chemist on a highly dangerous and pioneering expedition up the Orinoco river gathering curare poison from the Indians for use in medical research. Later, as a highly talented photographer (5H ☉–60–♆, 120–☿) with a keen interest in anthropology, he went to Guatemala to make a documentary film on the Lacandon Indians. From this grew his abiding interest in Central American archaeology and specifically the Maya, to whom he bore an uncanny resemblance. Much of his success lay in the close friendship he was able to establish with the Maya's descendants, the Lacandones. He won the Lacandones' confidence by taking them gifts and by the deep rapport he felt with them which led him to learn their language. Indeed, when he began his explorations of the nearly impenetrable forests with native guides he found in an uncanny way that he already seemed to know the tortuous and hidden paths, as though he had been there before. On several occasions he actually saw the paths he was to take in precognitive dreams. While in this and other matters he was constantly prone to suppress, and indeed at time hotly deny, his own undoubted psychic abilities, he was able to work with this 'sixth sense' to very good effect (5H $\odot-\varphi-\Psi$). To his own chagrin, this same facility was to surface later when he studied graphology and he was able to come to uncannily accurate character readings, allegedly following the rules, yet which tapped on a deeper level of perception.

During this phase of his life, in June 1946, he made his great discovery (UR–0–AS –120– $\varphi-\jupiter$ in 5H), in the north-eastern corner of the state of Chiapas in Yucatan, of the priceless coloured wall-paintings in a building on the site which Giles was to name Bonampak, Mayan for 'painted walls'. These Bonampak murals are by far the most important and masterly known paintings of ancient America. They had been miraculously preserved over the centuries by a unique combination of climatic conditions and good fortune, and amount in terms of Mayan archaeology to a Tutankhamun level of discovery. The richly coloured paintings completely cover the inner walls of a three-roomed building. If their happy discovery by Giles was itself a clear reflection of his own 5H chart's AS–$\uranus-\jupiter-\varphi$ and his radical $\moon = \jupiter/\pluto = \jupiter/\uranus$ (there was also a $\jupiter-120-\uranus$ in the sky involving his natal $\uranus-180-\pluto$ at this time), so too the themes of the paintings seem curiously appropriate to Giles's own life. In one room the fresco depicts the elaborate preparations for a ritual dance, consisting of the robing of those who are going to represent the Earth Gods (!), together with the great chief, the musicians and dancers. In another room is portrayed an expedition to take prisoners and a splendid battle scene which has been described as among the most beautiful expressions of Mayan art. If Bonampak was the highpoint of Giles's career as an explorer and archaeologist, it was only the jewel in the crown. He was also responsible for the discovery of twenty-one other major archaeological sites. Another major city site he spotted while on a reconnaissance by plane has still to be rediscovered, as details were lost and he was unable to return to follow them up himself. This is itself testimony to just how difficult of access is this area and the special combination of courage, tenacity, intelligence, and leadership that are required even now to explore this region.

As has been mentioned, Giles was at one time in the US cavalry. This was particularly on account of its polo facilities, a game to which he was passionately addicted, and at which he was supremely adept, and which he would practise at every available moment. We see here Giles's 7H vividly at work. Polo's dangers and the very high level of horsemanship, dexterity, and courage required to play it are well known. His passion for polo epitomized a central theme in Giles's life, that he was interested in anything so long as it was really demanding and challenging. The moment he had got to the top or mastered something he would be happy to drop it and move on. Polo held its attraction because it was endlessly challenging, a battle demanding total co-ordination, skill and almost foolhardy, disciplined courage. ♂–AS –120– ♇–♃, –90– ☉––180– ♄ in the 7H, could there be a better expression of the man who is turned on by the delights of courageous and totally demanding sporting challenge, and by the need for total discipline and training?

In relation to this 7H pattern Alfred Perles, writing to Henry Miller in *Reunion in Big Sur*, affectionately describes their mutual friend Giles as 'a bastard in his own right'. A high compliment from someone who wrote scathingly of the effects of American democracy, which levels every one down to being '100% pure, 100% efficient, and 100% vapid . . .' Vapid is the last epithet anyone could ever have applied to Giles. He could be tough and relentless. In later life Giles engaged in an unrelenting fight with neighbours over water rights at Big Sur. Like his battles with the tropical rain forests of Central America, one cannot but see this as all part of the same key myth, that for Giles life was at one very important level a challenge, a battle, a proving ground.

This guiding myth was to have its most remarkable manifestation when it was discovered that the amoebic dysentery that he had contracted in Yucatan was rapidly destroying his liver. Visits to top specialists throughout the USA, including the Mayo Clinic, confirmed that he had only a few months to live and that the only thing he could sensibly do was to write his will. This consensus was sufficient to galvanize Giles into action. He located an alternative practitioner, Dr Henry Bieler, author of *Food Is Your Best Medicine*, and asked him what he must do. Bieler put him on a diet of nothing but a particular kind of white grape, and within a few months, much to the astonishment of the assembled specialists, Giles's liver had been remarkably restored. Again can we think of a better symbolism for being inspired by a fight to regenerate the liver than ♃–0–♇–120–♂–AS?!

In the radical chart we were struck by the Moon rising in Taurus –120–♃–♄, a clear indication of the importance of the feminine element in his life, and suggesting a strong stable and nourishing relationship with his mother and in coping with the day-to-day world. This was certainly the case. Giles was immensely capable and adept at doing everything connected with the material world. He was very clever with money and worked for a stock market firm for a term and continued to keep in close touch with his Wall Street broker for most of his life.

Giles's mother seems to have been 'a sweetie', kind and generous, and as supportive of Giles and his brother as their father was callous and negligent, and though she could often irritate Giles, he was genuinely happy to look after her along with his own growing family during the later years of her life. But another aspect of the feminine in Giles is shown to be less easily satisfied. As Ψ–90– the ruling ♀, reinforced by ♀ = Ψ/♇ = Ψ/♅, and AS = ♀/Ψ and the ☽'s later planetary pictures, ☽ = ♄/♇ = ♄/♅, suggest, all was not entirely clear for Giles in this area of his life. He was married three times in all. The first two marriages were each in their own way tragically Neptunian. In the first marriage he found out that his new wife was already pregnant by another man. She was later to develop cancer, which involved over twenty major operations including the amputation of a breast and leg, and this drove her to the brink of suicide on many occasions. There were two daughters by this marriage. The first died of a galloping cancer activated by accidentally driving through a nuclear test zone in Arizona. The second became a chronic alcoholic with a fatal knack of attracting parasitic men. Giles was extremely closely tuned to her, so that though she lived in Switzerland he always knew when she needed help. This made her a constant source of concern to him. Following the death of his first wife Giles married a socialite and for a while lived a hectic social whirl in New York City. This marriage produced three children, a son and two daughters. The son seems to have taken after his grandfather and was jailed at one point for assaulting his mother. One of the daughters was to die suddenly of a stroke only four days before Giles. This marriage ended when his wife went off with another man. It was at this point in 1941 that Giles took himself off to Guatemala and it was there, on 6 December, that he was to meet his third wife, Sheila, an extremely talented portrait painter of Anglo-Argentine background, a remarkable woman who was to develop her own psychic sensitivity as vigorously as Giles continued to deny his own.

Appropriately for someone with $\Psi = \odot/\mathbb{D}$, this third and generally happy marriage took place during a trans-USA car trip, and was to be characterized by constant travel and in its latter years by a life lived half the time in Big Sur, California, and half in Sussex, England. (With characteristic 5H AS–0–$\mathbb{H}$ need for personal space, this often produced long periods of separation.) However, the long periods of separation earlier in their marriage, while Giles was off on his all-consuming archaeological explorations, cannot have been easy for either him or Sheila, and there is no doubt that this, and his past negative experiences of women, created considerable negative reinforcement to his $\Psi = \Psi/\hbar = \odot/\varphi = \mathbb{D}/AS$ picture. Over time this produced entirely unfounded preoccupations with imagined infidelities, something with which he was never able fully to come to terms, though at one level he was able to understand its aetiology and its astrological symbology. This third marriage produced four highly gifted and creative daughters. But even here Giles was not to be preserved from tragedy in connection with the female element in his life, and one of them, a ballerina with the Peruvian San Marcos Ballet, was to die suddenly of galloping cancer, the disease that was to fell Giles himself.

Much else could be said of Giles's career. He was an expert stellar navigator, a suitably mercurial skill which he originally developed in order to find his way through the dense forests and impossibly disorienting terrain of Yucatan. (The Ψ–Ψ–$\hbar$ T-square in 5H is highly relevant here as a signature for being able to manifest the knowledge by which one can fix one's position when travelling in uncertain terrain.) He was later to use these skills to teach navigation to the Navy during the Korean war. In this connection he was also later to draw upon his training in chemistry (which he had also used in his immediately postgraduate days to set up a laboratory for the analysis of alcohol and for work on contraceptives) to undertake freelance work in developing beryllium metal alloys for the US space programme. Through his expertise in celestial navigation he was also led into an interest in optics and astronomy generally. From there via the history of astronomy it was an easy step, for an innately Uranian maverick and outsider like Giles if not for most academics, to enter into astrology. In astrology during his later years Giles found a subject which linked his love and practical understanding of astronomy with his interest in personality. It also gave him a legitimate and scientific basis, via the work of John Addey and Michel Gauquelin, for probing further into a subject whose metaphysical implications undoubtedly fascinated him despite his protestations only to trust what he could touch and taste and see. In his last years this gap between Earth and Fire, and between Saturn and Neptune, was to be perceptibly closed. A short time before he died Giles had a starkly vivid dream that his brother, long dead, had contacted him to say with great enthusiasm how much he was looking forward to meeting Giles at the local church the following Thursday. Giles's funeral service was held that very Thursday, 6 March, in Bignor church.

As always it must be emphasized that the chart in its various guises reveals to us potential. That potential can and will manifest at many different points along the spectrum of possible effects inherent in the chart pattern. Taking any one major planetary picture within a chart and knowing the individual in question well, it is possible to see that picture working out in countless different ways. Thus taking Giles's $\math9 = \odot/\math010$, the mercurial qualities that this gave him were not immediately obvious in his build or manner. He was decidedly not the thin, nervous, type one associates with that planet. Yet he was a traveller, a navigator, from two different cultures, who spoke two languages fluently and several others passingly well, whose third marriage took place during a major journey. He lived in two houses 6,000 miles apart. He was ingenious and inventive. He played polo, a sport of great dexterity, and later in life was addicted to regular sessions of ping-pong with his good friend and neighbour the writer Henry Miller. He was never so happy as when acting as an agent for new ideas, communicating, bringing people together and putting them in touch, and providing news cuttings and photocopies, and the latest gossip and gadgetry and books and file indexes. He wrote an English at times as witty as P. G. Wodehouse. He was a man for whom phone and letter were his air and his healing.

Giles's love and delight in language was vividly expressed in his total obsession with Arthur Rimbaud (b. 20 October 1854, 6 a.m., 49N49, 4E43), the French poet, writer and traveller whose ambition was to live the life of a true Promethean 'stealer of Heavenly fire', and whose revolutionary, visionary, dream-like verse and prose-poems, such as *A Season in Hell*, anticipated the surrealists. Giles collected everything he could about the man, then, typically, presented his very fine collection of editions of works by and on Rimbaud to the University of California in Los Angeles for the benefit of other lovers of the poet. Yet despite this identification with such a muse, and his own deep aesthetic sensitivity, Giles himself would paradoxically seldom allow himself to communicate his own inner feelings. On the most seemingly trivial matters, such as a disagreement over colour (he had a phenomenal memory for the most subtle shades), he would periodically descend into a totally silent, dark mood in which for days he would seem surrounded by a black cloud of negative vibrations (shades of his 7H!). Such moods would lift as suddenly as they arrived, and he would be his genial, gentle, sensitive self once more.

Yet for all his failure to express his own personal vision, and his sense of guilt and impotence at his failure to develop his own artistic and spiritual side, Giles was a veritable psychopomp who led others by *le bon mot* and *le mot juste* to see truths about themselves and current affairs which put all into perspective.

CHAPTER 21

Looking Ahead

MICHAEL HARDING AND CHARLES HARVEY

While it is clear that even the most traditional signs/planets/aspects/houses approach to chart analysis can be very effective in the hands of a skilled astrologer, it should be apparent to the reader who has come with us this far that modern methods are opening up previously invisible dimensions of the chart. Harmonics, midpoints and Astro*Carto*Graphy are already able to reveal dimensions of space and time that are rich with a vitality and potency invisible to the casual astrological observer.

These discoveries call into question some of the ways we currently practise astrology while offering us a glimpse of new interpretative directions. How far these new borders can be extended depends on who is prepared to explore the territory and what – if any – excess baggage they are prepared to abandon. There would seem little doubt that there has to be a significant change within the attitude of astrologers if our art is to continue the advances it has made since the First World War.

In 1929 the cosmobiologist Karl Ernst Krafft wrote the following in the November issue of Leo's *Modern Astrology*:

> The development of a future science of the relations between the universe and mankind will hardly be based on astrology whatever attempts be made for its rehabilitation by statistical or other methods. For the edifice of astrology might be compared to a corpse whose resuscitation would be as mistaken as the raising of spirits or the driving out of devils in the days of psychoanalysis. Not that tradition and its practises are devoid of any basis, but the forms handed down do not conform to modern consciousness. Their mental premises are rooted in psychic strata which in modern man have become subliminal; i.e., withdrawn in favour of new possibilities.

Consequently, whatever archetypes again penetrate into the conscious, their manifestation must be made on methods of expression corresponding to the present day state of mind.

While this is undoubtedly an extreme view, it is also a remarkably fresh and apposite one with much to commend it. The wholesale, unquestioning absorption of everything that has gone before is equally extreme. There are many astrologers who cling to the rock of the past, oblivious of the rising tide, for no other reason than it *is* the past.

There are clear parallels with many other sources of ancient knowledge, and we should not ignore them. Medicine and physics have gone through innumerable changes, in the main to our enrichment. While we should suggest that the modern practitioner pay attention to the herbal remedies handed down through the ages, we must not overlook the fact that for every wise use of root or stem to heal the sick there are a dozen aphorisms which promise that bats' urine is a cure for the pox or the lard of a stoat taken at the waning moon will ensure an end to gout.

A gullible acceptance of such 'cures' has little to commend it – much less when they are taken twice. Many astrologers will parrot arcane rules which are demonstrably ridiculous. Indeed, they may well have performed the actual demonstration themselves in the course of trying to apply them, but a deep reluctance to jettison anything with 'astrology' stamped upon it ensures that the folly can only be repeated. While earlier traditions undoubtedly still hold much lost and misunderstood knowledge which we would do well to review, we inhabit a world that is in many respects the reflection of a far broader cosmos than our predecessors experienced. We cannot ignore this and appear reasonably intelligent at the same time.

Once the cosmos seemed simple; so likewise did the human body and psyche. Now, 'above', the known cosmos has grown from seven planets and the sphere of the fixed stars of the ancient and medieval cosmologists into the almost inconceivably vast interaction of wheeling systems each encompassed in yet larger orders of wholeness. So likewise 'below': the relative simplicity of the body, when viewed from the outside, has turned out on closer inspection to be a whole universe of quite extraordinarily complex interacting systems, capable of ever deeper and more detailed study. As with the body so too with the psyche. From being seen as a mixture of four humours and an assortment of fairly clear cut planetary character traits, it has burgeoned under the attention of the depth and height psychologists, Freud, Jung, Assagioli, Hillman, and others, into a full-blown pantheon worthy of a Hindu temple.

In these circumstances it is not surprising then that the old astrology can no longer suffice to describe these new complexities. When people rarely moved from the place of their birth there could be little practical significance in knowing that one had Venus in Rome, or Mars in Jerusalem, or Jupiter in Canterbury, though such information would have certainly assisted ambassadors, crusaders and pilgrims. In an age that knew nothing of the function of the pancreas and insulin, the relationship between 16 Cancer/Capricorn and these factors could have no meaning. In an age when relationships were, by-and-large, determined by parents and social factors, and when personal individuation and self-realization were unknown concepts, the outer and inner significance of the Sun/Moon midpoint could have no meaning. The same could be said of such concepts as the inner vision and 'inspiration' represented by the 7th harmonic and the 'personal choice' and individual approach represented by the 5th. But as we move deeper into the intricacies and mysteries of space and the cosmos, and expand our awareness of mankind's larger possibilities, so we can expect, and must demand, the growth in our understanding and perception of the intimate mirrorings of the macro- and micro-cosmic orders.

Each dimension of the chart which was familiar to the ancients is still there at the heart of our astrology: the heavenly bodies, the circles of the aspects, the zodiac, the houses. But our understanding of each of these categories is constantly being enlarged and extended, and we can only expect this process to continue, though, it is devoutly to be hoped, against an increasingly more coherent and philosophically satisfactory background. In this expanding picture John Addey's unifying harmonic model, and his vision of an integral astrology which comprises an understanding of all those essential archetypal principles on which the cosmos is woven, would seem to have a very important part to play. Addey's unified theory of astrology is summarized in his axiom that 'all astrological effects can be understood in terms of the harmonics of cosmic periods'. To meet the challenge of this vision it is essential that astrologers become more aware in their professional attitude towards the technical implications of their art.

Ours is an art of interpretation; we work with symbols. But these symbols of Sun and Moon, signs, nodes and planets are not scattered randomly about the solar system; they are following very precise paths, paths that are laid out mathematically. To make the best use of these symbols we must learn to recognize these patterns and how they interact as well as recognize the implications of this approach towards our understanding. In searching for repeating *patterns* of symbols we are moving away from the traditional astrology as a source of divination towards the creation of a recognizable knowledge system with the astrologer as a worldly professional working with symbol structures, not a priest relying on divine inspiration. This shift can only be healthy for astrology as a whole.

In pursuing the search for identifiable patterns within the orbits of the planets we have so far used only a few basic harmonic charts and concentrated almost solely on *aspects*. The *signs* in which the harmonic positions of planets are located have hardly been mentioned. These are, in fact, extremely complex relationships and suggest that a straightforward transposition of sign-meaning across the spectrum of harmonic charts is inadvisable.

In beginning to explore the relationship between the sign Scorpio, for instance, in the 7th harmonic chart with that of its radical position we are applying mathematics to a symbol in a way which is not immediately apparent and taking a great step towards one of the most intricate uses of harmonics, one which has not really been researched at all: how a symbol may unfold mathematically.

If someone has their 7th harmonic sun in Scorpio, does this in some way mean that they are turned on or inspired at a solar level by whatever Scorpio stands for? If so, what does this imply for their radical Sun, which may be in Gemini? Such blanket assumptions do not really seem to be justified by experience, and in fact are perhaps mathematically naive. It is the septile *aspect* relationship between two planets which seems to impart the inspiration, not the placing of the planets in their phasing to 0° Aries – though an exact harmonic of a body to the Aries point itself may have much to tell us, as we shall see later in a slightly different context.

What we are really looking at in a harmonic chart is the radical chart laid out in a different way; a way that is defined solely by *aspect*. For a harmonic position Sun to occupy a specific sign is in reality a reflection of the precise degree of its placement in the radical chart.

What must be recognized is that the sign position of the Sun in any harmonic is a statement about its original phasing from 0°

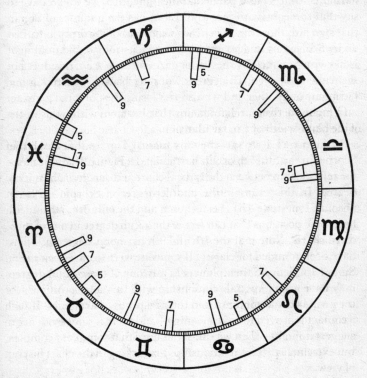

Figure 21.1 The only radical positions which will result in a Scorpio sun in the 5th, 7th or 9th harmonics.

Aries. For the 7th harmonic Sun to be anywhere in Scorpio it *must* be in one of the radical positions indicated in Figure 21.1. Thus we can see that it is impossible, for instance, for someone with Sun in Aries, Cancer, Virgo or Aquarius to have Sun in Scorpio in the 7th harmonic. They may have a Sun in Scorpio in other harmonics, but *not* the 7th.

Similarly, Aries, Gemini, Leo, Virgo, Scorpio, Capricorn, and Aquarius radical Suns can *never* show up in Scorpio in the *5th* harmonic. Someone with Sun at 6° Libra, however, will have a Sun in Scorpio in the 5th, 7th *and* 9th harmonic charts, for that is the one degree in which the clusters of the different harmonic groupings come together. If we were to suggest that the Sun sign in harmonic charts has a particular meaning, then we would have to say that someone with Sun at 6° Libra has the qualities of Sun in that sign plus those of someone who knows about Scorpio, is turned on by Scorpionic images *and* whose capacity for joy and fulfilment is likewise provided by the 8th sign. As we have seen, this does not seem the way to go; all degrees will refer back to Scorpio in one harmonic or another and we also risk losing the potential for exact and highly personal relationships that harmonics allow us in the wide band-width of a particular sign.

In Figure 21.1 we saw the only radical degrees that can fall in Scorpio in the 5th, 7th or 9th harmonic. In Figure 21.2 we can see the relationship between the radical chart and one *specific* harmonic degree. In this example the middle degree of Scorpio – 225° in absolute longitude – has been chosen and the only 5th, 7th and 9th harmonic positions that can *become* the 235th degree in one of those three charts. Note that the 7th and 9th harmonic degree positions have been rounded for clarity. If someone were to have their *radical* Sun at 15° Scorpio then planets in any one of these natal degrees may have a very special relationship with this solar position – for they will become conjunct it in their respective harmonics. If such a contact is proved to have meaning – and there is some evidence to suggest it might – then we can see at once that some very complex, but extremely precise relationships are lurking in the chart just out of view.

Note also the special relationship that exists between 15° of Scorpio and the 9th harmonic. A planet at 15° of any fixed sign will

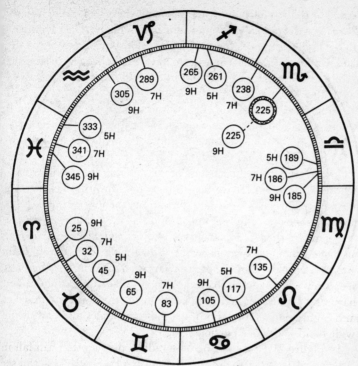

Figure 21.2 The radical solar positions for a Sun to be at 15° Scorpio in either the 5th, 7th or 9th harmonics.

return to that identical position in the 9th harmonic. Both 0° and 15° of any sign have very specific numerical relationships with certain harmonics which can produce such 'returns'. Other degrees of the zodiac also have specific resonances in harmonic charts; the implications of this for degree meanings, etc. are obviously considerable.

In Figure 21.3 we see just how intriguing such contacts can be. In this case a computer has calculated the radical/harmonic positions for each of the 360 degrees of the natal chart for the first 180 harmonics. This diagram shows how just one set of degrees are inextricably linked together. There are two series of degrees, the first including 12, 84, 156 and 228 and the second comprising of 132, 204, 276 and 348.

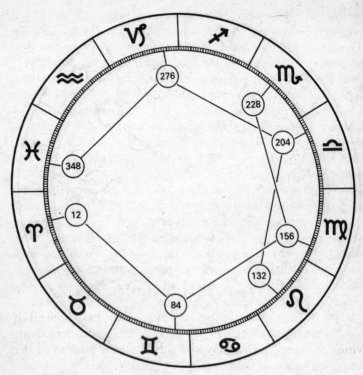

Figure 21.3 Certain interlocking harmonics can create a second series of quintile patterns in the birth chart.

If 12° is multiplied by 7 it becomes 84° – in other words the 7th harmonic position of 12° Aries is 24° Gemini. If 84° is multiplied by 7 it becomes 228° in the 7th harmonic chart. 228° multiplied by 7 becomes 156° which in turn becomes 12° again in the 7th harmonic. This sequence not only holds with a multiplication by 7, but also by any of the following numbers: 13, 37, 43, 67, 103, 127, 133, 157 and 163.

What we see here is an interlocking series of numbers spiralling through the multiples of any of these harmonics – yet remaining constantly separated by the *5th harmonic*. For all of these points are exactly 72° apart! The second series is also separated by quintiles and subject to the same consistency by the same series of harmonics. For those who believe that astrology may one day be seen as an expression of resonance phenomena these observations may be particularly interesting, even if at the moment they can do no more than whet appetites and spur further research.

If these observations seem daunting, or even in some way irrelevant, we should remind ourselves that traditional astrology has always been making claims for extremely complex mathematical structures within the birth chart, even if these have never been formally explored. These relationships involve the house cusps and their ruling planets together with the Ascendant, MC and their ruling planets. While this relationship is an expression of the symbolism concerned, it is without doubt that the actual degrees of planets and cusps are *purely* mathematical and treated as such when progressions and transits are employed. In other words, at certain moments in time traditional astrology allows for some extremely complex geometrics; furthermore, these are relationships which switch on and off quite abruptly as a change in sign transfers rulership or a progressed body reaches a specific relationship with the radix.

While it is true to say that only a very few steps have been taken towards using harmonics to clarify such involved interactions, Witte's followers in Germany and America have been using the images of resonance and complex pattern since the 1930s in their use of midpoints. The ideas which underlie the use of Arabic parts and those which are implied by the use of Antiscion degrees were brought together by the development of midpoint theory and offer the most cohesive image of integral astrology to date. Consequently this area of astrology has an enormous amount to offer the modern practitioner when it comes to the close examination of how a variety of symbols can interact.

For example the ♄/Ψ midpoint is related by Ebertin to 'suffering, renunciation, asceticism' and is generally considered to be a very negative combination, though it can equally be the hallmark of the individual who is able to channel some higher vision. In the chart of Swami Muktananda (Figure 21.4), the great Indian ascetic and sage, we find ☉ conjunct ♄/Ψ almost exact to the minute. A clue to the powerful and positive way in which he channelled this energy as a means to personal enlightenment is to

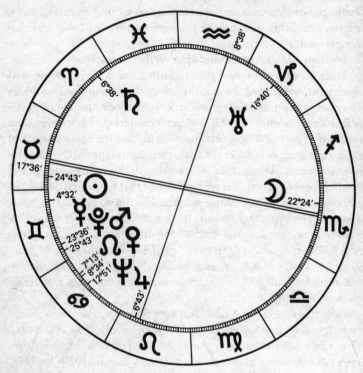

Figure 21.4 Natal chart for Swami Muktananda.

be found in the fact that his ☉ is almost precisely 24° degrees from both ♄ and Ψ and hence ♄, ☉ and Ψ are in a precise 15H resonance. Addey saw the 15H (3 × 5) as relating to 'delighting in the pursuit of intellectual beauty' and the kind of knowledge (5) which motivates (3) the individual, shown as trines in 5H (Figure 21.5).

Swami Muktananda chose to be a total ascetic as the path to self-discovery and enlightenment. He had no possessions beyond the simplest clothes he wore. He travelled throughout India on foot eating only what was given him and never deliberately asking for food. Through this highly conscious (5) and deeply motivated (3) denial of the outer world (♄) he was able to become a focus (☉) for vision (Ψ) and wisdom (♄). Such harmonic overtones occur with every close midpoint combination, and we must expect that future editions of *COSI* will include such refinements based on detailed observation.

We should also not forget that Witte's concept of planetary pictures went well beyond the kind of simple occupied midpoints dealt with in this book. He used, and his followers still use, a wealth of unoccupied midpoint structures which are considered to be important by virtue of their mutual symmetry and not because of the occupation of one midpoint by a third factor. As indicated earlier in Chapter 1, these are in fact another way of describing the symmetrical patterns of the Arabs' wealth of parts, few of which have been explored with any real rigour. There can be no doubt that sequences of unoccupied midpoints, and especially those

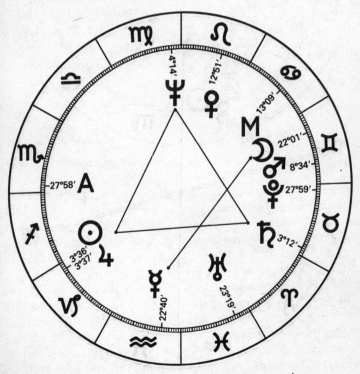

Figure 21.5 Swami Muktananda's 5th harmonic.

involving personal point combinations such as ⊙/☽ and MC/AS, can be important.

Two examples must suffice. First, considering figures of importance, Figure 21.6 is the chart of 'le roi soleil', 'le grand monarque', Louis XIV, the absolute monarch who reigned for 72 years and was the most prominent and influential figure in Europe of his day. He greatly expanded France's territories, and exercised an enormous influence on the politics, art, literature, and fashion of his age, surrounding himself with a court of the greatest, most brilliant and creative figures of his time. Embodying the self-evident truth of 'the divine right of kings', he was an autocrat of legendary pride and self-importance, who made the famous pronouncement 'L'Etat c'est moi', 'I am the State', and who built the sumptuous

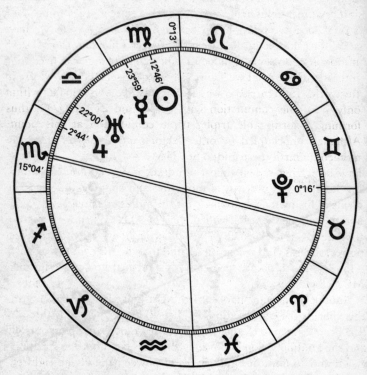

Figure 21.6 Natal chart for Louis XIV.

palace of Versailles and many other magnificent edifices of almost unparalleled wealth and extravagance. This is a valuable chart to study, for not only are Louis's life and character so well documented but his time of birth was taken precisely, as 11.11 a.m., by the great French astrologer Morin de Villefranche who, as the astrologer royal, was stationed on the balcony of the confinement room specifically to record the momentous event.

In astrological terms it could be said that Louis XIV is the very epitome of the Sun-Jupiter type. While $\mathrm{D}-0-\mathrm{\rho}$ in Ω $-90-$ 4 in M in the Gauquelin position is entirely appropriate for the sheer regal extravagance of Louis's instinctive, hedonistic and polygamous approach to the world, this does not account for the way in which he was able, so effortlessly, to embody his self-willed power, ambition and self-importance in everything that he did. Such intense purposeful achievement speaks, among other things, of a strong, positive relationship between MC and AS. As we have seen, for example in the case of Margaret Thatcher, the MC/AS midpoint represents that point where our being and becoming interact, where what we aspire to become meets the way we are in the world. In Figure 21.7 we see that this MC/AS is in fact within only 7′ of the conjunction with $\odot$/4 and 21′ of ξ/H, thus forming a formidable triple, triple conjunction at this point. Although unoccupied by other factors, day after day from the moment of birth these midpoints, $\mathrm{M/AS} = \odot$/4 $= \xi$/H, would have been triggered off almost simultaneously, continuously infusing his MC/AS process, of moulding and shaping the world in terms of his own aspirations, with the ambitious images of $\odot$/4 and the independent self-willed ideas of ξ/H. When we note also that the MC is itself exactly $-90-$ P (a conscious desire to actualize power, success, and recognition), and that the AS is almost exactly $-45-$ the Earth point (see below), we see just how powerful this MC/AS point is.

Another important unoccupied, tight-knit planetary picture in this chart is the combination Ψ/$\mathrm{M} = \Psi$/$\mathrm{P} = \odot$/D, all within 5′. Ψ/M can be seen to relate to our fantasies and myths about ourself and the guiding vision of our life. Ψ/P is related both to spiritual vision and to fantasies and myths of power ('the divine right of kings'!), and of transformation. Here exactly conjoined (3′) the

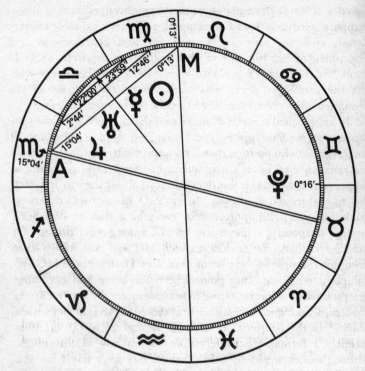

Figure 21.7 A closer inspection of Louis XIV's natal chart reveals a complex relationships of planetary pictures (see text).

all-important ⊙/☽ we can see how Louis could be entirely absorbed, body and soul, by his own myth: 'I am the State.'

Unoccupied pictures which closely involve the MC/AS and ⊙/☽ will always be important, but it is also invaluable to examine sharply focused pictures which contain ⊙/M, ⊙/AS and ☽/M and ☽/AS. Pictures involved with the ⊙/M can fill in important characteristics of our 'mission in life' and the focus of our conscious, purposeful aspirations, while those with ⊙/AS will indicate something of the way in which we meet the world as individuals. Winston Churchill's natural autocracy is well shown by his almost exact ♅ = MC/AS, but we also find in his chart the following unoccupied picture within the span of 25':

$$\sigma/P = \hbar/\Psi = \odot/AS = \odot/M = 2\!\!\downarrow/\mathbb{H}$$
$$3\Omega59 = 19\mathcal{H}01 = 4\mathfrak{M}13 = 19\mathfrak{M}19 = 19\mathfrak{M}24$$

This powerful and paradoxical picture is highly evocative of Churchill's speech on 13 May 1940, 'I have nothing to offer but blood, toil, tears and sweat', when the midpoint of transiting $\hbar$–90–P was at 18$\mathbb{I}$48, and of the imagery of his speech on 4 June 1940, when transiting $2\!\!\downarrow$ was at 4Υ15 –90– $\hbar/P$ 20$\mathbb{I}$15:

> We shall go on to the end . . . we shall fight on the seas and oceans, we shall fight with growing confidence and growing strength in the air, we shall defend our island whatever the cost may be, we shall fight on the landing grounds, we shall fight in the fields and in the streets, we shall fight in the hills; we shall never surrender.

This picture is also of course highly evocative of Churchill's proneness to swing within minutes between moods of violent exuberant energy (σ/P) to the blackest of depressions ($\hbar/\Psi$) and then back to supreme optimism ($2\!\!\downarrow/\mathbb{H}$). This combination is summed up in another way by his epigram, 'In war resolution; in defeat, defiance; in victory magnanimity; in peace goodwill'; and less portentously but equally characteristically in his perception of the Navy: 'Don't talk to me about naval tradition ($\hbar/\Psi$). It is nothing but rum, sodomy and the lash.' It is obviously not without significance that P was repeatedly transiting this potent picture during late 1940–43, and that this picture was exactly configured with Adolf Hitler's MC at 4Ω13.

The Aries or Earth point, 0° of the Cardinal Cross, and midpoints to this point, were considered by Alfred Witte to be of great importance in every chart, and will undoubtedly be found in the future to deserve far more attention than they receive at present. Their almost entire neglect, outside of Hamburg School circles, is no doubt attributable to the fact that Ebertin in simplifying and clarifying the Witte corpus decided to discard interpretations for these points. In *COSI* it appears only once, where Ebertin gives '$\hbar/\Psi$ = First point of Aries: Hysteria . . . As contrast to σ/Ψ: Infectious disease.' By contrast Witte considered 0° Aries and the Cardinal points as next in importance only to the MC, and in *Rules for Planetary Pictures* he gives systematic interpretations for midpoints involving 0° Aries and 0° Aries in midpoints.

Alfred Witte saw the Cardinal Cross as representing the Earth and our relationship to the world in general. He saw 0° Aries as part of a three-level hierarchy of relationship with the world shown by Ascendant, node, and Aries. His model is schematized in Jacobson's valuable *The Language of Uranian Astrology*, which shows Witte's hierarchical view of the personal points. The MC, ☽, ☉ are related to inner personal, emotional, and physical levels of being and consciousness, while the AS, ☊, ♈ he saw as being related to immediate, indirect, and impersonal external states of being.

In this hierarchy Witte saw Ascendant relationships as denoting immediate personal contacts. He saw nodal relationships as less directly personal contacts and associations. Aries relationships he saw as the most impersonal, as contacts with the world in general and the world around one. Thus for example he saw MC = the 'Ego' in relation to these three points as:

MC + ♈ = The relationship of the native towards the world in general. The 'I' embodied on the earth. The significance of the moment for the world . . .

as compared to:

MC + AS = The relationship of the individual to others. Joining with others for a common objective. Social and vocational relationships.

or:

MC + ☊ = Soul unions

The observations of mundane astrology going back to Ptolemy demonstrate the very great importance of the Cardinal points, and the charts for the moment of the Sun's ingress into the Cardinal signs are almost always found to be of very considerable value in judging the likely development of world affairs for the ensuing quarter and year. More especially, those periods when the outer planets cross over these points, or −45−/135 to them, often seem to mark critical epochs for the planet. Thus for example ♇ was at 0 Cancer at the time of the outbreak of the First World War (to be conjoined by ♄ in 1915), and hence was repeatedly in hard aspect with the Sun at each quarter for the next few years, while ♆ was close to 0° Libra, and with the Sun at the ingresses, during much of the worst fighting of the Second World War, from 1942–4. This period also saw the first steps in the formation of the United Nations on 1 January 1942, the day of ♆'s station at 29♍53, and the first release of atomic energy, and the formation of many other crucial developments for the post-war period. Neil Armstrong set foot on the Moon at ♃–0–♅ at 0° Libra. As we write, the major developments and changes taking place in the previously monolithic Soviet Union are occurring with the ♄–0–♅ entering 0° Capricorn with ♇ approaching 15 ♏.

The ♄–♅ is also on the USSR's ♀ at 0♑53, a classic Earth point placement for ♀ in several key world maps: the USA's ♀ is at 0♋24, the Treaty of Rome has ♀ at 29♓44, while Switzerland, renowned for its neutrality and willingness to act as an international mediator and banker, has its ♀ at 29♊54.

Individuals with factors conjunct the Cardinal points can make an appropriate impact. Thus for example we find ♄ at 29♓ in the charts of both Queen Victoria and her consort Albert, who were in some measure jointly responsible for the 'Victorian' ethos which dominated the nineteenth century. Using the ♈ point in planetary pictures can be very instructive, and especially where an individual or organization makes some contribution to the world at large. Thus Alexander Graham Bell, whose invention of the telephone has touched all our lives, had ♀ at 0♈35, but he also had the pictures ♈/AS = ☿ = ☽, which might be translated as 'contacts with the world, ♈/AS, of a communicative, talkative, even gossipy, kind'. Bell was of course, in addition to being an inventor, also an educator, who taught speech and music. His chart also contains the picture ♈/♇ = ♅ (orb 11′), which Witte gives appropriately as 'technical developments and changes'. ♈/♇ has much to do with 'transforming the world' and John Logie Baird, whose invention of the television, with its communication of information, advertising and propaganda, has also transformed our daily lives, has ♈/♇ = ☽ (6′) as well as ♈/☿ = ♈/♄ = ♇.

♈/♇ = ♃ is exact in the chart of H. G. Wells, who was preoccupied by the future development of the world and world government, and who saw human history as 'more and more a race between education and catastrophe'. He also had ♈/♃ = ♆ and ♈/♆ = ♂, a not inappropriate picture for a man who wrote *War of the Worlds*, a fantasy about the Earth (♈/♆) embroiled in a war with Mars. Witte relates ♈/☉ to 'people in public life'. This point can often seem to show something important about our conception of the world and our approach to it. H. G. Wells had ♈/☉ = ♀ = ♇, not inappropriate for his intense sex drive and notorious womanizing. ♈/☉ = ♈/☿ = ♀ = ♃ occurs in the chart of Daniel Berrigan, the Roman Catholic priest whose pacifist campaigning was so influential during the Vietnam war. Prince Louis de Broglie, who won the Nobel Prize for his discovery of the wave motion of the electron and who was responsible for developing the conception of the world (♈/☉) as vibration/waves, has ♈/☉ = ♆ = ♇ = ☿. A man whose personal vision of the world (M/♈, ♈/☽) has transformed our perception of the world in a very different way is Salvador Dali. The creator of those surrealist paintings of melting watches and disturbing fantasy images has ♈ = ♈/☽ = ♅/♆ = M/♈ = ☽ = M.

The ♈ point can be of particular importance when evaluating mundane charts, and the charts of countries, companies and organizations. For example, the British Astrological Association was elected to begin its existence on 21 June 1958 at 19.22 GMT in London. As far as we know neither John Addey nor Ronald Davison, who were responsible for choosing this date, nor Brigadier Firebrace, who fine tuned the chart, were *au fait* with the use of the Aries point, beyond the fact that they obviously recognized the importance of choosing the summer solstice. However, when we examine the chart we find that the midpoint which Witte relates to 'meetings', ♈/AS, is exactly conjunct ♅, clearly indicating that here is a moment and an organization which is concerned with astrological meetings.

In similar vein we must seriously doubt that Joan Quigley was taking any notice of the ♈/AS midpoint when she elected the time for Reagan and Gorbachev to sign the USA/USSR Arms Treaty in Washington DC on 8 December 1987 at 14.07 EST. Yet here we find ♈/AS 13♈49 exactly –90– the culminating ♀ at 13♑19, i.e. a 'peace meeting'! and ♈/M = ☿ which Witte gives as a 'public statement' or we could say a 'public signing'! This chart also contains a remarkable number of other pictures involving the ♈ point. These include the pictures ♈ = ☉/♀ = ♄/♆ = ☉/M; ♈/☽ = ♀; ♈/♀ = ♆; ♈/♂ = ♃; ♈/♄ = ♇ = ♅ 'world limitations on ♅–♇ matters'; and ♈/♅ = ☊. Almost all of these have a direct relevance to the picture of an event which has significantly changed the world, and the chances for world peace.

Mean points: We can study mean points between any number of bodies, so that the mean of ☉ + ☽ + ♅ may tell us something about the rhythm of radical change within the day and month, while the mean of ♂ + ♄ + ♆ may well be important for the study of cycles in infectious diseases. One might suspect that the cycles of influence of 'influenza' epidemics may be related to ☽ + ♂ + ♄ + ♆. Certainly W. D. Gann, in the work he was doing on the stock market in the last years of his life, was using the mean of 6 and 7 planets as key factors, a discovery which he considered as important as any he had previously made.

Other ratios and relationships: Harmonics theory seems to imply that integer (whole number) divisions of the circle can be used to explain all astrological effects. But, as Dr James S. Williamsen[1] pointed out, this cannot be the whole story. The importance of the Golden Section in the processes of nature has been known about since at least the Greeks, and these and other 'irrational' numbers, such as π, Planck's constant, and so on, can definitely be seen to play a vital part in the scheme of things. Various writers have independently pointed out the importance of the Golden Section (GS) ratio and have suggested that planets in GS ratio to each other at any time will have a very distinctive and creative resonance one with another. Such GS ratios are not easy to spot in the chart, and like the harmonic relationships depicted in Figure 21.3 above will almost certainly need to be located by computer.

All these approaches to quantifying or analysing the richness of the birth chart bring us back to the central question of its existence. Each new pattern that is discovered forces us to recognize anew that we are not looking at random effects; we are observing celestial order. The methods we use to decode this order will tell us something of its meaning.

Techniques that can successfully reveal the underlying patterns of our solar system must contain within them powerful clues about the inner construction of our own reality. This undertaking has the most profound implications. Developing approaches towards the systematic exploration of these dynamics is to take the next step beyond Darwin and Freud, towards the next major revolution in human awareness.

NOTE

1. Williamsen suggested that it was mathematically legitimate to create what he called an 'arc transform' chart, by which the whole chart is made to resonate in terms of the actual *exact* wave length between any two of its factors. To do this we: (a) take the exact distance between, say, Sun and Moon in the chart; (b) express this arc as a fraction of the circle; (c) multiply the whole chart by this factor to obtain the arc transform chart; (d) interpret the chart as showing the way in which the individual will approach life when their male/female aspects are working in unison. Charts for any pair of chart factors can be created in this way, and interpreted in accordance with the symbolism involved.

For those who prefer to stick to integer harmonics, a variation on the precise arc transform is to look at the nearest harmonic which brings the two factors under consideration together. This can be found by consulting Williamsen's indispensable *Astrologer's Guide to the Harmonics*, written with his wife Ruth, published by Cambridge Circle, and distributed by the AFA, Tempe, Arizona, USA. The *Guide* catalogues all the first 180 harmonics of the circle and their multiples sorted into degree order from 2°, the 180th harmonic, to 357° 59' 20", which is 178/179ths of circle, and 358°, which is 179/180ths. If for example one has SO and MO 63° 32' apart, this is not only a wide sextile but is also exactly 3/17th of a circle. A study of the 17H chart would help one to understand deeper subtleties about the process of self-integration. The *Guide* is an essential work for all kinds of research on harmonics. It includes valuable essays on calculating harmonic charts, on the use of *prime factors* to determine the meaning of the higher number harmonics, and a perspective on the distribution of 16,110 harmonics in the 360° circle. His other work, *Harmonic Chart Tables*, also available through the AFA, enables one to calculate any of the first 180 harmonic charts by hand, without use of calculator.

The late Dr James S. Williamsen (1941–88) was a brilliant mathematician and pioneer in the field of artificial intelligence as well as in astrology. His work in AI drew him into astrology, which he saw as a key to understanding the 'Cosmic Mind', and hence the human mind. His early death is a deep loss to astrology.

'Solution' to the midpoint case
given on p. 84

If you have not yet tried your hand at evaluating the planetary pictures for an event given on p. 84, you may like to do so before reading the solution below.

These are some of the main planetary pictures which were present at 12.30 p.m. LT, 16 February 1923 in the Valley of the Kings near Luxor, Egypt, when the English Egyptologists Howard Carter and Lord Carnarvon first entered the tomb of the eighteen-year-old Pharaoh Tutankhamun. This is probably the most exciting moment in the history of archaeology. The fabulous treasures that the outer and inner chambers of the tomb contained were of unparalleled profusion and are now familiar round the world from the various travelling exhibitions. They include the superb royal sarcophagus, various splendid canopies, a magnificent chair of state, amulets, scarabs and so on.

We can well imagine Carter's experience at this extraordinary moment in history, as he gazed upon these dazzling burial treasures which had lain undisturbed for about 3,000 years, since *c*. 1340 BC.

But as astrologers we do not have to imagine it all. When you look again at the midpoint structures for this moment the mixture of mystery, awe, joy and excitement leaps out at one. Note especially how this event, the entering of a burial chamber which is also a treasure trove, combines the contradictory messages of MC = ♄/☊, and its connotations of contacts with death, with the central joyous excitement of AS = ☉/☽ = ♃/♅, the midpoint which *COSI* relates to 'blissful realizations', 'fortunate turns in life', and 'fortune hunters'. ♃/♅ was named the 'Thank the Lord' aspect by Ebertin because it is so often present at moments when tension and strain are suddenly released. The tension prior to the opening of the tomb can be imagined. Would it be found to be what they thought it was? Would it still be intact? Or would previous tomb robbers have already removed the contents?

All is revealed, ♅, at this time and place, MC/AS.

Look again at these pictures on p. 84, first one by one and then as a total impressionist picture of the moment in which diverse shades and colours of ideas and potential emotions come together as one multifaceted experience. Just as you can reach back to the qualities of this moment through these pictures, so too in looking at the planetary pictures of your own birth, or at any other moment, you can learn to see not only the sparkling elements of the web of destiny but also something of the deeper meaning of that moment of space-time.

APPENDIX 1

Computer Program

```
100 REM    This program calculates the Cardinal/Fixed/Mutable
110 REM    sort. It is written in Microsoft Basic for IBM
120 REM    and compatibles, but will run under most other
130 REM    BASICs. It will be necessary to change the LPRINT
140 REM    command (which tells the printer to print a line)
150 REM    when some other BASICs are used. For instance, the
160 REM    Commodore 64 uses the instruction PRINT£4, for this
170 REM    command. It may also be necessary to put the planets'
180 REM    initials within double quotes "SO" etc. on line 220.
190 REM    It is not necessary to type in any line before 200.
200 CLS
210 DIM    C(100),F(100),M(100),C$(100),F$(100),M$(100),P$(13),
             P(13)
220 DATA SO,MO,ME,VE,MA,JU,SA,UR,NE,PL,NN,AS,MC
230 FOR I=1 TO 13:READ P$(I):NEXT I
240 INPUT"Enter Name ",T$
250 PRINT"Enter data as Sign, Degree, Minute"
260 FOR I=1 TO 13
270 PRINT"Enter position of ";P$(I);:INPUT " ",S,D,M
280 P(I)=30*(S-1)+D+M/60
290 NEXT I
300 CLS
310 REM *****Data is now loaded – Calculations begin
320 PRINT"Starting to calculate positions"
330 FOR I=1 TO 12
340 FOR J=I+1 TO 13
350 X=ABS(P(I)+P(J))/2:X$=P$(I)+"/"+P$(J)
360 IF X>90 THEN X=X-90:GOTO 360
370 IF X>60 THEN GOSUB 1320:GOTO 400
380 IF X>30 THEN GOSUB 1300:GOTO 400
390 GOSUB 1280
400 X=X+45
410 IF X>90 THEN X=X-90
```

```
420 IF X>60 THEN GOSUB 1320:GOTO 450
430 IF X>30 THEN GOSUB 1300:GOTO 450
440 GOSUB 1280
450 NEXT J
460 NEXT I
470 REM ****** Midpoints now Calculated and stored
480 REM ****** Now Planets are added *************
490 FOR I=1 TO 13
500 X=P(I):X$="*"+P$(I)+"**"
510 IF X>90 THEN X=X-90:GOTO 510
520 IF X>60 THEN GOSUB 1320:GOTO 550
530 IF X>30 THEN GOSUB 1300:GOTO 550
540 GOSUB 1280
550 X=X+45:X$=" ("+P$(I)+")"
560 IF X>90 THEN X=X-90
570 IF X>60 THEN GOSUB 1320:GOTO 600
580 IF X>30 THEN GOSUB 1300:GOTO 600
590 GOSUB 1280
600 NEXT I
610 REM ****************** Planets now stored
620 REM * Now Planets and Midpoints are Sorted
630 PRINT"Calculations finished – now Sorting"
640 REM ********** CARDINAL sort routine starts here
650 C=C1
660 I9%=C
670 I9%=INT(I9%/2)
680 IF I9%= 0 GOTO 780
690 FOR J9%=1 TO C-I9%
700 FOR K9%=J9% TO 1 STEP -I9%
710 IF C(K9%)>C(K9%+I9%) GOTO 740
720 K9%=0
730 GOTO 760
740 Q9=C(K9%):C(K9%)=C(K9%+I9%):C(K9%+I9%)=Q9
750 Q$=C$(K9%):C$(K9%)=C$(K9%+I9%):C$(K9%+I9%)=Q$
760 NEXT K9%:NEXT J9%
770 GOTO 670
780 PRINT"Cardinal Positions Sorted"
790 REM ********** FIXED sort routine starts here
800 C=F1
810 I9%=C
820 I9%=INT(I9%/2)
```

```
830  IF I9% = 0 GOTO 930
840  FOR J9% = 1 TO C−I9%
850  FOR K9% = J9% TO 1 STEP −I9%
860  IF F(K9%)>F(K9%+I9%) GOTO 890
870  K9% = 0
880  GOTO 910
890  Q9=F(K9%):F(K9%)=F(K9%+I9%):F(K9%+I9%)=Q9
900  Q$=F$(K9%):F$(K9%)=F$(K9%+I9%):F$(K9%+I9%)=Q$
910  NEXT K9%:NEXT J9%
920  GOTO 820
930  PRINT"Fixed Positions Sorted"
940  REM ********** MUTABLE sort routine starts here
950  C=M1
960  I9% = C
970  I9% = INT(I9%/2)
980  IF I9% = 0 GOTO 1080
990  FOR J9% = 1 TO C−I9%
1000 FOR K9% = J9% TO 1 STEP −I9%
1010 IF M(K9%)>M(K9%+I9%) GOTO 1040
1020 K9% = 0
1030 GOTO 1060
1040 Q9=M(K9%):M(K9%)=M(K9%+I9%):M(K9%+I9%)=Q9
1050 Q$=M$(K9%):M$(K9%)=M$ (K9%+I9%):
     M$(K9%+I9%)=Q$
1060 NEXT K9%:NEXT J9%
1070 GOTO 970
1080 PRINT"Mutable Positions Sorted − Now Printing"
1090 IF C1=>F1 AND C1=>M1 THEN TP=C1:GOTO 1120
1100 IF F1=>C1 AND F1=>M1 THEN TP=F1:GOTO 1120
1110 TP=M1
1120 LPRINT TAB(12);"Chart for: ";T$
1130 LPRINT TAB(12)"CARDINAL";:LPRINT
     TAB(34);"FIXED";:LPRINT TAB(56);"MUTABLE"
1140 FOR I=1 TO TP
1150  X=C(I):GOSUB 1210:IF C$(I)<>"" THEN LPRINT
     TAB(12);C$(I);Z$;
1160  X=F(I):GOSUB 1210:IF F$(I)<>"" THEN LPRINT
     TAB(34);F$(I);Z$;
1170  X=M(I):GOSUB 1210:IF M$(I)<>"" THEN LPRINT
     TAB(56);M$(I);Z$
1180 NEXT I
```

```
1190 LPRINT:END:REM ******Program ENDS here *******
1200 REM ******* Routine to convert to Degree/Minute
1210 A$=STR$(INT(X)):B$=STR$(INT(((X-INT(X))*60)+.5))
1220 IF X=0 THEN Z$=" 0 0"
1230 IF VAL(B$)=0 THEN B$=" 0"
1240 IF VAL(B$)<10 THEN B$=" "+B$
1250 IF INT(X)=0 THEN Z$=" 0"+B$:RETURN
1260 IF INT(X)<10 THEN Z$=" "+A$+B$:RETURN
1270 Z$=A$+B$:RETURN
1280 REM ***** This loads the Cardinal array
1290 C1=C1+1:C(C1)=X:C$(C1)=X$:RETURN
1300 REM ******This loads the Fixed array
1310 F1=F1+1:F(F1)=X-30:F$(F1)=X$:RETURN
1320 REM ******This loads the Mutable array
1330 M1=M1+1:M(M1)=X-60:M$(M1)=X$:RETURN
```

NOTE: This program is available as a midpoint option from Astrocalc
(see p. 453). This listing is for personal use only and may not be
used in a commercial program. © MKH

APPENDIX 2: TABLE OF EQUIVALENTS

Sign	360°	90°	45°	Sign	360°	90°	45°	Sign	360°	90°	45°
01° ♈ =	001 =	01 =	01	01° ♊ =	061 =	61 =	16	01° ♌ =	121 =	31 =	31
02	002	02	02	02	062	62	17	02	122	32	32
03	003	03	03	03	063	63	18	03	123	33	33
04	004	04	04	04	064	64	19	04	124	34	34
05	005	05	05	05	065	65	20	05	125	35	35
06	006	06	06	06	066	66	21	06	126	36	36
07	007	07	07	07	067	67	22	07	127	37	37
08	008	08	08	08	068	68	23	08	128	38	38
09	009	09	09	09	069	69	24	09	129	39	39
10	010	10	10	10	070	70	25	10	130	40	40
11	011	11	11	11	071	71	26	11	131	41	41
12	012	12	12	12	072	72	27	12	132	42	42
13	013	13	13	13	073	73	28	13	133	43	43
14	014	14	14	14	074	74	29	14	134	44	44
15	015	15	15	15	075	75	30	15	135	45	45
16	016	16	16	16	076	76	31	16	136	46	1
17	017	17	17	17	077	77	32	17	137	47	2
18	018	18	18	18	078	78	33	18	138	48	3
19	019	19	19	19	079	79	34	19	139	49	4
20	020	20	20	20	080	80	35	20	140	50	5
21	021	21	21	21	081	81	36	21	141	51	6
22	022	22	22	22	082	82	37	22	142	52	7
23	023	23	23	23	083	83	38	23	143	53	8
24	024	24	24	24	084	84	39	24	144	54	9
25	025	25	25	25	085	85	40	25	145	55	10
26	026	26	26	26	086	86	41	26	146	56	11
27	027	27	27	27	087	87	42	27	147	57	12
28	028	28	28	28	088	88	43	28	148	58	13
29	029	29	29	29	089	89	44	29	149	59	14
00 ♉	030	30	30	00 ♋	090	00	00	00 ♍	150	60	15
01	031	31	31	01	091	01	01	01	151	61	16
02	032	32	32	02	092	02	02	02	152	62	17
03	033	33	33	03	093	03	03	03	153	63	18
04	034	34	34	04	094	04	04	04	154	64	19
05	035	35	35	05	095	05	05	05	155	65	20
06	036	36	36	06	096	06	06	06	156	66	21
07	037	37	37	07	097	07	07	07	157	67	22
08	038	38	38	08	098	08	08	08	158	68	23
09	039	39	39	09	099	09	09	09	159	69	24
10	040	40	40	10	100	10	10	10	160	70	25
11	041	41	41	11	101	11	11	11	161	71	26
12	042	42	42	12	102	12	12	12	162	72	27
13	043	43	43	13	103	13	13	13	163	73	28
14	044	44	44	14	104	14	14	14	164	74	29
15	045	45	00	15	105	15	15	15	165	75	30
16	046	46	01	16	106	16	16	16	166	76	31
17	047	47	02	17	107	17	17	17	167	77	32
18	048	48	03	18	108	18	18	18	168	78	33
19	049	49	04	19	109	19	19	19	169	79	34
20	050	50	05	20	110	20	20	20	170	80	35
21	051	51	06	21	111	21	21	21	171	81	36
22	052	52	07	22	112	22	22	22	172	82	37
23	053	53	08	23	113	23	23	23	173	83	38
24	054	54	09	24	114	24	24	24	174	84	39
25	055	55	10	25	115	25	25	25	175	85	40
26	056	56	11	26	116	26	26	26	176	86	41
27	057	57	12	27	117	27	27	27	177	87	42
28	058	58	13	28	118	28	28	28	178	88	43
29	059	59	14	29	119	29	29	29	179	89	44
00 ♊	060	60	15	00 ♌	120	30	30	00 ♎	180	00	00

Sign	360°	90°	45°	Sign	360°	90°	45°	Sign	360°	90°	45°
01°♎ =	181 =	01 =	01	01°♐ =	241 =	61 =	16	01°♒ =	301 =	31 =	31
02	182	02	02	02	242	62	17	02	302	32	32
03	183	03	03	03	243	63	18	03	303	33	33
04	184	04	04	04	244	64	19	04	304	34	34
05	185	05	05	05	245	65	20	05	305	35	35
06	186	06	06	06	246	66	21	06	306	36	36
07	187	07	07	07	247	67	22	07	307	37	37
08	188	08	08	08	248	68	23	08	308	38	38
09	189	09	09	09	249	69	24	09	309	39	39
10	190	10	10	10	250	70	25	10	310	40	40
11	191	11	11	11	251	71	26	11	311	41	41
12	192	12	12	12	252	72	27	12	312	42	42
13	193	13	13	13	253	73	28	13	313	43	43
14	194	14	14	14	254	74	29	14	314	44	44
15	195	15	15	15	255	75	30	15	315	45	00
16	196	16	16	16	256	76	31	16	316	46	01
17	197	17	17	17	257	77	32	17	317	47	02
18	198	18	18	18	258	78	33	18	318	48	03
19	199	19	19	19	259	79	34	19	319	49	04
20	200	20	20	20	260	80	35	20	320	50	05
21	201	21	21	21	261	81	36	21	321	51	06
22	202	22	22	22	262	82	37	22	322	52	07
23	203	23	23	23	263	83	38	23	323	53	08
24	204	24	24	24	264	84	39	24	324	54	09
25	205	25	25	25	265	85	40	25	325	55	10
26	206	26	26	26	266	86	41	26	326	56	11
27	207	27	27	27	267	87	42	27	327	57	12
28	208	28	28	28	268	88	43	28	328	58	13
29	209	29	29	29	269	89	44	29	329	59	14
00 ♏	210	30	30	00 ♑	270	00	00	00 ♓	330	60	15
01	211	31	31	01	271	01	01	01	331	61	16
02	212	32	32	02	272	02	02	02	332	62	17
03	213	33	33	03	273	03	03	03	333	63	18
04	214	34	34	04	274	04	04	04	334	64	19
05	215	35	35	05	275	05	05	05	335	65	20
06	216	36	36	06	276	06	06	06	336	66	21
07	217	37	37	07	277	07	07	07	337	67	22
08	218	38	38	08	278	08	08	08	338	68	23
09	219	39	39	09	279	09	09	09	339	69	24
10	220	40	40	10	280	10	10	10	340	70	25
11	221	41	41	11	281	11	11	11	341	71	26
12	222	42	42	12	282	12	12	12	342	72	27
13	223	43	43	13	283	13	13	13	343	73	28
14	224	44	44	14	284	14	14	14	344	74	29
15	225	45	00	15	285	15	15	15	345	75	30
16	226	46	01	16	286	16	16	16	346	76	31
17	227	47	02	17	287	17	17	17	347	77	32
18	228	48	03	18	288	18	18	18	348	78	33
19	229	49	04	19	289	19	19	19	349	79	34
20	230	50	05	20	290	20	20	20	350	80	35
21	231	51	06	21	291	21	21	21	351	81	36
22	232	52	07	22	292	22	22	22	352	82	37
23	233	53	08	23	293	23	23	23	353	83	38
24	234	54	09	24	294	24	24	24	354	84	39
25	235	55	10	25	295	25	25	25	355	85	40
26	236	56	11	26	296	26	26	26	356	86	41
27	237	57	12	27	297	27	27	27	357	87	42
28	238	58	13	28	298	28	28	28	358	88	43
29	239	59	14	29	299	29	29	29	359	89	44
00 ♐	240	60	15	00 ♒	300	30	30	00 ♈	000	00	00

Addresses for Further Information

The central address for information on every aspect of astrology is:

The Urania Trust
Centre for Astrological Studies
396 Caledonian Road
London N1 1DN
(Tel: 071-700-0639)

The UT will send you on request a free copy of their latest annual *Calendar of Events and Directory* and updates. Please enclose a *stamped and addressed envelope* when writing for information, or two *International Reply Coupons* when writing from overseas.

The Centre has one of the most comprehensive collections of material on astrology anywhere in the world and can supply information about all the main schools and organizations in the UK and internationally.

This is also the central address for:

The Astrological Association of Great Britain and its **Book Service**. The AA is the outstanding international astrological organization and the main coordinating body in British astrology. Its membership is open to all levels of interest from students to professionals. Its bi-monthly *Journal* is considered to be one of the finest in the world and carries a regular section on midpoints and articles and studies which take account of the latest work and ideas in the field.

The Faculty of Astrological Studies, which is generally acknowledged to be the most outstanding teaching body in astrology anywhere in the world. Its patrons are Dr Baldur Ebertin, Dr Liz Greene, and Robert Hand. It runs regular courses and summer schools on midpoints and harmonics, and these methods form an integral part of their Diploma training programme.

The Centre can also supply you with the latest information on Computer programs for harmonics, midpoints and ACG. There is a growing range of software available. The Astrological Association issues a regularly updated booklet with addresses and information about all the main suppliers both in the UK and overseas. A copy of the latest edition is obtainable directly from the address above. There is a small charge for this and other AA information leaflets.

UK SUPPLIERS OF ASTROLOGICAL SOFTWARE

At the present time the addresses of some of the main suppliers of astrological software in the UK are:

ASTROCALC, 67 Peasecroft Road, Hemel Hempstead, Herts HP3 8ER (Tel: 0442-51809). Can supply software which produces midpoint trees as illustrated in this book; also graphic transits and progressions and many other programs.

ASTRO ADVICE BUREAU, Darrington Lodge, Springfield Road, Camberley, Surrey, GU15 1AB (Tel: 0276-21739 or 22000 or Fax 0276-61370). Supplies Robert Hand's Astrolabe range of software and specializes in Macintosh software.

ELECTRIC EPHEMERIS, 703 Finchley Road, London NW2 2JN (Tel: 071-435-4619). Provides a constantly updated integrated program which includes a wide range of options including midpoints and harmonics.

MATRIX SOFTWARE UK, c/o 396 Caledonian Road, London N1 1DN (Tel: 071-700-0639). Their wide range of software includes Blue Star which has comprehensive midpoint and harmonics features. Software is also available for producing Astro*Carto*Graphy charts.

COMPUTER SERVICES OFFERING CALCULATIONS

The UT Centre can supply an up-to-date listing. A few of the main international services are:

ASTRO-COMPUTING SERVICES, PO Box 34487, San Diego, California 92103-0802, USA (Tel: 619-297-9203). This is Neil Michelsen's pioneering service which is probably the finest of its kind. Write for a copy of their latest comprehensive catalogue. Within the USA use Freephone 1-800-826-1085.

ASTRO*CARTO*GRAPHY, Box 959, El Cerrito, California 94530, USA (Tel: 415-232-2525). Jim Lewis's original service. His ACG maps come complete with a listing of Latitude crossings and a valuable interpretation booklet. He can also provide personal reports regarding specific areas in the world. For supplies of Lewis's *Mundane Source Book* contact Astro-Numeric Services below.

ASTRO-DIENST ZURICH, Scheuchzerstrasse 19, CH-8033 ZURICH, Switzerland (Tel: 010-41-1-361-6464). This is the most sophisticated European computer service and has a very comprehensive catalogue of services including some very beautiful Astro*Carto*Graphy options.

ASTRO-NUMERIC SERVICES, 11163, San Pablo Avenue, PO Box 1020, El Cerrito, California 94530, USA (Tel: 415-232-5572). One of the oldest services, with a wide range of options including Astro*Carto*Graphy. Write or phone for catalogue. They are the agent for Jim Lewis's *Mundane Source Book* of ACGs for all ingresses and lunations. Issues are available from 1979 on. The following year is usually available from March of the preceding year.

For those interested in following up the work of the **Hamburg School of Astrology** this still flourishes under the direction of Udo Rudolph at **Olenland 24–26, 2000 HAMBURG 62, WEST GERMANY (Tel: 010-49-40-520-2234)**.

They can supply a wide range of books and material both in German and English. Their Computer Service provides chart print-outs covering the whole range of midpoint and planetary pictures and graphic ephemerides. Most of their material is also available from the AA Book Service at the UT Centre, address above. Those interested in keeping abreast with their work can subscribe to *Hamburger Hefte*, Olenland 24, 2000 Hamburg 62, W. Germany, and to *Uranian Forum*, 7671 NW 6th Court, Plantation, FL 33324, USA.

HARMONICS AND ASTROLOGY NEWSLETTER Essential reading for all astrologers wanting to keep in touch with the latest in harmonics and midpoints. For subscription details contact Archie Dunlop, B.Sc., DFAstrol.S, 9 Smallwood Road, London SW17 0TN, England.

Using the 90° dial: A leaflet describing the use of the 90° dial is available from the Urania Trust, at the address above, for £2 including postage.

APPENDIX 4

Chart Data

Addey, John: 8.15 a.m. GDT, 15 June 1920, Barnsley, England (ADIII).

Antonioni, Michelangelo: 9.45 p.m. MET, 29 September 1912, Ferrara, Italy. Source: birth certificate from GB.

Anne, Princess: 10.50 a.m. GMT, 15 August 1950, London, as given on official Buckingham Palace announcement.

Aurobindo, Sri: 5 a.m. LMT, 15 August 1872, Calcutta, India, given in *Auroville: City of the Future*, quoted in ADIII.

Bailey, Alice: 16 June 1880, Manchester. Time unknown. A speculative chart for 7.32 a.m. is given in POW.

Bernstein, Leonard: 6.06 a.m. EWT, 25 August 1918, Lawrence, Mass., USA. 'From him', quoted in ABC.

Catherine the Great: 2.30 a.m. LT, 2 May 1729 (Gregorian Calendar), Stettin, Pomerania, from WOL.

Chapman, Mark: 7.30 p.m. CST, 10 May 1955, Forth Worth, Texas (ADIII).

Collin, Rodney: 9 a.m., 26 April 1909, Brighton, Sussex. 'The source was almost certainly Rodney's widow', letter from his sister-in-law, the astrologer Joyce Collin-Smith, in the *Astrological Journal*, Vol. XIV, No. 1, p. 34.

Cousteau, Jacques: 1.15 p.m. Paris Time, 11 June 1910, Ste André de Dubzac, France (G).

Crane, Pamela: 9.18 p.m., 19 January 1943, Birmingham, England. Given by native in her *Draconic Astrology*.

Diamond, Legs: 2 a.m. EST, 10 July 1897, Philadelphia (or NYC?) (ABC).

Eichmann, Adolf: 9 a.m. MET, 19 March 1906, Solingen, Germany. 'From his mother' (ABC).

Fitzgerald, F. Scott: 3.30 a.m. LMT, 24 September 1896, St Paul, Minnesota (ABC).

Fitzgerald, Zelda: 5.40 a.m. CST, 24 July 1900, Montgomery, Alabama (POW).

Fleming, Alexander: 2.17 a.m. GMT, 6 August 1881, Lochfield, Scotland (AA).

Freud, Sigmund: 6.30 p.m. LMT, 6 May 1856, Freiburg, Germany (ABC).

Hemingway, Ernest: 8.00 a.m. CST, 21 July 1899, Oak Park, Illinois (AA).

Hendrix, Jimi: 10.15 a.m. PDT, 27 November 1942, Seattle, Washington. Birth certificate from CSH.

Hillman, James: Time of birth from mother. The ASC could be in the first degrees of Cancer within the possible margin of error.

Hitler, Adolf: 6.30 p.m. LT, 20 April 1889, Braunau, Austria, from birth certificate.

Hofman, Albert: 14.00 GMT, 11 June 1906, Basle, Switzerland. From him personally.

Joplin, Janis: 9.45 a.m. CWT, 19 January 1943, Port Arthur, Texas, USA. Birth certificate in POW.

Joyce, James: 6.25 a.m. GMT, 2 February 1882, Dublin, Ireland. From Richard Ellmann's biography *James Joyce*, time recorded by his father.

Jung, Carl: 7.30 p.m. MET, 26 July 1875, Kesswil, Switzerland (AA).

Keating, Tom: 'Midnight', 1/2 March 1917, Forest Hill, London. From his autobiography.

Kerouac, Jack: 5.00 p.m. EST, 12 March 1922, Lowell, Massachusetts (ABC).

Kubler-Ross, Elizabeth: 10.45 p.m. MET, 8 July 1926, Zurich, Switzerland. Birth certificate quoted in letter to Robert Chandler, correcting times previously given.

King, Martin Luther: 'High Noon', 15 January 1929, Atlanta, Georgia, according to his mother quoted in ABC.

Louis XIV: 11.11 a.m. LT, 5 September 1638, Saint-Germain-en-Laye, France. Source: Morin de Villefranche, who was present at the birth.

MacAuliffe, Christa: 9.13 p.m. EST, 2 September 1948, Boston, Massachusetts. From birth certificate.

MacLaine, Shirley: 3.57 p.m. EST, 24 April 1934, Richmond, Virginia, from birth certificate quoted in POW.

Manson, Charles: 4.46 p.m. EST, 12 November 1934, Cincinnati, Ohio. From AA.

Mao Tse-tung: 'at the hour of the dragon', approx. 7.30 a.m., LT, 26 December 1893, Siangton, according to Chinese biography quoted in ABC.

Miles, Sarah: 10.45 p.m. GMT, 31 December 1941, 51N41, 00W22. 'Between 11.30 and midnight' (=DST), according to the nurse who delivered her. Quoted in S&L.

Monnet, Jean: 8 p.m. GMT, 9 November 1888, Cognac, France. Source: G.

Napoleon I: 11 a.m. LT, 15 August 1769, Ajaccio, Corsica. Source: AB.

Pankhurst, Emmeline: 9.30 p.m., 14 July 1858, Manchester. Source: Edward Lyndoe in letter to AA said he had time from the family.

Piggott, Lester: 1 a.m., 5 November 1935, Wantage, Berkshire, from John Addey, whose source is not known.

Robespierre: 2 a.m. LT, 8 May 1758, Arras, France. Source: birth records given in AB.

Schweitzer, Albert: 11.50 p.m. LMT, 14 January 1875, Kayserburg, Alsace. Birth certificate alleged in ABC.

Stopes, Marie: 3.05 a.m., 15 October 1880, Edinburgh. From birth certificate (UT).

Teresa of Avila: 5 a.m. LT, 28 March 1515 (Julian Calendar), Avila, Spain. Official biography written shortly after her death.

Tesla, Nikolai: 'on the stroke of midnight' LT, 9/10 July 1856, Smiljan, Yugoslavia. As given in the biography *The Prodigal Genius* by J. J. O'Neill.

Thatcher, Margaret: 9 a.m. GMT, 13 October 1925, Grantham, Lincolnshire. From her press office.

Valentino, Rudolph: 3 p.m. LT, 6 May 1895, Castellaneta, Italy. Birth certificate from GB. NB: not 3 a.m. as often given!

Watson, James Dewey: 1.23 a.m. CST, 6 April 1928, Chicago, Illinois, USA. From birth certificate obtained by the late Dr James Williamsen.

SOURCES OF DATA

AA = Astrological Association Data Collection.

AB = André Barbault, *Traité Pratique d'Astrologie*, Editions du Seuil, 1961. This contains the charts of French monarchs and leaders with the historical sources of the data given.

ABC = Lois Rodden, *American Book of Charts*, Astro-Computing Services, 1980, an invaluable source book by a pioneer collector of accurate data.

ADIII = Lois Rodden, *Astro-Data III*, AFA, 1986.

CSH = *Contemporary Sidereal Horoscopes*, 1976, by Clark, Gilchrist, Mackey, and Dorminy, contains verified birth certificate data only.

GB = Grazia Bordoni, *I dati di Nascati interessanti*, Centro Italiano di Astrologia, in three volumes. An invaluable compilation of Italian and other data, mainly from the birth certificate.

G = Michel Gauquelin, *Birth and Planetary Data*, Series A. This remarkable publication contains the full birth data of many thousands of European notables as taken from the birth certificate.

POW = Lois Rodden, *Profiles of Women*, AFA, Tempe, Arizona, 1979.

S&L = Penny Thornton, *Sons and Lovers*, which gives charts, data, interviews and biographical studies of 24 figures in the public eye.

UT = Urania Trust data assembled from Scottish records by Paul Wright. Available on disc or print-out from 396 Caledonian Road, London N1 1DN.

WOL = Maurice Wemyss, *Wheel of Life*, L. N. Fowler, in 5 volumes. Gives sources, usually carefully documented, of a large number of historical figures.

General Index

Page numbers of illustrations are given in **bold** type.

Aalen, Cosmobiological Academy, 14
accidents, 47
addresses for astrological info, 452
anger, displaced, 49, 50
AIDS, 91
air crash, San Diego, 153
Alam Halfa, battle, 126
alchemist, 57, 63
anima, Hillman on, 270ff.
anorexia, 50
Apollo, 282
antiscia, 15
apple, and Number 5, 184
Arabic astrology, 8
Arabic Parts, 8, 433
arc transform chart, 442
Archetypal Man, 283
archetypes, 7, 275, 424, 425
Aries point, 437ff.
art, midpoints for, 11
artillery barrages, 11
As above so below, 41
Ascendant/MC, 79ff., 86, 87
aspects, 12
    hard aspects, 12
    officially approved, 41
aspiration, *see* harmonic charts: 3H
asteroids, 41, 223
Astro*Carto*Graphy, 305
    Aries ingress 1945, **319**, **320**
    case histories, 309ff.
    introduction to, 307

latitude correction for, 308
latitude crossings, 316, **317**
mundane, uses in, 317ff.
parans in, 316
Piper Alpha, for, **321**
planets in: Sun, **326**; Moon, **325**; Mercury, 312; Venus, 313, 318, 326, 327; Mars, 313, 317, 321, **326**; Jupiter, 313, 315, 318; Saturn, 311, 312, 313, 318, 321, **326**, 328; Uranus, 313, 317, 321, 322, **326**, 328; Neptune, 312, 313, 315, 317, 318, **326**; Pluto, 310, 311, 314, 315, 317, 318, 328
    Thatcher, Margaret, **325**, **326**
    transits activate, 313ff.
Astrological Association, 294
Astro-Numeric Services, 16
atomic bomb, 151ff.
atomic structure, 5, 22
autocracy, and Uranus, 75, 99, 107, 209, 327, 436
automatic writing, 71

Battle of Normandy, 126
Betelgeuse, gas explosion, 320, 323, 324
Bhagavad Gita, 256
birth chart, a distorted picture, 3
blind analysis, 395
bliss, follow, 297

Bonampak, discovery of, 417
British Journal of Astrology, 13

cause, and effect, 287
Cardinal Sort, 40ff.
Carmelite Order, reforms of, 257
Challenger, 52ff., 80, 90
China, 64, 65
Chiron, 348ff., 353ff.
Church of England, 83
clergymen, 225
cocaine, 111
Collective Unconscious, 275
composers, ♄–♅, 279
Combination of Stellar Influences
   (COSI), 13, 14, 51, 62, 100,
   101, 104, 110, 263
computer, program, 121, 445
   calculation services, 445
   software, 453
conjunctio, 57
consciousness, level of, 67
Conservative Party, 108
containment, planetary, 17, 18,
   70
coronation, of Elizabeth I I, 82,
   83
cramps, midpoints of, 49
creativity and ☉/☽, 57ff.
Cuba, 146
cycles, planetary, 7, 76, 91, 328ff.
   generational life of, 330

Dallas, 45° sort, 26
data, sources, 454ff.
death, contacts with, 84, 443
death, and Mars/Saturn, 88, 112,
   113, 114, 272
death, transits at time of, 74,
   119
declination, midpoints in, 14
degree areas, 16, 89, 90, 425, 429
dials, 90°, 360°, 16

directions, 136ff.
DNA, discovery of, 215, **248**
   fivefold, 223
Draconic Zodiac, 76, 174
drink, excesses and ♃=♆/♇, 62
drugs, 62, 74

Earth Point, *see* Aries Point
El Alamein, 125
electronic revolution, 92
Eleusinian mysteries, 282
encadrement, *see* containment,
   planetary
enneagram of Gurdjieff, 282
Equivalents, Table of, 450–51
entelechy, 254, 255, 280
epidemics, cycles, 441
Eternity, unfolded by planets, 7
evangelist movement, American,
   394
explosions, midpoints for, 12, 47,
   90
   Piper Alpha, 323

Fate, 288
Faust, 95
films, and Neptune, 72
flight, 5° Sagittarius as degree of,
   89, 90
forecasting, 118ff.
forgery, 70
framing, *see* containment,
   planetary
France, I V Republic, 196, **197**
   economic reconstruction, **198**
free enterprise and ♄–♅, 194

Gauquelin position, 62, 72, 396
genetic inheritance, 16, 190, 215
geoglyphy, 314
Gestalt, 128
Golden Section, 441
good fortune, 42

Good, and Will, 187
graphic ephemeris, 14, 128ff.,
132, **135**, **138**, 246, **360**
Greeks, 7

Hamburg Kepler Circle, 11
Hamburg School, 11, 15, 437, 454
harmogram, **250**, **251**
harmonics
art and, 230ff.
calculating charts, 181ff., 442
fantasy and, 226ff.
Hindu astrology and, 173
introduction to, 169ff.
midpoints in, 150ff.
signs in, 274, 291, 426
maths of signs, 426, **427**,
429, **430**
wave forms in, 155
zodiac degrees in, 426ff.
harmonic charts
2H, 286, 289
3H, **266**ff., 268
and aspirations, 279
and Heart, Beautiful, 286
and motivating ideal, 266
4H, 286ff., 288, **289**, 294
and Ideal of Good, 286; and
Will, 286, 288, 290, 295
5H, 176ff., 184ff., 290, **385**,
425, 426ff., **429**, **430**
6H, rhythms of life, 295
7H, 62, 224ff., **378**, 425, 426ff.,
429
8H, 176, 287, **290**, 294
9H, 173ff., 253ff., 426ff., **429**
Navamsa and, 173ff., 254,
256; image which draws
us, 274; marriage partner
judged by, 280; 9H
synastry, 369
12H, 295ff., **296**, **298**
14H, 353

15H, trines in 5th, 196
16H, 287, **291**, **292**, **293**, 294
18H, **299**
21H, **354**
24H, **297**
25H, **218**ff., **220**
27H, lunar mansions, 256
28H, 226, **355**, **386**
36H, 299
49H, 225
64H, I Ching aspect, 159, 287
hemisphere, left and right, 57, 75
herbal remedies, 424
Hindu astrology, 173, 280
Hiroshima, 91
horses, 189, 190
hot-air ballooning, 95
house systems, 14, 15
hypothetical planets, 15

I Ching aspect, 159, 287
Ideals, importance of, 67
and human faculties, 187
and 9H, 254
Ideas to be realized, 281
inbetweenity, *see* containment
India, Home Rule, 98
inflatus, 212
influenza epidemics, 441
inspirational energy, 73
insulin, and 16° Cancer/Cap, 425
integral astrology, concept of, 425
intuition and mystical faculty, 187
inventive genius and ♅, 201, 203
Iran, 147
Iranian Embassy, siege of, 80, **81**
Iranian airbus shot down, **148**ff.

Japan, 144, 145
Jupiter-O-Saturn cycle, 329ff.

karma, hard aspects and, 287
kidnap attempt, 50

laser, discovery of, 251
latitude, correction for, 308
League of Nations, 248
Long March, of Mao, 65
LSD, 160
lightning, obsession with, 204
Libya, People's Bureau, 81
listening, importance of, 93

Maine, sinking of, 143ff.
manifestation, harmonics of,
    285ff.
march, related to 4H, 286
marriage, ☉/☽ as point of, 57, 64,
    105, 124
    of Charles and Diana, 83, **84**
    5 as number of, 185
    partner, judged from 9H, 280,
        368ff.
    9H synastry, **369**
Mars, and self-assertion, 104, 105
    and 5H, 223
Mars-O-Pluto, and Piper Alpha,
    321, **322**, 328
Maya, discoveries of Giles
    Healey, 417
meditation, at same time each
    day, 117
mathematical talent, 11
medium, 71
micro-astrology, 46
midpoints, 2, 5ff., 77, 423
    artistic sense, as shown by, 11
    Ascendant/MC, *see*
        Ascendant/MC
    calculating, 22, 44
    Cardinal, Fixed, Mutable, 40ff.
    closest, 101
    consultation, using in, 78, 92,
        93, 94, 99, 100, 164
    in declination, 14
    definition, 7, 19
    degree areas and, 16

direct, 20
45° sort, 26
genetics and, 16
indirect, 20
interpreting, 100ff.
locating, 19
and marriage, *see* marriage
maths talent shown by, 11
mean points, of Gann, 369
mundane, in, 140ff.
orbs, 20, 26, 39, 121
outer planets, 126
paradoxical, 102
personal, 61, 101
planet/Angle, 78
repetition of, 87, 101
sequence, 16, 18, 27, 35, 78,
    101, 361ff.
slow-moving, 61, 90, 92
starting to use, 163
Sun/Moon, *see* Sun/Moon
transits to, 42, 46, 47, 48, 49,
    50, 51, 117ff.
trees, 93, 100ff.
unoccupied, 433ff., **436**
Modern Astrology, 423
mystics, Neptune and, 74, 75
myths, we enact, 269

Navamsa, *see* harmonic charts: 9H
Nazis, 75, 160ff.
Neptune, 69ff., 102
Node at USA Independence,
    141ff.
nuclear explosion, first, 151ff.,
    152, **153**
Number (*and see main chapters*)
    2 as first male number, 185
    3 and 3H, 266
        as first male number, 185
    4 and 4H, 285ff.
    5 and 5H, 184ff., 221
    7 and 7H, 224ff.

8 and 8H, 284ff.
9 and 9H, 253ff., 281ff.
  as utter perfection, 281; in
     myths and legends, 282; in
     European languages, 283
12 and 12H, 295ff.

Odin, 282
operations, midpoint for, 47
Opposition, Government and, 285
orbs for midpoints, 20, 26, 39, 121

pancreas, 425
paran, 315
paranormal, Neptune and, 72
parents, and Sun/Moon
Part of Fortune, 8, **9**, 41
Part of Spirit, **10**
Pearl Harbor, 145ff.
penicillin, discovery of, 245, **246**,
  247, **250**
pentagram, 222
personnel selection, 221
phobia and $\u263f = \u0127/\u03a8$, 205
Piper Alpha, gas explosion, **321**,
  322, **323**, 324, 328
planetary containment, *see*
  containment, planetary
planetary pictures, 8, 433
Pluto in Dallas, 310
police, killing of, **81**, 82
polo, passion for, 418
prayer, 68
prediction, 118
Presence of God, Practice of,
  258
progress as aspiration and effort,
  279
progressions, 136ff.
prohibition, 248
psychosomatic displacement, 49

quintessence of 5H, 218

quintile, *see* harmonics: 5H

ratios, irrational, 441
rectification, midpoints and, 80,
  101
religious conflicts, 259
relocation charts, 307
resignation and $\u2609-\u03a8$, 52
resonance and astrology, 429, 434
'reverence for life', 276
Rome, terrorist bomb, 90
Rules for Planetary Pictures, 12, 13,
  14, 437

San Diego, air crash, 153
SAS storm Iranian Embassy, **81**
Saturn, and self-questioning, 86
  as mother, 97
Saturn/Neptune images, 73
  as 'sickness' axis, 125
Saturn/Pluto, example of, 65
Saturn–Uranus and economic
  cycle, 194
septiles (*and see* harmonic charts:
  7H), 224ff., 249
  and creativity, 244, 245
serendipity, gift of, 404
sex education, 209
sexuality, confusion over, 71
sexual repression, 88
Shadow, concept of, 394
sheep, 41
signs of zodiac in harmonics, 274,
  291, 426
sort
  Cardinal, Fixed, Mutable, 40ff.,
     53, 117ff.
  45°, 26
soul, vision of, 280
Stark, USS, attack on, **147**
sub-personalities, 128
suffragettes, *see* women's
  movement

Sun/Moon midpoint, 57ff., 78, 101
  ☿ on, 69, 115, 399, 410, 415, 420, 422
  ♀ on, 71
  ♂ on, 58, 73, 102ff., 104ff., 324
  ♃ on, 60, 70, 72, 74, 115, 205
  ♄ on, 53, 59, 62, 358
  ♅ on, 67, 75, 86ff., 89, 147, 155, 157ff., 158, 294, 326, 327, 332
  ♆ on, 58, 69–75, 259
  ♇ on, 62, 64, **67**, 157, 158, 314, 324, 383
  ☊ on, 383ff.
  MC on, 399, 410
  AS on, 443
  adjacent midpoints, 125
  transits to, 58, 59, 124
Swiss metaphysics, 118
symbols, patterns of, 426
  mathematics of unfoldment of, 426
synthesis, art of chart, 393
syphilis, 91

Tao Te King, 253
techniques, 2
Terror, Reign of, 212
terrorism, 80, 90, 92, 95
tertiary progressions, 41
time, unfolded by planets, 7
  choosing time, 48
  experience of consciousness, 118
tobacco, 97
transcendent euphoria, 62
transits, 117ff.
  angles, 42ff., **81**, **83**, **84**

to midpoints, 121
Treaty of Rome, **199**
  5H chart, **200**
Tree of Life, 282
'Trinity', 151ff.
TUC, 246
Tutankhamun, entering tomb, 443
twoness, 285

Unconscious, 50
Uranian Astrology, *see* Hamburg School; Witte
Uranus–Pluto conjunction, 91
USA
  atom bomb and, 151
  independence, **141**
  navy, 143ff.
  Node position, 141ff.
United States of Europe, 192

vocational guidance, 221
volcano, 46
Vietnam, 146

Will, and 4H/8H, 255
woes, nine, of St Matthew, 282
women's movement, 105, 106, 107, 108, 210
world government, 193
World Astrology Watch, 323
World Tree, 282
Wu-Wei, 254
waltz, and 3H, 286

zodiac, degrees in harmonics, 426ff.

Name Index

Addey, John, v, 16, 170, 416, 421, 440
  Astro*Carto*Graphy, 313
  birth data, 454
  Rasi and Navamsa charts, **174**
  Sun-45-Neptune, 294
  straight line chart, **175**
  on integral astrology, 425
  on creativity and 5H and 7H, 244
  on 5H, 185, and genetics, 190
  on trines in 5H, 196, 432
  on 6H, 287
  on 7H in clergyman study, **225**
  on 9H, 254, 274, 283
  harmonic model, 16, 170, 425
  Harmonics in Astrology, 223, 225, 226
  transiting angles as final ward of lock, 122
  longevity study, 170
  Navamsa and marriage, 280
Addey, Tim, 284
Andersen, Hans Christian, 294
Anne, Princess, **50**, 454
Antonioni, Michelangelo, 72, **73**, 454
Aristotle's four causes, 288
Arthur, King, 282
Assagioli, Roberto, 128, 425
Aurobindo, Sri, 75, 454
Avila, Teresa of, 75, 257ff., 454
  midpoints, 259
  natal chart, **258**

  9H chart, **259**
  Gurdjieff reminiscent of, 260
  Mao Tse-Tung, 9H compared, 261, 262

Bader, Douglas, 394
Bailey, Alice, 75, 454
Bailey, E. H., 13
Baird, John Logie, 439
Baldwin, 107
Ballard, Ronn, 17
Becker, Boris, **51**
Belafonte, Harry, 71
Bell, Alexander Graham, 439
Bernstein, Leonard, 71, 72, 454
Berrigan, Daniel, 440
Besant, Annie, **98**, 106
Bieler, Henry, 419
Birkenhead, Lord, **96**
Bonati, Guido, 8
Brown, A. R., 16
Broglie, Prince Louis de, 440
Brummund, Ruth, 15
Buchan, John, 73

Caravaggio, Michelangelo Merisi da, 236
Carnarvon, Lord, 443
Carroll, Lewis, 241
Carter, Charles, 13, 16
Carter, Howard, 443
Catherine the Great, **99**, **292**, 454
Cerridwen, 382
Chapman, Mark, 75, 454

Charles, Prince, marriage, 83, **84**
Childrey, Joshua, 8
Christos, Archetypal Man, 283
Churchill, Winston, 293, 436, 437
Clay, Cassius, **296**
Collin, Rodney, 272ff., 454
    9H chart, **273**
    Gurdjieff-Ouspensky and, 272, 273
    Collin-Smith, Joyce and, 272, 274
Collin-Smith, Joyce, 272, 274
Cousteau, Jacques Yves, 69, **70**, 454
Cousteau, Simone, 69
Crane, Pamela, 62, 76, 223, 454

Dali, Salvador, 440
Darwin, Charles, 442
Davison, Marian, ix
Davison, Ronald, 440
Degas, Edgar, 71
Descartes, René, 58
Diamond, Legs, **68**, 69, 454
Diana, Princess, 83, **84**
Dilke, Charles, 106
DK, the Tibetan, 75
Dobyns, Zip, 348
Doyle, Arthur Conan, 97
Dwyer, Terry, 186, 226, 264, 283

Ebertin, Baldur, 15, 18
Ebertin, Elsbeth, 13
Ebertin, Reinhold, v, 13, 14, 62, 65, 203, 255
Eichmann, Adolf, **74**, 75, **162**, 454
Einstein, Albert, 215
    Jupiter on USA Moon, 153
    5H, **215**
Eisenhower, 126

Elizabeth II, Queen, Coronation, 82, **83**
Ellman, Richard, 340
Emerson, Ralph Waldo, 184, 253
Erlewine, Michael, 16

Ferrucci, Piero, 253
Firebrace, Brigadier, 440
Fitzgerald, Scott, 80, 85, 94, 454
    5H chart, **385**
    28H chart, **387**
    synastry with Zelda, **367**
    9H synastry with Zelda, **369**
    midpoint synastry with Zelda, **371**
Fitzgerald, Zelda, 454
    case history, 365ff.
    death of, 389
    5H chart, **377**
    7H chart, **378**
    9H chart, 369
    ☿ midpoints, **373**
    ♂ midpoints, **380**
    synastry with Scott, 366, 371ff.
Fleming, Alexander, 7H chart, 245ff., **246**, 454
Fletcher, PC Yvonne, 81, 82
Franco, Francisco, 293
Frederick the Great, 293
Freud, Sigmund, 88, 250, 357, 425, 456
    midpoints of, 108ff., 123
    meeting with Jung, 115
Fridthorsson, Gudlaugur, **156**ff.
Fritz, Robert, 284

Gann, W. D., 441
Gauguin, Paul, 394
Gauquelin, Françoise, 171
Gauquelin, Michel, ix, 72, 171, 396, 421, 457
Goad, John, 8
Goebbels, Joseph, 161, **162**

Goethe, 58, 95, **96**
Gorbachev, 440
Goulden, Emmeline, 105, *see*
    Pankhurst, Emmeline
Greaves, Doris, 16
Gudmundsson, Gunnlaugur, 156
Gurdjieff, 14, 260, 272, 273, 282

Hall, Manly Palmer, **96**, 294
Hamblin, David, 186, 226, 254,
    261, 283, 286, 294, 368, 388,
    408
    Harmonic Charts, 223
Hand, Robert, 16, 163, 226, 283
Hardie, Keir, 106
Harding, Judith, ix
Harland & Woolf, 246
Harvey, Suzi, ix
Healey, Giles, 395ff.
    birth data, 397
    midpoint trees, 398ff., **400**
    natal chart, 395ff., **396**, 413
    5H chart, 407, **408**
    7H chart, **409**
    8H chart, 410, **411**
    9H chart, 411, **412**
    Gauquelin position ♃–♄, ☽,
        396
    ♃–120–♃–♄, 397
    ☉–90–Ψ, 397
    ☉/☽=☿, 399, 415, 420, 422
    Addey, John, 416, 421
    Astrological Association,
        support for, 416
    astrology, and, 421
    Bonampak, discovery of, 417
    case history, 413ff.
    children, 419, 420
    marriages, 419, 420
    Miller, Henry, and, 418, 422
    polo, passion for, 418
    Perles, Alfred, and, 418
    Rimbaud, Arthur, and, 422

Healey, Sheila, ix, 420
Heath, Neville, 39
Hemingway, Ernest, 86, 87, 456
Hendrix, Jimi, 73, 456
Hillman, James, ix, 268ff., 425,
    456
    natal chart, **269**
    9H chart, **271**
    on anima, 270
Himmler, Heinrich, **162**
Hitler, Adolf, 65ff., 265ff., 290ff.,
    392, 437, 456
    MC axis, **98**
    natal chart, **66**
    Sun/Moon axis, **67**
    3H chart, **266**, 281
    4H chart, **289**, 290
    5H chart, 222ff.
    8H chart, 289, **290**
    9H chart, **265**
    12H chart, **296**
    16H chart, 290, **291**
    24H chart, **297**
    Leo–Aquarius in 16H
    Churchill, Winston, and, 437
    Mao's 9H compared, 267
    Napoleon's midpoints
        compared, 294
    natal chart an enigma, 65
    Pluto/Node in 3H, 267
Hofmann, Albert, 160, 456
Holmes, Sherlock, 97
Howe, Gregg, 16
Huber, Bruno, **97**

Jackson, Eve, 348
Jacobson, Roger, 438
Jones, Daphne, 223, 224
Jones, Marc E., 17
Joplin, Janis, 59ff, 456
    Jupiter's importance, 59ff.
    natal chart, **60**
    5H chart, 205ff., **206**

Joplin, Janis – *cont.*
  Sun/Moon midpoint,
    importance of, 60, **61**
  Crane, Pamela, and, 62, 76
  Rodden, Lois, on case history,
    59
Joyce, James, 456
  Astro*Carto*Graphy of, **340**
  case history of, 335ff.
  death of, 363
  midpoints of, **339**, **342**, 358
  natal chart, **337**
  5H chart, **346**
  7H chart, **347**
  14H chart, **353**
  21H chart, **354**
  28H chart, **355**
  Bloomsday transits, **358**, **360**,
    361
  Ellman, Richard, and, 340
  Freud, Sigmund, and, 335
  Jung, C. G., and, 335, 362
  Norah and, 337, 341, **361**
Jung, C. G., 113, 114ff., 123, 255,
    425, 456
  7H chart, **350**
  9H chart, 274ff., **275**
  Sun–90–Neptune, 294
  on Fate, 288
  feminine and, 276
  Joyce, James, and, 335, 362
  Mao, Tse-Tung, contrast with,
    276
  Ulysses and, 357ff.
  and Hillman, James, 268, 270

Keating, Tom, 70, **71**, 74, 456
Kennedy, John F., 146
  Astro*Carto*Graphy of 309ff.,
    317
  Pluto in Dallas, 310
Kepler, Johannes, 173
Kerouac, Jack, 86, 456

King, Martin Luther, 213ff., 456
  midpoints, 214
  5H, **214**
Kollerstrom, Nick, 245, 248
Krafft, K. E., 170, 423
Kray twins, 393
Krishna, Sri, 256
Kubler-Ross, Elizabeth, 74, 456

Lambert, John Heinrich, 139
Landscheidt, Theodore, 15, 159,
    175
Leo, Alan, 423
Leonardo da Vinci, 192
Lennon, John, 75, 245
Lewis, Jim, ix, 308, 317
Lefeldt, Hermann, 11, 12
Lilley, John C., **97**
Louis XIV, 293, **434**, 435, **436**,
    456

MacAuliffe, Christa, 52ff., **53**, 87,
    89, 94, 456
MacLaine, Shirley, midpoints, 207
  5H **208**, 456
McPhail, Jamie, ix
Manson, Charles, 37ff., 85, 87,
    109, 111, 455
Mao Tse-Tung, 62ff.
  birth data, 64, 456
  Saturn in Gauquelin position, 62
  Sun/Moon=♄=♇, 62, **63**
  5H chart, **219**, 223
  7H chart, **243**, 244
  9H chart, 261, **262**
  25H chart, **220**, 221
  Cultural Revolution of 1966, 91
  permanent revolution, 65, 221
  St Teresa 9H chart compared,
    261, 262
Marx, Karl, 255
Meyer, Michael, 17
Michelangelo, 192

Michelsen, Neil F., 16
Miles, Sarah, 72, 456
Miller, Henry, 418, 422
Milarepa, 393
Monnet, Jean, 192ff., 457
  natal chart, 194
  5H chart, 195
  architect of European unity, 192
  China's railways, 196
  EEC, instability in material
    things, 201
  European Coal and Steel
    Community, 193, 196
  France, economic
    reconstruction of, 198
  French IV Republic and, 197
  League of Nations Secretary
    General, 193, 196
  Treaty of Rome, and, 199, 200
  United States of Europe, 192
Montefeltro, Count of, 8
Montgomery, Field-Marshal, 125
Morin de Villefranche, 435
Morris, William, 106
Morrison, A. H., 348
Mozart, Wolfgang Amadeus, 192,
  223
Muktananda, Swami, 431ff. **432**
Mussolini, Benito, 293

Napoleon Bonaparte, **293**, 457
Nielsen, Dennis, 393
Niggemann, Hans, 14
Nixon, Richard, **51**, 52

O'Neill, Mike, 245, 248, 250ff.
Ouspensky, 14, 272, 273

Palmer, Samuel, 71
Pankhurst, Emmeline, 102ff., 210,
  457
  midpoints structures, **102**
  5H, **211**

Moon–MC axis, 102–4
Sun/Moon midpoint, 104
autocracy of, 107
Baldwin on, 107
Conservative Party, joins, 108
husband, 105, 106
parents, 105
suffrage work begins, 106
Pankhurst, Christabel, 106, 107
Pankhurst, Richard, 105, 106
Pavlov, 35
Perles, Alfred, 418
Perls, Fritz, 128
Picasso, Pablo, 95
Piggott, Lester, 187ff., 457
  5H chart, 188, **189**, 223
  7H chart, **191**
  family, riding in blood of, 190
  genetic factor, 190
  horses, mastery of, 188, 189, 190
  luck, 191
  money, and, 191
  style, 188
Plato, 253
Proclus, 253
Ptolemy, 11
Pythagoras, 184, 185, 281, 283

Quigley, Joan, 440

Reagan, Ronald, 327, 440
Reinhart, Melanie, ix, 348
Rilke, Rainer Maria, **98**
Robespierre, 211ff., 457
  midpoints, 213
  5H, **212**, 213, 223
  Scorpio emphasis in 5H, 213
  Sun/Moon=Pluto, 212
Robson, Vivian E., 13
Rodden, Lois, 59, 457, 458
Rommel, Erwin, **162**
Roosedale, Alfred G., 14
Roosevelt, Franklin, 193, 318

Rothko, Mark, 233
Rudolph, Ludwig, 11
Rudolph, Udo, ix

Sandbach, John, 17
Sasportas, Howard, ix
Sayre, Zelda, 80, 94
Schweitzer, Albert, 276ff., 457
    natal chart, **278**
    9H chart, **277**
    Sun–90–Neptune, 294
    Bach and, 277, 279
    Nobel Prize, 278
    'reverence for life', 276
Seymour-Smith, Martin, 283
Sieggruen, Friedrich, 11, 15
Sissons, Douglas, ix
Speer, 161
Sri Aurobindo, 75
Stein, Zane, 348
Steiner, Rudolf, 75
Stewart, Jackie, 223
Stopes, Marie, 208, **209, 457**
St Matthew, 282
St Paul, 283
St Teresa of Avila, *see* Avila,
    Teresa of
Svehla, Richard, 14

Tarnas, Richard, ix, 203
Taylor, John Russell, 72
Teresa of Avila, *see* Avila, Teresa
    of
Tesla, Nikolai, 201ff., 457
    natal chart, 201, **202**
    5H, 204, **205**
    Virgo sign emphasis in 5H, 205
    midpoints, 203, 205
    phobias and $\text{☿} = \text{♄}/\text{Ψ}$, 205
    Uranus–Prometheus and, 203
    Edison and, 202
    Marconi and, 202
    Prometheus, a modern, 202

Thatcher, Margaret, 79, 457
    Astro*Carto*Graphy, 324, **325,**
        326
    Mars=AS/MC, 79, 328, 435
    midpoint, 327
    9H chart, 262ff., **263**
    18H chart, **299**
    and Jupiter/Saturn cycle,
        329ff., **331**
    as Saturn/Uranus radical
        reformer, 263
Thérèse of Lisieux, 75
Thornton, Penny, 458
Tito, Marshal, 293
Tomaschek, Rudolf, 14
Tompkins, Sue, ix
Tutankhamun, 84, 443
Twain, Mark, 204

Valentino, Rudolph, 72, 457
Vico, Giambatista, 335
Victoria, Queen, 439
Vitti, Monica, 73
Volguine, Alexandre, 16, 17, 70

Walter, Hans-Jorg, 15
    on 5H and Mars, 223
Watson, James, 215ff., 457
    natal chart, **216**
    5H, **217**
    25H, **218**
    septiles and discovery of DNA,
        249ff.
Wells, H. G., 193, 439, 440
Wemyss, Maurice, 458
Whitman, Walt, 393
Williamsen, James S., 283, 441, 442
Windsor, House of, 82
Witte, Alfred, 8, 10, 11, 14, 15,
    79, 159, 255, 431, 433, 437, 438
Wodehouse, P. G., 422

Yariv, Gaila, ix

Midpoints Index

☉/☽ (*and see General Index for other references*)
  ☿ on, 69, 115, 399, 410, 415, 420, 422
  ♀ on, 71
  ♂ on, 58, 73, 102ff., 104ff., 324
  ♃ on, 60, 70, 72, 74, 115, 205
  ♄ on, 53, 59, 62, 358
  ♅ on, 67, 75, 86ff., 89, 147, 155, 157ff., 158, 294, 326, 327, 332
  ♆ on, 58, 69–75, 259
  ♇ on, 62, 64, **67**, 157, 158, 314, 324, 383
  NN on, 383ff.
  MC on, 399, 410
  AS on, 443
  adjacent midpoints, 125
☉/☿, 98, 102ff.
☉/♀, 342, 399, 401, 420
☉/♂, 95, 152
☉/♃, 66, 67, 126, 147, 342, 372, 435
☉/♄, 154, 358
☉/♅, 52, 64, 65, 98ff., 108, 371
☉/♆, 48, 51, 52, 84, 99, 342, 214, 327, 347, 405ff.
☉/♇, 50, 81, 83, 102ff., 339, 405ff.
☉/☊, 152ff.
☉/AS, 47, 50, 80, 108ff., 147, 294, 437
☉/MC, 46, 51, 126, 332, 341ff., 408, 437

☽/☿, 23, 116, 214, 259, 342
☽/♀, 48, 83, 102ff., 108, 358
☽/♂, 49ff., 50, 339, 345, 373ff.
☽/♃, 83, 84, 96, 327, 380
☽/♄, 83, 84, 119ff., 152
☽/♅, 48, 81, 102ff.
☽/♆, 93, 214, 325, 341, 358, 372, 389
☽/♇, 96, 327, 341ff.
☽/☊, 84, 96, 108
☽/AS, 207, 214, 371, 388, 401, 420
☽/MC, 66ff., 80, 207, 358

☿/♀, 11, 54, 86, 108, 357, 401ff.
☿/♂, 87
☿/♃, 24, 37ff., 99, 102ff., 213, 294
☿/♄, 23, 85, 87, 96, 102ff., 342, 384, 401, 420
☿/CHIRON, 349ff.
☿/♅, 46, 54, 148, 152, 383, 435
☿/♆, 84, 147, 154, 383ff., 401ff.
☿/♇, 108ff., 213, 267, 332
☿/☊, 66ff., 147
☿/AS, 55, 80, 108, 147, 152
☿/MC, 90, 402

♀/♂, 60, 61, 62, 84, 96, 152, 373ff., 399ff.
♀/♃, 84, 97, 327, 342, 361, 380, 402ff.
♀/♄, 30, 33, 36, 38, 81, 84, 96, 358, 403ff.

♀/♅, 54, 141ff., 148, 351, 361ff.
♀/♆, 84, 97, 102ff., 158, 342, 405ff., 419
♀/♇, 48, 116, 327, 342, 373ff.
♀/☊, 125, 152, 399ff.
♀/AS, 84, 158, 388
♀/MC, 51, 102ff., 342

♂/♃, 55, 96, 108, 122, 123, 154, 166, 401ff.
♂/♄, 87ff., 110, 112ff., 116, 147, 158ff., 162, 166, 339, 351ff.
♂/♅, **11**, 30ff., 37ff., 47, 50, 80, 94, 358, 372, 388
♂/♆, 29ff., 51, 81, 90, 102ff., 108ff., 141ff., 166
♂/♇, 30ff., 37ff., 52, 81, 125ff., 158, 283, 294, 324, 437
♂/☊, 153
♂/AS, 81, 155, 342, 383, 403ff.
♂/MC, 29, 33, 38, 81, 327

♃/♄, 81, 87, 96, 342
♃/♅, 42, 51, 84, 90, 102ff., 123, 141ff., 259, 404ff., 415, 437, 443
♃/♆, 95, 98, 102ff., 160, 206, 342, 403ff.
♃/♇, 84, 87, 96, 152, 166, 404ff., 415
♃/☊, 82ff., 401ff.
♃/AS, 81, 83
♃/MC, 81, 84, 294, 342

♄/♅, 90, 147, 194, 213, 380ff., 402ff., 419
♄/♆, 54, 95, 125, 147, 205, 373ff., 431ff., 437
♄/♇, 63, 84, 95, 152ff., 161, 213, 221, 342, 402ff., 405ff., 419
♄/☊, 98, 327, 372, 380, 443
♄/AS, 51, 52, 97, 147ff.
♄/MC, 37, 52, 342

♅/♆, 30, 152, 339, 380, 419
♅/♇, 91ff., 95, 102ff., 108ff.
♅/☊ ,102ff.
♅/AS, 47, 80, 97, 148, 342, 362, 371
♅/MC, 60, 61, 83, 90, 102ff., 148, 339, 371

♆/♇, 30, 48, 49, 60, 81, 84, 90, 97, 116, 154, 294, 419
♆/☊, 90, 102ff., 154, 380, 435
♆/AS, 152, 207
♆/MC, 33, 38, 60, 207, 341ff., 435

♇/☊, 207, 267, 339, 372
♇/AS, 46, 80, 98, 102ff., 154, 383
♇/MC, 52, 80, 81, 108, 267

☊/AS, 83, 152, 327, 358, 402ff.
☊/MC, 62

AS/MC, 79, 81, 83, 84, 85ff., 87, 108ff., 123, 124, 148, 155, 389, 401, 435, 436, 444